The Victim's Fortune

Inside the Epic Battle
over the Debts of
the Holocaust

JOHN AUTHERS *and*
RICHARD WOLFFE

HarperCollins*Publishers*

HarperCollins books may be purchased for educational, business, or sales promotional use. For information, please write: Special Markets Department, HarperCollins Publishers Inc., 10 East 53rd Street, New York, NY 10022.

FIRST EDITION

Designed by Joseph Rutt

Printed on acid-free paper

Library of Congress Cataloging-in-Publication Data

Authers, John.
    The victim's fortune : inside the epic battle over the debts of the Holocaust / John Authers and Richard Wolffe.—1st ed.
      p. cm.
    Includes index.
    ISBN 0-06-621264-2
    1. World War, 1939–1945—Confiscations and contributions—Europe. 2. Jews—Europe—Claims. 3. Restitution and indemnification claims (1933–) 4. Jewish property—Switzerland. 5. Banks and banking—Corrupt practices—Switzerland—History—20th century. 6 Holocaust, Jewish (1939–1945)—Reparations. I. Title: Battle over the debts of the Holocaust. II. Wolffe, Richard. III. Title.

D810.C8.A88 2002
940.53'18—dc21

                       2001051935

02 03 04 05 06 WB/RRD 10 9 8 7 6 5 4 3 2

For Sara,
and
For Paula and Ilana

You have committed murder and now you wish
to inherit the victim's fortune as well.

—ELIE WIESEL,
quoting from the First Book of Kings

Contents

Cast of Characters

Larry Kill *Fagan's associate*
Anderson, Kill & Olick in New York
Michael Hausfeld *Son of Holocaust survivor, millionaire attorney*
Cohen, Milstein, Hausfeld & Toll in Washington
Martin Mendelsohn *Simon Wiesenthal's lawyer, Hausfeld's close friend*
Verner, Liipfert, Bernhard, McPherson & Hand in Washington
Morris Ratner *Hausfeld's intense young associate*
Lieff, Cabraser, Hyman & Bernstein in New York
Melvyn Weiss *King of the class action lawsuit*
Milberg, Weiss, Hynes, Bershad & Lerach in New York
Deborah Sturman *Pugnacious associate of Weiss*
Milberg, Weiss, Hynes, Bershad & Lerach in New York
Burt Neuborne *Broker between rival factions of lawyers*
Professor of Law, New York University
Stephen Whinston *Independently filed his own lawsuits*
Berger & Montague in Philadelphia

AMERICAN OFFICIALS
Stuart Eizenstat *Administration's obsessive Holocaust point man*
Undersecretary of State, later Deputy Treasury Secretary
J. D. Bindenagel *German specialist and career diplomat*
U.S. special envoy for Holocaust issues
Bennett Freeman *Wordsmith and ebullient political strategist*
Senior adviser to Eizenstat
Alfonse D'Amato *Populist politician who led the attack on the Swiss*
U.S. Senator for New York, special master in German case
Alan Hevesi *Led sanctions threats against the Swiss and others*
Comptroller of New York City
Steve Newman *Hevesi's right-hand man, former NASA engineer*
Deputy Comptroller, New York City
Eric Wollman *Veteran of South African sanctions campaign*
Legal counsel to Hevesi, New York City
Elizabeth McCaul *Workaholic pursuer of Swiss banks*
New York State banking superintendent

SWITZERLAND
Hans Baer *Senior Jew in Swiss banking, negotiated with Singer*
Chairman, Bank Julius Baer

Georg Krayer *Professorial president of Swiss Bankers Association*
  Chief Executive, Bank Sarasin
Bob O'Brien *American inside Swiss bank, D'Amato's friend*
  Managing Director, Credit Suisse
Robert Studer *Patrician and undiplomatic banker*
  Chief Executive, Union Bank of Switzerland
Paul Volcker *Former Fed chairman who led Swiss bank inquiry*
  Chairman, International Committee of Eminent Persons
Michael Bradfield *Dogged leader of investigation into Swiss banks*
  Legal adviser to Paul Volcker
Thomas Borer *Tried to sell Swiss government policy to Americans*
  Swiss ambassador on World War II issues
Curtis Hoxter *Worked for both Baer and Singer*
  Public relations consultant
Greta Beer *First victim to testify against the Swiss banks*
  Retired travel guide
Gizella Weisshaus *First survivor to sue Swiss, critic of campaign*
  Romanian Jewish survivor of Auschwitz
Edward Korman *Banged heads together in the Swiss bank lawsuits*
  Chief Judge, Eastern District of New York, in Brooklyn
Christoph Meili *Whistleblower who stumbled upon fame*
  Night watchman, Union Bank of Switzerland
Roger Witten *Tough attorney for Swiss banks, German companies*
  Wilmer, Cutler & Pickering in Washington

INSURANCE
Lawrence Eagleburger *Exasperated former Secretary of State*
  Chairman, International Insurance Commission
Neil Levin *Architect of international insurance commission*
  New York State insurance superintendent
Chuck Quackenbush *Volatile member of Eagleburger Commission*
  California State insurance commissioner
Deborah Senn *Vocal critic of insurers and Eagleburger*
  Washington State insurance commissioner
Giovanni Perissinotto *Charmer who mollified Generali's antagonists*
  General Manager, Assicurazioni Generali
Guido Pastori *Urbane head office lawyer*
  Chief legal counsel, Assicurazioni Generali

Kenneth Bialkin *Generali's negotiator, former Jewish leader*
 Skadden, Arps, Slate, Meagher & Flom in New York
Scott Vayer *Generali's American lawyer, former kibbutznik*
 Sole practitioner in New York
Bobby Brown *American immigrant who led Israeli policy*
 Adviser for Diaspora Affairs to Prime Minister Netanyahu
Martin Stern *Self-appointed critic of Generali and Singer*
 Property developer and grandson of Holocaust victim
Michael Melchior *Successor to Bobby Brown*
 Adviser for Diaspora Affairs to Prime Minister Barak

F R A N C E

Jacques Andréani *Gruff, former ambassador to the U.S.*
 French government envoy on Holocaust issues
Claire Andrieu *Leading historian on banks under Vichy*
 Professor at Institut des Études Politiques in Paris
Frederick Davis *Legal bulwark for the French banks*
 Shearman & Sterling in New York
Lionel Jospin *Created the commissions on Jewish plunder*
 French Prime Minister
David Kessler *Young Jewish liaison to the Prime Minister*
 Senior cultural adviser to Lionel Jospin
Theo Klein *Former Resistance fighter turned bank lawyer*
 Klein Goddard in Paris, former Jewish leader
Kenneth McCallion *Environmental lawyer turned Holocaust attorney*
 Goodkind, Labaton, Rudoff & Sucharow in New York
Owen Pell *Peacemaker for the French banks*
 White & Case in New York
Christian Schricke *Influential French bank executive*
 Secretary General, Société Générale
Ady Steg *Former Jewish leader who guided the French response*
 Vice-chair of Mattéoli historical commission
Harriet Tamen *Gung-ho warrior against the French*
 Sole practitioner in New York
Richard Weisberg *Intellectual critic of the Vichy regime in France*
 Law professor, Yeshiva University in New York

GERMANY

Gerhard Schröder *Promised to resolve the lawsuits before his election*
German Chancellor

Bodo Hombach *Overly optimistic, high-profile fixer*
Chancellor Schröder's first envoy on Holocaust issues

Otto Graf Lambsdorff *Tough-talking envoy, former German soldier*
Former economics minister and successor to Hombach

Michael Geier *Lambsdorff's minder*
German foreign ministry official leading Holocaust issues

Manfred Gentz *Brains behind the German industry foundation*
Chief Financial Officer, DaimlerChrysler

Wolfgang Gibowski *Pollster and Gentz's mouthpiece*
Spokesman, German industry initiative on Nazi labor

Rolf Breuer *Agreed to an early deal with Singer*
Chairman, Deutsche Bank

Herbert Hansmeyer *Bitter opponent of compensation payments*
Head of North American operations, Allianz

Shirley Wohl Kram *Maverick judge in German and Austrian cases*
U.S. District Judge, Southern District of New York, in Manhattan

AUSTRIA

Jörg Haider *Demagogue whose party entered government*
Leader of far-right Freedom Party

Charles Moerdler *Attorney for both Bank Austria and Vienna's Jews*
Stroock, Stroock & Lavan in New York

Ariel Muzicant *Property developer and sharp critic of Chancellor*
Leader of Vienna's Jewish community

Maria Schaumayer *Former central banker with Chancellor's ear*
Austrian government representative on forced labor issues

Wolfgang Schüssel *Determined to restore his government's image*
Austrian Chancellor

Ernst Sucharipa *Veteran diplomat with little authority*
Austrian government special envoy on Jewish property issues

Hans Winkler *Leading official on Nazi compensation deals*
Legal adviser to the Austrian foreign ministry

The
Victim's
Fortune

Prologue

The unassuming seventy-one-year-old New Yorker looked at his $5,000 check with disdain. It was meant to compensate him for the time he had toiled in a Nazi labor camp, sorting coal from rocks that passed on a conveyor belt. Jaime Rothman was just a teenager when he was deported to Auschwitz alongside his three brothers and his parents in 1944. Almost a lifetime later, he found himself standing in a wide, windowless conference room off Lexington Avenue in Manhattan, recalling his descent into hell one more time for the reporters huddling around him.

"Truly it's not a big thing," he said, dismissing the payment with a wave of his hand. "It's not justice. Whenever you touch the subject and you put the money and the suffering together, it's not the way to do it."

Rothman was typical of the handful of aging victims present at a staged ceremony on June 19, 2001, intended to mark the crowning achievement of a campaign begun six years earlier. None of them rejoiced as the meager payments began to flow to thousands of former slave laborers across the world. After half a century of waiting, none of them breathed a sigh of relief, or even saw the money as a small measure of justice.

Mendel Rosenfeld, an Orthodox Jew in a broad-brimmed black hat and full white beard, laughed at the mere suggestion that the German payments represented some form of justice. The proprietor of a take-out food store in Brooklyn, Rosenfeld was forced to spend the war years building tunnels under the Austrian Alps to protect German munitions factories from Allied bombings. "This is very far from justice. It's very far from that," he said with a wry smile. "There's no such thing as money that can pay for what I went through in my life."

Yet money was precisely what a small group of dedicated, mostly Jewish Americans had sought on behalf of survivors like Rothman and Rosenfeld since 1995. They had traveled from country to country and from company to company, confronting those who had profited from the Holocaust and failed to settle with its victims. Their odyssey had started in Switzerland, where the secretive banks were still clinging to victims' savings held in hidden accounts. Soon they were traveling across Europe in pursuit of insurers who had refused to pay off the policies of those murdered in the concentration camps. They challenged stubborn French banks, dismissive German businesses, and the far-right demagogues at the heart of the Austrian government.

With the help of the New York courts and some of Washington's most skillful power brokers, they humbled mighty corporations trading in the new global economy. Economic sanctions were threatened on a scale unseen since the boycott of apartheid-era South Africa. Friendly foreign governments were forced to confess to their complicity in Nazi-led plunder, arousing fierce controversy across Europe. Companies that claimed to bear goodwill toward survivors often believed they were being blackmailed.

Nothing about the deals that emerged was inevitable. Except, perhaps, the gnawing feeling that they could never be enough.

For Israel Singer, the mercurial mastermind behind the compensation campaign, the money was only the means to an end. "We need moral and material restitution for one reason and one reason alone," he explained. "The Nazis dehumanized the Jews. It became legal to steal their property because they no longer were human. What we are doing today is rehumanizing these individuals posthumously and saying that the grand theft that took place in fifteen countries was not permissible. That rehumanization and rebreathing of life into these people, into these dry bones, is what our activity is all about. It's not about money."

But as the fight over the victims' fortune unfolded, Singer's lofty ideals were increasingly set aside while the negotiations descended into bitter disputes over money. The campaigners clashed with European Jews and they clashed with one another. They bickered over who truly represented the survivors of the Holocaust—the attorneys filing lawsuits on their behalf, or the Jewish groups looking after their welfare. Meanwhile, the victims found themselves confined to the sidelines of their own battle and distrustful of those who claimed to speak for them.

Roman Kent, an Auschwitz survivor, was so dissatisfied with the German payments that he threatened to walk out of the Manhattan press conference in June 2001. He bridled at the suggestion that he might feel happy to have won some kind of victory. When he was finally called to the podium, Kent—who represented the victims in the German compensation talks—seized the microphone in despair. "I am ashamed," he said. "I am ashamed that I was participating in those negotiations.

"Let me ask you these questions. Why did it take the German nation sixty years to engage the morals of the most brutal form of death, known as death through work?

"Why call the agreement an initiative when in fact the need for accountability was brought about by the recent demands of survivors, linked to economic and legal issues?"

Kent stood back, staring at the journalists in the front row to ask his final question. "Why don't you look in your soul and stress our moral and ethical values that we survivors fought for, rather than stressing the glitter of gold?"

Kent was not alone in asking such questions. Why did it take so long for the compensation to flow? Why now, when so many survivors had already died? Why the focus on money?

This is the tale of the lawyers, businessmen, government officials, Jewish leaders, and victims who hold the answers to those questions. It is a story of people striving for justice, and people squabbling over money. It is a story of people searching for historical truth, and people hurling historic abuse. It is their struggle to write the final chapter of the Holocaust before the last survivor dies.

As Kent left the podium, it seemed as if that last chapter might be about nothing more than money. But Singer followed him to the microphone and deftly seized on Kent's disgust to justify his own aggressive pursuit of billions of dollars in compensation.

"Roman was right," he said, abandoning his notes. "From the very outset, all of these negotiations focused on the moral rather than the material aspects of the crimes committed against the Jewish people. We are not celebrating, we are not congratulating, we are not thanking. But we do thank God that there are still some alive today to show their anger and the anger of all those who have died.

"You heard the anger and you heard the hope. Anger and hope are what drove these talks."

For Want of a Chair

I t was a little after one o'clock on Thursday, September 14, 1995, when Israel Singer stepped out of the Swiss presidential palace in Bern. A sprightly figure, with a black yarmulke perched at a rakish angle over his white hair, Singer relished what lay ahead of him. As he bustled along the cobbled streets, the fifty-three-year-old rabbi from Brooklyn was leading a group of six Jewish leaders toward lunch with some of the most powerful men in the financial world.

Singer and his friends hurried as they turned into Theater-platz, a narrow arcade ending at the Zytglogge, a huge clock tower that has efficiently ticked out perfect Swiss time since 1530. It reminded them how late they were. Ignoring the Alpine peaks of the Eiger and the Jungfrau towering in the distance, their Swiss host guided them to the Théâtre de Musique, an ornate eighteenth century building decorated with carvings of lyres and mandolins, and steered them through an unmarked door to an unremarkable vestibule. The men climbed a broad flight of stairs leading to a pair of heavy wooden doors, which bore a discreet plaque bearing the inscription: *Cercle Privée de la Grande Société.*

Singer was no stranger to the exclusive circles of power and money. For more than a decade as secretary-general of the World Jewish Congress, he had courted some of the wealthiest business-people in America and cultivated the country's most influential politicians. Always immaculately presented in tailored suits and monogrammed shirts and sporting a fresh splash of cologne, Singer was no ordinary rabbi.

Beside him was Edgar Bronfman Sr., an urbane Canadian who strode into La Grande Société with the confidence of the fabulously rich. Bronfman was ready to hand over to his son the reins of Seagram, the family's huge distillery and entertainment conglomerate, and was throwing his estimated $3.3 billion personal fortune behind Singer. As president of the World Jewish Congress, Bronfman had even used his private jet to fly the delegation from Brussels to Switzerland that morning.

Together Singer and Bronfman were proud of the international battles they had already fought and won for Jewish causes. They had helped to free Jewish dissidents in the Soviet Union and successfully exposed the hidden war record of the Austrian president, Kurt Waldheim. Now they were ready for the biggest battle of their lives—confronting Switzerland's secretive banks about something buried in their vaults for fifty years. The Swiss banks, for centuries a refuge for the wealth of Europe, were clinging to money deposited by desperate Jews on the eve of the Holocaust. Rather than return the cash to bereaved families at the end of the war, Singer and Bronfman believed, the banks had brushed the victims aside with decades of pettifogging excuses.

Inside La Grande Société, the Swiss Bankers Association waited to meet their accusers. Singer's allegations were not new. Indeed, suggestions that the banks had profited from "dormant assets" had rumbled through the Swiss body politic for decades. In the first seven years after the war, the banks had conducted surveys three times to try to identify accounts that might be dormant. Since then, Switzerland had carefully cultivated a wholesome image based on its finest institutions: the International Committee of the Red Cross, the nation's highly democratic local government, and its neutrality in times of hot and cold war. Now the banks found themselves in the firing line as Switzerland began to admit that its record during the Nazi years was less than snow-white.

Only a few months earlier, on the fiftieth anniversary of the end of the war, Kaspar Villiger, the Swiss president, apologized to the many Jewish refugees refused entry to Switzerland during the war.

But his noble act provoked a new wave of international scrutiny into the banks' conduct, both during and after the Nazi years. *Globes,* Tel Aviv's biggest business newspaper, claimed that as much as $7 billion in Holocaust survivors' money lay dormant in Swiss banks, while the *Wall Street Journal* printed a front-page article on the struggles of Holocaust survivors to retrieve their accounts. Even some of Switzerland's bank regulators were agitating to clear the record. Feeling stung, the Swiss banks launched an internal audit, and they had just released preliminary results. They found 893 dormant accounts worth only 40.9 million Swiss francs, or about $24 million.

Singer and Bronfman entered the red-carpeted, chandeliered splendor of La Grande Société, convinced that there was more money waiting to be found. As they headed straight for the feast waiting for them in a far room, Georg Krayer, president of the Swiss Bankers Association, gestured for them to stop. First, he said, they should go to the anteroom for aperitifs and his welcoming speech. A charming if somewhat professorial man, Krayer headed Bank Sarasin, the largest private bank in Basel, where he was familiar with extremely wealthy clients like Bronfman. He had labored over his brief speech of welcome, aiming to seem open to discussion while firmly denying the Israeli media's wilder estimates of the missing money. As the association had no offices in Bern, Krayer had chosen La Grande Société, an elite private club often used by Bern's diplomatic community. He reasoned that meeting in the club's ornate corridors would be almost like inviting the Jewish dignitaries into his private circle, and made sure to order a kosher meal.

It perturbed Krayer that his guests were late—a cardinal sin in Switzerland. Moreover, despite an agreement to keep the meeting private, a group of journalists accompanied the Jewish delegation and were gathered in the cobbled street outside. The supposedly private meeting felt like an ambush in the making.

The two groups clutched their cocktails and lined up uncomfortably in the small anteroom, which Bronfman angrily noted had no chairs. Next to Krayer stood Hans Baer, the chairman of Bank Julius Baer and a rare Jew in the upper echelons of Swiss banking. Recovering from back problems at the time, he felt similarly uncomfortable. The slow reading of Krayer's "brief" five-page welcome speech, in carefully enunciated English, only intensified his discomfort. Bronfman began to fume. But Krayer was confident that the charges being hurled at the Swiss were largely groundless. He told his guests that the purpose of the meeting was to exchange information, "since a lot of time has been spent responding to comments, some justified and some not, which had found their way into the media."

"The huge sums mentioned in the media have no basis in reality," he said. "We ask those who continue to use them and, in doing so, encourage unfounded hopes or expectations, to check the proven facts."

Krayer told them that the banks had followed a Swiss government decree of 1962 "as diligently and completely as possible under the circumstances." That decree forced banks and other companies to report all assets of "foreign or stateless persons subject to racial, religious or political persecution." It had unearthed 9.8 million Swiss francs, or about $5.6 million at the time, in 739 accounts. Of this, 3.7 million Swiss francs had been returned to heirs, and the rest given to charity.

But now there were new demands from Israel based on an assumption of Swiss guilt, and the banks almost felt under siege. He explained that the banks were introducing a new system to allow Holocaust survivors to claim money in dormant accounts. Though not free of charge, he said, the service would be "reasonably priced and transparent."

He ended with a challenge. "Mr. Bronfman," he said. "We would very much like to hear which were your thoughts and expectations of this gathering. And we would appreciate it very much if you could give us a brief summary of actions taken in your country or community with regard to this problem."

Bronfman stood speechless. Accustomed to deferential treatment, he found this welcome demeaning. He still did not have a chair and wondered whether he would even be offered any lunch. His entourage started to confer, worried that he would lose his temper. One of his companions leaned over and whispered, "Edgar, say that was a most interesting speech, let's discuss it over lunch."

The tension among the bankers seemed to dissolve a little, and they settled down to enjoy the kosher feast. Bronfman, however, found himself squinting into the sunlight and noted that his nameplate said "Bronfmann," spelled in the German style.

When asked how much money he thought might be involved, he left his options open by saying, "It's more than $50 million, and less than $50 billion." Instead Bronfman repeated several times, mantralike, that he wanted to discuss a process not an amount of money. He left it to Singer to talk details.

As they talked, Swiss banking secrecy—not money—proved the sticking point. Krayer repeatedly insisted that the banks had no desire to hold on to even one Swiss franc that did not belong to them. But Krayer and his colleagues saw no reason to let outsiders monitor the books of one of the world's greatest banking systems. The Swiss banks could be trusted to audit the money. After all, their entire business was based on trust.

In reply, Bronfman used the analogy of President Ronald Reagan's approach to the Soviet Union on nuclear arms control. He was prepared to work with the Swiss, but only on a cold war understanding: "Trust, but verify."

By the time Singer, Bronfman, and their colleagues left La Grande Société, to be greeted by a mob of reporters, they thought they had agreed on a way forward. The bankers would continue their investigation of dormant accounts in conditions of total secrecy. A joint committee, including Israel Singer, would hire auditors and examine the process. Neither side was to discuss the findings in public until they were complete.

Both sides left their lunch at La Grande Société feeling vindicated and self-righteous. The Jewish delegation refused to leave the final auditing of Holocaust accounts to the banks. Meanwhile, the proud bankers, believing they had nothing to be ashamed of, refused to allow anyone to violate their secrecy.

Bronfman departed with a clear image of Swiss arrogance. His account of the meeting, and particularly the failure to offer him a chair, appeared in newspaper articles and books over the ensuing months. "They weren't decent enough to provide us a chair to sit in while we waited ingloriously for their august presence," Bronfman complained. In 1997, he even joked that he would devote a chapter to the incident in any future memoir, entitling it "For Want of a Chair."

To the Swiss, Bronfman's behavior looked like deliberate exploitation. "If you want to apply public pressure," Hans Baer said, "you have to complain about the chairs. Otherwise the man on the street doesn't know what you're talking about. If you're out to make trouble you have to use an opportunity like that."

Krayer felt stung by the suggestion that he had been personally rude. He wrote to Bronfman complaining of an "embellishment of things past" and saying his account of their meeting bore "little resemblance to fact." He threatened to make public his own version of the lunch at La Grande Société if "biased, incorrect and incomplete stories continue." He said: "As you undoubtedly remember, there was some difficulty in keeping to the schedule, as an unplanned visit by you to the president of the Swiss Confederation had been fitted in just before our meeting. This is the reason why the welcome cocktail and introduction—as is customary in Switzerland (and in the United States)—did in fact take place 'standing.' "

He apologized for not having invited him to be seated on one of the many chairs in La Grande Société. Bronfman never replied.

Israel Singer spent the next few months shuttling from his native New York to Switzerland, monitoring the investigation. He was in his element, declaring that his life's task was to "comfort the afflicted, and afflict the comfortable." The Nazis had forced his parents, Austrian Jews, to scrub the streets of Vienna while an anti-Semitic mob jeered at them. He believed he had been "appointed by my parents, to make the lives of those [perpetrators] who are here and still with us miserable. Both allies and neutrals as well as those who are opponents, criminals and varied villains." His agenda included the Swiss but was not confined to the tiny mountain nation. In fact, he hoped the battle with those who had profited in Switzerland would lead to a historical reckoning for Holocaust crimes throughout Europe.

Strictly Orthodox from birth, Singer tried to run his life with a "relatively fundamentalist view." He described himself as "far to the right on religious principles," but eschewed what he called "one-size-fits-all Judaism." Although he had been ordained, Singer chose to be a "rabbi without a pulpit," living up to his calling as an aggressive spokesman for Jews, and for other minorities as well. He knew the importance of economic power, he knew how to negotiate, and he knew how to win the world's press over to his side of the argument. He also knew how to wage the guerrilla campaign he was about to unleash on the Swiss.

Before his ordination, he had marched in the civil rights movement with Martin Luther King Jr. on twenty-six occasions, a dangerous activity for someone who wore a yarmulke at all times. He took the bruises he had received during a beating in Tallahassee—a worse experience for him than Selma or Montgomery—as marks of pride. In the late 1960s he embarked on parallel careers in business, politics, and academic life. Enjoying a highly successful stint in real estate, he invested in construction from Toronto to Miami, while earning a doctorate in political science and teaching in both Israel and New York. In the 1970s he grew active in New York politics and Jewish affairs.

While campaigning for the rights of Soviet Jews in 1969, he met Nahum Goldmann, the charismatic founder of the World Jewish Congress. Established in 1936 to coordinate international efforts against Nazism and anti-Semitism, the WJC became the main Jewish body negotiating Holocaust reparations with German chancellor Konrad Adenauer after the war, but it had lapsed into quiet irrelevance by the time Singer started working there in the early 1980s. The onset of the cold war had effectively scotched any hopes of further compensation for Holocaust victims. In the East, the United States blocked the flow of cash to survivors now living in the Soviet bloc, and in the West it had no desire to antagonize its European allies against Communism. Meanwhile, the Jewish community had another battle to fight, and was concentrating on the survival of the new state of Israel.

The organization was almost insolvent by the time an aging Goldmann gave way to Bronfman in 1981. Singer seized the opportunity, and persuaded Bronfman to pour his energy, and money, into making the WJC a vital player in the Jewish Diaspora once more. Singer, in day-to-day control of the World Jewish Congress, became Bronfman's guiding spirit and "brother." In his youth, Bronfman had been so far from observing Judaism that he even ate pork on Yom Kippur, the day of atonement when Jews are expected to fast. Singer helped bring him to Judaism, patiently discussing the Torah during innumerable long-distance flights. In return, Bronfman gave him sweeping freedom of action at the WJC.

Still, the WJC had a tiny membership, and did not command the automatic loyalty of world Jewry. Others had been campaigning against the Swiss for years. Israeli politicians had taken on the Swiss banks at different times and Dan Tichon, chairman of the Knesset's finance committee, had spent much of the last ten years shuttling to Switzerland, collecting testimony from survivors and writing letters to Swiss banks, but with little impact. Tichon even suspected that the Jewish Agency, the Israeli agency charged with working for Holocaust restitution, was deliberately covering up its own past failures.

Singer, however, had several advantages. Chief among them was Bronfman himself, who gave him access to American businesspeople and politicians with real clout. As Singer launched his campaign against the Swiss, Bronfman was rapidly becoming one of the biggest donors in American politics. In the 1996 elections, Seagram's U.S. subsidiary was the biggest donor of soft money to the Democratic Party and President Bill Clinton's reelection campaign.

Singer admitted that nothing could have happened without Bronfman. "He's the nine-hundred-pound gorilla with the smiling visage," said Singer. "When he came to see politicians as a multibillionaire, this meant to everyone that this was a serious subject, and we meant business. This is the industrial establishment taking on the banking establishment. They could not say this was just from a rabbi or a philosopher. I could never have run this without him."

Singer had other advantages. As an American, he was free to alienate and attack any government—unlike Israeli politicians who remained heedful of the life-and-death struggle on their own borders. He also understood the Swiss. His wife, Evelyne, was a Swiss Jew—a fact that he never ceased to mention to his Swiss adversaries.

Ultimately, Singer's greatest advantage was his own theatrical performance. He dazzled friends with witticisms, and charmed adversaries as he looked for compromise. But in public, Singer's oratory was demagogic and passionate, often angry and always forceful. He believed that Jews needed to show they could not be "pushed around," and made no apology for using Jewish organizations' political and economic power in any way he could.

"There is a new brand of Jew alive today that believes that God gave the Jew power and that power needs to be used and exercised," he once proclaimed to a group of Jewish law students. "At times it needs to be abused, because the abuse of power by everyone else has brought the results that we are studying today, and if we do not abuse our power at times for good, we shall not be able to protect ourselves." As he campaigned across the world for Jewish causes, he frankly admitted that the end sometimes justified the means, no matter how extreme they might appear to fellow Jewish leaders. It was a stance that sometimes made him enemies in the Jewish world.

In private, he used aggressive tactics, borrowed from Lyndon Johnson. "I learned from Johnson that there are two options," Singer said. "You can either be outside the tent or you can be inside the tent. I found a third place, and that was outside, as well as inside the tent, urinating on the president's shoe." During the campaign to free Soviet Jews, he practiced this third option vigorously, and he did so many more times during the restitution campaign. "I was outside with the demonstrators," he said. "I was inside negotiating quietly, they thought; and I was also doing what I had to do."

As his 1995 winter of shuttle diplomacy between Switzerland and New York continued, Singer felt the Swiss were not taking him, or the WJC, seriously. He made contingency plans.

In December, Singer took Bronfman to Washington to meet

the Republican New York senator Alfonse D'Amato. A feisty and populist Long Island politician, D'Amato chaired the Senate Banking Committee, giving him oversight of all banks operating in the United States—including the Swiss banks' lucrative Wall Street operations. D'Amato had survived three six-year terms in the Senate by persistently making sure that he delivered for New York's voters, and he was proud to be known as Senator Pothole. As his visitors spoke, D'Amato began to grasp the explosive possibilities of the story of survivors deprived of their bank accounts for half a century, and rubbed his hands with glee. Brooklyn, near D'Amato's political heartland, was home to the world's largest concentration of Holocaust survivors.

He could hold hearings with aged Holocaust survivors, standing up for them against the faceless bankers in Zurich. "This was made in heaven!" he shouted several times at Singer and Bronfman. He wanted to schedule Senate hearings right away.

Bronfman professed to find D'Amato's behavior distasteful, but Singer convinced him to swallow his doubts. To give the Swiss investigation a chance, they persuaded the senator to hold off his hearings, but they left Washington confident that they had his political firepower at their disposal.

Within weeks, they would need it. The Swiss Bankers Association lost the chance to resolve the affair quietly and with dignity on February 7, 1996, five months after the lunch at La Grande Société, when it gave its semiannual briefing for the press over coffee and croissants at Zurich's Savoy Hotel.

Singer, who thought that he was still helping to run the investigation, was asleep at home in Queens, New York, at the time, utterly unaware of what was happening. After a *tour d'horizon* from Krayer, the stage was given over to the results of the association's "investigation" into the dormant accounts issue.

The banks offered precise statistics. Their survey had found 775 accounts with a total value of 38.7 million Swiss francs (about $22 million) that had been deposited by foreign clients before 1945 and were now dormant. Of these, 516 accounts, with a total value of 28.5 million Swiss francs, originated from Germany and German-occupied territories.

"These numbers confirm our forecast of last September," the

association said. "The rumors about huge assets hidden at Swiss banks belonging to Holocaust victims are totally unfounded. Finally, it is not accurate to blame Swiss banking secrecy as being the reason why victims could not get adequate information. On the contrary, every Swiss bank is obliged by law to give descendants all information available."

The association said it was trying to find a "fair solution" that "does not infringe on anyone's legal rights" for disposing of the assets, in collaboration with the "international Jewish community." The bankers hoped their statement would at last close the historical episode, and persuade their Jewish accusers to abandon the hunt.

It had exactly the opposite effect. By treating the claims of Holocaust survivors like any other business, to be settled without fanfare in a routine meeting, they betrayed a deep misjudgment of the depths of the campaigners' emotions. Even within the bankers' ranks, Hans Baer was annoyed not to have been advised in advance of the press conference and felt sure the Jewish side would feel slighted.

In Queens, an enraged Singer awoke early to the news that the Swiss had published their report. He started his day by giving a succinct order to Elan Steinberg, his executive director at the WJC: "Kill them."

Singer then called Bronfman. "Fuck them, kill them, they are a bunch of bastards," Bronfman yelled into the phone. Finally, Singer called Avraham Burg, the head of the Jewish Agency for Israel, a fellow member of the delegation to Bern. "We must go to war," Singer said.

Barely six months earlier, the issue of dormant accounts had been the subject of civilized conversation over lunch in Bern's most exclusive private club. Now Singer had moved the battle from La Grande Société to terrain where he could win: America.

Singer marshaled his troops, giving D'Amato the go-ahead to hold a hearing—D'Amato set it for April 23, 1996—and enlisting other friends from New York politics for support. Elan Steinberg, who handled press relations for the WJC, started peppering journalists with declassified U.S. intelligence reports from the 1940s, gleaned from the National Archives, sometimes with the help of

D'Amato's researchers. These revealed U.S. suspicions that the Swiss had held on to the assets of Holocaust victims after the war.

The day before D'Amato's hearing was scheduled, Bronfman saw the opportunity to widen the scope of his attack on the Swiss when he and his wife hosted a Democratic Party fund-raiser at his Manhattan apartment. The guest of honor was First Lady Hillary Rodham Clinton. Asking for five minutes of her time, he proffered an article on the banks torn from the latest issue of *New York* magazine, published that day, drawn largely from documents released by the WJC's Elan Steinberg.

Clinton read the pages quickly, then looked up at him. "Edgar, is there any chance we can get the Swiss banks?"

"With your husband's help, yes."

Bronfman explained how he was finding it hard to reach President Clinton directly to enlist his support.

"I would be more than pleased and even privileged to arrange it. It's an issue I have very strong personal feelings about and I know that Bill will, when he has an opportunity to learn more about it."

Clinton knew a little about the issue, but only from books. As soon as she left the Bronfmans', she phoned her husband to arrange a meeting with Singer and Bronfman the next day. In the midst of the frenetic fund-raising of the 1996 campaign, the Clinton White House was only too ready to open its doors to one of the party's most generous donors.

It did nothing to raise the spirits of the Swiss delegation, freshly arrived in Washington for D'Amato's Senate hearing, to discover that Bronfman could not meet them due to a prior appointment with the First Lady. They were under greater pressure than they had ever thought possible.

The star at D'Amato's hearing, though, would be a very different lady. Greta Beer, an elegant retired travel guide from Jackson Heights, Queens, was about to bring the Swiss banks to their knees.

Born Greta Beligdisch in Romania, before the war, she had enjoyed a privileged childhood, living off the fruits of her father's extensive textile business. He had traveled all over Germany and the old Austro-Hungarian Empire on business, and could even afford to send her to boarding school in Switzerland. Before dying, of natural causes, in 1940, he confidently assured his children that his money was safely deposited in Switzerland. The family had spent the rest of the war in hiding, and could not cross the Swiss border until after hostilities had ceased.

Despite repeated attempts after the war, Greta and her mother never managed to retrieve the money, but a *Wall Street Journal* reporter wrote a front-page story about her in the summer of 1995, ratcheting up the pressure on the banks. Steinberg, knowing that the story of Swiss perfidy needed a human face to sustain public interest, telephoned to ask if she would be willing to testify. Beer, who had made her living by charming large crowds as an international tour guide, promptly accepted.

The day before the hearing, as Bronfman was talking to Hillary Clinton, Steinberg's secretary greeted Greta Beer in Queens and transported her to Washington where she would stay the night. Beer, an elegant dresser who spoke English with only a slight Eastern European accent, charmed everyone she met, including Senator D'Amato. Talking to her before the hearing, he quickly felt the power of her story.

Senate hearings take place in a formal atmosphere not unlike a courtroom, and some of the Swiss felt as though they were on trial. One of D'Amato's staffers later said that the bankers were "on our turf and conveniently, we were judge, jury, and executioner."

For dramatic effect, D'Amato arranged for Beer to speak first. Hans Baer, speaking for the Swiss banks, would go last, after all the charges had been levied. With a bang of the gavel, D'Amato launched the proceedings. "Good morning. This morning the committee meets to take up an important matter that has implications that go back to World War II, the Holocaust, and it involves more than money, more than millions and tens of millions and maybe hundreds of millions and maybe more than that. But it involves the systematic victimization of people."

He plunged straight into the story of Greta Beer, "a Long Islander from Queens, Long Island, Jackson Heights, New York," whose victimization at the hands of the Nazis had continued at the hands of the Swiss banks. "She and her mother went from city to city and from bank to bank back in the '60s in Switzerland looking for accounts that her father had placed in trust with the Swiss banks. That trust was broken. And because of that broken trust, she and her family have been forced to deal with the evasions and excuses over 50 years."

In barely a minute, D'Amato had thumped out a devastating indictment of the Swiss and their behavior. The message sounded even more poignant from Beer herself. She silenced the room as she told of her father's illness, of her family's travails when the Communists seized Romania, and of her repeated trips to Montreux in Switzerland to look for her father's *chiffres*, or numbered bank account.

As a seasoned tour guide, she told the assembly about Switzerland, its ancient democracy, and how it had inspired Thomas Jefferson. She ended: "How come Swiss banks, I don't say Switzerland, but the Swiss banks perpetuate the same things we thought was *tempe posti*, a thing of the past? And now the Swiss banks perpetuate the same things toward people who have suffered in one way or another. The only thing I can say, I do hope Senator D'Amato, that the Swiss banks will see the light—and so many people have died in the meantime—and will see the light to correct what has been done—so long. I'm sorry I don't read, I just speak from my heart, albeit a very heavy heart."

As she sat down, Hans Baer, as moved as the rest of the room by her story, impulsively offered to take her to Switzerland to help her track down her account.

Edgar Bronfman, with Singer at his side, spoke next. "I hope it will not sound presumptuous, Mr. Chairman," he said, "but I speak to you today on behalf of the Jewish people. With reverence, I also speak on behalf of the six million: those who cannot speak for themselves."

He recounted Georg Krayer's promise made at their meeting in Bern that the banks did not want to keep "a single Swiss franc that is not their own," and took the senators through the Swiss banks' sporadic attempts to clear up the issue since the war. Then he declared: "Swiss institutions cannot be permitted to come back and say once again that they will create such a process but that they want to be the ones who appoint the auditors. Their repeated failure of integrity over 50 years has forfeited for them such a privilege. There must be an arm's length process that is credible to the entire world."

Barbara Boxer, the senior Democrat on D'Amato's committee, asked more about the history. "My instinctive judgment," replied Bronfman, "is that they said in 1962, here's some money, now go away. And they're trying to do that again in 1995. Here's a lot more money, and please go away and leave us alone."

Finally, Hans Baer got the chance to speak for the Swiss Bankers Association. Baer had been brought up in America as a war refugee, and regarded English as his mother tongue, although he spoke it with a gravelly German accent. Careful to avoid any more public relations gaffes, he furnished D'Amato with a résumé detailing all his donations to Jewish and Israeli causes, and launched his speech with an account of how the World Jewish Congress had commended Bank Julius Baer in 1944 for its work safeguarding the Jewish faith.

A large man with a craggy and expressive face, Baer looked tired under the lights, showing the fatigue of crossing and recrossing the Atlantic three times in the last week in his attempt to sort out the problem. One of D'Amato's staffers unkindly noted his resemblance to Peter Sellers's mad bomb-making character in *Doctor Strangelove*. He made a lengthy presentation, setting out his hopes that an independent audit (jointly overseen by the WJC and the Swiss banks) could solve the problem. In a show of openness, he even read out the fax number for the Swiss banking ombudsman.

During cross-examination, D'Amato brandished intelligence reports from the National Archives showing that 182 Jews from the Balkans had Swiss accounts worth $20 million in 1945. Another report showed that the Swiss National Bank had taken 21 tons of German gold in 1942. Baer knew nothing about the documents, and he could say little about them.

Then Senator Boxer asked him about stolen goods "that landed in Sweden," deeply confusing Baer, who knew nothing about Sweden. Boxer admitted that she had misspoken, but she was not the only one who struggled through the hearing. Baer stumbled through his responses from this point on. None of the senators liked his plan to hold an independent audit.

"It is not good enough to say, 'Take $32 million' on the basis of an examination that has admitted, I think, deficiencies, areas that were not accounted for," D'Amato said in conclusion. "That's what the committee is looking for, a methodology of establishing a legitimate, bona fide accounting."

The meeting ended with a second bang of the gavel. D'Amato had staged a perfect piece of political theater.

Bronfman and Singer did not witness Baer's ordeal. They had slipped out early to make the short trip down Pennsylvania Avenue to the White House to meet with President Clinton. The two Jewish dignitaries had only a brief slot in the late afternoon as Clinton changed before a diplomatic reception—a decidedly more informal and intimate setting than their meeting with the Swiss president the year before. The only other person in the room was Leon Panetta, then Clinton's chief of staff.

Clinton crisscrossed the Oval Office while Bronfman and Singer stood. The president had no great desire to help D'Amato, who had made himself an annoyance and an enemy with his dogged hearings on the Whitewater affair, involving a failed real estate venture that threatened to engulf the Clintons. But like his wife, he was keen to help Holocaust survivors. And Bronfman was a hard man to ignore.

"What's Senator D'Amato doing in this?" Clinton asked.

"Mr. President, this matter may require legislation."

"Okay, you tell Senator D'Amato that if this needs legislation, I'll be honored to work with him."

Bronfman had a biblical analogy for this: Clinton working with D'Amato was like Esther saying she would dance with Haman. With this unholy alliance, Singer and Bronfman had united the president, the Senate, and much of the U.S. press behind a struggle against the Swiss banks. Now it was time for the Swiss to respond.

The Final Accounting

The Swiss banks found their man for the hour in the unlikely figure of the sixty-eight-year-old Hans Baer, their hapless representative at D'Amato's hearing. Baer had planned to retire that year, stepping down as chief executive of Bank Julius Baer, the family bank which he had nurtured from a tiny private concern with less than thirty employees during the war into an international operation in twenty-five cities with a staff of more than three thousand. A life of relaxation beckoned. Baer, who cheerfully described himself as an "inherently lazy person," had no desire to hurl himself into the affair of dormant accounts.

Fortune conspired to change his plan. Bank Julius Baer figured prominently in the front-page *Wall Street Journal* article of the previous year that had helped to turn international attention toward Switzerland. Baer read with horror its revelation that in 1987 his bank demanded a fee of 100 Swiss francs (about $57) to search for the account of a Dachau internee called Moses Blum. The bank had told Blum's daughters that it was only obliged to keep records for ten years. Baer demanded to see the account file immediately and when it arrived promptly on his desk, he realized that his and many other banks must still be holding on to a lot of wartime records. The incident left him with an uncomfortable feeling that the banks, even his own, had deliberately obstructed victims from obtaining readily available evidence about their accounts. Unlike many of his colleagues, Baer appreciated that Singer was raising a genuine issue.

Baer was the most senior Jew in Swiss banking and although not a religious man, he had a strong sense of his Jewish identity. As a young man, he had even been a friend of the WJC's founder Nahum Goldmann, who spent much of his life in Switzerland. However, Baer felt no great respect for Goldmann's successor, Edgar Bronfman, and he found shocking Bronfman's frank admission in his book that Judaism had meant little to him as a young man. He had no desire to fight the WJC now over the way his own banking community had mistreated his fellow Jews.

However he was given little choice. Shortly before D'Amato's Senate hearing, as the world's media focused on the world of Swiss banking, Baer received a phone call from Kurt Hauri, chairman of the Swiss Federal Banking Commission and the nation's chief banking regulator. Hauri issued a strict instruction: "It's your duty to sort this out."

Hauri reminded him of his status as the only Jewish member of the executive committee of the Swiss Bankers Association. Baer, yielding to the inevitable, phoned his contacts in Israel. They agreed that the only person who could help him was a man named Curtis Hoxter. He would turn out to be the perfect bridge between Hans Baer and Israel Singer.

A German-born public relations expert who had emigrated to New York in 1939 and was now in his seventies, Hoxter had made a living for half a century out of smoothing the path of difficult deals for Swiss, German, and Austrian companies in the United States. Every few months he would swing through central European capitals, holding court in the best hotels. Hoxter often visited Hans Baer, who was on his "hit list" for frequent contacts.

Crucially, Hoxter had worked as the go-between for Singer and Chancellor Franz Vranitzky of Austria during Singer's vocal campaign a decade earlier to uncover Kurt Waldheim's Nazi past. While Singer and Vranitzky attacked each other publicly, they used Hoxter as a private channel of communication. During that episode Singer and Hoxter had developed a deep mutual trust. Hoxter became Singer's most trusted adviser on the restitution campaign, while cheerfully continuing to advise his Swiss client Hans Baer. He regarded it as his duty to help find a resolution.

On the morning of D'Amato's hearing, despite a ban imposed

by Edgar Bronfman on WJC talks with the Swiss, Hoxter presided over negotiations between Israel Singer and Hans Baer. In the breakfast room of a Washington hotel, Singer and Baer sat at different tables while Hoxter, cunning as ever, shuttled from table to table, offering Singer and Baer new revisions of a proposal he had written to sort out the situation.

Their plan was simple. International accounting firms would audit the banks, as Bronfman had requested at La Grande Société in Bern. The Swiss Bankers Association and the WJC would each appoint three members to an "Independent Committee of Eminent Persons" (ICEP) which would oversee the audit and decide on a fair amount of money for the Swiss to pay. A respected and neutral chairman would cast tie-breaking votes.

The three men, all the sons of German-speaking Jews who had spent much of their youth in New York, struck up a quick rapport. They had already negotiated over capuccinos in a bar in midtown Manhattan, where they found a sense of common ground. Baer considered Singer a brilliant man and enjoyed his company, but noted that he was deliberately dragging his feet.

Singer badly wanted to get the Swiss to sign up to a process, but he could not show weakness. His Israeli colleagues from the mission to Bern were keen to force a confrontation, while signing a deal straightaway might annoy D'Amato. If he signed too quickly, Singer suspected, the senator would cancel the hearing, relieving the pressure on the Swiss at just the wrong moment. As a result, a discontented Baer had to return across the Atlantic, only to recross it days later to face D'Amato.

Baer kept on the phone to the Swiss Bankers Association in Basel. Of the several hundred banks in Switzerland, many were tiny, serving only their local cantons, but three huge institutions—Union Bank of Switzerland (UBS), Credit Suisse, and the Swiss Bank Corporation (SBC)—dwarfed the rest. They each owned big investment banks on Wall Street, where they needed to hire, and retain, Jewish employees. Any damage to their reputation could therefore cripple their ability to compete in the world's capital markets, and so they needed a solution quickly. Baer made sure that the big three knew what they were about to sign.

On May 7, two weeks after the circus in D'Amato's hearing

room, the Memorandum of Understanding, a concise document that fit onto one sheet of letter-sized paper, was ready for signing. Swiss secrecy laws would be lifted, but only for the auditors of the new committee, and only for the purpose of hunting for dormant accounts. The auditors would get "unfettered access to all relevant files in banking institutions regarding dormant accounts and other assets and financial instruments deposited before, during and immediately after the Second World War."

These were huge concessions for the Swiss, striking at the foundations of the way they did business. They could not imagine going any further.

Baer flew back to New York for a special signing ceremony, accompanied by Georg Krayer. On short notice, Josef Ackermann, then chief executive of Credit Suisse, also flew out for the signing, underscoring that Switzerland's international banks supported the new committee. Bronfman, in cheery mood now that the Swiss had acceded to his core demands, hosted the signing at the Four Seasons restaurant on the ground floor of the Seagram Building, the modernist glass-and-metal palace his father had commissioned. Each Swiss banker carefully signed the memorandum. It would prove one of the most expensive pieces of paper any of them would ever handle.

As the bankers dined on some of New York's most expensive cuisine, Bronfman proposed to convene the committee's first meeting at his French château. Baer delicately suggested that this might not look good in Switzerland, and the plan was shelved. Instead, they discussed the membership of their new committee. Singer and Baer, as the architects of the committee, would both serve on it, although officially as alternates, not full members. Baer had a slate of Swiss members he had drawn up in a New York taxi. Two were Jewish, as he attempted to ensure balance, and none was directly employed by a Swiss bank. Instead he opted for regulators, academics, and accountants, none of whom had a direct financial stake in the outcome.

Singer, on the other hand, drew up a list of nominees tied to organizations working for restitution for Holocaust victims, including Ronald Lauder, the WJC's treasurer and heir to the

Estée Lauder fortune, and Avraham Burg, head of the Jewish Agency for Israel.

Singer had a deep attachment to Burg, a Young Turk on the left of Israeli politics, who would shortly become the speaker of the Knesset. A generation earlier, Burg's father, Yosef, had led the Mizrahi religious Zionist movement in interwar Germany, while Singer's father had run the Austrian counterpart. After Germany's annexation of Austria, Burg's father attempted to use the contacts he had developed with the SS to help the Singers escape, signing a certificate to allow them passage from the country. Yosef Burg became a giant of Israeli politics, helping to found the right-wing National Religious Party and serving as a cabinet minister for thirty-five years.

Avraham Burg did not share his father's politics. But, like Singer, he wore his yarmulke all the time, had more than his fair share of charm and charisma, and could be intimidatingly aggressive. Even in the calm surroundings of the Seagram Building, he saw fit to bluster that he could never trust the Swiss.

Months earlier, Burg's inflammatory rhetoric had provoked the Swiss president into retracting an invitation for him to accompany Bronfman to Bern. Burg reinstated his invitation by coolly telling the presidential press office: "Okay, we're coming tomorrow to Bern. Now if the president will continue this selection policy of the Nazis to distinguish between Jews and Jews, we are calling an international news conference on the steps of the presidential palace to tell the world how we feel about it." Singer took advantage of Burg's volatility by telling the Swiss he was the voice of moderation who could save them from the aggressive Israeli.

Burg's attitude, however, was dovish compared with that of the final Jewish nominee to the committee, Zvi Barak. A former fighter pilot who flew thirty-five missions during the 1973 Yom Kippur War, Barak was now cochairman (with Singer) of the World Jewish Restitution Organization, an umbrella group set up in 1992 to seek compensation from formerly Communist countries in Eastern Europe.

As far as he was concerned, Singer was too moderate, having been nurtured in the safety of North America. Barak's own upbringing on Israel's front line gave him a different perspective. "I was born in a minority and I live in a minority," he said. "I am a fighter pilot and you know fighter pilots fly alone. Singer is coming from a consensus place." Barak, a lawyer and a director of Bank Leumi, Israel's biggest bank, was also the Jewish "details" man on the committee. Over the next four years, he would never miss a meeting, and never afford the Swiss any benefit of the doubt.

With such a polarized and dysfunctional lineup of eminent persons, the choice of chairman grew more important. The Swiss shortlist had several names, including Brian Mulroney, the former Canadian prime minister, but Curtis Hoxter was clear about the first choice: Paul Volcker, the former chairman of the Federal Reserve.

A bearlike bald-headed Texan, at six feet eight inches Volcker had a huge profile in more ways than one. As a non-Jewish American with close contacts both in Switzerland and in the Jewish community, he seemed ideal. For almost a decade he successfully steered the world's financial system, navigating the straits of the early 1980s and showing his independence with repeated hikes in interest rates.

Now sixty-eight, Volcker had worked since leaving the Fed as a partner of the New York investment banker James Wolfensohn, president of the World Bank and a friend of Edgar Bronfman. Swiss bankers also knew Volcker well. In the early 1980s, he had flown into Basel and Zurich many times to negotiate resolutions to the world banking crisis. He even sat on the board of Nestlé, the giant Swiss consumer products company.

When Hoxter phoned to offer him the job, Volcker needed convincing. He believed the two sides were absurdly far apart, with the Swiss offering $5 million in compensation for victims' accounts and the American team demanding $50 billion. He canvassed his Jewish friends, all of whom warned him not to touch the job with a ten-foot pole.

Bronfman even phoned him from his private jet to lobby him. But the man who tipped the balance proved to be Fritz Leutwiler, who headed the Swiss National Bank while Volcker was at the Fed. Leutwiler told his good friend Volcker that it was his duty to take on the task: the honor and integrity of the Swiss banking system was at stake.

He also reassured Volcker that the job would not be onerous. The panel would appoint auditors, who would enter the banks, looking for documents. Swiss law allowed the destruction of documents more than ten years old (a common practice in other jurisdictions), so they both believed it would be impossible to pinpoint the number of dormant accounts. Once auditors had established that there was not enough hard evidence, he would simply broker a settlement. The process would take no longer than two years, ending in mid-1998 at the latest.

Once the Swiss central banker had made his pitch, Hoxter phoned Volcker, telling him he had already had four weeks to decide. The next day, Volcker accepted, on the condition that he could appoint his own legal adviser. Nobody objected, and so Volcker appointed Michael Bradfield, a colleague for more than twenty years at the Treasury Department and the Fed, as his general counsel in a move he subsequently described as "the one smart thing I did." It was a description with which the Swiss banks would totally disagree.

Bradfield became the effective general manager for the inquiry, and the public face of the investigation in Switzerland. A dogged man who had spent decades amassing piles of data to ensure that banks were run properly, Bradfield, although battling cancer at the time, was determined to subject the Swiss banks to a stringent investigation. He ceaselessly traveled to Switzerland, often flying overnight and then heading straight to a meeting, where he would doodle constantly without ever losing the flow of the meeting around him.

The Swiss bankers did not realize they had invited a tough American banking regulator to manage the investigation, and Hans Baer complained that Bradfield's appointment was "like bringing a child into a marriage without talking about it." Another commented: "Nobody realized that when we engaged Paul Volcker we bought at the same time a person called Mike Bradfield. We were naive."

Volcker soon discovered that his board of "eminent persons" did not behave with the civility of his fellow governors at the Fed.

For example, the two Israelis did not wait for others to stop speaking before talking themselves. Zvi Barak, in particular, regarded Volcker with suspicion. "An American chairman believes that he *is* the commission," he complained.

Meanwhile, one of the Swiss Jewish members resigned after only two meetings, apparently alarmed at what he thought would prove an unmanageable and intrusive investigation. He left saying, "This is not going to be the possible thing I thought it was."

Even the task of hiring accountants grew politically charged, and deadlocked the committee for more than six months. Zvi Barak refused to appoint Swiss auditors, and eventually forced a change in Swiss law to permit accountants not certified in Switzerland to audit the banks. The huge international accounting firms appointed to carry out the investigation responded by staffing the audit mostly with English speakers from the United Kingdom, the United States, Australia, and New Zealand. Auditors arrived fresh from long journeys, with no knowledge of Swiss banking regulations and often no command of French or German. Swiss bank managers, most of whom spoke English fluently in addition to French and German, resented the time they had to spend translating documents for outside auditors who knew nothing about their business. Rubbing salt into the wound, the auditors billed by the hour for taking these language lessons. The banks paid all the expenses, as they had agreed in the Memorandum of Understanding.

Agreeing on a mandate for the accountants proved no easier. Volcker eventually required his auditors to examine not only dormant accounts but also "accounts that would otherwise have been dormant" that had been "extinguished by actions that, whether or not inadvertent or deliberate, were illegal or in breach of fiduciary duties." This innocuous sentence, largely unremarked at the time, had immense consequences by broadening the scope to include accounts that had been closed, and for which there might legitimately be no remaining records. It was a far harder task than looking at the open accounts that had not been touched since the war.

With an army of auditors descending upon them, the banks felt under attack. Since few relevant documents had been transferred to computers, accountants spent hours looking through archives that had lain untouched for half a century. The Swiss banks, it emerged, had held more than six million accounts at the onset of war. Under their mandate, the accountants were required to find records for every account opened from 1927 until the outbreak of war. Then they needed to find records—seldom in the same place—to show what had happened to those accounts.

Four hundred eighty-one Swiss banks survived from the war era, and many had since merged, leaving large banks with disorganized archives spread across the country. UBS alone had more than eight hundred buildings in Switzerland, and Volcker's auditors searched all of them. By the time the audit was over, UBS had accumulated a pile of papers twelve kilometers long.

As the auditors came to terms with the scale of the task, they upped their staffing, eventually employing hundreds of people. Bradfield hired almost all the world's biggest accounting firms— Arthur Andersen, KPMG Peat Marwick, and Price Waterhouse were involved, later joined by Coopers Deloitte and Ernst and Young. By the end of 1999, when it began to wind down, the Volcker Commission had spent 310 million Swiss francs, or about $177 million. Adding in the costs of the audit itself, which the banks had to pay directly to the audit firms, took the bill to slightly above 1 billion Swiss francs, making it the biggest and most expensive audit ever held. Even this number excluded the amount of time the banks' employees needed to devote to helping the auditors. Both Hans Baer and Georg Krayer, the two Swiss bankers who had signed the Memorandum of Understanding, now admit that they had had no idea of what they had signed. But, as Volcker put it: "If you want the truth, you have to pay for it."

While Volcker had assumed that this task would prove impossible, the auditors returned from their first trawl of the banks' records with conclusive results. Far more documents had survived than Volcker expected; they possessed the records for more than four million accounts, out of a total of about six million. This meant that Volcker had enough evidence to settle the historical issues with a true forensic audit; the question was how long it would take to do it.

Volcker later commented ruefully, "That was the problem when the auditors went into the banks—they found quite a lot."

While Volcker girded for this massive investigation, the Swiss belatedly attempted to counter the public animosity building against them in the United States. Thomas Borer, an energetic young Swiss diplomat whose American fiancée was a former Miss Texas, was tapped to head a special government "Task Force" on Switzerland's wartime behavior. During 1997 he reached out to American Jews, addressing Saturday services at New York synagogues. Donning a yarmulke, he would tell skeptical but responsive audiences about his country's acceptance of its wartime guilt and answer questions over kiddush.

The Swiss parliament also set up a second commission, the International Commission of Experts, to look more deeply into questions about Switzerland's war record. Switzerland was already wrestling with a highly public debate about its position in a rapidly changing Europe, and whether with the end of the cold war and the rise of the European Union, its long policy of neutrality could still be justified. Now it was struggling with a crisis of confidence about the war itself. Had the country turned back Jewish refugees? Did the banks indeed launder looted gold for the Nazis?

This commission was no fig leaf. The chairman, Jean-Christophe Bergier, was a respected Swiss historian while his panel included leading Jewish American scholars of the Holocaust, and it started on its own lengthy quest for the truth. Its first report would not appear until 1998.

Meanwhile, Singer complained loudly that needy Holocaust survivors would die while they waited for Volcker to complete his audit. The Swiss government responded by offering money. It endowed a $200 million humanitarian fund for needy Holocaust survivors, overseen jointly by Swiss and Jewish representatives, and headed by Rolf Bloch, leader of the Swiss Jewish community. The big banks contributed $70 million.

During 1997, Volcker published two lists of names of dormant account–holders (not necessarily Holocaust survivors) from before the war. The first, with 1,872 names, covered large accounts, while a second list, of 3,687 names, had much smaller accounts: numbers that made a mockery of Georg Krayer's assertion at La Grande Société that only 752 dormant accounts remained. In an awful public relations blunder, the released lists included the names of several Nazi war criminals, including Heinrich Hofmann, Hitler's personal photographer.

Krayer, an honorable man, felt ashamed to find that so many accounts remained dormant. Years later, he still agonized over the complacency and insensitivity he and his colleagues had shown, and kept thinking of the letters he himself had written, asking survivors to "send the proof." He had never thought what such a letter would mean to someone when all that was left of their relatives were "two photographs and from time to time a visit from a cousin who said, 'I remember Aunt Rebecca.' "

"Looking into the list I felt and I still feel ashamed," he said later. "In some of the cases it would have been quite easy—just taking a phone book or just using some retired bank employees to look after this and we could have reduced it by a large percentage. This complacency is something I feel shame about. We at the beginning said, 'It's some small leftovers.' And we found out it was not some small leftovers. It was a pile of work that had never been done and should have been done."

With the Volcker and Bergier Commissions, the publication of new accounts and the humanitarian fund, Singer and Bronfman had everything they had asked for—an impartial accounting of the bank vaults, relaxation of secrecy laws, a rigorous reinvestigation of the historical record, and immediate aid for Holocaust survivors in need.

Even with these measures, however, Switzerland could not avoid the crisis. Instead, a series of crassly insensitive comments by some of the nation's most powerful men deepened its public relations difficulties in the United States.

Robert Studer, the patrician head of Union Bank Switzerland (UBS), Switzerland's biggest bank, gave a corporate press conference where he dismissed sums involved in Holocaust survivors' dormant accounts as "peanuts." From a corporate point of view, he was right: even the highest sums being mentioned would inflict minimal damage on UBS's profits. But to Holocaust survivors kept waiting for their accounts for half a century, the statement sounded cruel and obtuse.

In late 1996, outgoing Swiss president Jean-Pascal Delamuraz gave a retrospective interview as he was leaving the presidential palace, describing Bronfman's demand for a humanitarian fund as "no less than oppression and blackmail." He said such a fund would be treated as an admission of guilt and added: "When demands are made not in good faith, they must be rejected."

Avraham Burg called Delamuraz's comments anti-Semitic and threatened a Jewish boycott of the banks. By the time Delamuraz had published a carefully negotiated letter of apology, the damage had been done.

In January 1997, a Swiss newspaper published a secret memo that Carlo Jagmetti, the veteran Swiss ambassador in Washington, had written a few weeks earlier. "This is a war which Switzerland must win," he said, "both on the external front and on the internal front. Most of our enemies cannot be trusted." Jagmetti's comments were splashed over the front pages of newspapers in the United States and Israel, and within days he announced his decision to quit. At sixty-four, he had been due to retire six months later in any case. Ironically, Singer and his colleagues also believed they were at war, but were too smart to say so in public.

Studer, Delamuraz, and Jagmetti were pillars of Switzerland's banking, political, and diplomatic establishments. But the gravest damage to the Swiss reputation was inflicted by a twenty-eight-year-old night watchman.

At about 4:30 A.M. on January 8, 1997, Christoph Meili deviated from his usual route guarding a UBS building under renovation in the center of Zurich, and entered the shredding room of one of the bank's main administration buildings. In the years to come, bank officials would question why he changed his path, but Meili explained that security guards were often asked to move around, to avoid the impression that they were congregating in one place.

The shredding room was popular because it was warm, and there were often old magazines lying around.

There he found two large plastic pushcarts, full of old-looking documents waiting to be shredded. The main ledgers had titles like "Federal Bank, 1870–1926." Growing curious, Meili leafed through a large, heavy black-bound book with the years "1945–1965" written on the cover. In it he found the names of German chemical companies, with records starting as of February 1945. Some entries were for as much as 44,000 Swiss francs. In a separate ledger on real estate he found entries dating back to 1930, covering transfers and deposits, as well as details of bankruptcy auctions.

Noting the dates, he ripped out the entire real estate part from both books, which he then replaced in the pushcart hoping nobody would notice. He dragged the real estate pages and a book dated "1920–1926" to his locker in two trips, and then took the real estate section home, where he and his wife inspected it with great curiosity. Two days later, he returned to the shredding room to find that the other documents had been destroyed.

Like most in Switzerland, Meili had read about the investigation of the Holocaust accounts, and he had recently seen Steven Spielberg's Holocaust movie, *Schindler's List.* He had also been given his notice—in routine cutbacks the previous year, UBS had said that he and other security guards would soon be asked to leave. He decided he must go public with the information.

Meili would later testify:

> I was convinced that documents were being destroyed illegally. I wished to prevent the Swiss people from suffering harm, and to make the documents and actions known to the public. I also wanted the oppressed Jewish population—the Holocaust victims— to get justice.

He offered the documents to the Israeli consulate, which refused them, and then to the Zurich Jewish Community Center who advised him to go to the police. At the police station, Meili was advised not to go back to work the next day, while officers referred the case to the district attorney, who started investigating

UBS for destroying documents, and Meili for stealing bank property. The next day, his employers at his private security firm told him he was suspended.

The prosecutor's decision to investigate Meili—even though UBS had requested him not to do so—made him a martyr in the eyes of the American press. In Switzerland, however, he was viewed as a traitor. This response, in combination with his revelations about shredding, disastrously undermined all the efforts the Swiss had made to restore their reputation. Death threats started to arrive for Meili at the offices of the Jewish community in Zurich, and his name and face became so well known that he abandoned hope of finding work in Switzerland. Robert Studer, UBS's ever-undiplomatic CEO, compounded the hurt by speculating about his motives on a television chat show. Many in Switzerland believed that Meili was simply a glory-hunter.

The documents proved to relate to Eidgenössische Bank, which UBS had bought some years before and which had had strong connections with Germany. They had no relevance to dormant accounts, but they were covered by a law working its way through the Swiss parliament at the time that barred banks from destroying documents relevant to Bergier's historical commission. The bank's archivist had apparently acted on his own initiative, despite recent management memos outlining a new policy against destruction of documents. Years later, a former UBS executive looking back on the events said, "It was probably all a coincidence: just very, very bad luck."

Meili flew to the United States with his family, where he sought asylum—the first Swiss citizen ever to do so on grounds of political persecution. "Let's play games," he thought. "There are Jews in the U.S. who appreciate what I do and I can help them, so let's make a lot of trouble and do it. It's better than staying in Switzerland and living on welfare."

Congress rushed through a law, speedily signed by President Clinton, to grant him citizenship. In May of 1997, Al D'Amato proclaimed Meili a "noble hero" and "righteous man," and called a special hearing in the Senate, with Meili and Israel Singer as the only witnesses. An attractive and studious-looking young man in wire-rimmed glasses, with his wife, Giuseppina, and two young children watching him, Meili enunciated his English slowly and carefully. He unfolded a detailed account of his adventures, and said he was acting in the best interests of the Swiss people.

Then D'Amato spoke. "Let me tell you what has taken place," he said. "This young man has been threatened, coerced, received death threats. His children have been threatened with kidnap. He has not been able to get a job. He has been branded as a traitor, as a pariah.

"Just two weeks ago we were informed by his lawyer in Switzerland that he should not come back there, that the state prosecutor is threatening him with prosecution for the taking of these documents and revealing them. Imagine that!"

The hearing ended with Meili's appeal: "Please protect me in the U.S.A. and in Switzerland. I think I become a great problem in Switzerland. I have a woman, two little children, and no future."

Edgar Bronfman offered Meili a job as a security guard in Florida, which he turned down, suspecting that the big Jewish groups wanted to keep him away from the center of the action in New York. Instead, he found part-time work as a security guard on Wall Street, supplemented with a steady stream of honoraria for speaking to Jewish groups. For the next year, Meili persistently embarrassed the Swiss, appearing regularly at campaign meetings, and even launching a lawsuit against UBS for slander.

A man who had never met Jews before his trip to the shredding room, he traveled the Jewish community circuit in the United States, and even ventured to Israel. However, he grew suspicious of the big Jewish organizations, who he felt used him as a "pawn in the chess game," hailing him as a hero but failing to appreciate his advice on how they should run their campaign against the Swiss.

In 1998, many months after the impulsive act that made his name, Meili made a speech at a law school in southern California. Members of the 1939 Club, a Los Angeles club made up largely of Polish Holocaust survivors, heard him speak about the impact *Schindler's List* had made on him and offered donations of more than $10,000 on the spot. Then they arranged for him to become a student. He was given a full-tuition scholarship at Chapman University, a commuter college in Orange County, while a new group called the Christoph Meili Humanitarian Tribute Committee raised money at a gala at the Beverly Hilton to pay his living expenses. His English fast improving, Meili slipped easily into junk culture, and like his fellow students became an expert in finding ever more bizarre sites on the Internet. He was unlikely ever to return to Switzerland.

His distrust of the most powerful figures in the American Jewish community intensified. "I've met nice people here," he said, "but I've also met ugly ones. The more money they have, the uglier they are. I get supported by normal people. Little synagogues are collecting money. But the rich Jews, they don't get so helpful. You know how many billionaires I've met? They just shake your hand."

Increasingly embittered despite his comfortable new California existence, Meili came to believe that the American campaigners needed him not only for his one moment of instinctive moral courage but also for his strategic advice once he arrived in the United States. He said: "Without me they wouldn't get one penny from the Swiss banks. They needed my knowledge. I told the lawyers what to do. I was the guy who controlled the newspaper articles and who told them how to be strategic and increase pressure on the Swiss people."

Even if these claims seem hopelessly exaggerated, it remains hard to overstate the impact of Meili's trip to the shredding room and its appallingly handled aftermath. After the Meili affair, the Volcker Commission and the $200 million humanitarian fund were no longer enough to win peace for the Swiss. Instead, the dispute turned from a historical debate into a contemporary cover-up. To the American press and public, weaned on scandals like Watergate and Iran-Contra, the spectacle of a bank shredding documents and then attacking the whistle-blower looked terrible.

In the United States, lawyers were already planning to launch lawsuits as their own line of attack, but they needed to undermine the legitimacy of the Volcker process to do so. Meili came as a godsend to them. Now, the lawyers could claim that the Volcker audit was not enough, because documents had been destroyed. As Franz Zimmermann, legal counsel for UBS, admitted: "Meili opened the floodgates in terms of the litigation, because there were allegations that they've destroyed everything. This is why Meili is so important."

THREE

A Pride of Lawyers

I n the summer of 1996, Ed Fagan, a New York personal injury lawyer, was intrigued to read an article in the *New York Times* about D'Amato's inquiry and the Volcker investigation. Surely, he reasoned, litigation offered the best way to make the Swiss pay. All the Swiss banks had Wall Street branches and plenty of Holocaust survivors lived in New York, so they could easily be pursued in a New York court. File the case in Brooklyn, and the jurors for any trial would be drawn from the world's largest Jewish community.

Fagan's actions would have a profound effect on the dynamics of the campaign against the Swiss. Until this point, Israel Singer and the Jewish organizations had controlled or guided all the efforts to make the banks pay. But if Fagan launched his lawsuit, there was nothing Singer or anyone else could do to make it go away until a federal judge dismissed it.

A Texan Jew who had once considered rabbinical training before enrolling at Yeshiva University's Cardozo Law School, Fagan needed a high-profile lawsuit to inject life into the small and struggling personal injury practice he ran from offices on the eighty-first floor of the World Trade Center. Taking on the cause of Holocaust survivors seemed perfect. A lanky and untidy man in his mid-forties with a shock of curly hair that was just beginning to gray, Fagan was already looking beyond American shores for a big case, flying to Colombia in 1995 in search of plaintiffs after an Andean air crash. His trip prompted complaints from bereaved relatives. Fagan's taste for publicity could land him in trouble, and he once even faced a libel lawsuit from the movie star Sylvester Stallone over material he leaked to the press in a lawsuit.

The Friday after reading the *Times* article, a client of his named Gizella Weisshaus dropped by his office as she often did before the Sabbath. Fagan had worked for her three years earlier when she had challenged the order of a rabbinical court in a dispute over a building she owned in Brooklyn. Now sixty-eight, and the only member of her Romanian Jewish family to survive Auschwitz, Weisshaus had settled in a Hasidic community in Brooklyn. A stern figure, usually dressed in black and wearing dark hats above Orthodox wigs, she retained great energy.

Fagan asked her what she thought of the *Times* article, and she replied, to his delight, that she had a claim against the Swiss banks. Before her father was separated from her and loaded into a railcar, he told her he had saved money for the family in Switzerland. After the war, Weisshaus made three trips to Switzerland looking for the money, but never received any help from the banks. She said, "After all that, I don't want to wait another five years for my money."

Weisshaus was happy for Fagan to sue on her behalf, and also offered to help. Over the next eight months, she would go to work in his World Trade Center office almost daily, wear a beeper so she could be summoned at any time, and make herself available to the press. She even baked Fagan cakes.

Fagan was overjoyed. After two weeks of research, largely gleaned from the growing volume of press cuttings D'Amato and Singer had generated, Fagan had a lawsuit. On Friday, October 4, 1996, he filed a complaint, *Weisshaus v Union Bank of Switzerland et al.*, in the Brooklyn courthouse of the Eastern District of New York, alleging that the Swiss deliberately stole the accounts of Gizella Weisshaus and others. He demanded $20 billion in damages. Fagan had no staff to help him research the complaint, or to deal with potential plaintiffs, and he had no expertise in international litigation, all insuperable obstacles to running a class action that could involve tens of thousands of people. But that did not bother him for now. The press gobbled it up, and Judge Edward

Korman, chief judge for the district, was assigned the case. The only mystery for Fagan was why nobody had thought of it before.

Someone had. All summer long, a team of the nation's top class action lawyers had been working on an almost identical complaint under the leadership of a Washington lawyer named Michael Hausfeld, who had built his reputation leading complex class action cases against corporations. In late 1996, as Fagan filed his complaint against the Swiss, Hausfeld was nearing victory in a draining campaign against the oil giant Texaco. Armed with tapes of Texaco executives making racist comments, he forced the company to pay $167 million to its ethnic minority employees and admit bias against them.

The cause of Holocaust survivors, however, lay closer to his heart. Named after his uncle who was killed during the Holocaust, Michael Hausfeld had known no grandfathers or grandmothers, and on his father's side, no uncles or aunts. He had lost ten relatives to the Nazis, and he treated suing the Swiss banks as a moral crusade. Hausfeld grew up in Brooklyn, in a community dominated by Holocaust survivors, where parents would show each other their camp tattoos. As a child he assumed that he too would have a number on his arm in later life. At synagogue during Kol Nidre, the opening service of Yom Kippur, he had vivid recollections of ambulances waiting outside to collect those overcome by grief for the loved ones they had lost in the death camps.

Nervy and intense at the best of times, Hausfeld's grief for Holocaust survivors drove him to displays of emotion in negotiations, and tears often welled in his eyes.

In the early 1980s, he tested the waters of international law by drafting a case against a suspected Croatian war criminal backed by the Nazis. The case failed, but he remained bent on finding a way to hold the Holocaust's perpetrators to account in American courts. Once D'Amato's hearings started, he returned to the problem, searching through books of transcripts from the Nuremberg trials.

Hausfeld believed he had the perfect opportunity to apply his legal expertise in the cause of Holocaust survivors. Flush with funds from recent victories, he could even afford to work pro bono, refusing a fee. He grew so preoccupied with the Swiss case that at one point he found himself driving aimlessly around the Washington area, utterly lost on his way to pick up his daughter.

During the summer of 1996, before Fagan even thought of the Swiss banks, Hausfeld built a legal dream team to take on the Swiss. Martin Mendelsohn, a friend for twenty years and a former federal government Nazi-hunter, offered to help, as did the Simon Wiesenthal Center. Based in Los Angeles, the Wiesenthal Center applied Hollywood techniques and financial acumen to Nazi-hunting, and boasted a mailing list of more than four hundred thousand donors. Marvin Hier, the Orthodox rabbi who founded the center, feuded with Singer's World Jewish Congress over its pursuit of Kurt Waldheim, which Simon Wiesenthal himself strongly opposed. Joining the lawsuit would give the Wiesenthal Center a role in the pursuit of the Swiss banks, and signal that the case was not the exclusive domain of Israel Singer.

Hausfeld also contacted Lieff, Cabraser, Heimann and Bernstein in San Francisco, another of the largest class action firms in the United States. Their chief partner, Robert Lieff, donated the firm's services, and offered one of his brightest young attorneys, Morris Ratner, to help. At twenty-nine, Ratner boasted glittering credentials, with honors degrees from Stanford and Harvard Law School to his credit. Possessed of a swift intelligence and a driven personality, Ratner became Hausfeld's chief workhorse, often drafting the legal documents other members of the team would use.

Ratner's firm suggested another name for the team: Mel Weiss. Based in New York, Weiss truly ruled the world of class action, and had expanded the scope of mass litigation in a series of aggressive pursuits of Wall Street transgressors from Prudential Insurance to Michael Milken's Drexel Burnham Lambert. Fabulously wealthy, he was both a stalwart contributor to the Democratic Party and a passionate supporter of Jewish causes. Although controversial for his entrepreneurial attitude in filing lawsuits, his name carried great weight with federal judges in New York. Weiss agreed to work pro bono, completing the core of Hausfeld's team.

Hausfeld's researchers diligently constructed their case against the banks, often working cheek by jowl with researchers from the World Jewish Congress and from D'Amato's office as they leafed through ancient files in the National Archives in Maryland. They intended their complaint to be a substantial work of historical research, which would force the Swiss banks to take this lawsuit seriously.

News of the case of *Weisshaus v Union Bank of Switzerland* hit Hausfeld's team like a thunderbolt. They were putting the finishing touches to months of research, but none of them had heard of Ed Fagan. After an hour of running searches on the Lexis-Nexis legal database, Morris Ratner found only routine personal injury cases.

These legal battalions refused to let a small-time personal-injury lawyer impede their historic task. Two weeks after hearing of Fagan's suit, Hausfeld filed his own *Friedman v UBS* complaint with Judge Korman in Brooklyn. Running to 109 pages, roughly ten times the length of Fagan's *Weisshaus* complaint, it was a profoundly more impressive piece of work. Unlike Fagan, Hausfeld sued the Swiss banks for far more than mere dormant accounts, alleging that they should pay for their role in laundering Nazi gold and in banking profits from slave labor in the concentration camps. Hausfeld hoped the power of the lawyers enlisted in the *Friedman* case would persuade the judge to make him lead counsel, trusting him to pursue the Swiss.

Ed Fagan did not see it that way. He had gotten there first. Besides, with the entry of Hausfeld and his team of top litigators, he felt like he was "playing with the Yankees at last." In the two weeks after filing his complaint, he made fresh discoveries about the scale of the undertaking. Holocaust survivors knew each other well and had great support systems, so he needed only to talk to one community group and he would soon sign up another hundred plaintiffs. He and Mrs. Weisshaus took more than a hundred calls from prospective claimants each day. Despite the overwhelming evidence that the case was too big for him to handle, he saw no reason why a bunch of wealthy lawyers who made their living extracting money from Wall Street should elbow him out with a "me-too" case.

But Fagan had minimal financial resources, and he grasped that he needed help. It came in the form of Bob Swift, who was much harder to dismiss. Based in Philadelphia, Swift had made a career out of innovative human rights litigation, most recently with an epic suit against the estate of Ferdinand Marcos, the former president of the Philippines, over civil rights abuses. Much of the Marcos millions had come to rest in the coffers of Swiss banks, and Swift had already spent many days in Zurich battling with Swiss bankers. After Marcos's fall in February of 1984, Swift reached the Philippines within a month, and embarked on a decade of complicated litigation, culminating in a 1995 trial in Hawaii, where the jury found for the plaintiffs and against Marcos. A huge framed account of that trial still hung above his desk, including press accounts, maps of the Philippines, and the formal court announcement of the verdict in his favor.

Swift found Fagan's lawsuit interesting and phoned to offer his help. He still had appeals from the Marcos litigation to deal with, and he had launched other cases, including a pursuit of Radovan Karadzic, the leader of the Bosnian Serbs, but he wanted to contribute to the Swiss litigation. Swift would act as Fagan's legal brain.

Unlike any other senior lawyer in the case, Swift was not Jewish and had more ecumenical motivations than the others. He considered Hitler an equal opportunity persecutor and noted that the Star of David was one of twenty-four emblems worn by concentration camp inmates. Although he cultivated a laid-back negotiating style, Swift added an incendiary element to the contest between Fagan and Hausfeld—Swift and Hausfeld had once worked together at the same law firm but the firm had split, amid acrimonious circumstances. The two men treated each other with wary distrust.

Fagan and Swift soon developed an effective working relationship, with Fagan generating as much heat as he could in the media, leaving complex legal drafting and negotiating to Swift. In public, he turned up the volume. Behind closed doors, Fagan rarely said a word in negotiations. European businessmen would leave meetings astonished that Fagan, their most vocal accuser, portrayed in Europe as the leader of the campaign against them, had remained mute.

Much wealthier than Fagan, Swift saw no reason to work pro bono. Cases like this could get expensive. He had already run up a $500,000 bill in personal expenses for his Marcos litigation. That gave him a financial incentive to settle with the Swiss, giving rise to a fear among Hausfeld and his colleagues that Swift was staking out a position for himself as the friendliest lawyer for the Swiss to talk to, the one willing to settle for the smallest sum. Such a strategy would make him a central figure in the process, but might also undercut the efforts of Hausfeld and Weiss to extract the most they could.

Swift tried to build a legal team to match the forces arrayed around his former partner Michael Hausfeld. On the advice of a friend, he made a call to Burt Neuborne, a professor at New York University's law school. A former legal director of the American Civil Liberties Union and a true legal heavyweight, Neuborne was not known as a class action lawyer. Instead, he specialized in the First Amendment, which he supported so strongly that he often took positions unpopular with liberal colleagues, such as defending the right of Nazis to march through the Holocaust survivor community of Skokie, Illinois. His long career also included winning an injunction against the government to halt bombing during the Vietnam War. A man who frequently testified before Congress on campaign finance reform and argued before the Supreme Court, Neuborne could add intellectual heft to the team around Fagan.

A nonobservant Jew with no close relatives who had died in the Holocaust, Neuborne was moved to take part by personal tragedy. His daughter had rebelled against his brand of secular Judaism by training as a rabbi. Neuborne was truly thankful that she had chosen such a harmless form of rebellion and took great pride in her choice. He was devastated when she suffered a heart attack and died, while studying at rabbinical seminary.

Still grieving, Neuborne saw the fight for Holocaust restitution as a chance to complete the arc of his daughter's chosen life. While he still felt little religious conviction himself, he knew that his daughter would have been delighted to know that he had taken this course. He did not realize that he was being recruited primarily to help one faction of lawyers prevail over the other.

In January, life grew more complicated as a third lawsuit, brought by the World Conference of Orthodox Jewish Communities, arrived in Brooklyn. The Philadelphia lawyer behind it, Stephen Whinston, would evolve into another significant player. Three separate lawsuits, all making essentially the same allegations, now sat on Judge Korman's desk, along with a burgeoning correspondence from dueling attorneys. Bob Swift complained that "the Friedman and World Council complaints have more law firms than clients," and criticized Hausfeld, saying: "He's been secretive and divisive and we would have no confidence in his judgment going forward."

The feelings were mutual. At a legal conference at a southern California law school, Hausfeld was disgusted to hear Fagan introduce a speech by admitting that he had never really known about the Holocaust until he researched his lawsuit. For Hausfeld, who had lived with the consequences of the Holocaust all his life, somebody who "never really knew about the Holocaust" had no business in this case.

Hausfeld further retained deep suspicions of anyone trying to earn a fee from Holocaust-related work. Later, he recounted how Swift once asked him, "What are you getting so emotional about? This is just a matter of money." For Hausfeld, the case was always more emotional than financial.

Judge Korman realized that no lawsuit against the Swiss could be effective if the lawyers were not reading from the same page, and he tried to prod them into working together. In January 1997, he called the first of many conferences in his courtroom. Korman arrived to find more than a dozen lawyers arrayed in two polarized groups, with the familiar faces of Burt Neuborne and Mel Weiss chatting amicably in the front row.

For Korman, Neuborne was a figure from a previous existence. Korman, a conservative, had worked in the Solicitor General's Office under President Reagan, giving him the difficult task of defending campaign finance laws against attacks from Neuborne. The two men did not share a political philosophy, but the experience left Korman with profound respect for Neuborne's character and intellect. A pattern was soon established in which the judge attempted to give his old adversary as much responsibility as he could, and even sought him out for private advice.

The judge was also familiar with Weiss, who had argued before him many times. Weiss had a simple, written proposal to bridge the gap between the competing attorneys—an executive committee of ten lawyers whom Korman should appoint to run the case. In the event of disagreement, each of the ten would have one vote.

Neuborne looked at the paper in his friend's hand, and noted that seven votes belonged to Weiss's own team, giving them a built-in majority. Neuborne protested. So did Swift. "The important thing is that to go ahead there must be at least parity. We were the first filed case."

Weiss wasn't having that. "The fact that the *Weisshaus* action was the first filed I think is meaningless," he barked. "If you look at that complaint and you look at our complaint I think you can make a comparison as to where the work went."

Korman asked if the lawyers were working pro bono. Most said they were. But Swift answered crisply, "I don't intend to, nor does my group, nor should that matter. Are they doing it for their costs as well? In the Marcos case, I've run up over half a million dollars in costs."

Swift thought the issue of fees was a ruse to help Hausfeld and Weiss take over the case, and he believed that working for a fee aligned his interests with the survivors. Besides, a sole practitioner like Ed Fagan simply could not afford to work pro bono; he was already deeply in debt, and financing himself with loans from factors.

Neuborne attempted to build a bridge. "I agreed to do this because it seems to me a sacred trust at this point," he said. "I didn't consider myself bound to one side of lawyers or another side of lawyers. It should be roughly equal and let's get on with the business of making this happen. Judge, this is embarrassing. Could I suggest something? Can you give me a couple of days to come up with a governing structure?"

An exasperated Korman happily accepted his friend's offer. Neuborne would become the mediator on an executive committee of ten lawyers, with Hausfeld and Swift installed as co-lead attorneys. Weiss would manage communications with the judge. But Fagan was frozen out of leading the litigation he had first filed, although he at least had a place on the ten-member committee.

Neuborne commented later, "As soon as it was clear to everyone that nobody could drive anyone else out, then with the precision of an army of ants these people swung into line. Fagan had the good sense not to try to throw his weight around." As far as Neuborne could see, Fagan was a "guy who essentially stumbled into something bigger than he was" and "understood that this was something he wasn't very good at."

Nobody, however, could stop Fagan from appointing himself as an agent provocateur. Shuttling back and forth across the Atlantic, making friends with the Lufthansa staff at Newark International Airport, he made himself deeply unpopular with most of the other Europeans he met.

Fagan proved a master of public relations, and persuaded a number of his clients to go public with their stories, taking them to Europe to embarrass the Swiss. Fagan stewarded half a dozen elderly women, who all testified to the same cruel story. Like Greta Beer, their father had assured them that there was money in Switzerland, but they did not know exactly where. After the war the banks had stood in their way. Fagan skillfully exploited their moving stories to show to the world's media that there was a pattern to the banks' behavior.

Fagan also befriended Christoph Meili, the Swiss night watch-man, and his wife, Giuseppina, whom Fagan called "Juicy," and persuaded them to launch a suit against UBS for slander, assur-ing them they would be rich within months. He even brought Meili to New Jersey and installed him in a Travelodge, until the hapless young guard was forced to leave when the credit on Fagan's credit card ran out. Meili could not believe the desperate measures to which his lawyer would resort in an attempt to raise cash. After negotiating first-class tickets to Europe from a televi-sion company, Fagan would sell the tickets, pocket the cash, and travel economy.

Crucially, however, Fagan kept himself and Meili before the gaze of the U.S. and European press. He staged theatrical stunts like reading from the Torah while wearing a yarmulke in Zurich's main square, cementing Fagan in European minds as the leader of the lawsuits, at a time when he had ceased doing virtually any legal work on it.

Israel Singer and his colleague Elan Steinberg perversely almost approved of Fagan's public relations campaign, as it put restitution firmly on the European agenda, while simultaneously casting all the lawyers in a bad light. It made Singer seem reason-able by comparison. But the lawsuits also created a problem for Singer because they fostered the impression that the entire cam-paign was only about money. Moreover, the lawyers were the one group that Singer could not control.

The lawsuit also created difficulties with his Israeli allies on Paul Volcker's commission. Zvi Barak believed the lawyers would cut a deal, and save the banks from facing a true accounting from the Volcker Commission. "I'm a lawyer, I know how it works," he warned Singer. "Lawyers come to compromises." Avraham Burg dismissed the American class action lawyers as "shylocks" and demanded that the Jewish organizations should launch their own lawsuit.

By now, however, the litigation had developed its own momen-tum. Once forced to work together, the lawyers managed to com-bine their firepower unaided by Singer or other Jewish politicians. "There's a reason why in the English language a group of lions is called a pride," Burt Neuborne later commented. "You should have a pride of lawyers as well. There were the usual egos and mistrusts, but by and large people worked together fairly well." Their priority now was to persuade Korman to grant them powers of discovery—the right to enter the Swiss banks and see documents. They calculated that the Swiss would rather settle the case than lose their precious secrecy.

The Swiss, meanwhile, prepared their response. The lawsuit scared them far more than any of the tactics yet unveiled, as U.S. federal judges or U.S. juries were both powerful and unpredictable. The sums involved, given American courts' propensity to award punitive damages, dwarfed anything they might have to pay under the Volcker process. Ed Fagan also contributed to the incessant flow of bad publicity. Fighting the lawsuit became the banks' top priority and they appointed American attorneys to direct their defense.

The Swiss Bankers Association tapped its existing Washington lawyers, Wilmer, Cutler and Pickering, one of the most politically connected firms in the capital, to manage its case. Lloyd Cutler, formerly White House counsel to President Carter and special counsel to President Clinton, gave them general guidance, but the task of planning the campaign fell to the firm's chief litigation partner, Roger Witten.

Witten's liberal political credentials were arguably as strong as those of Weiss and Hausfeld. After serving as an attorney in the office of Archibald Cox, the Watergate special prosecutor, he carved out a career as a political lawyer in Washington, often working for international institutions. His specialty was campaign finance reform, and he had worked for many years as a counsel for Common Cause, the public interest group, occasionally preparing briefs with Burt Neuborne, who was now one of his opponents. As a Jew, Witten understood his opponents more clearly than his clients at the Swiss banks. He soon became a key figure, constantly talking with the head offices in Zurich. Witten became a tireless defender of the Swiss banks, secure in the conviction that it was in the best long-term public interest of everyone—including Holocaust survivors and the Jewish community—to ensure that the issue was resolved fairly.

Settlement talks in early 1997 proved short-lived. They made halting progress on the structure for an out-of-court deal, but the talks came to an abrupt end when Mel Weiss asked for clarification on the kind of numbers the banks were willing to pay. He assumed the banks stood ready to pay "multiple billions."

"Did you say *billion* with a *b*?" asked Witten, aghast at the idea.

"We've argued him down from the end of the alphabet," deadpanned Hausfeld. "He started with a *z*."

From that moment on, Witten's strategy was clear. The cases should stay where they were in court, and go no further. If the judge could not be persuaded to dismiss them—and a Brooklyn judge would need great courage to throw out this particular case—he could at least delay the litigation while Paul Volcker's committee looked for a resolution. Witten reasoned that the appropriate venue for a trial was in Zurich, Bern, or Basel, not Brooklyn. Furthermore, the trial should have been held decades earlier, he argued. After half a century, the evidence from aging Holocaust survivors would almost certainly not be reliable enough for a court of law, and in any case the Volcker Commission was trying to settle exactly the same issues. Israel Singer and other Jewish leaders sat on Volcker's board, so the plaintiffs' interests were protected.

Witten's first response was to file a motion that the case should not proceed. He even persuaded Paul Volcker to write a letter to the court asking for the case to be dropped, on the grounds that a lawsuit could undermine his work by giving the banks an excuse not to cooperate. Further, his auditors feared they might face lawsuits of their own if the plaintiffs' lawyers did not like the result of the investigation.

Hausfeld and Swift countered that the case should continue on an expedited basis, given the age of the plaintiffs, and called for discovery to start immediately. They did not believe a consensual process like Volcker's commission could possibly serve the needs of their clients as well as a fully argued litigation. Besides, they were suing about looted assets and other financial crimes, not just the dormant accounts covered by Volcker's strictly circumscribed terms of reference. Volcker's letter seemed to them to prove that he was firmly in the Swiss camp.

The two sides came to court in July of 1997, and battered each other with well-prepared legal arguments. Korman listened and left with an announcement that he was reserving his opinion. He hoped to rule on the case shortly.

But Korman made no announcement that month, or even that year. As summer turned to autumn, no word was heard from him. Korman knew that other moves to settle the issue were already afoot, and hoped it could be resolved somewhere other than his courtroom. By refusing to rule either way, he kept the pressure on both sides to settle amicably and out of court.

His tactics frustrated both groups of lawyers. However, it suited Israel Singer for the litigation to stay in limbo. He had another ally in Washington, whom the Swiss would need to treat with the utmost respect. They could dismiss self-interested lawyers— particularly small-time personal-injury lawyers like Ed Fagan— easily enough. But Singer knew that they would find it much harder to answer an indictment from the U.S. government. While the lawyers bickered in Brooklyn, Singer helped to persuade one of the most politically skillful figures in the Clinton administration to prepare his own charges against the Swiss.

Rewriting History

Israel Singer stood at the back of the State Department's briefing room in Washington and purred with delight. It was little
more than a year since he had spoken with President Bill Clinton inside the Oval Office to press his case against the Swiss banks.
Now, on May 7, 1997, the Clinton administration was delivering
the most detailed and authoritative indictment to date of Switzerland's war record.

Standing before him, on the other side of the television cameras
and journalists, was the man he had urged President Clinton to
tap as point man on Holocaust issues. Stuart Eizenstat, a rare veteran of the Carter years among Clinton's New Democrats, was exe-
cuting a vital part of Singer's strategy for shaming the Swiss into
paying compensation. Media campaigns and congressional hearings were all very well. But nothing could match the forceful voice
of the U.S. government—the world's only superpower—in pushing Switzerland toward a final reckoning with its wartime history.

Speaking slowly in a southern drawl, Eizenstat read from his
new report on U.S. and Allied efforts to retrieve property looted
by the Nazis. Despite its title, his report concentrated not on the
United States, but on Switzerland's behavior before and after the
war. Eizenstat accused the Swiss National Bank—Switzerland's
equivalent of the Federal Reserve—of knowingly receiving gold
looted from Holocaust victims and occupied countries. Switzerland had prolonged the Nazi war effort, he said, by laundering
gold for the Third Reich. When the war ended, it was one of

Europe's wealthiest nations, and it was still profiting because it had failed to make amends.

A gaunt and balding figure, Eizenstat was one of the most experienced and single-minded members of the Clinton administration. Eizenstat had championed American Jewish causes since his years in the Carter White House as the chief domestic policy adviser. On reentering government in the first Clinton administration, he returned to Jewish causes while serving as U.S. ambassador to the European Union. There, besides his duties related to economic issues, he began to negotiate the return of Jewish community property in the newly free countries of Eastern Europe. Like Singer, he was a strongly observant Jew, and their careers had intersected for almost thirty years. In his private career as a lawyer, Eizenstat had even handled the legal work for Singer in a real estate dispute.

When he returned from Brussels, Eizenstat worked not among the career diplomats of the State Department but among the trade lawyers at Commerce, where he carried on his pursuit of stolen Jewish property. In suggesting Eizenstat's name to President Clinton, Singer was sure that he would grow into a determined and principled critic of the Swiss. "I trusted him," recalls Singer. "I believed that he would write a strong report. He was horrified by what he found."

The details Eizenstat enunciated in a flat and emotionless tone that morning would have horrified almost anyone. He found that Germany had transferred gold worth about $400 million (or $3.9 billion in 1997 money) to the Swiss National Bank in Bern during the war. The Swiss, he alleged, kept three-quarters of it and used the rest to buy goods and raw materials for Germany. It should have been obvious to the Swiss that some of the gold they received was stolen—Germany's total gold reserves were less than half that figure at the war's outset.

"Despite repeated Swiss protestations after the war that they had never received any looted Nazi gold, this report is incontrovertible," Eizenstat said. "The Swiss National Bank and Swiss bankers knew as the war progressed that the Reichsbank's own coffers had been depleted and that the Swiss were handling vast sums of looted gold."

Most shockingly, he revealed that some looted Nazi gold was stolen not from bank vaults, but from the homes and even the mouths of Holocaust victims. A dry man not given to theatrics, Eizenstat held a blowup of a page from the account where the SS kept its looted gold in Switzerland, which government researchers had retrieved from microfilm records at the German Reichsbank only weeks earlier. One receipt read: "On behalf of the Reich Finance Ministry, 854 rings, one trunk of silver objects, one trunk of dental gold, 29.996 grams."

When the Nazis overran countries, he explained, they seized gold and deposited it in the account of SS officer Bruno Melmer. They smelted and resmelted this "Melmer Account" gold until it could pass, under false markings, for legitimate Reichsbank gold.

Eizenstat did not merely attack Swiss conduct during the war. Indeed, he found their feeble attempts to make amends in the postwar years the hardest to forgive, or as he put it, the "least understandable." His report covered the drawn-out negotiations on restitution held in Washington after the war, where he said the Swiss "used legalistic positions to defend their interests, regardless of the moral interests also at stake." Eizenstat even seemed to leave the door open to renegotiating the 1946 Washington Accords, under which Switzerland handed the Allies $58.1 million in payment for that laundered gold.

Eizenstat complained that this sum was far less than the looted gold that the Allies believed the Swiss National Bank still held at the war's end, estimated at between $185 million and $259 million. He even held that the Swiss had reneged on their agreement to pay the Allies 50 percent of the German assets left in Switzerland after the war. In 1952, Switzerland made a token payment of $28 million, while the Allies estimated that German assets in the country were worth possibly as much as $500 million.

The report also criticized the Allies. Eizenstat said that at least some "victim gold" had found its way into the stocks of the Tripartite Gold Commission, a postwar organization set up by the United States, the United Kingdom, and France to return plundered gold to the central banks in liberated Europe. More than fifty years later, the commission still held about $55 million in Nazi gold, mostly in the vaults of the Bank of England and the

New York Federal Reserve. Some of the gold wrenched from Holocaust victims might still lie buried deep inside a New York safe.

This gold helped Singer and Edgar Bronfman to force the White House to take a role. As Eizenstat recalled it, Bronfman "educated the White House," claiming that some of this gold belonged to victims. "This became a matter of practical importance and here Bronfman had a very important role while I was at Commerce," Eizenstat recalled. "He wrote to the president and asked him to stop the payment of the remaining 6 tons of gold that were in the Tripartite Gold Commission." Under pressure from one of the Democrats' biggest contributors, the White House was happy to delegate the issue to Stuart Eizenstat.

Eizenstat's calm denunciation belied the chaos that attended the writing of the report. In early 1996, Senator Al D'Amato's banking committee had asked the administration to collect all documents related to the role of neutral countries in handling Nazi loot. William Slany, the State Department's chief historian, decided to do more than just assemble a heap of documents, and sought to write a narrative study. By September 1996, Eizenstat had taken over the historical project and turned it into a huge, interagency effort. Over the next seven months, Slany's team picked through fifteen million pages of documents in the U.S. National Archives, piecing together the awkward compromises the State Department had negotiated with neutral nations after the war. It was a monumental effort, drawing inputs from across the federal government. Apart from the State Department, Eizenstat asked for contributions from the CIA and the FBI, the Departments of Commerce, Defense, Justice, and Treasury, the Federal Reserve, the National Security Agency, the National Archives, and the U.S. Holocaust Memorial Museum.

Almost inevitably for a report written by committee, agendas clashed. Eli Rosenbaum, head of the Justice Department's Nazi-hunting unit, agitated for the report to tackle American complacency, as well as the failings of the Swiss. Rosenbaum, a former colleague of Singer at the WJC, went off on his own tangent, convinced that the postwar State Department had misled Congress and the White House about the total amount of gold handled by Switzerland. He also unearthed the Melmer account records.

With competing agencies and departments fighting over the details of the 210-page report, Eizenstat decided to highlight his conclusions in a foreword, and tried writing a draft himself. For the sensitive political and diplomatic task of completing it, he drafted Bennett Freeman, former chief speechwriter to Secretary of State Warren Christopher and a member of Bill Clinton's campaign-strategy team and debate team in 1992. Freeman, an ebullient political appointee with a cackling sense of humor, was on New York's Upper East Side when the call came in the early afternoon of April 15. He immediately returned to Washington and met with Eizenstat from 4:30 till about 9:00 P.M. Eizenstat already had a first draft, but was unhappy with the summary and foreword, which he considered rough and incomplete. Freeman had a reputation as a wordsmith and expected it would take three or four nights to rewrite the report's ten-page foreword, along with the summary—the only parts of the report the media were likely to read.

The task in fact took three weeks. Virtually every evening, Eizenstat, desperate to be accurate, would call in at least ten people, from the State Department and sometimes other agencies, to analyze every change to the draft. Eli Rosenbaum lobbied for a tough critique while the State Department's specialists on Switzerland despairingly tried to tone it down. They knew one devastating sentence written by Eizenstat himself would antagonize the Swiss more than any other:

> Whatever their motivation, the fact that they pursued vigorous trade with the Third Reich had the clear effect of supporting and prolonging Nazi Germany's capacity to wage war.

As German military defeat became more and more certain toward the end of the war, the slaughter of Jews and others had accelerated. Effectively, Eizenstat was holding the Swiss responsible for the loss of millions of lives because they kept trading with

Hitler after decisive setbacks like Stalingrad in 1942 or the invasion of Italy in 1943.

Eizenstat's foreword contained one other explosive sentence:

> In the unique circumstances of World War II, neutrality collided with morality: too often being neutral provided a pretext for avoiding moral considerations.

For the Swiss, whose four-hundred-year-old neutrality was central to their national identity, the accusation would cause grave offense. Originally adopted as a means to maintain unity between the fractious mountain valley communities in the early sixteenth century, the country's policy of neutrality went further than barring Switzerland from taking one side against another in Europe's wars. It even required that the nation have no active foreign policy in times of peace. Swiss policymakers regarded this as a moral position, requiring many to swallow their natural sympathies for either the French or the Germans.

Bennett Freeman instantly recognized that the phrase "neutrality collided with morality" could be explosive when he invented it one Sunday afternoon while sipping iced capuccinos on the sidewalk Java Café near Dupont Circle in Washington, D.C. Since the sentence did not mention Switzerland, he could defend it by saying it applied to other neutral nations, such as Portugal, Sweden, and Turkey. Further, his sentence did not say which of the two values, morality or neutrality, had won. He had read and reread the summary, and felt it finely balanced.

Eizenstat agreed. "The morality language was important," he recalled, "because we were dealing with a country that had convinced itself that its history was that it was neutral. They had to face the fact that there were limits to neutrality, that neutrality was not an agnostic or completely fine dream." Both sentences remained in the published report.

The U.S. officials knew their report would be, as Freeman put it, "the biggest turd to drop in the Swiss punch bowl ever." However, with so many last-minute revisions and delays, they discarded the courtesy of showing them a copy until a few hours before its release. Eizenstat did not want the report to leak and did not trust the Swiss. Working out of the Commerce Department, he was also unhindered by the diplomatic protocols of the State Department.

News of their report appeared on the front page of the next day's *New York Times* and other papers across the nation. A *Washington Post* columnist even described it as "a Matterhorn of integrity and truth-telling" in a "moral wasteland."

Those who negotiated the original accords, however, felt it unfair to criticize an agreement forged half a century earlier. Seymour Rubin, deputy head of the State Department's postwar negotiating team, thought the 1946 agreements "a pretty good deal at the time." For Rubin, now an elderly man living in a rambling Georgetown home, the Eizenstat report brought back vivid recollections of his hard-fought deal in a Europe decimated by war. Compromises that looked disgraceful in the peaceful and prosperous world of 1997 seemed far more reasonable in the chaos of 1946.

"You have to remember, this was the close of World War Two," Rubin said. "Europe was a devastated area. Here are the Swiss, who sat the war out, and have a fairly strong economy, and so forth, and they were in a position to help. You don't really want to piss off an ally, if you're in that position."

Toward the end of the war, the Allies had geared up for an aggressive attempt to reclaim all the looted German assets in the hands of the neutrals. But in 1946, Rubin's team faced the same dilemma that would confront Israel Singer and others in the 1990s: the urgent need for some funds straightaway, balanced against the desire to exact full justice. In the face of intransigent Swiss negotiators, Rubin said, they had taken what they could get. The Swiss had already walked out of negotiations once.

The onset of the cold war vitiated American attempts to push for every last cent in their confrontation with Switzerland. "Wartime objectives were replaced by new Cold War imperatives," said Eizenstat. It was only after the collapse of the Soviet Union that Eizenstat and others would pick up these issues once more.

It might have been different, Rubin thought, if there had been class action lawyers and determined political leadership in 1946. "If you had back in those days a Stu Eizenstat and a variety of characters like that, and all the class action lawyers up in New

York fighting that sort of thing, it probably would have been a much rougher deal on the Swiss."

Meanwhile, Thomas Borer, Switzerland's special ambassador on Holocaust issues, had somehow to craft a diplomatic response to a report that most of his countrymen found devastatingly offensive. In his own view, the report was "totally" unfair, and "portrayed Switzerland and Swiss neutrality during the war in a totally unobjective way."

Only a few hours after Eizenstat released the report, Borer shared a platform with Israel Singer at a Washington hotel. He said Swiss foreign policy had taken a "legalistic view" during the war, and Eizenstat had "made it clear that one should have taken a more moral attitude." He said he was shocked to hear that resmelted gold stolen from victims had found its way into the Swiss banks. But he added that the Nazis, and not the Swiss, had committed the Melmer account crimes.

Borer stressed that the Swiss wartime government had upheld its independence "at a price." "Trading with Germany was inevitable," he said. "Concessions had to be made. It was incumbent upon us to determine to what extent these concessions went beyond the limits of the inevitable."

Armed with a map of Europe, Borer tried to show skeptical American journalists that Switzerland was at risk of a German invasion. Basel and Zurich, Switzerland's biggest cities, lay in lowlands within easy reach of the German border and so remained at risk even after the Normandy landings. The Nazis, in a desperate plight by this point, could have invaded to gain extra supplies had Switzerland cut off trade with Germany.

In Switzerland, the reaction to Eizenstat's report was visceral. Swiss newspapers lambasted the gross hypocrisy of criticizing Swiss neutrality when the United States had itself stayed neutral for more than two years after Hitler had invaded Poland. One historian alleged that U.S. neutrality in the 1930s had directly "led to the aggressors—Italy in Abyssinia, Japan in China, Germany in Europe—being encouraged to carry out further shameful acts."

Books soon appeared detailing acts of Swiss wartime courage during the war. Yad Vashem, Israel's main Holocaust memorial, had named thirty-seven Swiss men and women as "righteous gentiles" for their actions in saving Jews during the war. As a neutral nation, Swiss writers pointed out, they had taken in more Jewish refugees during the war than the vastly bigger United States. They had also given Allied spies a base for espionage efforts, while Swiss ambassadors in Eastern Europe had helped to rescue many more Jews.

The Swiss also picked apart the equally damaging assertion that Swiss trade had prolonged the war. Once the Allies invaded France in 1944, Germany had no means of obtaining raw materials. Even if it could get hard currency from Switzerland, it could not buy anything with the money.

Jacques Rossier, the head of the exclusive Geneva private bank of Darier Hentsch, was already suffering the annoyance of Paul Volcker's auditors at the time Eizenstat delivered his report. At a speech in Boston, Rossier said that he could at least understand the behavior of the Jewish organizations and the class action lawyers. But he found it much harder to understand why the Clinton administration had joined in the "Swiss bashing exercise."

"The quantities of materials delivered by Switzerland for the German war machine were negligible in view of the total German war effort, amounting to only about 0.1 percent," he said. "The Clinton administration's assertion that Swiss trade with Germany prolonged the war does not withstand the test of historical fact."

The vast majority of the Swiss population "deeply resented" the report, Rossier said. "It opened wounds that will take some time to heal."

Responding to allegations that the Swiss National Bank knowingly accepted stolen gold from the Germans, Rossier pointed out that the U.S. government had impounded two-thirds of total Swiss gold reserves in June 1941. That left the bank with no choice but to purchase gold from the only source available—Germany.

Curt Gasteyger, an international relations expert who sat on Paul Volcker's committee, found the U.S. government's intervention "hardly helpful," saying that Eizenstat had converted debates among the commissioners into "a highly emotional and politicized confrontation." He complained, "U.S. foreign policy has both a very legalistic and moralistic dimension. Together they tend to push the administration to 'punish' the other side with sanctions or simple bullying if it doesn't behave as America thinks it should."

Even the Swiss Jewish community would have preferred a more moderate approach. "It fostered two things—anti-Semitism and anti-Americanism," asserted Rolf Bloch, the head of the community, who accompanied Singer when he confronted the Swiss bankers in Bern. "It was seen as Jewish organizations together with the American government hurting Swiss feelings."

Eizenstat later defended his analysis, although he conceded that it might have been more diplomatic to soften the blow. "The only thing I would have changed was when we said the actions of the Swiss *extended* the war effort," he said. "We should have said *helped sustain* the war effort. I believe it clearly extended the war effort but at a diplomatic level it probably would have been better to use a more neutral term like sustained."

But it was too late. Until the Eizenstat report, it was possible to pretend that only a group of self-interested campaigners were targeting some technical irregularities at Switzerland's commercial banks. Now, the entire policy of neutrality, one of the building blocks of the Swiss nation's identity, was under fire.

The report marked a watershed in the Swiss response. Until now the Swiss press, usually aggressive and fractious, had been evenhanded, analyzing the flaws of the banks in detail, while public opinion was divided on the issue. However, the intervention of the U.S. government served to unite the fractured nation. Eizenstat appeared to be almost universally unpopular in Switzerland. His report barely touched on the dormant accounts issue, but it dramatically altered the dynamic for the banks as they sought a compromise. Swiss public opinion shifted firmly against the American campaigners, and the notion of reaching any accommodation with them. If the banks were to sign a deal that appeared to admit any guilt, they would face stiff opposition. The banks could not take the risk of setting a legal precedent against other Swiss companies, or against the nation itself.

State Department officials would hear the offending two

sentences repeated back to them, in aggrieved tones, innumerable times over the next twelve months. Freeman began to believe that the Swiss had willfully misread and misunderstood them. "The Swiss persisted in a self-centered way in misreading those two sentences as being directed solely at them," he complained, instead of "all the wartime neutrals."

In the wake of his report, Eizenstat received an approach from Lloyd Cutler and Roger Witten, the two Washington lawyers for the Swiss Bankers Association. They wanted Eizenstat to intervene to end the class action litigation by saying to the judge, "Stay your hand. This is the business of governments and not the court."

Eizenstat was glad to be asked to take part, but he began to plot a very different role for himself—as a neutral broker who would mediate a settlement. He cared about Holocaust survivors no less than Israel Singer himself, and he badly wanted to be the man who finally won them some justice. Intervening in a private lawsuit would be an unprecedented step for a State Department official, but he thought it could be justified. With anti-American sentiments suddenly rife in Switzerland, he could claim that any action to heal the diplomatic rift was in America's national interest.

However, Bennett Freeman noted a deeper driving force behind Eizenstat's approach. "There was a willingness that at some point became a desire and then at some point became a commitment and even an obsession for Stu to try to do the deal," Freeman said.

As Eizenstat began sounding out class action lawyers about taking a role, he was burdened by his report. Whatever its merits as a historical document, it was a diplomatic disaster that eroded Swiss trust in him and undermined his efforts to mediate a resolution. In large part, he had contributed to the very anti-American sentiment he was now determined to heal.

On May 8, the day after he published the report, Eizenstat phoned Hans Baer, the senior Jew in Swiss banking, to ask him how people in Switzerland were responding. Baer struggled for the right words. "I hate to tell you this, Stuart," he said, "but you're public enemy number one."

Shot across the Bow

As Switzerland reeled from Stuart Eizenstat's report, Israel Singer prepared what he hoped would be the knockout blow against the Swiss banks. He decided from the outset that if all else failed, he would threaten the banks with sanctions—a direct attack on their bottom line. New York was both Singer's political bailiwick and the capital of the world's financial markets—no bank could survive in the global financial industry without doing business on his patch.

However, by nature and politics, Singer disliked sanctions. The state of Israel had long suffered Arab boycotts, and Singer believed they should only be imposed "where life and limb were in danger—not in a historical case." The fight against Switzerland was important, but not even Singer could say that it was a case of life or death. Besides, once sanctions were imposed, nobody would want to negotiate a deal.

Instead, Singer crafted a strategy of threats to support his demands for compensation. "Sanctions should be used as a threat," he said, "but whether sanctions should be implemented is something I had a different interest in." He needed to ratchet up the pressure on the Swiss with the clear and present danger of financial punishment. After all, he declared, "I don't believe in shooting blanks."

Singer would go to great lengths to deny supporting sanctions, while often in the same breath urging Jews to boycott companies with outstanding debts to Holocaust survivors. "I'm going to say that I don't believe in boycotts," he once said. "I just don't want you to buy this company's goods, because they're not nice people. Just buy from the nice guys."

The WJC did not have the power to launch any meaningful sanctions campaign on its own, so Singer contacted an old friend from his days in New York politics—Alan Hevesi, the comptroller of New York City. Singer respected Hevesi, who he hoped would move on to be mayor. The feeling was mutual, and Hevesi, who considered Singer a "hero" for his work on restitution, happily agreed to launch what he called a "team effort."

Despite his old-fashioned title, Hevesi wielded sweeping political power. One of only three directly elected city officials, his job required him to borrow money on behalf of New York City, one of the world's biggest borrowers, bestowing huge fees on investment banks in the process. He also controlled the city's pension funds, which were among America's largest, giving him a stake in companies across the world. If Hevesi chose to impose sanctions, he could inflict real pain on any international bank.

In Singer's master plan, Hevesi would play "good cop" to Senator Al D'Amato's "bad cop," roles which suited both men. D'Amato was the aggressive and street-smart populist, a rabble-rouser who used the Senate as a bully pulpit, while Hevesi was altogether more statesmanlike, possessing survival skills drawn from three decades in New York politics. A soft-spoken man, Hevesi had worked as a professor at Queens College and still lectured on economics and social policy at New York's Columbia and Fordham Universities.

While D'Amato was holding hearings in the glare of Washington publicity, Hevesi wrote discreet letters to the heads of the big three Swiss banks, expressing concern about Singer's allegations and asking for details of their response. He left the threat of sanctions unspoken.

As the grandson of a chief rabbi of Hungary, Hevesi had lost many of his ancestors in the Holocaust, and fiercely advocated Jewish causes. When a member of the New York State Assembly in 1985, he had led a delegation of twenty-seven American politicians to West Germany, where they stood outside the Bitburg cemetery to protest President Reagan's decision to honor the graves of nearly two thousand soldiers, including several dozen SS troops. Moreover, he took on multinationals while advocating disinvestment from South Africa during the apartheid era. For him, the campaign for restitution boiled down to a simple question of justice. Those who profited from crimes, he said, should not go unpunished. Just as the Israeli government had hunted down the perpetrators of the 1972 Munich Olympics massacre, so he believed it was vital to hunt down those still profiting from the Holocaust.

A Democrat, Hevesi was not a natural political ally of the Republican D'Amato, but both were pragmatic. In early 1997, as Christoph Meili inflamed passions on both sides of the Atlantic, Hevesi invited D'Amato to lunch to discuss dormant accounts. D'Amato nominated a favorite Italian restaurant in Long Island City, Queens, safely across the East River from Manhattan, in an attempt to avoid prying eyes. It proved unsuccessful: a group of city councilmen interrupted them, and immediately suspected the two men were discussing the 1997 mayoral election. But the lunch left Hevesi with a clear plan—he would visit Switzerland to attempt to persuade the Swiss to make a moral gesture and to assure them that the fury in the United States was not contrived. Meanwhile, he would prepare to take economic action and test the city's financial power.

In May 1997, Hevesi, accompanied by his deputy, Steve Newman, set off for Switzerland, amid the tension surrounding Christoph Meili's possible prosecution. They wanted to administer the message diplomatically. Newman, a bald-headed former NASA engineer, and Hevesi, a gray-haired academic, looked and sounded very much like the kind of people Swiss bankers were used to dealing with.

Shuttling along the scenic route from Zurich to Bern, they found the Swiss to be courteous hosts, who mostly spoke to them in fluent English. In meetings at the Swiss Bank Corporation and Credit Suisse, almost everyone complained about the way the Union Bank of Switzerland (UBS) was behaving.

After meeting UBS's chief executive, Robert Studer, they could understand why. He met them in a conference room next to the elevator, and never turned on the lights or offered his guests tea or coffee. Unlike the other bankers, Studer conducted the meeting without any other legal or political officials present, bringing along only his secretary to take notes. He remained encased in a military bearing and, as Newman remembers, clammed up when Christoph Meili's name came up in conversation. Hevesi left with the impression that Studer thought his former security guard was an agent for Mossad.

On their return to New York, the two men read an interview in the *New Yorker* in which the chairman of UBS's board, Robert Holzach, voiced the sentiments they suspected were shared by Studer. Holzach boasted that there were no Jews at the top of the three big Swiss banks and claimed that the campaign over dormant accounts was "really to do with the Jewish conspiracy to take over the world's most prestigious financial centers." Hevesi wrote to Studer, demanding Holzach's ejection from the UBS board.

Meanwhile, Newman recruited legal help from the office of the city's general counsel. In the 1980s, Eric Wollman had helped Newman to draft the New York pension system's disinvestment campaign against South Africa. Since then, Wollman—a burly man who worked as an auxiliary New York policeman in his spare time—had become an effective corporate governance activist, showing public pension funds how to push companies into improving their records on issues like employment rights or environmental protection. Newman had a hunch that Wollman's expertise was about to come in very handy.

Wollman established that New York City's pension funds held shares worth $69.55 million in the three big Swiss banks. At Newman's behest, he built a database of officials who controlled public finance across the United States, including city, state, and country treasurers and banking and insurance regulators. Among them, these officials exerted great influence over the flow of money in the United States to Wall Street and international banks. He started sending them bulletins titled "Swiss Monitor," which updated them on negotiations. Wollman also contacted other public pension funds to suggest that they write to any Swiss companies in which they held stock, to ask if they were contributing to the government's humanitarian fund. With these tactics in place, the Swiss would know exactly what anger they could face from their U.S. shareholders.

Hevesi's armory was well primed, but it was not until October 1997 that a routine event triggered the first shot of an international trade war. Steve Newman, Hevesi's deputy, needed to borrow some money to bolster city finances, and he invited Wall Street banks to underwrite a loan, or "letter of credit," to the city. Since the amounts involved were big, banks would bid for the business as a syndicate, with one bank taking the lead. A veteran of municipal finance, Newman had executed this financial maneuver countless times before, but the identity of the winning bank gave him a jolt. It was the Union Bank of Switzerland.

Newman took his problem to Hevesi, who, as he expected, could not stomach giving new city business to an outfit like UBS. Although they barely realized it, they were about to administer a sharp lesson in the realities of operating in the global economy: banks in Switzerland would be made accountable to elected municipal officials in New York.

Initially, Hevesi believed that Wollman's well-oiled corporate activism tactics would apply sufficient pressure to force the Swiss into making the concessions he wanted. But after Studer's behavior, Hevesi could not bring himself to reward UBS with new business when the bond issue arose in October. If he asked UBS to underwrite the letter of credit, the deal would give the syndicate of banks a total of about $1.5 million in fees. That meant that UBS stood to earn at least $300,000 from the transaction—perhaps a tiny amount for an international bank, but still more than Hevesi wanted to award to UBS. "I was presented with a situation where UBS became a symbol for bad behavior," Hevesi said. "It wasn't disrupting existing incumbent relationships, it was new business, and I wasn't going to reward them with new business."

Had SBC or Credit Suisse been named at the head of the syndicate, he would have done nothing, but UBS was different: Studer had blackened the bank's name forever in Hevesi's mind.

Instead, he determined to take the opportunity to send the bank a message.

As Hevesi's chief financial officer, Newman was required to work within New York's procurement rules, which meant accepting the lowest bid. Any new proposal would have to be cleared with the mayor, Rudolph Giuliani, a Republican who had at times a confrontational relationship with Hevesi's office.

Newman saw that J. P. Morgan, one of the biggest commercial banks in New York, also appeared in the syndicate. He phoned them with an offer. Their syndicate could still have the business, but only if UBS was removed. Morgan—or some other banks—would have to cover UBS's portion of the loan, and the final price tag must not be any higher than that of the original UBS-led deal.

The next day, J. P. Morgan phoned back to say that they could lead a new syndicate but there might still be a problem: a German bank would replace UBS. Was that all right? Newman laughed and said that he was not fighting the Germans just at the moment.

They did not publicize their action. "It was a sort of shot across the bow," Hevesi said. "Enough people in the banking community knew we had done it." UBS was only poorer by about $300,000 but the mere fact that a city with New York's power and financial clout might take such action was a terrifying proposition for the Swiss.

Hevesi's warning shot caught the attention of Wall Street's gossipy bond traders, who eagerly spread the news of his tactics to promote restitution for Holocaust survivors. From there, word leaked to journalists, who understood the implications. Clearly, Hevesi had the ability to launch costlier sanctions: as head of the New York City public pension fund, he could send shock waves through the market if he should ever start divesting shares in Swiss companies. The tactic that had worked so well to discourage Western companies from dealing with apartheid-era South Africa might prove effective once again.

Within days, Hevesi had attracted an impressive following. Matt Fong, the Republican state treasurer of California, announced that he had barred the California Public Employees Retirement System (CALPERS), the biggest U.S. pension fund, whose investment strategies and corporate governance postures were copied all over the world, from buying new Swiss stocks. Hevesi had never heard of Fong but quickly got into contact. They needed to coordinate.

The State Department was furious. Trade sanctions and foreign policy came under its purview, not under the control of financial officers in New York City, or even state treasurers in Sacramento. Stuart Eizenstat, still buffeted by the furious Swiss reaction to his report on looted gold, sent irate letters to both Hevesi and Fong, urging them to stop playing with foreign policy. He said that sanctions would be counterproductive and praised the actions the Swiss had already taken. "Sanctions and boycotts, taken after the many steps outlined above to correct past mistakes," he said, "have led to a negative reaction in Switzerland, creating the impression in the Swiss populace that they are under unfair attack."

In private, Eizenstat suggested that the message had been sent, and continuing with sanctions might be unhelpful. "This is a little bit like an atomic bomb," he told Hevesi. "It's an important deterrent. But when you use that club there is a lot of collateral damage and you cannot use it again. Once you drop an atomic bomb, a lot of innocent people get hurt."

Hevesi responded with a stock answer: "I'm a loyal American: I agree with my State Department most of the time." In private, he thought Eizenstat's objections boiled down to one simple objection: "Stay off my turf." Hevesi's team, remembering they had imposed South African disinvestment only over fierce opposition from the Reagan administration, did not feel too abashed about trampling on Eizenstat's territory.

Hevesi also had his finger on a broader trend. Globalization had increased the power of multinational corporations in the world economy, and correspondingly lessened the power of individual governments. Well-organized interest groups were now better equipped to take on companies than sovereign states, who were restricted by legal and diplomatic concerns. Nike, the sporting goods manufacturer, suffered severe damage to its reputation after labor rights organizations publicized its use of child laborers in Southeast Asia, for example. Moreover, the State Department itself used sanctions often, usually against Third World totalitarian governments such as Burma or Iraq, and almost invariably with negligible effects. According to Washington's Institute for

International Economics, the United States had imposed economic sanctions on other countries at least 110 times during the twentieth century, and by the end of 1999 it had sanctions against twenty-six countries, accounting for more than half the world's population.

For the record, Hevesi announced that he was not involving himself in foreign affairs, simply exercising his right to determine which people he did business with. But he had no desire to antagonize Eizenstat. Hevesi talked to Fong, and persuaded him to withdraw his threats.

By then, however, the movement to enact sanctions, fanned by Eric Wollman's bulletins and by press coverage of Hevesi's initial riposte to UBS, had spread beyond New York's borders and out of Hevesi's control. Massachusetts legislators were proposing a law to block state pension funds from investing in Swiss banks, as were lawmakers in New Jersey and Illinois. Since the Swiss banks generally did little or no business in those states, which all had significant populations of survivors, lawmakers had little to restrain them from taking a principled stand against Swiss banks.

Hevesi and his team needed to establish control. They invited all 900 financial officers in their database to an "educational gathering" in late December at the Plaza Hotel in Manhattan, a grand bronze-roofed turn-of-the-century edifice. There they planned to let the officials hear from all the leading players, including the Swiss banks, and draw their own conclusions. Within weeks, more than 150 of the most powerful U.S. financial officers had replied that they would make the trip, at their own expense. With this kind of interest, the conference needed to provide the structure to make decisions—and push forward their campaign.

Israel Singer saw an opportunity. He phoned Hevesi with a suggestion: The conference could back a "moratorium" on sanctions for a fixed period, maybe three months. Hevesi, who did not intend to impose further sanctions, considered the suggestion a magnificent way to extract leverage by delaying an action he had no plans to take.

Hevesi was not the only New York official flexing his muscles. Elizabeth McCaul, recently appointed by Governor George Pataki as New York's acting banking superintendent, was a workaholic former Goldman Sachs investment banker who combined her job with raising a family, which included six children. Earlier in 1997, Pataki—acting in part on the prompting of Israel Singer—had called for an investigation to find whether Nazi loot or dormant accounts had passed through the Swiss banks' New York branches during the war, and McCaul was vigorously fulfilling her mandate. In 1939, the Swiss Bank Corporation had opened a branch at 120 Broadway, in the building formerly occupied by the New York Federal Reserve, and McCaul suspected that they chose it for its large vault, which could hold plenty of valuables. Credit Suisse opened its own New York bank in 1940.

Wartime records could legally have been destroyed after ten years, but amid the fear of nuclear war in the 1950s, SBC copied its documents and buried them fifty floors underground in a working salt mine in Kansas. McCaul's chief investigator, Irwin Nack, traveled down the mine shaft, ducking his head to avoid the chunks of salt falling from the walls, to find an extensive archive in mint condition. Despite this experience, he found SBC highly uncooperative, with clerks at one point denying they possessed the documents he needed. However, at last he found exactly the records he wanted.

On the eve of Alan Hevesi's conference at the Plaza, McCaul issued a "consent order" against SBC. Only one degree less severe than removal of their license to trade, the order gave her department sweeping powers to compel the bank to submit to an independent audit. Another order followed against UBS a few months later. This investigation would take a heavy financial toll on the banks. Credit Suisse alone—which cooperated with McCaul's inquiry without the need for a consent order—spent $28 million on the investigation, which revealed no dormant accounts.

For the conference, Hevesi's staff hired the Plaza Hotel's ballroom, a vast space surrounded by a stucco balcony. The ballroom rarely staged dances anymore, but the hotel had found a niche for it as a site for corporate conferences; it was loved by planners of such gatherings for its 1920s grandeur and rich crimson deep-pile carpets. F. Scott Fitzgerald had set several scenes from *The Great Gatsby* in the hotel, which sits just across the street from the line of horse-drawn carriages that take tourists for rides through Central Park.

Camera crews were camped outside while the delegates slowly pushed their way through the hotel's narrow staircases and corridors. Ed Fagan, who was not scheduled to address the conference, had reserved a small conference room where he served Plaza refreshments to some of his clients, most of them Holocaust survivors. When the bill for the drinks and cookies at Fagan's reception arrived at Hevesi's office a few weeks later, Wollman refused to pay it.

Outside, their breath forming clouds in the cold New York air, a group of anti-Zionist Hasidim angrily demonstrated against the Jewish organizations inside. On the hotel steps, a pair of New Jersey assemblymen announced their own draft legislation to bar the state's pension funds from investing in Swiss banks.

Inside, the delegates sat on the Plaza's plush seats and listened to an array of speakers from the dais, including Christoph Meili, whose brief speech in halting English received a standing ovation.

Israel Singer spoke first, and apologized for the absence of his billionaire boss, Edgar Bronfman. "There are several billion reasons why I am sorry I am not Edgar Bronfman," he began, with a grin spreading across his face. He took the time to thank Hevesi who, he said, would make an excellent mayor.

Sharply dressed, with a handkerchief neatly folded in his breast pocket, Singer switched into his most belligerent mode. He said he would give the Swiss ninety days, and then sanctions might follow. "We don't like boycotts of any kind and we oppose them," he said. "But we understand those who believe economic pressure is successful as a means of bringing results. We describe the next ninety days as a period when we will talk to anyone to resolve every last issue." Hevesi and Singer had worked out their plan carefully, and nobody mounted effective opposition.

The executives from SBC and UBS arrived looking flustered.

That morning their banks had announced they would merge their $595 billion operations in the biggest deal of its kind in European history, and a rival press event was taking place only a few blocks away to explain the deal to journalists. It was an event that loomed much larger in the banking world than the investigation into Holocaust victims' accounts, although the two would intersect in the office of Elizabeth McCaul. The newly merged bank could not operate on Wall Street without first getting a license from the state banking commissioner, and so the proposed merger greatly increased McCaul's power over the Swiss banks. Apparently stunned by the merger's implications for their own careers, the bankers looked oddly disengaged, while struggling to deal with heckling from Holocaust survivors in the audience.

Thomas Borer, the Swiss ambassador, was defensive. Sanctions against Switzerland, he said, were "unfair and against international law." Speaking over an insistent murmur from the Holocaust survivors in the front row, he inveighed against any deadlines for settling the issue. During the question-and-answer period, one of Fagan's clients took umbrage when he mentioned the Swiss government's humanitarian fund. "Where were the Swiss when I came out of Belsen?" she asked, jabbing her finger. "The Swiss didn't help us then. How can you call this humanitarian when it comes fifty-two years later?"

While the argument continued from the podium, Steve Newman put the final pieces of Hevesi's strategy into place. If he declared a moratorium on sanctions, someone would have to decide what to do at the end of it, and such a decision could not rest with Hevesi alone. Neither could it practically be left to a vote of several hundred people. Newman's mission that afternoon was to recruit an "executive monitoring committee" of five officials who would sit in judgment, and he wanted as balanced a group as possible. He could scarcely believe his own success. By the end of the day, he had recruited two Republicans, a Democrat, and an Independent to join the Democratic Hevesi. The New York City comptroller would be the only Jew on the committee, which included two women, an African American, and an Asian American. Nobody could dismiss this as a liberal Jewish conspiracy.

While Newman worked the floor, Hevesi parried questions from the often hostile crowd. Councilmen from Chicago and New Jersey complained that the Swiss banks were getting another three months when they had already been given fifty years too many to seek a resolution. But Hevesi, fresh from talks with the class action lawyers, explained that simply imposing sanctions might force the Swiss into intransigence, crushing the chance to settle the lawsuit out of court. The meeting ended with a show of hands on his plan. Nobody voted against.

In only two months, Hevesi had parlayed an almost symbolic gesture against UBS into a vehicle that would let him quietly exert control over Holocaust restitution for years to come. Soon Hevesi would have the opportunity to wield that power. The pursuit of the Swiss had now carried on for two years, and the time was ripe to force a settlement.

Take It or Leave It

Three days after Hevesi's conference at the Plaza, Mel Weiss paced his corner office on the forty-sixth floor of Penn Plaza, the spike of the Empire State building shining blood-red behind him. He had too many things to do. He was flying to Zurich the next morning to meet the CEOs of the big Swiss banks, and the trip, planned at short notice, had thrown other plans awry. Every five minutes, his personal assistant Lois thrust a new Post-it note under his nose for his attention while he tried to focus on the difficult mission ahead.

His body language betrayed intense emotional commitment. Weiss, an elegant, gray-bearded man with broad shoulders and the well-centered stance of a boxer, punctuated his comments with jabs of his right hand. His thick eyebrows knitted beneath a stormy forehead as he recounted how he intended to deal with the Swiss bankers. Any settlement would give Weiss the most satisfying victory of his career, but he feared his Swiss excursion would only be a waste of his time. "Frankly," he said in his clipped Brooklyn accent, "I find it hard to be optimistic."

Above his desk, Weiss had hung a framed newspaper profile of himself, headlined "Crocodile Lawyer." It said that lawyers recognized him as the master of the class action lawsuit, a status that gave him great pride. Companies caught in his litigation felt as though they had dropped into the mouth of a crocodile. Educated in the law in New York's public universities, Weiss had founded his own firm and steadily extended the frontiers of class action lawsuits to force billion-dollar sums out of Wall Street financiers, often on behalf of middle-class plaintiffs who could not have afforded to sue on their own. Almost always, he achieved his results through backroom negotiations, as his opponents badly needed to avoid appearing in open court. He took all the risks himself, often spending millions of dollars investigating a corporate miscreant.

Weiss typically charged a percentage, a contingency fee amounting to about one-third of whatever defendants would pay to his clients. Over the preceding decade, his firm had pulled in $692 million, of which his share alone came to $102 million. Large chunks of it went to the Democratic Party and to building a large collection of Picasso's works of art, whose full-blooded approach to life Weiss admired. Even though he would act pro bono, he could afford to pursue the Swiss banks for years.

He felt he might need to. Weiss had scant confidence in Israel Singer and the World Jewish Congress, which he thought people only took seriously because of Bronfman's influence. Many other American Jewish organizations were better known, and Weiss did not think the WJC public relations campaign would scare the Swiss. But the gnomes of Zurich—as British Prime Minister Harold Wilson once labeled them—might be shocked to confront America's king of class action law.

As far as Weiss was concerned, the search by Paul Volcker's commission for dormant accounts was a well-designed trap, and the WJC had naively fallen into it. He found it absurd even to think about auditing documents that had lain in filing cabinets for more than half a century. "If we get trapped into thinking this is about that which we can justify with precision, we aren't doing justice to those who suffered these wrongs," he said, pounding his right fist into his left hand, "because fifty-two years of obfuscation make it impossible to reconstruct with precision. We aren't going to play that game."

He believed bank employees had stolen and looted Holocaust survivors' money in the intervening half century, but he wanted to hold the Swiss government accountable, not just the banks. Volcker had no mandate to touch the government's role. Besides, Weiss pointed out contemptuously, Volcker himself sat on the board of Nestlé, the huge Swiss manufacturer of Nescafé and many other goods, alongside the chairmen of all the big three Swiss banks. So Weiss believed that only the American courts could provide a "just process" to resolve the issue.

Weiss was growing to appreciate Alan Hevesi. But he saw little chance for sanctions to work without the tangible threat of a lawsuit claiming billions of dollars. He also noted that many American Jewish leaders felt happier backing a lawsuit than risking accusations of hypocrisy by signing up for a boycott, after so many years of opposing Arab boycotts of Israel.

From his office, Weiss enjoyed a view sweeping across lower Manhattan from the Empire State Building, only two blocks away, downtown to the lights of Wall Street. He turned off the lights, so that the room seemed to float in a sea of neon.

"We are seasoned lawyers," he growled. "And we're not going away."

As his plane touched down at Zurich airport in the early hours of a Sunday morning, Stuart Eizenstat prepared to embark on one of the biggest gambles of his thirty-year career in public life. Having decided to intervene in the lawsuits, he was hosting a secret meeting between the class action lawyers and the banks' CEOs. After talking to Swiss diplomats and bankers, he believed a meeting could produce results. Other State Department business beckoned, and he would be leaving Zurich for Israel, the West Bank, and Gaza that afternoon for talks on rebuilding the Palestinian economy. But first he wanted to bring the Swiss bankers face-to-face with their American accusers, and he had arranged a rendezvous for them at the Savoy Hotel in the Paradeplatz, the ornate square at the city's center.

If all went well, he hoped to make himself the mediator who brokered a "global settlement," resolving the lawsuit and all the other complaints against the Swiss. But it was unprecedented for the State Department to intervene in a lawsuit between private parties, when there was no foreign government involved. Eizenstat was determined to lead the talks, and he effectively browbeat the administration's attorneys at the State and Justice Departments into dropping any objections to his intervention. He also needed to work hard to justify his presence to the rival parties themselves. The Swiss, still smarting from his accusation that they had prolonged the war, did not consider him an impartial broker, while the lawyers preferred to work before a judge rather than a government official. For now, as his aide Bennett Freeman put it, he just "wanted to see if these guys could sit in the same meeting together."

The Savoy belongs to Credit Suisse and sits at right angles to Credit Suisse's headquarters, while the head office of UBS faces it across Paradeplatz. Not a likely site for a secret meeting, its elegant lobby is usually thronged with visitors, and the hotel faces onto the city's busiest tram intersection. Eizenstat met Freeman in the lobby and the latter ushered him into the breakfast room to meet Paul Volcker, a friend from the Carter administration. The news was grim: Volcker's audit would take at least another year, so there was no imminent chance of hard numbers to break the impasse.

Credit Suisse had reserved the hotel's largest private dining room for the morning, and most of Eizenstat's guests were already seated around one long table, waiting for him to take his seat at the head. To his right—looking uncomfortable—were the CEOs of the three biggest Swiss banks. Mathis Cabiallavetta of UBS and Marcel Ospel of SBC were both recently appointed and remained preoccupied by the merger their banks had just agreed, which had required several weeks of secret negotiations. They looked detached. Lukas Muehlemann of Credit Suisse, by contrast, seemed keen to assess the American accusers he was meeting for the first time.

Facing each other farther down the table were the banks' legal team, led by Roger Witten, and a formidable triumvirate of plaintiffs' lawyers: Mel Weiss, Michael Hausfeld, and Bob Swift. However, Israel Singer, the man who more than any other had built the campaign, was notable by his absence. Eizenstat, keen to insert himself and stamp his own authority on the negotiations, had chosen to exclude him. The lawyers felt happy to leave him out, but the Swiss were nervous. They would need some guarantee that any deal this process produced would be acceptable to

Israel Singer. Without him, there could be no global settlement and no closure.

Ospel chain-smoked throughout the meeting much to the irritation of the Americans, who were used to no-smoking policies, while Hausfeld fidgeted in his seat, sensing that the Swiss were not taking him, or his lawsuit, seriously. He could not understand why Ospel and Cabiallavetta—who had spent the last week flying between Zurich, London, and New York promoting their merger—seemed so offhand, and he did not appreciate being told by the bankers that he was talking to the busiest businessmen in the world. No U.S. executive would say anything like that if such a deadly trio of lawyers had arrived to discuss a class action lawsuit. Swift was thinking much the same thing, and wondering why he was there.

Roger Witten, leading for the bankers, wanted to use the "exploratory meeting" to find a way to combine a court settlement with the Volcker committee's work or the government's humanitarian fund. He did not want to talk about money.

But Witten's ideas were poorly received by the lawyers on the other side of the table. Weiss passed a note to his colleagues while Witten was speaking: "This guy is a schmuck." When Weiss himself came to speak, he advised the banks to pay a big sum and walk away. "Putting myself in the shoes of the other side," he said, "what's the best way to get rid of the problem? How? Create a fund which the court has the responsibility to distribute. The focus is then on the courts and not on the defendants, and on how and when the dollars are distributed as opposed to what was done and by whom."

Eizenstat carefully avoided any talk of figures. The lawyers wanted several billion dollars, while the Swiss, having set a huge and definitive audit in process, saw no reason why they should pay any more than the total amount the Volcker investigation found in dormant accounts. Bargaining over numbers now might therefore torpedo the talks before they had begun. Eizenstat suggested they should discuss the structure of a settlement first, and invited the participants to meet again in Washington the next month.

Ospel, Cabiallavetta, and Muehlemann agreed. They would not travel to the United States themselves—they hired lawyers to do that—but were happy to keep talking under the State Department's aegis.

Eizenstat faced another problem. Despite the attempts at secrecy, news had leaked, and several journalists stood outside in the alpine air. To the great amusement of their Swiss hosts, Eizenstat and Freeman attempted to escape through the hotel kitchens. Then, accepting that the press knew they were there and needed to be told something, Freeman scribbled a brief statement on hotel stationery to explain their presence. Eizenstat proclaimed that the U.S. government wanted to see "justice done to victims of the Holocaust" and a "strong and positive bilateral relationship" with Switzerland. Those two laudable motives might be at odds, but that did not matter for now. It was the first time they had publicly laid out a statement of U.S. interests.

By working as an intermediary for the plaintiffs' lawyers, Eizenstat hoped he could apply pressure on Switzerland that would normally be impossible while maintaining good relations with a friendly government. Despite the frosty atmosphere in the hotel room, Eizenstat left for the Holy Land feeling the meeting had served its purpose: the two sides had a dialogue now, and he thought he controlled it.

However, talks dragged on under Eizenstat's auspices for three months without moving beyond wrangles over structural issues. It turned out that Eizenstat needed Israel Singer. Roger Witten, plagued by the "nightmare scenario" of making a legal settlement only to find that it was rejected by the Jewish community at large, was determined to involve the World Jewish Congress, against the opposition of the plaintiffs' lawyers. Besides, Eizenstat knew that the true political power lay in Singer's hands.

"What gave Singer a role was Bronfman's having such an impact and because Clinton had such a good relationship with him," Eizenstat recalled. "It was his communication with D'Amato that would keep D'Amato spinning. It was his relationship with Hevesi that led to the threat of sanctions. His role, as far as I'm concerned, was oftentimes very undefined. But because he was stirring up these sanctions, he was indispensable. It would not have happened without him."

Breakthrough only came on March 26, the last week of Hevesi's three-month moratorium on sanctions, when the New York City comptroller convened his "monitoring committee" of financial officials from across the country. He had to decide whether to extend their moratorium. During the day, witnesses trooped into Hevesi's boardroom to testify to the committee, while the outlines of a settlement fell into place in negotiations in the cluttered municipal offices outside.

The Swiss bankers arrived bearing a one-paragraph letter from their CEOs committing them to a search for a "global settlement" with Singer and the World Jewish Congress, under the auspices of Stuart Eizenstat, not the judge. They expected a slew of Jewish organizations, not just the WJC, to endorse any agreement that was reached, in order to guarantee legal peace for Switzerland. In effect, Eizenstat would negotiate the settlement, but Singer would hold a veto.

Alongside the bank officers in Hevesi's office, Thomas Borer, the Swiss ambassador, was in a belligerent mood, but Eizenstat and Freeman successfully pleaded with him to be diplomatic with Hevesi. Borer's words in the boardroom, and his very presence at the gathering, left Hevesi with the impression that the Swiss government was ready to be a party to the talks. He now believed that any legal deal would be a true global settlement, covering the banks, the Jewish organizations, and the governments of the United States, Israel, and Switzerland. He toasted the diplomatic success with his colleagues. But the Swiss government in fact never contemplated becoming involved. Swiss officials believed they had agreed to a global settlement for the banks, not for Switzerland.

Hevesi retained his guiding influence by imposing another moratorium on sanctions. The new deadline would be July 1.

Eizenstat convened the first round of talks toward a global settlement at his State Department offices in Washington several weeks later, all the parties having first sworn themselves to secrecy and deposited their oaths with Judge Korman in Brooklyn. As with the Dayton peace accords that had ended the Bosnian war a year earlier, Eizenstat put the two teams in separate rooms. In State Department vernacular, these were proximity talks—all each team would know about the other's position would come from Eizenstat, who would shuttle between the rooms. The strong point from the Swiss banks' point of view was that their numbers could not find their way directly to the Jewish side, and thence to the pages of American newspapers. The downside was that both sides would become totally reliant on Stuart Eizenstat. If either side ever doubted what he was telling them, the talks would collapse.

The Jewish group sat in Eizenstat's wood-paneled and windowless conference room. Decorated with photos of Stuart Eizenstat chewing the fat with American presidents and Israeli premiers, the room was small, seating a maximum of only about twelve on worn brown 1970s-style acrylic-covered sofas. The Swiss bankers sat in an even less joyful room across the corridor. They had to sit in institutional surroundings, negotiating with the ascetic Stuart Eizenstat.

Both sides, accustomed to face-to-face bargaining, chafed under these arrangements. Eizenstat would ask each team to agree on a number, write it down, and seal it in an envelope, an arrangement that polarized postures still further. None of the lawyers wanted to be soft, so they gravitated toward the highest common denominator, while the Swiss lawyers across the hallway became ever more intransigent.

Among the plaintiff lawyers Mel Weiss played the elder statesman, confident a deal could be done at the right price. He could argue details easily enough. But he could also lean forward, stare down Eizenstat, and say, "That ain't good enough." When an early negotiation grew bogged down in the minutiae of different kinds of accounts and safe deposit boxes, Weiss interjected with a simple question they all had to keep in mind: "How tight can we squeeze their balls, and how much can we get from them?"

The acerbic Hausfeld was more volatile. He would fall quiet as Eizenstat related the last words he had heard from the Swiss side, minimizing their duty to the survivors. Then, Hausfeld's eyes would redden, moisten, and glisten, and his face would flush, as if tears were falling down his cheek. Some began to suspect he had developed a lawyerly trick, switching on emotion at will to disarm his opponents.

Bob Swift, a pragmatic figure compared with his two colleagues, found Hausfeld and Weiss's demands unrealistic, and he was privately known in the State Department as the "acceptable face of Faganism." Eizenstat kept Fagan, whose publicity antics with Holocaust survivors he found ever more embarrassing, out of the building at all costs.

Next to the lawyers sat Israel Singer, always immaculate, wearing a tailored shirt with a bright tie. Singer knew that Swift was working for a fee and disliked the fact. The distrust was mutual; Swift only reluctantly accepted Singer's presence, and suspected he wanted money for the WJC, not individual claimants. Singer had warmer feelings toward Weiss, recognizing that he could easily be making millions suing Wall Street and was making a genuine moral commitment. Both savored aggressive negotiating. Together they found a measure of mutual trust.

But differences persisted. Singer wanted grand moral gestures, while Hausfeld and Weiss thought they had a simple duty, to gain the most valuable settlement possible for their clients. They did not see a place for the rabbi in the talks, especially as Singer did not have a plaintiff to represent. But Singer claimed to represent the world's Jewish population and leaned on his long friendship with Eizenstat. As if to underscore his chutzpah, he would put an arm around Eizenstat, and say, "I am the plaintiff, and Stuart is my lawyer." He was referring to an episode years before when Eizenstat had acted as his lawyer on a real estate deal, but the gesture seemed highly presumptuous to the lawyers.

Singer's fast and abrasive witticisms occasionally reduced everyone in the room, apart from Eizenstat, to laughter. But he could also inspire fear. When his temper snapped, he would curse abusively. Between them, Singer and the lawyers agreed on an opening demand of $5 billion in addition to anything Volcker found as "rough justice" for the looted assets the banks held, and for all the dormant accounts that would remain undiscovered. They expected the banks to open the bidding at about $800 million, with a ceiling of $3.5 billion. Weiss wanted at least that much. At their first meeting, Eizenstat predicted that the Swiss would start the bidding at $500 million, and settle at $1 billion.

Events in New York soon hamstrung Eizenstat's State Department talks. To focus attention, Senator Al D'Amato had demanded that regulators block the Swiss banks' merger until they settled with Holocaust survivors. George Pataki, New York's Republican governor, seconded his call. The New York State Banking Commission needed to approve any deal if the merged bank wanted to trade on Wall Street, and Elizabeth McCaul, the state's banking superintendent, obdurately refused to put the UBS-SBC merger on the commission's agenda. By June she had passed on the first four opportunities for the commission's board (staffed entirely with Pataki appointees) to vote on the merger at its monthly meetings, and each month cost the banks about 300 million Swiss francs (or about $180 million).

The banks despairingly tried to persuade her that they were cooperative. In 1998, SBC appointed a former air force general, Roger Peterson, to supervise their response. An expert in operations management, he ensured that paper began to flow as it should. The banks' CEOs flew to New York to meet McCaul, as did the Swiss president and the Swiss ambassador. Her objections to the merger remained.

If UBS and SBC could not complete their merger by the end of June, they could not be united under Swiss law until the next financial year. UBS managers even discussed moving their Manhattan offices to neighboring Connecticut, in a move that would allow them to escape the clutches of McCaul and the New York State Banking Commission. To settle with survivors in these circumstances was out of the question. Thus, the Swiss refused to make any offer at the Washington talks until the merger had been cleared, prompting Eizenstat to phone McCaul repeatedly to ask her to desist from her opposition to the merger. Israel Singer, with his links to New York's political establishment, kept his own counsel as to whether the merger should be allowed.

In early June, Eizenstat wrote Singer a letter saying that he had received a "firm and concrete offer" from the banks for a "prompt and just resolution" once the merger had been cleared. For the first time, the banks were to name a number. Singer assumed they would offer a payment in the range that was being discussed by the plaintiffs' lawyers, from $1 billion to $3 billion. After discussing it with his colleagues at the WJC, he made it known on the eve of McCaul's June meeting that he wanted the merger to proceed.

When McCaul's board members arrived at their meeting, they found themselves surrounded by the television lights and microphones of the Swiss media. However, the chances of clearance for the merger did not look good, as it needed eleven votes to clear, and only twelve members of the commission had showed up. They heard first from officials who confirmed that very few accounts were at stake—the department had submitted twelve dormant account claims to SBC and sixteen to UBS. Since McCaul had imposed her "consent letter," UBS, which had previously dragged its feet, had acknowledged every claim individually within three days of its being presented.

After the presentations, the commissioners started to argue, with at least four of them showing skepticism. They mentioned the guard Christoph Meili and asked about the risk that the banks were still shredding documents. They also wanted to know whether holding up the merger longer would improve claimants' chances of reclaiming their dormant accounts. The deputy superintendent, Edward Kramer, even asked about the moral capacity of the banks' management. McCaul agreed that the character of management was "paramount" and she now found it satisfactory.

At the end of the meeting, they cleared the merger by the smallest permissible number of votes: 11 to 1. The Swiss banks had their deal.

The Swiss bankers believed the episode was politically motivated from start to finish, with D'Amato calling the start of the effort to block them, and Singer calling the end. But McCaul denies that political factors played any role. "With all the regulation we do of exotic and sophisticated financial instruments, our most fundamental job is protecting individual deposits, whether these accounts are fifty years old or one year old," she says. "We are talking about an institution operating under our jurisdiction that flagrantly used the deposits for its own ends. You don't allow institutions that steal money to operate in a business-as-usual manner. That has nothing to do with politics."

Pointing to the negligible amounts that her investigation had revealed, at huge cost, one Swiss lawyer said, "She did as much good for survivors as if she'd walked in there and burned $100 million in cash."

The next day, Friday, June 5, in a suite of meeting rooms in New York's Four Seasons Hotel, Singer learned the terms of the Swiss offer. It was $450 million, less than half what he had expected. This, Singer fumed, was all the Swiss were prepared to pay for all their actions in bankrolling the Nazi war effort.

Until this point, Singer had been cautiously prepared to trust the Swiss. That was over now. Without Eizenstat's assurances, Singer would never have recommended clearing the merger, and he felt duped. "We believed him," Singer said. "*He* believed them himself! But for whatever reason, they burned us. That's what made us angrier. That was it. Once burned, if you make the same mistake you are a fool."

With Singer newly intransigent, Eizenstat's attempt to control the negotiations was effectively dead. The Swiss number looked meager next to a report in the *New York Times* detailing the $1 billion the Jewish side thought the banks would offer. When negotiations started early in the morning, an irate Eizenstat entered and looking at Singer, demanded that nobody discuss numbers in the press for the next ten days.

"It wasn't us who leaked it," protested Singer.

"You're not credible," Eizenstat replied.

Once Eizenstat shuttled up and down the hotel's elevators, the truth dawned on the American negotiators. The $450 million offer, paltry though they thought it, was "concrete, firm, and irrevocable." The room erupted.

"Don't be impatient!" Eizenstat shouted at Hausfeld. "I've worked hard to get them here—give them a chance."

"If I were impatient, we'd have left this process weeks ago," Hausfeld replied.

Singer felt that he had been misled and betrayed. "They are paying us with our money," he shouted. "We stood mute yesterday while they got their merger."

Eizenstat left to press the Swiss once more. When he reappeared, he suggested that it might be possible for the banks to guarantee $600 million. "That's 50 percent of our demand," countered Weiss. "Our reduced demand, our take-it-or-leave-it number. It's 50 percent less."

Singer, by now incandescent with rage, tried to use the Volcker Commission as a weapon. "If this breaks down," he shouted, "then on Monday we'll have the audit go into every pubic hair of those banks, from the bottom up! It'll cost them hundreds of millions of dollars."

Weiss, meanwhile, hammered out his counteroffer. He set up a new "take-it-or-leave-it number" of $1.85 billion, "minus a few deductions." Eizenstat retreated with the lawyers snapping at him, and headed back upstairs to the bankers, who had failed to reach their bosses in Switzerland, and had no clearance to make a new offer. Both negotiating teams had arrived thinking they were on the verge of a settlement, and left suspecting that Eizenstat had misled them. They now believed he had systematically understated the plaintiffs' demands and exaggerated the banks' offers.

Trust among the members of the Jewish negotiating team also broke down. On June 8, three days after the merger was cleared, Eizenstat held a conference call without Swift. When he found out, Swift told his colleagues that he was "chagrined and annoyed" and made a damaging allegation: "This method of negotiating raises the specter that a secret deal is being forged which includes compensation for NGO's." Swift believed he was being excluded to allow Singer to negotiate a sweetheart deal for the World Jewish Congress.

Meanwhile, Hausfeld set a deadline, saying he expected an offer from the Swiss by midday the following Friday. Otherwise he and Weiss would not appear again.

Roger Witten, witnessing the collapse of the fragile unity among the plaintiffs' lawyers, decided that his clients should no longer negotiate through Stuart Eizenstat. He disliked the report in the *New York Times* as much as Eizenstat did, especially its confident prediction that the banks would pay at least $1.6 billion, including a lump sum for Jewish groups to spend as they saw fit. These numbers wildly exceeded anything the banks would contemplate paying. Since State Department mediation had already disintegrated, Witten opted to keep Hausfeld's deadline, but do away with the cloak of secrecy that had led to so many misunderstandings. Going public with an offer would also help to prepare the Swiss public for the reality that their banks would soon be paying a big sum of money to their American accusers.

On June 19, a few hours before the deadline, Credit Suisse and the newly merged UBS announced a "final" offer of $600 million (just below a billion Swiss francs) to redress all their historical wrongs. This included the $70 million the banks had paid early the previous year to the government's humanitarian fund—in a gesture that at the time they had thought might settle the issue, but was already largely forgotten in the United States. Any money found by Volcker would also be paid.

The offer was greeted with a wail of outrage in the United States, and forced a united stand by Singer, the lawyers, and those who proposed sanctions. Hevesi organized an impromptu press conference and, flanked by Singer and Weiss, announced that he was reconvening his monitoring committee in New York City Hall on July 1, when they would consider sanctions. He showed reporters a crudely anti-Semitic cartoon culled from the Swiss press—proof, he claimed, that the Swiss government was ducking its moral responsibility to counter the ugly intolerance in its country. Titled "Helvetia Unter Druck" ("Switzerland Under Pressure"), a fat Hasidic Jew, with thick lips, beard, ringlets, a hooked nose, and wearing a yarmulke, was turning the screw on a large press. This pushed down with seven arms, like an inverted menorah, onto the back of a trapped Swiss man, who was vomiting gold and coins.

Weiss, meanwhile, announced that peace could be bought for $1.5 billion, down from the $1.85 billion take-it-or-leave-it number he had unveiled at the Four Seasons only a few weeks earlier.

Gizella Weisshaus, the lead plaintiff, was sitting in the office of her lawyer, Ed Fagan, that morning. When a journalist called seeking comment, Fagan offered the receiver to her, and she immediately complained that the Swiss were still dictating how much they should pay, while she had no say—she just had to wait while lawyers argued among themselves, and all they wanted was fees. Fagan grabbed the receiver back.

Eizenstat, excluded from the unfolding events in New York, could not get the talks back on track. He tried to rally the American lawyers behind a call to reopen the 1946 Washington accords—a move that might have goaded the Swiss government into taking a role. But the lawyers were too painfully divided. On June 26, Hausfeld and Weiss refused to appear at a new round of negotiations. Swift arrived and floated a new figure of $1.25 billion, which would include anything Volcker found. News of the meeting incensed Hausfeld. On June 29, Mel Weiss, Michael Hausfeld, and Israel Singer ended Eizenstat's disastrous attempts at mediation, saying that no person had the authority or right to represent or speak on behalf of the group as a whole. They wrote:

> This is not the first time that you and your office have attempted to exploit perceived differences within the group by segregating its members. It is one thing for the banks to try to divide our interests. It is a disgrace for you to do so.

Eizenstat's erstwhile friends were signaling that his cause was hopeless. He phoned the Swiss foreign minister in a last attempt to persuade the Swiss government to take a role, but Swiss public opinion effectively barred the government from being seen anywhere near a settlement. Swiss ambassador Thomas Borer explained the reasons bluntly to the *New York Times.* "The mood in Switzerland has changed in the past year," he said. "Most Swiss don't even want to talk about a global settlement. They know that whatever we do, no one gets credit."

A few weeks later, with the sides refusing to meet each other, Eizenstat publicly conceded defeat before Senator D'Amato at a hearing of the Senate Banking Committee. "On June 20, the plaintiffs informed the Court that the settlement negotiations under my auspices had concluded without a resolution. I therefore consider my role in this phase of the matter closed." It was possibly the most public defeat of Eizenstat's long and distinguished political career.

Almost unnoticed amid the acrimony in the State Department, Jean-Francois Bergier, who led the historians appointed by the Swiss government, reported his findings on the Swiss banks' role in laundering looted Nazi gold. Bergier's estimate of the total laundered was even higher than Eizenstat's of the year before, suggesting the Swiss National Bank alone had received Nazi plunder worth $280 million in wartime dollars, now worth roughly ten times that much. UBS and the other commercial banks had handled only $61.2 million (in wartime dollars).

The findings allowed Hausfeld to open another front in his battle against the Swiss commercial banks. On June 29, he sued the Swiss National Bank, calling on it to disgorge all "the unjust profits" it had made as an accessory to robbery and looting. By implication, they were claiming billions. It was a huge escalation.

Hausfeld's legal problem was how to establish grounds for suing the Swiss National Bank in the United States, where it had no subsidiaries. He stressed that it held gold worth $64 billion in the New York Federal Reserve's vaults, but even his colleagues thought his argument threadbare. Swift refused to join the lawsuit, fearing the law barring attorneys from bringing frivolous lawsuits. Burt Neuborne, the law professor who was attempting to keep the warring groups of attorneys together, joined the action, but had little doubt that the case would be dismissed if it ever came to court. But he still thought it worth a try; it could only increase the pressure on Credit Suisse and UBS.

Alan Hevesi now effectively controlled the process. Angered by the refusal of the Swiss government to negotiate, no amount of objections from Stuart Eizenstat could now deter him. The second meeting of his monitoring committee took place on one of the hottest days of summer, when the tiled Victorian corridors of city hall grew uncomfortably sticky. Witnesses emerged from the elevators to pass through the ornate metal gate that separates the comptroller's office from the rest of the building. They were greeted by armed guards and a knot of European journalists. Fagan arrived with two of his frail clients.

A chandelier hung high above Hevesi's spacious but dusty conference room where Greek figures stared down from friezes. Five state and city treasurers sat on one side of the table: Matt Fong, campaigning to become California's Republican nominee for the U.S. Senate, was impatient for action. Barbara Hafer, Pennsylvania's state treasurer, seemed to simmer with fury at the bank's behavior, while Carl McCall, the New York State comptroller, leaned back in his chair, apparently unruffled by the commotion outside.

Edgar Bronfman was the first witness. He did not like sanctions but he would not object to them, he said, and Eizenstat's opposition to them was "irrelevant."

Bennett Freeman, representing Eizenstat, powerfully challenged Hevesi's right to act. "We believe that state and local sanctions in this matter are wrong both in principle and practice," he said. "Wrong in principle because our nation should speak with one voice in matters of foreign policy and international commerce and because they are not warranted; wrong in practice because they may be counterproductive and fail to advance the goal of a prompt and just settlement."

Having made his statement for the record, Freeman attempted to persuade Hevesi to play a game of brinkmanship. He knew Hevesi would announce sanctions but wanted him to give the Swiss a grace period before imposing them. This would heap more pressure on the Swiss without provoking retaliation.

Representatives of UBS and Credit Suisse followed, and criticized the lawsuit against the Swiss National Bank. Richard Capone, head of U.S. operations for UBS, felt that UBS and Credit Suisse were being singled out only because they were within Hevesi's reach in a "crass exercise of economic leverage over us."

He made clear, however, that $600 million was not a final offer. Ducking to avoid the reporters, Capone and Bob O'Brien, his colleague from Credit Suisse, spent hours in the office of Steve Newman, Hevesi's deputy, trying to patch together a deal. They made frantic phone calls to Switzerland, bearing the news that a billion dollars might buy peace. Newman noted that the bankers most wanted extra time: a few more weeks to win around their head offices.

The outcome of Hevesi's deliberations was so predictable that a secretary for the Swiss Bankers Association distributed a statement headlined "Swiss Banks Express Outrage about Sanctions" before the treasurers had finished their meeting. After conferring for less than half an hour Hevesi confirmed that he would impose sanctions, because the negotiators had reached a "stonelike impasse." UBS and Credit Suisse responded that they would not be pressured into paying "exorbitant and unwarranted sums of money that do not bear relation to the facts simply because politicians, plaintiffs' lawyers, and the World Jewish Congress demand it."

Afterward, Hevesi's lieutenants, Steve Newman and Eric Wollman, sat down to draft their sanctions, using the South African disinvestment campaign as a template. In the 1980s, New York's politicians had been divided over whether to impose full sanctions straightaway, as a moral gesture, or to impose them selectively and retain more power by keeping the threat to escalate sanctions on firms that did not comply. Believing that sanctions could be a subtle weapon, Newman and Wollman had drafted measures that steadily increased the pressure on South Africa; and with the Swiss pleading for time, Newman used that strategy again. They would play brinkmanship, just as the State Department had hoped.

On July 2, Hevesi announced that the sanctions would go into effect on September 1, when he would bar overnight investments by pension funds with Swiss banks, and refuse to borrow from them through bond offerings. True economic pain would commence on November 15, when he intended to block city and state investment managers from making any trades through Swiss firms.

On January 1, Hevesi would drop Swiss banks as managers of New York pension funds—a much more lucrative and profitable business for both UBS and Credit Suisse. Hevesi also wanted the state legislature to write a law that would, on January 1, block both the New York City and State governments from purchasing any Swiss goods.

On July 1, 1999, New York City would impose an economic boy-cott as severe as that of South Africa years before, forcing its pen-sion funds to divest their stock in all Swiss companies. The New York State pension fund alone held $416 million in Swiss stocks. If other states followed Hevesi's lead, many billions of dollars' worth of Swiss shares would be sold, critically damaging Swiss compa-nies' ability to raise money on international markets.

For Switzerland, home of huge exporters like Nestlé and the Novartis and Roche drug companies, this was a horrendous pros-pect. The United States was Switzerland's biggest trading partner, with more than four hundred Swiss companies doing business there. In the preceding five years, Swiss companies had invested 27 billion Swiss francs (about $15.4 billion) in the United States, more than three times as much as they had invested in Germany, their second biggest target for exports.

Swiss companies planned retaliation, however little they might dent the mighty American economy. Denner, a large Swiss grocery chain, advertised that it would no longer carry four American products: canned sweet corn, California wine, and two brands of whiskey, Jack Daniel's and Four Roses. Swatch, the watchmaker, said that it would boycott American products if Hevesi took his action. At least the Swiss public could feel their companies were taking some form of revenge, even if no one in the United States noticed.

Within weeks, the New York officials had word of sanctions in New Jersey, Massachusetts, Illinois, and even Kansas City, not a tra-ditional center of Jewish influence. Steve Newman even received calls from companies that provided services for the city under contract, worrying because they also did business with Swiss banks. Would they be hit by the sanctions?

Newman disliked organizing a boycott of any description, and would never support running a secondary boycott like this. How-ever, the lesson was clear: New York's actions were escalating with-out any help from Alan Hevesi, and the pressure this put on the Swiss would soon prove intolerable.

———— •◦• ————

Meanwhile, the rift between the plaintiffs' lawyers opened wider. Bob Swift saw little chance of pushing the banks above $600 million, and decided to extend an olive branch to UBS and Credit Suisse, hoping to deliver a deal before the sanctions began to bite. On July 15, Swift announced, with Ed Fagan, that they were prepared to "come off the $1.5 billion figure" named by Weiss, provided the Swiss banks would increase their offer. Neither of them bothered to inform in advance the other eight members of the committee running the lawsuit.

An apoplectic Weiss wrote the other nine attorneys on the committee, calling Swift's conduct "the most outrageous flaunting of a Court-appointed Executive Committee mandate that I have ever encountered." In his view, the WJC and the lawyers were "winning the fight hands down," and such a display of "weakness" undermined Hevesi's drive to impose sanctions. He proposed removing both his colleagues from the committee.

Swift responded: "Some of you may be so emotionally wound up that you cannot appreciate that my statement gives the Swiss banks and government a graceful way to resume negotiations," he wrote. "In any event, the Swiss banks have responded saying they are willing to resume negotiations."

Holocaust survivors themselves were excluded from all this infighting. Gizella Weisshaus, in whose name the suit had been brought, expected her attorneys to fight the Swiss banks, not each other. Her scorn for Fagan, her own lawyer, and for Israel Singer, now seemed to equal her disgust for the Swiss banks. She wrote a letter to Judge Korman, apparently now the only person who might force a deal and avert sanctions, demanding that he intervene. Her neatly typed letter was punctuated by the raw emotion of her suffering fifty years before:

Dr. Singer and Mr. Fagan are involved in the negotiations with the banks and the Holocaust survivors are <u>outraged to be left in the dark</u>. We will be in the dark for eternity—WHY MUST WE BE SUBJECTED TO THIS TREATMENT WHILE WE ARE STILL ALIVE AND HAVE SUFFERED UNIMAGINABLE HORROR AT THE HANDS OF MONSTERS?

The Price of Peace

On a sultry August evening in 1998, Judge Edward Korman took nineteen lawyers, accompanied by Israel Singer and Elan Steinberg of the WJC, to dinner at Gage and Tollner, a favorite local restaurant near the courthouse in Brooklyn. Unfortunately for many of Judge Korman's guests, Gage and Tollner was not kosher. Singer, an Orthodox rabbi, had to walk past a display case filled with lobsters on a bed of ice, and he spent the evening nibbling fruit and sipping at a Coke, grinning wryly at the implausibility of the situation. Steinberg, seated next to him, munched on a steak. Korman, meanwhile, sat at the head of the table, looking judicial even without his black robe. Effectively appointing himself the warring parties' new mediator only weeks after Stuart Eizenstat had admitted defeat, Korman had made his dinner invitation to give both sides the chance to discuss the next day's negotiation in his courtroom.

Unlike Eizenstat, Korman had teeth. Eizenstat needed to balance American interests against his attempts at gaining a just outcome, and could not threaten either side. But Korman was interested only in hammering out a just settlement, and had a track record of toughness. As a prosecutor in Queens in 1982, he prosecuted and imprisoned Joseph Margiotta, the legendary Republican boss of Nassau County, for an insurance kickback scheme. As a judge, he was known for unorthodox attempts to bring parties together informally and force compromises. He knew that the men around him had reached an impasse, and that Hevesi's sanctions were due to bite in only three weeks. The only alternative to a settlement appeared to be a trade war, while every day more Holocaust survivors died uncompensated. They must be able to agree on something better than that.

He had chosen a local landmark for the meeting. In the 1930s a restaurant critic had said that Gage and Tollner was to Brooklyn what the Statue of Liberty was to New York Harbor. Sandwiched between video stores on Fulton Street, a few blocks behind Brooklyn's courthouse, and modeled on a Pullman dining car, the restaurant served a traditional menu of seafood and steak. Freshly refurbished, it still retained its old-fashioned trimmings, like gas lamps and oak paneling. Its waiters, clad in tuxedos and white aprons, made a great ceremony out of lighting the gas lamps early in the evening.

It did not, however, provide the most comfortable venue. Monday, August 10, was one of the hottest and must humid nights of the year, almost all of the participants were wearing dark suits, and the newly mended air-conditioning system was malfunctioning. Korman had reserved a private upstairs room, and the atmosphere soon became stuffy. The main restaurant was empty by the time they left, after midnight, by which time the twenty-two men had drunk only two bottles of wine among them.

That morning, Bob O'Brien, the Credit Suisse executive charged with representing the banks in the United States, had met Hevesi in his office, pointing out that the bank employed more than twelve thousand people in New York. Hevesi regarded this as a crude attempt at blackmail, and did not respond. With Wall Street in the midst of a boom, the other big investment banks would soon pounce on all the new employees if a couple of big Swiss banks were to leave town. He showed no sign of budging. Asked what he thought a fair settlement amount would be, Hevesi replied, "I'll give you an answer if you'll agree to pay that much."

The Swiss government, unrepresented at Gage and Tollner, created another problem for the banks. UBS and Credit Suisse wanted a deal for the sake of their U.S. operations, but politicians

felt differently. If the banks settled, they would face a public out-
cry at home for increasing the risk of legal action against other
Swiss companies.

The divisions among the survivors' lawyers remained unreconciled, while Israel Singer wanted an emphatic admission of
responsibility from the banks, but was not particularly concerned
with the precise amount of money they surrendered. Privately, he
had a figure in mind: $1 billion. This was well below what he
thought the Swiss banks owed, but he was confident that it would
cover all the claims from living heirs. He had even floated the figure of $990 million with the Swiss, sensing that they did not want
to breach the $1 billion barrier.

Korman's attitude was restrained. He started the proceedings
with a brief speech. He told them that he had no desire to see the
crimes of the Holocaust come to trial in his court. They had happened on another continent, fifty years earlier, and he did not
believe a courthouse in Brooklyn was the right place to decide
such historic matters. Both sides took him seriously. No judge
would want to try this case, as it would involve making unpopular
rulings on the validity of evidence from elderly witnesses like
Gizella Weisshaus. Who could rely on her shaky recollections of
the details of complicated financial events that had taken place
when she was still a child?

Korman told them that both Holocaust survivors and the Swiss
people had much to gain by a settlement, and that he had discussed the matter with Senator D'Amato, who agreed. Then he
asked them to proceed with what was in effect a mock trial. He
wanted everyone to visualize how the evidence would appear in
open court.

Michael Hausfeld, leading the discussion for the victims,
wanted to respond to Roger Witten, the banks' lead lawyer, who
had produced research showing that capital flight to Switzerland
had fallen during the war. As high-strung as ever, Hausfeld treated
the occasion as if he were in court, projecting his voice and distributing large briefing books for everyone to follow. His food
remained untouched.

In the analysis he presented in Gage and Tollner, dormant

accounts were insignificant compared with other services the banks had rendered to the Nazi Reich. He listed the assets stolen by the Nazis: paintings, necklaces, jewelry, religious artifacts from synagogues and homes, gold fillings from Jews' teeth. His analysis rested on broad abstractions rather than precise evidence. Well over half of Jewish assets were marketable and easily movable, so he assumed that half of these assets, or $5 billion, could be sent to neutral countries. He "conservatively" projected that 60 percent, or $3 billion of this went to Switzerland. Big commercial banks he estimated would have taken $1.3 billion of this, which would be worth $13 billion in 1998 dollars.

As for dormant accounts, Hausfeld estimated that Jews who would later become victims of the Holocaust had deposited $100 million in Switzerland. He guessed that survivors withdrew $25 million, leaving the rest to accumulate to a current value of $3.8 billion. By the time he finished his presentation, Hausfeld alleged that the banks owed a total of $16.8 billion.

The others heard his speech mostly in silence. Ground rules negotiated in advance barred them from interrupting Hausfeld as he spoke, or from laughing. Marc Cohn, one of Witten's partners, raised objections a few times and started short arguments before the judge called them to order. Steinberg occasionally winced when he felt Hausfeld had misstepped. He also found it difficult to stay silent as Cohn attacked Hausfeld's theories. "So I suppose you're telling us there are no dormant accounts at all and all these people should be happy?" he asked.

"There may be responses to any one element of this business," Hausfeld concluded, "but when you put them all together, they create a picture for which the banks had no excuse."

His oratory was heartfelt, but Witten and the others remained unmoved, and even mildly amused. If sweeping extrapolations were the best Hausfeld could throw at them, they believed, his case could never stand up in court. Roger Witten responded with his standard line. This case should be tried in Switzerland, not Brooklyn, he said. Hausfeld's arguments might help the plaintiffs in the court of public opinion, but a court of law required tougher standards of proof. Some of Hausfeld's fellow attorneys agreed. Swift, seated next to Hausfeld, privately felt that any presentation that started with an estimate of the total wealth of all Jews in prewar Europe sounded like a weak argument.

If Witten was unimpressed by Hausfeld's rhetoric, however, he was mightily taken by the determination of the judge to press for a settlement, and the Swiss side all noted that Korman now seemed to be operating beneath the wings of D'Amato's authority. Korman made occasional interjections about particular items of evidence that would not be admissible in court, but otherwise he allowed both sides to sit and calculate what might happen if they did not settle. Swiss banks could contemplate the damages a jury of laypeople, selected from the world's largest Jewish community, might award. The steady drip of bad publicity alone could destroy their reputations. Meanwhile, the plaintiffs' lawyers knew that time was against them, that they had already lost the goodwill of clients like Gizella Weisshaus, and that the judge disapproved of their litigation. The meeting stayed orderly, and Korman invited suggestions.

Weiss offered a critical concession. If Credit Suisse and UBS paid enough, he said, it could cover the Swiss National Bank's obligations, and possibly even all claims against the Swiss government and other Swiss companies. In effect, even though the Swiss government refused to talk, he would allow the banks to bail out their politicians.

For the Swiss banks this was great news. It provided an excuse to increase their "final" offer of June, which had covered only the banks, for the sake of Switzerland and not just of their own self-interests. Witten realized that he could "buy peace for the nation," which would be much easier to sell to a skeptical Swiss public.

Weiss knew what he was doing. He said afterward that his offer to release the Swiss National Bank was "a deliberate move to defuse any feeling on the other side that this was just going to be a repeated attack on their side and that they could not buy peace ever." Moreover, his concession took away the political excuse for the banks not to settle. In the process he would get what he wanted: an acknowledgment from Swiss institutions of their nation's culpability. Weiss did not fear that he would appear soft.

Two days of negotiations in the courtroom lay ahead of them, and Witten would soon see that he would yield no further.

Korman saved his judgment for the end of the evening, by suggesting two possible settlement figures. The banks could either pay $1.25 billion, to cover all their liabilities, to be paid in installments, or they could pay $1 billion plus a sliding scale of other payments to cover compensation for dormant accounts found by Volcker. This amounted to more than thirty times what the Swiss had said they kept in their vaults in 1996, and it was more than double what they had offered to pay two months earlier. It easily covered all claims from accountholders who were still alive. But it was also less than a tenth of the $16.8 billion that Hausfeld thought they owed to Holocaust victims.

Once Korman uttered the word "billion," any chance to settle for less than that figure vanished. Both sides left Gage and Tollner confident that they would have a settlement before the week was out. Virtually assured of his $1 billion, and the hefty implicit admission of responsibility it brought with it, Israel Singer felt happier than he had been for months, even if he went home hungry.

The federal courthouse for the Eastern District of New York is an unlovable concrete box set in a windswept stretch of Brooklyn's Cadman Plaza. The blue struts of the Manhattan suspension bridge loom in the distance, but the building itself is charmless and institutional, providing a much less convivial atmosphere than Gage and Tollner. Korman's dinner guests would spend the best part of two days in virtual incarceration there, as he forced an agreement out of them.

The morning after their late-night dinner, the participants arrived early at the courthouse after little sleep, passing lines of immigrants waiting for a naturalization ceremony. Their discussions would be as secret as the meetings in the State Department, but this time they could talk openly and face-to-face. The teams based themselves in different rooms—both normally used for jury deliberations—and readied themselves for tough decisions.

Witten and his team arrived full of optimism. He had awoken early to hold a conference call with Credit Suisse chairman Rainer Gut, who was at his holiday home not far away in Long Island, as well as Cabiallavetta and Ospel of UBS, who were still in Switzerland. They were cleared to settle at $1.25 billion, with a preference for Korman's option of paying one lump sum, to include anything Volcker had found. In effect, the banks' CEOs were declaring Volcker irrelevant, risking the ire of Volcker himself in the process. The grand audit they had set in motion two years earlier, costing them more than $500 million, would now have no effect on the sum they would pay to buy peace. As Mel Weiss had wanted, the Swiss had abandoned the attempt to fix their liability "with precision."

As the day wore on, progress proved slow and Witten's optimism dissipated. While the outlines of a deal grew clear, the numbers were a problem. Witten started the day by offering $1.25 billion, but then deducting several "credits" to leave only about $1 billion in new money for survivors. For example, he wanted to deduct the $70 million the banks had already paid to the government's humanitarian fund. Witten also proposed paying in four installments, to cushion the financial hit for the banks and lessen the total present value of the payout. Aided by calculators the two sides made painful progress toward a compromise.

Witten wanted the settlement to be as broad as possible, insulating the Swiss from any conceivable legal attack on their war record. As the talks ground on, he won the inclusion of two extra classes of potential claimants: refugees turned back at the border, and slave laborers forced to work for Swiss companies. Promises of future compensation for these big groups of people were thrown into the agreement like bargaining chips.

He also wanted to settle on behalf of insurers, and that posed a problem. Eighteen months earlier, Swift and Fagan had sued three Swiss insurance companies, alleging they had failed to pay out life insurance policies written on the lives of Holocaust victims. These included Winterthur, an insurance company owned by Credit Suisse.

The bank wanted to buy legal freedom for its insurance subsidiary, but Swift balked. He knew there was a chance of extracting significant extra money from the insurers, and did not want to be rushed into setting too low a precedent for the other European insurers in his sights. It took most of the day for the lawyers to agree on a clause specifically excluding the three insurers Swift had already sued: Winterthur, Zurich, and Basler Leben. Every other company in Switzerland would be released from future American legal action related to the Holocaust.

They also hammered out a settlement for Christoph Meili, the night watchman who still had a lawsuit outstanding against UBS for slander, brought the previous year by Ed Fagan. Swift suggested that a payment of $1 million would be appropriate. But UBS could not countenance being seen to pay any money to Meili; it would have been politically unsellable. So Swift suggested a compromise, which became the subject of a short, sealed agreement that would remain secret. The banks would pay lawyers' fees, including $1 million for Meili in recognition of the service he had done to the campaign against the banks. The lawsuit against UBS would be withdrawn without the bank making any acknowledgment of causing harm to Meili or directly paying him any money.

With the issues of insurance and Christoph Meili resolved, they still had to agree on a number. Weiss and Hausfeld finally agreed—very reluctantly in Weiss's case—on $1.25 billion, to be paid in installments.

That meant that they would also have to agree on interest payments. Weiss, now firmly in his element, wanted an interest rate well above inflation and refused to budge. Singer and Steinberg watched aghast as two groups of lawyers argued over tenths of a percentage point. For the Jewish leaders, who had already won agreement in principle for what promised to be the greatest triumph of their careers, wrangling over percentage points seemed distasteful and a waste of time.

Now that the Swiss had agreed to everything he wanted, Singer could tolerate no more delays. Ever keen to exclude lawyers from the process, that night he held a conference call with D'Amato and Bob O'Brien of Credit Suisse, while the negotiations continued in the courtroom. Singer said he was happy to settle for $1.25 billion, with no interest payments. D'Amato agreed to apply pressure on Weiss to take the lower number. After all, none of the plaintiffs' lawyers wanted to see D'Amato appear on television to blame them for failing to get the money Holocaust survivors needed. D'Amato phoned Witten with news of the new offer.

As Wednesday dawned, word of the impending settlement spread. Television crews assembled in Cadman Plaza and basked in the sunshine outside the courthouse. Plaintiffs journeyed in to await developments, accompanied by Christoph Meili, who had helped their cause so much.

Bennett Freeman of the State Department was in New York paying a visit to Abraham Foxman, national director of the Anti-Defamation League, and heard to his delight that a settlement was in sight. Freeman grabbed Foxman's telephone and called his boss, Stuart Eizenstat, in Washington. Why not jump on the next shuttle? It would be good for him to be in the public eye, in the throng outside the courthouse as the final points were added to the settlement he had done so much to build. Eizenstat demurred. He did not want to go without being invited. If someone cared to call him, he would head for Brooklyn. The call never came; other politicians had arranged to take the credit.

Meanwhile, Foxman looked out over the glittering expanse of the East River and pondered what he should say about the settlement, a subject on which his views were growing stronger. The horse-trading over money disturbed him. For Foxman, a child Holocaust survivor sheltered during the war by Polish Catholics, the arguments brought back youthful memories of his mother opting to take German compensation after the war while his father denounced it as blood money. The new campaign against the Swiss risked giving the wrong impression about the Jewish community's attitude to the Holocaust, and about the nature of guilt.

He had a set-piece comment: "Six million Jews died because they were Jews, not because they had money or bank accounts. Six million Jews, 99.9 percent, didn't have Swiss bank accounts, didn't have gold, didn't have jewelry, or art. They perished because of who they were. This debate, this discussion, as important as it is, skewed the whole message, the lesson, the truth of the Holocaust. I do not want the last sound bite of the history of the twentieth century to be Jews and their money."

Alan Hevesi was keeping a low profile, phoning D'Amato early that morning to assure him he would be keeping to their deal. D'Amato would announce the settlement in Brooklyn, they had agreed, while Hevesi would wait to take his own glory at a press conference the next day, at which he would announce the calling off of sanctions. His key helper, Eric Wollman, took the day off to catch a day game at Yankee Stadium. Sitting in the sun in shorts, T-shirt, and baseball cap, and listening to commentary on his radio, Wollman heard that a deal with the Swiss banks was imminent. To the mystification of the baseball fans around him, he emitted a whoop of joy and punched the air.

Back in Korman's courtroom, however, the deal suddenly looked further away. Witten and the Swiss lawyers arrived confident in their $1.25 billion interest-free deal. The Swiss CEOs had cleared them to settle at the number, and while they might still have to make a few small concessions, they thought they knew the extent of the damage.

Hausfeld and Weiss, however, knew nothing of the interest-free offer, and were outraged that D'Amato appeared to have offered it on their behalf. They made it clear they would not accept any such deal. Hausfeld felt betrayed. Witten's team felt equally angered that an offer had been retracted almost as soon as it had been made. Two teams of intransigent lawyers, newly embittered, hunkered down in their respective jury rooms.

It was time for Al D'Amato to make an appearance. After his phone conversation with Hevesi, the senator phoned Korman to tell him what the numbers would be. D'Amato had his own reasons for wanting a quick settlement. He faced a tough reelection campaign in November against Charles Schumer, a well-funded and high-profile Jewish opponent from Brooklyn. After a few words with the judge, D'Amato bustled into Witten's room, and embarked on a spirited presentation telling them why they should pay some interest. After all, he pointed out, it was not the end of the world. Banks paid interest all the time. When D'Amato had finished, Witten icily suggested that he should make the same presentation to the plaintiffs' team. The Swiss had been offered their interest-free deal, and they were keeping it.

D'Amato's reception in Hausfeld's jury room was even frostier. Weiss had left to go on a cruise vacation with his wife, leaving Hausfeld as the effective leader of the Jewish side. Hausfeld felt that D'Amato wanted a deal at any price and that he was railroading him into agreeing to a number. He threatened to walk out. To break the impasse, someone suggested choosing a money market rate published in the *Wall Street Journal,* a key measure for financiers but generally lower than the rate borrowers would pay on a loan. Someone looked up the rate in the paper. It was 3.78 percent. D'Amato rushed to the Swiss jury room with the new offer. Witten decided to take it and live with the irony that the Swiss banks' noisiest and most persistent critic, D'Amato, of all people, had told him, "You've got a deal."

Then the plaintiffs' lawyers burst in with the news that they had misread the section in the newspaper and wanted to ask for a higher rate.

"Too late!" barked D'Amato. He had offered the lower rate now.

At five-thirty that afternoon, Witten and Hausfeld informed Korman that they had a settlement. The stenographer was summoned, and a group of disheveled lawyers piled into the courtroom. They had been together almost constantly for the past two days.

Witten read the terms of the agreement they had thrashed out into the record, occasionally pausing for Hausfeld, who looked furious, to bark his acceptance of each point. That was enough for Korman. He looked along the line of lawyers, proclaimed that settlement had been reached with the words "That's it," and banged his gavel. The banks had bought peace for Switzerland.

In less than forty-eight hours an agreement on dormant accounts had been turned into a national settlement for Switzerland. The Swiss National Bank and government, far more culpable on any measure than the commercial banks, had been freed from all legal claims. Neither showed any contrition. The following week, the national bank's board voted to refuse to contribute toward the $1.25 billion. "By participating in such an agreement, SNB would give it an official stamp, which is not in the best interest of the country," its president, Hans Meyer, said in a formal statement. The campaigners had failed utterly to extract either moral or material restitution from the central bank, which had reason to be thankful to Credit Suisse and UBS. Meanwhile, hundreds of thousands of people had suddenly been given a claim against the commercial banks. All refugees to Switzerland and all concentration camp laborers could now expect some money. The complexities were enormous, but they could wait.

By settling the litigation, UBS and Credit Suisse had set a precedent for the rest of Europe's corporate establishment. They had also provided the perfect tactical template for the Jewish advocates. The deadly matrix of strategies used against the Swiss—lawsuits backed by high-pitched public relations, governmental pressure, and threats of sanctions—could be used again and again.

Israel Singer had always fixed his eyes beyond Switzerland, and could now move against any other country or company that had failed to settle the debts of the Holocaust. The settlement by the Swiss did not end the restitution campaign: rather, it signaled the beginning of an attempt to reopen the history books across Europe. The list of those who could now expect the same treatment was long: insurers who never paid out Holocaust victims' life policies, German industrial groups who never paid compensation to people who toiled as their slaves, and banks in other countries that seized Jewish assets.

On that sun-dappled afternoon, everything looked very simple as D'Amato rushed out to announce the agreement to an excited crowd of reporters. Ed Fagan bragged that Europe's insurance companies would be the next to be forced into a reckoning with survivors. Just as Hitler's army had launched a blitzkrieg to conquer Europe, he said, he would launch his own blitzkrieg to recover survivors' possessions.

Hausfeld had devoted his life to the cause for the past year and—unlike Fagan—would receive no money in return. Asked about D'Amato's role, he paused, looking for words. Then he said, "He's certainly very good at showing up and taking the credit."

Meanwhile, Estelle Sapir, a Holocaust survivor who had only just retrieved her father's money from Credit Suisse, remained angry. "This is not charity from the Swiss," she told the television reporters when they clustered around her. "My father deposited money there. It is my money."

Gateway to Zion

Israel Singer was not the only New Yorker pursuing compensation for Holocaust victims. Among the congregation at Singer's synagogue in Queens was Adolf Stern, a retired clothing salesman who had lost his father, wife, and daughter in the gas chambers at Auschwitz. Without the aid of New York politicians and class action lawyers—without even the help of Singer and the World Jewish Congress—Stern and his large family were determined to press their claim against an Italian company little known in the United States.

Adolf remembered only too well how his father, Mor Stern, had carefully prepared for the worst as war loomed in 1939. Mor, the owner of a Czech rum and liquor company in Uzhgorod, now in Ukraine, had paid several years of premiums on a life insurance policy. It might not have been a Swiss bank account, but the family set great store by his policy with the Italian insurer Assicurazioni Generali.

In 1945, Adolf was liberated from Buchenwald, his sixth camp, and hitched a ride to Prague with some American soldiers. There he presented a claim on his father's policy at Generali's branch office in Brun, a Prague suburb. Adolf said that the Generali officials asked for copies of his father's policies and death certificate. "Hitler don't give us death certificates," he replied.

"So I start to cry and I stayed there," Adolf later recounted. "One of the guys got so nasty. He pushed me out—he take me and put me out on the street. Because I don't want to move out. Because I don't have nothing."

Later, in August 1945, Adolf's younger brother Rudy, who had spent the war in Britain, approached Generali through the Czechoslovakian embassy in London asking for payment on his father's policy. He needed money to help pay for the medical treatment that a third brother, Bart, was receiving for the tuberculosis he contracted in the camps. Again he was asked for a death certificate, as was Bart when he appeared in the Brun office a year later. Three times the Stern brothers asked about their father's policy, and three times they were rebuffed.

The surviving Stern children scattered after the war, with Rudy staying in London, Bart heading for Beverly Hills, California, and Adolf making a home in New York, where he bought a tie store on Forty-second Street. Their sister, Edith, settled in Petah Tikvah, Israel. Among them they built a substantial family fortune, largely through Rudy Stern's real estate interests in southern England. But their resentment of Generali's treatment continued to fester. Edith obtained written confirmation in 1972 that the company could not trace any policy covering her father's life. They had reached an impasse, but none of them felt inclined to leave the matter there.

The Sterns were not the only Eastern European Jewish family to place their trust in Generali. Utterly unlike the Swiss banks, Generali was founded by Jews and took pride in its Jewish heritage, growing strong in Eastern Europe as the insurer of choice for the sizeable prewar Jewish population. Antoine Bernheim, its chairman in the late 1990s, spent the last months of the war as a prisoner in Auschwitz. Based in Trieste, a port city tucked into the mountainous northeast of Italy, Generali looked across the Alps and into the lands of the Austro-Hungarian Empire. In the early nineteenth century, Trieste offered the Mediterranean's only access to Austria-Hungary and became a nexus of trade for Eastern Europe, while a hundred years later the Jews flooding through Trieste en route to Palestine called it the gateway to Zion.

Generali's founder, Giovanni Lazzaro Morpurgo, set up the

company in 1837 with financing from Jews in Trieste and Venice, under a Jewish board of directors. He broadcast his international ambitions in its original name: Assicurazioni Generali Austro-Italiche. Mindful of the experience of his father, a banker, who had needed a special dispensation from Pope Benedict XIV to enter and leave the Vatican without wearing a Star of David, Giovanni Morpurgo decided instead to put down roots for his company in the Jewish communities.

Generali became the most powerful insurer in Eastern Europe by spreading with the Jewish Pale of Settlement, the area in which largely Orthodox Jewish societies were tolerated, building itself into one of the essential institutions of the Jewish communities in the region. In those days, before mutual funds, the poor and the middle classes saved mostly through life insurance. Paying their premiums in person and in cash, they would buy a policy that carried a guaranteed payout at the end of a fixed term, and would also compensate their family if they died earlier. Generali's agents would staff booths at the marketplaces frequented by Jewish farmers from the shtetls in Czechoslovakia, Hungary, Poland, and Romania, and collect premiums each market day. A web of offices grew to support their operations. Franz Kafka, the novelist who captured the nightmarish power of bureaucracies, developed his ideas during a long career in Generali's Prague office at the turn of the century.

In 1938, Mussolini's Races Act barred Jews from running public companies, forcing Generali's chairman, Edgardo Morpurgo, to stand down. It ushered in the only period in the company's history without a Jewish chairman. Morpurgo's mournful white marble bust still stands alongside those of Generali's other chairmen at the company's ornate headquarters in Trieste. Another Morpurgo, Carlo, the secretary of Trieste's Jewish community, remained in the synagogue when the Germans started deporting Jews, warning people to hide. He was deported, never to return.

German troops also plundered Generali's companies in Eastern Europe, seizing Jewish assets. In Prague, the Gestapo reported that it had confiscated Generali policies worth more than 20 million koruna by the middle of 1942 (equivalent to $20 million today). This was almost double the amount taken from any other insurer, demonstrating Generali's influence among Eastern European Jews and suggesting that the incoming Nazis had targeted Jewish companies. But if the war was disastrous for Generali, its aftermath was even worse. Communist governments in Eastern Europe nationalized insurers along with other private businesses, and Generali lost fourteen separate insurance companies that it had bought or built up over the preceding decades. In the process it also lost 184 buildings, including several grand headquarters buildings in capitals like Prague, where the Generali lion still stares proudly from several rooftops. It received sporadic payments in compensation from the Polish and Czech governments after the war, but still felt a sense of loss. To Generali's employees, their company was a victim of the war, and the mere suggestion that they had deliberately robbed Holocaust survivors was horrifying.

While other European insurers turned their strategic attention to the United States, Generali looked east, to Israel. It had helped to found the Migdal insurance company in Palestine before the war, and the company quickly grew to be Israel's biggest insurer, with Generali holding a stake even after the Israeli government took control of the company. In early 1996, a new law barred banks from holding shares in insurance companies, so Bank Leumi, Israel's state-owned bank, put its stake in Migdal up for sale. In June of that year, Generali offered to pay $330 million for the shares, in what was at the time the biggest direct foreign investment in an Israeli company. It seemed a good investment, but it was to catapult the company into many years of battling over its Holocaust legacy.

When Martin Stern read about the proposed deal in the Israeli newspaper *Ma'ariv*, something clicked in his mind. The grandson of Mor Stern, he had often heard his uncles and aunt complain about their treatment by Generali in the past. For all he knew, Migdal, a pillar of the Israeli economy, was about to be bought with money stolen from Holocaust victims. The idea was anathema to him.

Stern was driven by more than a desire to see justice for his family. His father, Rudy, who had died several years before, had brought him up to distrust Jewish politicians, or *machers* as he called them. After his father's death, Martin Stern had been deeply upset to find that much of the money his father had donated to an Orthodox Jewish charity in Israel was being misused. Although a passionate Zionist, Stern distrusted the Israeli political and business establishment and considered the entire Israeli banking system to be corrupt. The Migdal deal reeked to him of some cozy and sleazy arrangement made in a smoke-filled room.

Martin Stern was also deeply suspicious of the World Jewish Congress, even though he had never met any of its leaders. Reading of their campaign against the Swiss banks, then in its early days, Stern felt furious that Edgar Bronfman—whose son had married a non-Jew—could pretend to represent world Jewry. The tiny scale of the WJC also annoyed him. "It was obviously an insignificant organization," he said. "It really bothered me in fact that in 1995 the person who walked in to the Swiss banks was a person who represented eight workers and eleven secretaries. I felt he had no standing at all—I think he had chutzpah."

Stern believed that Singer and Bronfman had achieved their results because the Swiss knew them to be close to the Clinton administration, not because they legitimately represented world Jewry. While he was determined to extract justice from Generali, he was possibly even more determined to ensure that he, and not the Israeli or American Jewish establishments, should be the agent of justice. Stern became a self-appointed gadfly buzzing around Singer and his friends.

Speaking with a perfect cut-glass English accent, Martin Stern controlled a large residential real estate company, which he had inherited from his father, in the south of his native England. Every week he commuted between Jerusalem—where he usually spent the Sabbath with his wife and children—and a home he shared in the leafy north London suburbs with his mother. Jovial and bearded, he was a born storyteller and loved passing on every latest tidbit. He had contacts in the Knesset and, more important, in the British and Israeli media, who succumbed to his ceaseless and frequently very irritating requests for coverage. As the Swiss

banks scandal rumbled into its second year, arousing little attention in Israel, he determined to put Generali in the headlines.

Shortly after the Migdal purchase, Martin's Uncle Bart died,
occasioning a family reunion in Jerusalem for his memorial service. The memorial, a predictably somber occasion, took place in
the harshest heat of the Israeli summer, but Martin Stern found
the time to talk to his aging relatives about Generali. Both his
Aunt Edith and Uncle Adolf had clear recollections of their suffering at the company's hands. Martin now resolved to fight for
the family patriarch's money.

With their wealth and connections in Israel, the United Kingdom, and the United States, the Sterns could make a misery of the
lives of Generali's executives. Martin wrote to Bank Leumi, in
which Generali had a large stake, asking if the funds Generali was
using to buy Migdal were "in fact Jewish moneys."

This led to an acrimonious correspondence with Guido Pastori, Generali's chief legal counsel, who decided to reply to the
Bank Leumi letter. Pastori, an urbane lawyer who made his career
working in the Trieste head office, explained that Generali's
entire business in Czechoslovakia was nationalized in October
1945, and therefore the company no longer felt responsible for
policies issued there before World War II. Pastori also checked
with the company's life insurance department, and added a fate-
ful paragraph:

> Assicurazioni Generali made efforts to find records relating to the
> insurance policy of the late Mr. Morris Stern, allegedly issued in
> Prague in 1929/30. Unfortunately, no such records were found, as
> the documents and details relating to specific policies were nor-
> mally kept in the Prague Branch Office.

Pastori was denying that the company had any record of the
policy, and implying that there could not be any records in Trieste. This provoked a response from Martin's mother, Celia, who
wrote to Bank Leumi suggesting that Generali let the Stern family
ask the Czech government to hand over the deeds of any proper-
ties that had belonged to the company.

Generali's anger at the Communist nationalizations continued to vitiate its response. Again Guido Pastori replied, conceding that Generali had indeed been paid some compensation by the Czech Republic—$8,453,497 in total. But he added: "It can hardly be contended that Generali possesses any material amounts which can be ascribed to premiums paid by Holocaust victims." He ended with another assertion that would return to haunt the company:

> We would like to state that in view of the very considerable number of years which has elapsed we cannot relate to your claim as a legal claim. However, being fully aware of the special and tragic circumstances, we believe that Generali has to explain to you the reasons for our being of the view that, unfortunately, we cannot entertain your suggestion, even on moral grounds.

By now Martin Stern had the bit between his teeth. He disliked the legalistic tone of the correspondence and refused to believe that Generali no longer had the documents to assess his family's claims. An English friend in the life insurance business explained the complexities of life insurance records to him. Life policies stay open until the insured person dies and cannot become "dormant" like a bank account. If Generali had really required a death certificate of every Holocaust victim, Stern was told, then "nobody ever died." Generali could not have thrown out Holocaust victims' policies, because they would not have known which policies to throw out. They might still have millions of unpaid policies belonging to people who had officially never died.

Bending to the persistent pressure from the Sterns, Pastori asked his staff to dig through its Trieste archives. Reasoning that any policies would be held in a warehouse near the company's Trieste headquarters, Martin Stern also hired two private detective agencies to find his grandfather's policy.

The search led the different hunters to a small, low-slung modern warehouse, near Trieste's waterfront. Over the years, Generali had used it as a dump, and crates of promotional CDs and records filled the ground floor, next to cases of celebratory wine. An echoing series of metal stairs led to an upper floor, containing the company's old maritime and real estate records. On the top floor, tucked below the white arched ceiling, lay the life insurance department's prewar records.

On the evening of December 10, 1996, a clerk presented a copy of Mor Stern's life insurance policy to an embarrassed Guido Pastori, who promptly faxed it to Martin Stern in Jerusalem. The next day, Generali announced that it still held written single-page records, neatly bound with brown paper, recording the policies sold to 301,000 people before the war. Printed on wafer-thin white paper, typed in turquoise or purple ink, the policies were written in several languages and often carried handwritten addenda by the policyholder or the Generali agent. They documented the family relationships and the financial infrastructure of Jewish communities that no longer existed. The company started the laborious process of transferring them to computer databases—a job that took twenty people six months.

Meanwhile, Martin Stern launched a media offensive against Generali in Israel, where it was already a famous company. Generali was not so well known in the United Kingdom, but Stern prevailed on friends at Channel Four television to make a documentary out of the case. Guido Pastori had never experienced anything like this before, and he could not countenance negotiating with Martin Stern under the glare of the media, even though he now acknowledged the company had insured Stern's grandfather.

On December 23, Celia Stern wrote to Pastori saying she had made arrangements to travel to Trieste to meet him, accompanied by a film crew from Channel Four. Pastori responded by saying that Generali was considering a gesture in memory of Holocaust victims, but was not under "any legal or strict moral obligation" to do so. Losing patience, he completed his letter to Celia with the words:

> If you wish to come to meet us (not at our expense), we are still willing to meet you, but only if we are satisfied of your being truly interested in the facts, rather than in a TV production.

Celia responded by asserting a formal claim "on behalf of my late husband and his sister in Israel and two brothers in the U.S.A.—all Auschwitz survivors." She said that Generali was welcome to discuss the matter with her solicitors in London.

Pastori, increasingly angered, replied tersely:

> Kindly be advised that we have no intention of coming to London to meet with you, or with your solicitors. We will gladly meet you personally in Trieste (not as our guest) should you decide to come, with or without your solicitors.

Martin Stern now pressed for the Israeli government to block Generali's acquisition of Migdal, for which he enlisted the help of Michael Kleiner, chairman of the Knesset insurance committee. Kleiner, a bearlike, bearded man, was known as a nationalistic firebrand and was proud that his office staff lived in Hebron, the most bitterly contested Israeli town in the heart of the West Bank. At the time he was a member of Benjamin Netanyahu's governing Likud Party.

Investigating further, Kleiner swiftly lost patience as he heard Generali's lawyer in Israel repeatedly contend that his company had no legal liability to pay. At first, said Kleiner, the case was marginal to him—"one of a hundred acts that I do in the Knesset to help groups of people who approach me." It soon became a priority thanks to the "disgusting, immoral, offensive attitude of Generali."

In early 1997, Kleiner held a full public hearing—televised live in Israel—to investigate whether Generali's acquisition of Migdal should be blocked. Dan Tichon, the speaker of the Knesset, who had spent the preceding decade in a fruitless search for Swiss bank accounts, was first to address the hearing. He alleged that Migdal had been deliberately undervalued, and that Generali had inside knowledge of the firm's real value from its initial stake in Migdal and was trying to buy Israel's biggest insurer on the cheap.

Elisheva Ansbacher, a young Jerusalem lawyer, testified that a client of hers seeking property restitution from the Hungarian government had come to her with a complaint against Generali similar to the Sterns'. Ansbacher stated that her client had asserted a claim on his policy in the 1950s, and Generali had responded that its Hungarian assets had been nationalized. After doing some research, she said, some hundred families could be affected.

For Kleiner, it now became a matter of principle to beat Generali. "If they had started in the beginning and they had put forward one million or two million dollars and paid those one hundred families, they could have finished it very easily," he said. "But it became like a snowball."

Stern even tried to reach Benjamin Netanyahu, then Israel's prime minister, and was directed to his adviser on diaspora affairs, Bobby Brown. Brown, a practical-minded immigrant from the United States, was initially skeptical, but Stern argued that the Israeli government should take on the cause of insurance policy–holders even though it had deliberately remained quiet during the Swiss banks controversy. Money hidden in Swiss numbered accounts was probably *treif*, or nonkosher, he said. But money placed by small savers in insurance policies was kosher. Brown cautiously agreed with him.

Government regulators waved through the Migdal acqusition, but Kleiner only escalated his campaign. Stern pushed him to call a boycott, something Kleiner was reluctant to do, until Stern twisted the arm of a friendly journalist who phoned Kleiner to ask if a boycott was at hand. If Generali would not put the names of unpaid policyholders on the Internet, Kleiner announced, then Migdal should be boycotted. It was not at all clear that Kleiner could deliver a consumer boycott, but Migdal's share price dipped on the Tel Aviv stock exchange. The threat also extracted from Generali an offer to set up a fund to make *ex gratia* payments, admitting no liability, to Holocaust survivors. The Knesset could have ultimate control over the fund.

Negotiations over the money Generali should place in the fund proved bad-tempered. Kleiner asked Elisheva Ansbacher how much the total file of Generali's business might be worth, and she hazarded a guess at $10 million, thinking the problem would affect a few hundred families. Kleiner therefore opened the bidding at $10 million, while Generali responded with $1 million.

Pastori brought the matter to a head in an all-day Saturday

meeting in Generali's boardroom in Trieste, an elegant chandeliered room lined with cases containing artifacts and various items
of historical interest, including Franz Kafka's résumé from his initial job application in Prague.

Scott Vayer, a New York lawyer whom Generali had recently
hired, flew in and urged a radical policy: if Generali was being
asked to pay $10 million, then it should pay $12 million. "It's
really inappropriate for us to do what's demanded of us in this
context," he said. "So we should do better. We can hardly be criticized for that."

After a day of argument, the board of directors agreed. The
$12 million would go toward a humanitarian fund for Holocaust
survivors. Pastori now accepted that the company's approach had
been too narrowly legalistic: they had to try something more.

The Knesset had still to approve the deal, forcing Generali to
enter the labyrinth of Israeli party politics. The company proposed a board of five trustees, to be selected by the Knesset's leading financial and restitution figures—among them Michael
Kleiner himself, and Rabbi Avraham Ravitz, chairman of the
Knesset Finance Committee. Dov Levin, a retired supreme court
justice, would chair the trustees. Levin, a onetime fighter in Menachem Begin's Zionist militia, had ten years earlier pronounced
the death sentence on John Demjanjuk, the Ukrainian suspected
of being the Ivan the Terrible guard at the Treblinka death camp.
After paying the money into the trust, Generali would have no
control over the fund whatever.

The stratagem worked. Ravitz liked the idea. On a Saturday
evening, just after the Sabbath had lifted, he telephoned Martin
Stern at his home in Jerusalem and asked him to come to a meeting. Stern was due to fly to London the next day, on his regular
commute, but he agreed to drive over in a hurry, with Elisheva
Ansbacher, arriving at Ravitz's house shortly after eleven o'clock.

Ravitz detailed the plan before them. The Generali Trust could
be used to fund good works, memorials, and humanitarian gestures
throughout Israel. But both Stern and Ansbacher thought the
money would be better spent on paying claimants against Generali directly. They said they would agree to the idea only on this
condition.

Kleiner agreed with them and fashioned a compromise. The Generali Trust could indeed be used for humanitarian work, and for commemorating the Holocaust, but only after "goal one"— paying claimants with Generali insurance policies—had been satisfied.

In June, Pastori received a letter, signed by Kleiner and Ravitz, which said that Generali had fulfilled its obligations to Holocaust victims. He believed this meant that Generali could at last consign its Holocaust problems to the past. They wrote:

> We wish to confirm as most praiseworthy the establishment by you of the fund in Israel in memory of people insured by Generali who perished in the Holocaust. We realize this to be a fulfillment of Generali's public obligation in memory of the Holocaust victims. We are pleased that the unfortunate misunderstandings have been cleared. We wish to greet Generali's presence in Israel as a most welcome contribution to Israel's economy and to the insurance industry in this country.

There was still one more alarum to come, when Kleiner arrived at the signing ceremony for the fund and found that there was no mention in writing that the goal of paying policy claims must take priority. Kleiner shouted that this was cheating and threatened to walk out, before being pacified.

Once Kleiner had signed the trust into being, Pastori and the other Generali executives believed they had at last settled their debts with the people of Israel. They were wrong. Instead, they would soon face trouble on the other side of the Atlantic.

Falling like Dominoes

Generali's troubles in the United States began when Marta Cornell, a sixty-nine-year-old from Queens, New York, read about Ed Fagan's lawsuit against the Swiss banks and decided to call him. She had a story to tell, and it bore a close resemblance to the story of Adolf Stern.

Cornell's childhood in the former Czechoslovakia had ended with internment in Theresienstadt and Auschwitz. All her family except her grandmother had perished during the war. However, in 1945 she found a piece of paper with scribbled numbers in her father's handwriting. An insurance agent told her these were the numbers of policies issued by Generali and another Italian insurer, Riunione Adriatica di Sicurtà. She filled out forms for both companies—three years before the Communists national-ized insurers in the former Czechoslovakia—but neither was pre-pared to pay. Cornell said she was given no explanation.

She made more inquiries after emigrating to New York in 1964. Again neither company would pay. They said that payment was not possible due to the "extraordinary circumstances of the war," that her father had failed to pay all his premiums, and that the policies had been nationalized by the Communists. "By refusing to pay the insurance proceeds or benefits that were due upon my demand in 1945," she said, "these companies broke the insurance contracts and stole or profited from my father's money."

Cornell was not alone. Busily collecting plaintiffs for his Swiss lawsuit, Fagan noticed that more survivors complained about insurance policies than bank accounts, and that Generali's name recurred more than any other. In March 1997, he filed a suit, *Marta Cornell v Assicurazioni Generali*, in New York, and the case was assigned to Judge Michael Mukasey, an observant Jew famed for his erudition, who would quote the philosopher Wittgenstein in his decisions. Fagan enlisted the help of Bob Swift, his colleague in the Swiss case, and also brought in the New York lawyer Larry Kill, who specialized in complex litigation against insurers.

Fagan took Marta Cornell unannounced to Trieste, where he demanded entry into Generali's headquarters. To his surprise, they were invited in. Guido Pastori sat down with Marta Cornell, whom he found to be a very nice lady, and introduced her to Jewish colleagues. He tried to explain their positions. From there, Fagan journeyed to Israel where he met Martin Stern in a seafront hotel in Tel Aviv, and suggested that the Stern family should become star plaintiffs in the class action. Stern was unimpressed, gaining the impression that Fagan and his entourage had done little research and that their plaintiffs possessed little or no evidence. He also took exception to their failure even to order him so much as a glass of orange juice. He decided to ignore them and stopped them from looking through Michael Kleiner's archives of claims against Generali in his Knesset office. Fagan and his colleagues parted believing that Martin Stern's only desire was to further the cause of Martin Stern.

Generali had encountered its own problems with lawyers in the United States. No American lawyer Guido Pastori contacted would touch the case, and a succession of lawyers at big Manhattan firms could only give embarrassed excuses. The lawyer they fixed on—Scott Vayer—ran a small private practice in Manhattan. But he also possessed numerous business contacts in Israel. A former kibbutznik, Vayer was not an obvious candidate for defending large corporations against attacks from the Jewish community. Brought up a Zionist, he had spent his youth developing radical political ideas and even led the student socialist movement at Amherst College. When the Yom Kippur War broke out in 1973, he left Amherst for Israel, where he arrived shortly before the end of the fighting, and spent time working on a kibbutz. Once back in America, he worked full time for the United Jewish Appeal, raising funds for Israel.

He was not worried about taking on Ed Fagan, who had been only a year behind him at Cardozo Law School (part of New York's Orthodox Jewish Yeshiva University), and he had plenty of friends in the world of Jewish politics. But it bothered him that no American lawyer would defend Generali. Once he did his home-work, he felt comforted that Generali had done the right thing. Looking through payment ledgers from 1946, 1947, and 1948 he found numerous entries under the heading *"Osservazioni,"* which read *"Morte in Campo Concentramento"* or *"Morte in Campo Concen-tramento, Mauthausen."* In Western Europe, where their assets were not seized by Communists, it appeared that Generali had paid Holocaust victims' claims.

Vayer enlisted Wayne Berman, a lobbyist and Republican fund-raiser who enjoyed close links to Senator D'Amato and who con-vinced the senator that Generali's intentions were good. Go easy with Generali, he said, and there was every chance of an eye-catching settlement. He also started talking to Bob Swift and Ed Fagan.

Trouble now brewed on the West Coast. Deborah Senn, insurance commissioner for Washington State, read an article about Fagan's lawsuit on a plane from New York to Seattle and struck her fore-head. Why had she not thought of this before? As soon as she landed, she phoned a friend who worked at the Anti-Defamation League and asked him to investigate.

About five hundred Holocaust survivors lived in the Seattle area. Local survivor groups were alerted and within weeks Senn had heard from about fifty who thought they had unpaid insur-ance policies. Few of them, however, had documentation, and many did not even know the name of the company—their parents never discussed financial matters with them. Unless companies chose to publish the names of unpaid policies, they could never make a claim.

Senn, who had enjoyed a strongly religious Jewish upbringing in the Midwest, was a liberal Democrat who had undergone her political education fighting her own party's apparatus in Chicago. She had a feisty attitude toward regulating insurance companies and gloried in her rating by Ralph Nader as the nation's best insurance commissioner. She cultivated a maverick image, driving around Olympia, the Washington State capital, on a motorbike.

Insurers in the United States are regulated separately by each state, not at the federal level. No insurer can do business in a state without first getting clearance from its commissioner, who is either elected or appointed by the governor. Senn thus wielded enormous power over the industry and was determined to exert it over European insurers accused of mistreating Holocaust victims. Her first step was to set up a working group, which she chaired, of commissioners from twenty-eight states, aiming to force insurers to publish names of unpaid policyholders. In Washington State she drafted a law allowing her to revoke the license of any European insurer which would not publish Holocaust victims' names. New York, California, and Florida—states with the biggest survivor populations—drafted similar laws.

Senn organized a series of hearings across the country, each of them carefully orchestrated political spectacles. She recalled, "To corner public support, it's always good to shine the sun on things." Martin Stern liked the sound of this undertaking, and sent her a detailed pack of his correspondence with Generali, appealing to her to use her power to "right this historic wrong." The letter started a friendship, and Stern later invited Senn to stay with his family in Jerusalem.

The hearings followed a structure similar to Senator Al D'Amato's inquiries into the Swiss banks. First, victims were asked to tell their stories, with representatives of the insurers left until last. As the road show moved through the biggest centers of Holocaust survivors—from Seattle on to Los Angeles, Miami, and Skokie, Illinois—the ill feeling that existed between the insurers and the commissioners steadily deepened.

The insurers suspected Senn and her colleagues of distorting the issue for political advantage. Senn was eyeing a run for the U.S. Senate, but she vehemently denied any suggestion that she was motivated by a mere search for political capital. Nevertheless, the relationship between the insurers and Senn continued to deteriorate.

James Davis, a lawyer for the Swiss insurer Basler Leben, appeared at Senn's first hearing in Seattle, where he made a magnanimous speech about the suffering of Holocaust survivors. But he quickly grew wary of the attitude the commissioners were taking. On January 6, 1998, he wrote to say he wished to decline from appearing at future hearings. The letter complained of "the open hostility conveyed to the European insurers by some commissioners—from a moral high ground they have claimed as their sole province." Davis said it was "an impractical place from which to start a dialogue." He added that Basler Leben, one of the many companies named in Ed Fagan's lawsuit, had decided not to open its books for inspection by the commissioners. Winterthur, the insurance subsidiary of Credit Suisse, sent her a similar letter, saying examinations by U.S. commissioners would be "violations of Swiss sovereignty."

Davis's letter angered the insurance commissioners. Senn adamantly denied that any commissioner in the United States had behaved with such moral superiority toward the insurers and derided Davis's letter as "name-calling." She and her colleagues were protecting the policyholders, not playing at politics.

The hearings reached a climax in February 1998, on Presidents Day, when Senn convened a hearing in a New York hotel. Neil Levin, the Republican commissioner for New York, was in the chair. Copies of the letters from Winterthur and Basler Leben were distributed among the audience before the hearing. As Davis arrived, already feeling uncomfortable, he saw a Holocaust survivor stand up and say, "Where's that villain, James Davis? I want to look him in the eye."

Flanking Levin in the chair were a bristling Senn, and Chuck Quackenbush, the Republican insurance commissioner for California, strongly tanned even in February. They heard testimony from local survivors and from Senator D'Amato who, the insurers noted, faced reelection that year. The letters from Basler Leben and Winterthur outraged him. He waved the letter from Winterthur and yelled, "This letter is morally bankrupt, it is morally bankrupt. Bankrupt. Morally. I have to tell you something, as commissioners, if I had these guys doing business in my town, I would do everything I could to let people know how morally bankrupt and deceitful they are!"

Then Levin called on the representative from Basler Leben. Davis rose to his feet, and said good morning. Several voices rose to tell him it was already afternoon.

"Ladies and gentlemen. I think I'm sufficiently uncomfortable at this point that I might be capable of mistaking morning for afternoon or afternoon for morning."

Senn started the questioning. What mystified her, she said, was Basler Leben's reluctance to open its books. "Mr. Davis," she said, "why would you be fearful, or concerned about allowing us to examine your books and records if you're certain that we will find nothing more than you claim that you have been able to find?"

"Well, there are two responses to that," Davis replied. "The first is somewhat visceral but I think meaningful. If you're being called morally corrupt, if you're the subject of charges that you believe are unjustified, I suppose you could open the door. Another way of looking at it, I suppose, is that you may not be inclined to invite the person who's making the charges into your living room."

Davis warned that she was leveling charges at his company, and that might not help survivors. "When you make charges like that, sometimes people want to put up their dukes."

Senn told him he was creating a "diversionary tactic and a red herring," but Davis continued on his course. "Actually, when I was sitting here today, I heard someone say from the audience: 'Are these people going to be here? James Davis, Are we going to see his face?' I'm fifty-one years old. Never in my life have I felt a villain. I don't think I deserve to be a villain. I know Basler Leben does not deserve to be a villain.

"We do have an obligation to pay what we owe. We will pay that. But good claims policy also means not paying what you don't owe. And we would like to be able to follow that policy without being villains."

Quackenbush gestured that he wanted to say something. "I'm just incredulous that you would take that kind of an attitude toward us," he said. "The letter that you sent to Commissioner Senn was really something. You said you were uncomfortable and you didn't want to show up because it wasn't a place where we facilitated dialogue. I'm not interested in having a friendly dialogue. I am a regulator. I expect to see consumers in California paid for any policy that you may have issued to them. That's all I've got to say."

Quackenbush was greeted with a round of applause. As it died down, Davis said, "Well, if you're interested in a dialogue and you find my comments amazing, I think it's fair to say a certain amount of amazement ought to be allocated to your response to me."

"I'd be very careful how you respond to me. Very careful."

"I'm trying to speak flatly, because that's the way you've spoken to me. Basler Leben is not in California."

"Don't count on being there soon, either."

Levin attempted to calm the atmosphere, but his message was clear. "I may speak more gently than my colleague from California," he said, "but I have to tell you I agree wholeheartedly with everything he said."

The two American campaigns against Generali—by the lawyers and by the insurance commissioners—were now set on a collision course. The ambitious politicians among the insurance commissioners had no desire to cede control to fee-hungry lawyers, while Swift, Fagan, and their colleagues believed the commissioners lived in the pockets of the insurers they regulated.

Vayer sped up his attempts to reach an agreement with the lawyers. The outline of an agreement with Fagan and Swift emerged during meetings in the summer of 1998: Generali would open its Trieste archives and set up an arbitration committee to look at every claim. Their talks had the advantage of secrecy and—thanks largely to Vayer—cordiality, especially when compared with the Swiss banks negotiations taking place at the same time. Vayer repeated that Generali felt the postwar Communist nationalizations left it with no liability.

Vayer recalled, "They had to understand that they didn't have the case legally that they thought they had and that we really did have a certain level of empathy for their clients and their clients' plight. We had a vested interest in maintaining a relationship with the Jewish community."

However, the insurance regulators' power made them the ultimate arbiters of any settlement, and they had divisions of their own. Neil Levin of New York emerged as their most powerful force. A former legislative assistant for Al D'Amato in Washington, he had only recently left his old job as New York's banking commissioner. There he had negotiated with the Swiss banks and observed the Volcker Commission at close quarters. Appalled by the expenses Volcker had incurred, he believed he had a better blueprint for insurance. A selective "top-down" audit would assess a rough overall figure for the insurers' total liability, coupled with a claims process that would allow those owed money to get what was theirs.

He set about canvassing D'Amato and Israel Singer, as well as New York Governor George Pataki, about setting up an international commission for insurance. They agreed, giving Levin's idea the blessing of the political establishment that had campaigned against the Swiss banks. Now he needed to win over his fellow insurance commissioners.

He resented Deborah Senn's hearings, although he had agreed to chair one of them. "I felt it was outrageous," he said. "We all knew there was a problem. We didn't need to slow the process down for six to nine months so they could do a road show. What were they going to find out at the end of the day? We already knew there were survivors with claims."

Levin decided to work through the National Association of Insurance Commissioners (NAIC)—normally a bloodless organization that harmonized insurance standards. Glenn Pomeroy, its chairman, whose state of North Dakota was home to exactly one Holocaust survivor, threw himself into the campaign, following Levin's lead. They drew up a Memorandum of Intent outlining their idea for a new international commission. All U.S. insurance regulators would sign up for it. So would Jewish groups, European regulators, and—critically—the insurers themselves. Like the Volcker process, a balanced group of Americans and Europeans would look through the books, and move by consensus.

The U.S. government also took a hand. Stuart Eizenstat's

attempt to mediate a settlement in the Swiss banks case was col-
lapsing at the time, and he now wanted a less antagonistic remedy
for settling insurance claims. He entrusted Ambassador J.D.
Bindenagel, a longtime German specialist, with the task of looking for a compromise. The Swiss experience had left Bindenagel
determined to avoid both litigation and a repetition of the expensive Volcker Commission. The idea of a consensual international
commission seemed far more attractive to the veteran diplomat
than the alternative of dealing once more with aggressive class
action lawyers. After putting its weight behind the lawyers in the
Swiss case, the State Department under Bindenagel's influence
quietly tried to bypass them in the insurance case.

Senn opposed the idea, which she felt would voluntarily surrender the great power the commissioners already had. But with the
State Department smoothing the way for them by hosting meetings in Europe, Pomeroy and Levin soon had an agreement in
principle from six insurers, none of whom had yet agreed firmly to
be ruled by a commission's decisions. When it was unveiled, the
chairman handling it was North Dakota's Glenn Pomeroy. Levin,
pulling the strings, was his deputy. Senn, fuming, was left out.

Like the Volcker process before it, an international commission
ran the risk of slowing down the wheels of justice and could potentially derail Scott Vayer's attempt to negotiate a capped settlement
for Generali. He agreed to $65 million as an appropriate number
with Swift and Fagan. Now, Vayer needed to make sure the deal
could stick with the broader Jewish and political establishment.

He talked to Neil Levin, who said he could live with a legal settlement provided the company joined the international commission. Then Vayer talked to D'Amato, who in turn spoke to Israel
Singer. Singer was adamant that $65 million was not enough.
D'Amato told Vayer that an extra digit, increasing the payout to
$100 million, might do it.

These negotiations ignored the other line of attack against
Generali: Israel and the Sterns. News of the planned settlement
began to leak. Martin Stern thought it crazy to let Generali sign

up to a capped number without first gathering evidence on the total number of policies the company held, and he determined to break the settlement.

On the evening of Tuesday, August 18, six days after the Swiss banks deal in Brooklyn, Vayer hammered out a tentative $100 million agreement with Bob Swift and Ed Fagan. The next step would be to allow D'Amato to take the credit for the deal. On the morning of Wednesday, August 19, Vayer and Guido Pastori arrived in D'Amato's offices in downtown Manhattan, hoping to sign a final deal. Instead, they were told the deal had tanked; Singer could not endorse a deal without support from Israel, while Levin was determined that Generali should commit to join the international commission.

D'Amato, however, had a strong interest in getting a deal done that day. The senator's small suite of offices grew overcrowded as Singer and Steinberg from the WJC arrived, along with Neil Levin. Meanwhile, the plaintiffs' lawyers, including Ed Fagan and Bob Swift, arrived bearing a draft of an agreement with only the final numbers needing to be inked in. The partition wall in D'Amato's office was so thin that they could hear D'Amato on the other side remonstrating with Levin to accept the settlement. Fagan phoned journalists and told them a deal was in the offing: they knew that with journalists waiting outside the courthouse, the pressure on D'Amato to agree a settlement would increase.

Pastori needed the approval of his board to raise the settlement sum from $65 million to $100 million and to join the commission, and he placed a long-distance call to Trieste. Early in the afternoon, having caught his colleagues at the end of the day in Italy, he got the green light: Generali's board was prepared to pay, but if they sensed that their settlement would not end the matter, then the deal was off. Generali's directors thought they owed nothing, and they were quite prepared to be intransigent.

Over the next few hours, the men caucused in side rooms. Singer, under pressure from D'Amato, reluctantly agreed to accept $100 million, of which $15 million went to a humanitarian fund. But Singer would not let Generali use the money to escape the commission. After another round of talks, Pastori signed a letter of intent with Neil Levin, agreeing to join the commission, and agreeing that Generali would pay its share of its administrative costs. In the light of the huge bill the Volcker Commission had amassed, Pastori felt that this was another big concession, and a potentially big extra expenditure on top of the $100 million. The money for survivors, however, remained capped at $100 million.

Swift thought the deal was a "door-opener." Generali would allow him and the other lawyers to conduct a forensic examination of corporate records using professional insurance detectives. The process of the lawyers' discovery would be merged with the investigation by the international commission, presumably making Judge Mukasey the ultimate overseer of the process. He hoped to draft Elie Wiesel, the Nobel Peace Prize–winning chronicler of the Holocaust, to chair the committee that would assess Generali's liability.

Once in Mukasey's courtroom, which offered views out over New York Harbor to the Statue of Liberty, D'Amato addressed the other insurers that had been sued, many of whose lawyers sat watching. "There may be those of their colleagues who are upset, very much like the tobacco litigation where one company came forward. It's about time though that all came forward in an honest effort to settle the outstanding grievances so that we can say that in this day and age of enlightenment we put the interest of justice first and foremost."

D'Amato carefully praised a number of insurance commissioners, but did not mention Deborah Senn. Swift hurried off early to board a flight for the Philippines, where he was due to speak with the new president in his continuing marathon lawsuit against the estate of Ferdinand Marcos. En route, he dropped in at Stuart Eizenstat's office in Washington to ask him to support the Generali settlement.

As soon as the hearing was over, a gathering formed on the steps outside. It seemed as joyous as the gathering to celebrate the Swiss banks' settlement in Brooklyn only a week earlier. Holocaust survivors flocked to the scene shedding tears of joy. One of them, Margaret Zentner, even kissed Senator D'Amato in full view of the cameras. As D'Amato basked in the adulation, Fagan predicted that other insurers would fall "like dominoes," adding that his clients wanted the last company to settle to face "another Nuremberg."

———•◆•———

Deborah Senn heard of the deal via a phone call from the *New York Times,* just as she was leaving Prague for Israel where she was due to speak at an international B'nai B'rith convention. Once in Jerusalem, a phone call from Bobby Brown alerted her to change course and head for a press conference. Brown had been feeling the heat from Martin Stern for months. He had spent the morning fielding calls from journalists about the Generali settlement and decided to make a formal statement, hastily booking the government press office in Jerusalem for a news conference.

From the sketchy details in front of him, he could not tell if the $100 million was a capped amount or a first installment. "Because the names hadn't been published and we had never looked into it, we really didn't know anything about their exposure," he said. "Was it generous or was it just a token amount?" The money for humanitarian causes did not help. "You may morally have the right to gamble with some of the money," Brown said, "but you have no right to gamble with the money of legitimate claims. And we didn't want to be in a situation to tell the 101st million-dollar claim: 'Thank you very much but we ran out of money.'"

Martin Stern, scared that a deal with Generali might short-circuit his own right to sue the company, went through his address book phoning seemingly every journalist in Israel to inveigle them into attending. He arrived at the conference carrying a photograph of his grandfather.

From the platform, Senn said that claims against Generali policies belonging to Holocaust survivors might "easily be within the billion-dollar range or more." She would "absolutely not" sign the agreement if Generali wanted it to be a ceiling on their payments.

The intervention from Israel swung the political momentum in the United States. By the end of Thursday, North Dakota's Glenn Pomeroy said that Generali could not limit its liability to $100 million. The settlement was almost dead within twenty-four hours of its signing.

With Swift out of the country, Ed Fagan had to negotiate with Neil Levin for a merging of the legal process with the new international commission. The two men hated each other. Levin found Fagan's media stunts with his Holocaust survivor clients exploitative. "My biggest problem with the settlement was the fact that the class action lawyers were in there for a chunk," he said. "Some of these guys sat around the settlement table like jackals. I wanted a mechanism constructed that didn't include class action lawyers." The feelings were totally reciprocated—Fagan commented that he would rather have sex with one of his septuagenarian clients than meet with Neil Levin. This hostility communicated itself, and his protests that the lawyers would "only" be charging 10 percent, or $10 million, did not help. Levin called Fagan to a series of increasingly antagonistic meetings, extinguishing any chance of merging the two processes.

On Tuesday of the following week, August 25, five other insurers—Allianz of Germany, Axa of France, and Basler Leben, Winterthur, and Zurich of Switzerland—agreed to join the international commission. They would be bound by the commission's decisions, all of which would be reached by consensus. For the time being, nobody thought much about the difficulty they might experience finding a consensus among Jewish campaigners and insurance executives.

Israel Singer had agreed to the deal with Generali, but preferred the commission to the legal settlement led by Fagan and Swift, whom he could not abide. The commission would leave him with a clear say in how the insurance issue was finally settled. "That settlement was put together by one of D'Amato's friends," he said. "He didn't have all the lawyers, and frankly it wasn't thought through. At that time it could have been a breakthrough, and D'Amato was desperate for a deal, but the lawyers never worked out the details."

If $100 million would not buy them legal closure, Generali's directors decided, they would rather take their chances. On August 28, Generali's board met in Milan, with Antoine Bernheim, an Auschwitz survivor and the company's chairman, in the chair. It stressed that the issue was "nonexistent" because the question of unpaid policies was limited to the Central and Eastern European countries where Communists had expropriated its assets. "If the agreement fails to obtain the endorsement of all parties involved," Generali's directors said, "then it will not take effect." The management was, however, authorized to join the international commission.

Fagan implored Judge Mukasey to call all the parties to a conference, but Neil Levin and Glenn Pomeroy wrote to the judge to say that Generali had agreed to be subject to their own investigation. They said the commission would be the best way to pay the plaintiffs quickly, and that it "does not intend to become a vehicle for plaintiffs' counsel to generate lawyers' fees."

The lawyers bitterly admitted defeat. Morris Ratner, who had worked on the insurance deal, thought an opportunity had been missed to combine the commissioners' regulatory power with litigation to produce massive benefits for survivors. "The companies would have been forced to do a real claims program. They passed it up out of pettiness, in my view," he said. "By competing with us, and setting up this process from which we were specifically exempted, they had to entice the insurers to go with them. They didn't entice them by threatening them. They enticed them by offering a cheaper option. They sold out."

In October, the ballroom of the New York Sheraton was bedecked with flags of all fifty states for the annual meeting of the National Association of Insurance Commissioners, which doubled as the launch meeting of the newly created International Commission on Holocaust-Era Insurance Claims. In a coup for the commissioners, Lawrence Eagleburger, secretary of state in the first Bush administration, agreed to chair it. Now, the talk was of pushing Eastern European governments, which had nationalized the insurers, to join the commission. Singer gave a passionate speech defending the restitution campaign.

Amid the crowds in the lobby outside stood Ed Fagan and a group of Holocaust survivors. They were barred from the hall and hotel security men arrived to remove them from the premises, but

Fagan bellowed his message to journalists. "The reason the insurers are going with the insurance commissioners is that they think that will give them an out," he said.

Fagan got his clients to write letters to the commissioners, as well as the WJC and Senator D'Amato, on paper drawn from the stalls around them. Margaret Zentner, who had kissed D'Amato on the steps of the courthouse two months earlier, addressed her letter to the "gentlemen" of the NAIC, WJC, and World Jewish Restitution Organization. She wrote:

> Again you shut us out of your meeting, even though *we* should be the ones to negotiate with the Insurance Companies since they are our policies. We did not retain you as our representatives, therefore you have no legal right to receive our money.
>
> None of you can imagine what we had to go through!
>
> I hate to say this to you, but what you are doing, somewhat reminds me of those times.
>
> Please change your course and include us, the survivors and owners of these policies.

Marta Cornell, in whose name Generali had first been sued in America, also wrote a letter, in an elegant and flowing handwritten script:

> I am Marta Drucker-Cornell,
> My father paid policies of Generali and Riunione from 1924 to 1942. In 1942 the entire family was deported to various concentration camps, where they were killed. Only I survived—I was only 16 years old.
>
> Germans took everything, communists took the rest. Now you are deciding what to do with the money which belongs to me?
>
> You people have no idea what suffering I went through.
>
> Where am I?
>
> After I thanked Senator D'Amato for the settlement—now you killed it? Is it right?

The Last Prisoners of War

If the Italians felt besieged over insurance, the French felt positively victimized over something far more esoteric. Three months after the collapse of the Generali deal, Ady Steg and his French delegation were being hounded around the corridors of the State Department. For three days over the course of the Washington conference on Holocaust plunder, the French were cast as Nazi collaborators clinging to their war loot. France was being pilloried alongside Switzerland and condemned more loudly than Germany itself. A former resistance fighter and head of the Jewish community in France, Steg had suffered enough. A proud Frenchman, he felt as if the French were being accused of behaving worse than the Nazis.

And what was the cause of the public mauling? Not France's wartime complicity in blocking and then robbing Jewish bank accounts. Not the French bureaucracy's role in aiding the "Aryan" takeover of Jewish businesses. Not even the roundups and deportations of poor "foreign" Jews who immigrated to France, like Steg's own Czech family. But works of art. Masterpieces by Monet, Rembrandt, Renoir, and Degas: in fact, almost two thousand pieces originally looted by the Nazis, now hanging on the walls of French museums and government buildings.

Two attacks stung the dark-eyed, diminutive professor of urology more than any other, as he stepped to the lectern in the cavernous State Department amphitheater on December 2, 1998. Steg was the guiding hand behind an official French historical commission investigating looted Jewish assets, which he hoped would lift the lid on France's years of wartime collaboration. The historical researchers were attempting to unearth the truth about the French state's complicity in the plunder of Jewish property during the Nazi years. Drawing on hidden French government records, the historians were trying for the first time to detail the nation's full role in the persecution of its own Jewish population. But in Washington, Steg was instead being portrayed as part of a government cover-up.

The attacks were led by Israel Singer's World Jewish Congress, fresh from its triumph over the Swiss and claiming to represent Jews across the world. "There are two reasons for having a commission," Elan Steinberg of the WJC told reporters, as he brandished declassified U.S. military reports on looted art from 1945. "One is to resolve a problem. The other is to bury a problem. The French have to decide what kind of commission they have." For the WJC, the unclaimed works of art—temporarily in the hands of the French government for almost fifty years—were "the last prisoners of war." They needed to be freed immediately, either to their rightful owners or by auction, with the proceeds flowing to needy Holocaust survivors.

Clutching two pages of handwritten notes, Steg responded bitterly to the charges that the paintings were prisoners. "The French museums are not jails," he said in his heavy Gallic accent. "In France we know what it means. We were jailed. Our fathers were tortured. We know exactly. And we consider that someone from over the Atlantic to come and give lessons has to be more cautious and more measured, with modesty." He told the hastily arranged press conference that his commission was no less committed to survivors than the WJC. "Clearly we do not protect any institution or organization or corporation," he said. "Only the victims."

Few people present that day were as qualified to discuss what it meant to be a prisoner during the war. Named Adolphe at birth— a name he loathed—Steg had seen his father arrested and deported to Auschwitz. He was a teenager in Paris when a school friend warned him of the dire threat he faced, the night before the mass roundup of Jews in July 1942. Forced to wear the yellow star and prevented from escaping during the nighttime curfew, Steg hid in a neighbor's empty apartment and later fled to Lyon. There he was arrested and jailed for using false papers, but was released and thrived because—unlike his fellow immigrant Jews— he spoke French without a foreign accent. He later joined the Resistance guerrillas of the Maquis in the Dordogne region of southern France.

After the war, Steg became a pillar of the Parisian medical establishment. He rose to become one of the city's leading urolo- gists and counted the Parisian elite—including President François Mitterrand—among his patients. At the same time he scaled the establishment of the French Jewish community, rising to be presi- dent of CRIF, the community's umbrella group. Now in his seven- ties, the feisty Steg lived on the Quai d'Orsay, overlooking the River Seine, in a vast apartment filled with oriental antiquities. With his impish smile and infectious optimism, Steg could cajole those around him without obvious coercion. Not bad for a poor Czech immigrant who arrived in France at the age of seven.

From almost the moment they landed in the United States, the French delegation to the Washington Conference on Holocaust- Era Assets felt besieged. Instead of focusing on one area of Nazi theft, the American conference took a shotgun to a range of issues—insurance, art, books, community property. Insurance should have been at the top of the conference agenda, at a time when Lawrence Eagleburger was completing preparations for his new insurance commission. But it was the rarefied issue of art that actually stood out—thanks in part to a blockbuster exhibition of Monet paintings at Boston's Museum of Fine Art.

The exhibition was billed as the greatest single display of Monet's water lily canvases in almost ninety years. Among the twenty-four canvases was a serene painting of white lilies in a pond, which carried the accompanying label: "Recovered after World War II." Behind the sparse description lay a wartime tale that was anything but serene. Untold by the exhibition, the canvas had come into the hands of the French government by way of the

Nazi Ministry of Foreign Affairs in Berlin, where it had been part of the von Ribbentrop collection. Over the course of half a century, it became one of around two thousand pieces in the Musées Nationaux Récupération (MNR) living in a legal twilight zone. In the custody of the French government, the artworks were not technically owned by anyone and therefore could not be sold.

The WJC felt the unclaimed canvas was just the tip of the iceberg and prompted the *Boston Globe* to publish details of the Monet's past on the eve of the Washington conference. The news report came complete with a claim of ownership by the American heirs of Paul Rosenberg, a French Jewish collector who had purchased the masterpiece before the war. The disputed canvas underlined how the French authorities had failed to resolve the issue of looted art for half a century. It also mirrored the controversy that engulfed two paintings by Egon Schiele, exhibited at New York's Museum of Modern Art earlier that year. On loan from Austria, the canvases were subpoenaed in a blaze of publicity by Manhattan's district attorney when they were claimed by heirs of the original owners, whose collections were looted by the Nazis.

Ronald Lauder, the cosmetics magnate and chairman of the Museum of Modern Art, told the State Department conference that "*every* institution, art museum and private collection" contained unidentified Nazi-looted art. He estimated there were some 110,000 lost artworks, worth between $10 billion and $30 billion. As the WJC treasurer and the head of its commission for art recovery, he lambasted the French government for selling some 13,000 unclaimed items after the war and keeping the 2,000 most artistically important pieces for itself. Art institutions must now ask themselves a new set of questions, he said: "Is the art genuine? Is the art genuinely theirs?"

"We must set the record straight, and put art back in the hands of the families from whom it was stolen, simply because they were Jewish," he argued. "For many members of this generation, art is the only connection they have to members of their family who perished in the Holocaust."

Stuart Eizenstat and his State Department officials feared the dispute could undermine what they hoped would be the single achievement of their high-profile conference—a set of eleven principles for dealing with looted Nazi art. After the spectacularly hostile reaction to their Swiss-gold report, they sorely wanted to approach the issue on the basis of consensus. But the principles were feeble diplomatic posturing. Countries were merely "encouraged" to deal with contested ownership. They were only expected to "make efforts" to publicize Nazi-looted art.

The French delegation objected even to these weak guidelines. In an early morning meeting in Eizenstat's windowless conference room, the French explained how the Napoleonic legal code would not allow such interference with the property rights of current owners. In stark contrast to their approach toward Switzerland, Eizenstat and his team agreed to preserve the consensus. The tame principles were prefaced with an opt-out clause, recognizing that all countries should act "within the context of their own laws." The reaction from the WJC was withering. "You can't water down water," said Steinberg.

However, the public pressure brought results. Within four months, the Monet was returned to the Rosenberg family by the French government after half a century on display in museums in Paris and Caen. In contrast, the Schiele canvases were bogged down in a legal quagmire. One painting was sent back to Vienna the following year, while the other—*Portrait of Wally*—was still in storage pending a legal resolution three years later.

The public pressure left the French with a lingering resentment that would haunt those in America pursuing Holocaust claims. The cultural gap between the American campaigners and the French contingent widened over the course of their first contact in Washington. "To see that during the whole conference, in the press, especially in Boston, there was one story of one painting by Monet," said Steg. "This was so different from the people who were deported, and from the suffering of the poor Jews. Who had the paintings? They lost one painting but they have more. It was a gap between the real problem of justice for the Jews and this extravagant, extraordinary problem."

Inside the French government, the fate of the MNR artworks was seen less as a sign of French greed than of the country's tortured relationship with its wartime past. Amid all the legal wrangles over the artworks' status, the state had simply preferred to set aside its wartime years. Few in government wanted to reopen the book on the nation's history, weighed down by the moral horrors of collaboration and the heroic status of the resistance. David Kessler, senior cultural adviser to the French prime minister at the time, says, "I think it was more like a symbol of what had been going on, especially in France. The MNR are ambiguous. You can say it is to the credit of the museums, the way they dealt with it, because they were never integrated into the French collections. Or you can say that the museums treated the MNR as if they were their masterpieces because they are shown in the collections, and nobody knows that they don't belong to the collections. I think it was a symbol for something—the ambiguity of France towards its past."

In Steg's eyes, the attacks from America seemed especially unfair as France had at least attempted to clear up that ambiguity far earlier than any other country caught in the crossfire of the Holocaust compensation claims. In July 1995, the newly elected President Jacques Chirac dropped a historical bombshell. Two months into his term of office, he abruptly tackled the Republic's worst taboo for fifty years—the issue of France's complicity in Jewish suffering, and the role of the Nazi puppet regime of Vichy. Speaking at a ceremony marking the roundup of Parisian Jews that Steg had escaped, Chirac acknowledged a "never-ending debt" to those who died. In a stroke he tore up the entrenched excuse of postwar France that Vichy had been an aberration, an illegitimate regime that the French Republic was not responsible for. "Those dark hours sully our history forever and are an insult to our past and our traditions," he said. "Yes, the criminal madness of the occupier was aided by the French, by the French state."

France's never-ending debt seemed all the greater in the light of an official 1944 report unearthed by the Nazi-hunter Serge Klarsfeld on the eve of Chirac's speech. Klarsfeld cited the war-era report to accuse the French state of holding on to cash and other possessions stolen from 80,000 prisoners herded into the notorious camp in Drancy, near Paris. Drancy became a transit point for around 67,000 people on their descent into the hell of Auschwitz, and until the SS took control in 1943, it was in effect a French concentration camp. Among those who suffered there were 4,000 children separated from their parents in August 1942. Under scrupulous French supervision, cash taken from Drancy's prisoners was seized and placed into individual government accounts. More than 12 million francs were stolen at the camp, representing just a fraction of what was seized. The bulk of the cash remained unclaimed at the end of the war and was simply inherited by the French government.

Chirac was horrified by the emerging picture of French complicity in the persecution of its Jewish citizens. But he was also appalled by the comments of his socialist predecessor, François Mitterrand, who had served in the Vichy regime at the start of his career and earned its highest civilian medal. In his final days in office, Mitterrand had begun to rehabilitate Vichy, to the dismay of supporters and opponents alike. In 1992, soon after the fiftieth anniversary of the mass arrests in Paris—when thousands were held in abominable conditions at the Vélodrome d'Hiver stadium before deportation—Mitterrand sent a wreath to be laid at the tomb of Marshal Philippe Pétain, a war hero in World War I. The gesture commemorated those who had died in the Great War, but Pétain was also the idolized head of the Vichy regime. Around the same time, Mitterrand pointedly refused to bend to a public campaign to acknowledge the French Republic's responsibility for the fate of the murdered Jews. Two years later, in Pierre Pean's explosive book on the president's wartime past, Mitterrand claimed ignorance about Vichy's anti-Semitic laws and revealed his enduring friendship with René Bousquet, the Vichy chief of police. Bousquet was killed by a deranged gunman in 1993 as he was preparing to stand trial on crimes against humanity for his role in the deportation of several hundred Jewish children.

"What Mitterrand said in the last years of his life was—and I weigh my words—terrible, undignified and shameful," said Claire Andrieu, history professor at the Institut des Études Politiques in Paris and herself the daughter of Resistance fighters. "The more he was speaking, the more he was rehabilitating Vichy. If you are a historian and can read between the lines, you see how committed he was to Vichy. Very deeply committed. Chirac's speech was a sort of response to Mitterrand. The country had to be washed of the words of the president of the country. If he had said the same thing after he retired, they would have been the words of an old man. But as president of the Republic, it was dreadful."

Chirac's speech represented a generational shift among French politicians who were too young to face the question of collaboration. But it also reflected a deeper trend in French society, which led a younger generation to revisit how their parents had dealt with Vichy. Thirty years after the riots of 1968, they were posing new questions about the war, focusing not on Germany but on the seventy-six thousand French Jews who were deported to the death camps.

"What changed is that a new generation came," said Steg. "You see, the claims were not from the old people, but the new generation saying, What happened? What happened with our parents? They had been told that France was not Vichy. But suddenly, they became very aggressive wanting to know what Vichy was. And the final factor was also the international situation. They began to hear what was happening to Switzerland."

Steg and his fellow Jewish leaders wanted to capitalize on Chirac's speech to push forward with a broader review of France's Vichy past. But the reaction to the president's emotional address was hardly favorable. From former Resistance fighters to his own right-of-center Gaullist Party, there was widespread disbelief that Chirac had broken with a fifty-year-old French government tradition of distancing itself from Vichy.

"His party, many among his own people, and I may say even the left were so surprised with the story about Vichy," said Steg. "France is not Vichy, they were saying. It was the same old story— it's the Jews again. There was no sympathy."

Steg met with a group of his fellow former leaders of the CRIF Jewish umbrella group to discuss how to move forward. Their conclusion was to press the government to create a commission to investigate Vichy's treatment of the Jews. It took almost eighteen months for the French government to agree to create the historical commission, and when it did, Steg was asked by the then prime minister, Alain Juppé, to become its chairman. Steg refused, saying that he wanted to demonstrate that it was "not a Jewish business." This was a matter for France to deal with collectively, as a country. Instead, Steg suggested his friend Jean Mattéoli, a fellow member of France's prestigious Economic and Social Council and a Resistance hero in his own right. Mattéoli did not hesitate to accept.

But by late 1998, as Steg journeyed to the Washington conference, his historical commission had run into the ground. Starved of resources, its work had barely begun to move after a year. With few researchers and even fewer computers, Steg told the new prime minister, Lionel Jospin, that the Mattéoli Commission stood little chance of reporting back before the government's own deadline of the year 2000.

Days before the Washington conference, France's Jewish leaders told Jospin in blunt terms that his government was frustrating his well-intentioned aims for an exhaustive analysis of the looting of the Jews. Close to the Champs Élysées in Paris, at the annual dinner of CRIF, its president Henri Hajdenberg urged the prime minister to intervene personally. Jospin heard privately that his own finance ministry—which held thousands of documents on looting—was being obstructive. In public, Jospin told the Jewish community to be patient, to wait for the historical research. As a compromise, he boosted the research funding by 10 million francs ($1.8 million) and announced the outline of a process for settling individual claims. Jospin firmly rejected their proposal of buying the looted artworks and donating the proceeds to Holocaust education in France. Steg and his fellow Jewish leaders were stymied—caught between relying on the French government's support and pushing against its inertia.

For the researchers in the historical commission, the situation was bleak. Claire Andrieu, the history professor, joined the commission in March 1998, with just "one and a half" researchers. She was forced to confront head-on a series of reluctant government departments. "You know, the government was perfect ideologically," she said. "Everything that was said to us was perfect. But they did not supply the necessary means for us to carry out our historical work. Also the climate was not always excellent. Not at the highest levels, but the civil servants sometimes didn't understand what we were doing. Every ministry had the same first reaction—we never did anything wrong. We had to use so much diplomacy and energy to convince them that it was in their own interests to cooperate with us. We couldn't close the shop and say we couldn't complete our research."

It was only a matter of time before the class action lawyers turned their fire from the Swiss to the French. In January 1998, a group of New York lawyers sued nine international banks, including France's big three—Société Générale, Crédit Lyonnais, and Banque Paribas—as well as the British bank Barclays. By the end of the year, the case had broadened to include Chase Manhattan and JP Morgan in the United States, both of which had operated French branches during the Nazi occupation. The lawsuit accused the banks and the Vichy authorities of "systematically plundering cash, gold, foreign exchange, securities, jewelry, art treasures, businesses, equipment, and other real, personal and/or intangible property." Through 143 laws and regulations, the Vichy government sought to strip its Jewish citizens of their property and their livelihoods, before stripping them of their human rights and handing them over to the Nazis to be murdered. Vichy established its own racial laws, some of them more anti-Semitic than corresponding German laws. In France, for instance, the "Jewish race" was defined broadly to include someone of partial Jewish heritage who had simply married someone Jewish.

The banks actively participated in this state-sponsored plunder, identifying clients as Jewish, blocking access to their accounts, and ultimately turning over their assets to the authorities. French bank supervisors even preempted the initial blocking of Jewish accounts by acting ahead of a German order by several days. Moreover, the banks had "failed to account to the Holocaust survivors or their families for many, if not most, of these assets." The lawyers, suing on behalf of French Jews now living in New York, sought a full accounting of all looted assets as well as their return, in addition to the disgorging of the banks' unjust profits. As in the Swiss case, the lawyers were suing the banks on behalf of an entire country.

However, these were different class action lawyers with very different relationships to the Holocaust. Ken McCallion, the lead attorney against the French, made his living from environmental litigation, representing the victims of the 1984 Bhopal gas disaster in India and Native Americans in the 1989 Exxon Valdez oil spill in Alaska. McCallion was a soft-spoken, slightly built Irish-American with a previous career as a U.S. attorney investigating Mafia crimes. By his own admission, his only previous interest in the Holocaust was his role in a school stage show of *The Diary of Anne Frank.*

His son Brendan provided a crucial link with a law professor who had recently published a study of Vichy laws. One of Brendan's high school basketball buddies was the son of Richard Weisberg, from the Cardozo School of Law at New York's Yeshiva University, one of the foremost Orthodox Jewish institutions in the country. Weisberg had begun his academic career teaching French literature at the University of Chicago before taking his law degree. Inspired by Albert Camus's allegorical novels about Vichy, he began to research Vichy's anti-Semitic laws to test Camus's theories. "The first thing I did while I was getting my law degree, was to go to the Columbia law library and look up these law books," Weisberg said. "And I saw that Camus's insight was correct, which was this very elegant, eloquent system of logic and language that just proceeded as though there weren't anything really morally different. It was fully integrated into their discourse, into their day-to-day practical life as lawyers, and this fascinated me."

In Weisberg's book, McCallion discovered a small chapter on property law that told how the French banks anticipated German orders to block Jewish accounts. It appeared to prove that the banks had willingly adopted anti-Jewish policies to persecute their own customers.

McCallion's interest remained intellectual until a friend introduced him to some real-life survivors—Anna Zajdenberg and Fernande Bodner. Both had survived the war as children by hiding with other families after their fathers were deported to concentration camps. The thought dawned on McCallion that his case involved not just the taking of property but a breach of international law.

Instead of seeking other lawyers with experience in Holocaust litigation, McCallion reached out among his friends for the technical expertise he was missing. He felt troubled by the Swiss bank litigation, which he was watching from a distance. In particular, he was disturbed by reports of infighting among the class action lawyers, who included his cocounsel in the Exxon Valdez case, Michael Hausfeld.

McCallion contacted a friend of his ex-wife with extensive banking experience and fluent French—both of which he lacked. Harriet Tamen had worked for five years as in-house counsel for Crédit Lyonnais in New York. Although she had never been hired as a litigator before, Tamen brought intense passion to the case. Her family had escaped the Holocaust by leaving Poland and Hungary before the war, and she was fired with moral fervor against the banks because of their flat denials of the cases against them. As the litigation dragged on, she became the hard-line litigator in the case, infuriated by what she saw as the lies and evasions of the French banks in denying their guilt from the Vichy years.

"We started talking to people and to a certain extent it was an intellectual interest, until we saw the papers from the French banks, in which they said they had been following orders," Tamen recalls. "That's when it stopped being an intellectual interest of mine and became an emotional interest. Don't do that. Don't tell me—fifty-five years after the Nuremberg trials said that's not an excuse—that it was the occupiers."

The French opted for a hardball defense: no liability, no negotiations, no quarter given. They based their arguments on the established postwar view of Vichy in France. In the first instance, the

Germans were to blame. The banking sector had been closely monitored by the German Oberkommando services working from the Hotel Majestic in Paris. The Nazis controlled French banks and no one could escape their power. Moreover, within months of France's liberation, the government of General Charles de Gaulle ordered the nullification of all anti-Semitic plunder and the return of any seized assets. Restitution was therefore a thing of the past. If by chance any cash was left in dormant accounts, the banks were legally obliged to transfer the balance to the French state after thirty years. Indeed, the paperwork surrounding those accounts could be legally destroyed after forty years—more than a decade before the lawsuits were filed. Above all, the banks argued that no U.S. court could possibly extend its reach to the French state. If any cash or paperwork survived, it was in the government's hands. In short, the courts would be better advised to leave it up to the Mattéoli Commission.

At Société Générale's ultramodern headquarters overlooking Paris, Christian Schricke had just joined the bank as its secretary-general when the lawsuit was filed. Together with his counterparts at competitor banks, he joined legal forces to present a single argument. "We felt the case should be settled in France," said Schricke. "The difficulty was to demonstrate that, first of all, the French situation was not the same as the German or the Austrian or the Swiss case. But we also had to give enough time to the Mattéoli Commission and allow the process that had been set up by the French government to conclude—before the case in the New York court was decided. The attitude was to avoid a ruling before the end of that process."

As the most active French bank in New York, Société Générale had good reason to take the litigation seriously, and had already begun its own archival research. But the banks were also engaged in a political alliance with the government and the historical commission. The French government told them it wanted the issue resolved in France, while members of the Mattéoli Commission insisted that they wanted to see their research to the end. A negotiated settlement was out of the question.

That was a feeling shared by the French banks' American lawyers, Shearman and Sterling. Fred Davis, the leading attorney for the defense, took a dim view of the class action lawsuit. "Bottom line, I think that the litigation as such was a polite form of ambulance chasing," Davis said. "Were there victims of the Holocaust in France who didn't get their money back? Yes, clearly. Therefore, is there a legal or moral imperative that they get paid back? The answer is yes, absolutely. So it's not that anybody was saying the suit doesn't have merit. But the notion of resolving those particular issues in a courtroom in Brooklyn with lawyers who don't speak French, in front of a judge who doesn't speak French, and jurors who don't speak French is pretty ridiculous."

Davis traveled to Paris in March for an all-day meeting to outline a defense strategy to the banks. The aim was not to deny the claims of Holocaust victims, but to suggest that it was "a cruel illusion" to pretend that a class action could solve the issue. Besides, Davis told the banks' lawyers, "you can't lose this litigation, but in a sense you can't win it, either. You can't lose it because the notion that ultimately these lawyers can go through all the legal hoops, having a trial, proving liability, and sustaining appeal is very, very slim. If you want to spend the money, and take the time, the biggest impact will be attorneys' fees.

"On the other hand, you'll never win it because there is an implacable nature to the overall desire for closure in the U.S. Even if you win the first round, there's going to be an appeal, and no judge is going to lightly want to say 'Holocaust victims have no remedy, get out of here.' Plus, you have Alan Hevesi, Alfonse D'Amato. You've got a number of other constituencies out there that won't take kindly, even if you were to win in court."

In their first round of combat with the banks, the class action lawyers grew ever more passionate about their cause. France had shirked its responsibility for Vichy and its horrors for half a century. It was only now, under pressure from American lawyers, that there was any sign of movement. It was too little, too late.

But they were missing a vital piece of the compensation puzzle: French victims. By chance, the door opened to those victims through an American organization in Paris. The Simon Wiesenthal

Center is a strangely complex hybrid in Paris—a Los Angeles-based group, named after an Austrian Nazi hunter, with a French office run by a British-born former academic. Shimon Samuels works from a small set of chaotic offices in the Maison France-Israel, a community center for Parisian Jews. Close to the Champs Élysées, it is more securely protected—fenced with metal railings and a permanent presence of riot police—than most government buildings.

Samuels—who maintains an academic appearance thanks partly to his bearded, chubby face and ill-fitting suits—had spotted a news story about the French lawsuit. He was intrigued by the name of one of the plaintiffs—Zajdenberg—which was close to his original family name. Believing he might be related to her, Samuels contacted the lawyers and offered his services soon after the lawsuit was filed. He was not impressed by their first meeting. McCallion seemed too laid-back, as if he couldn't be taken seriously. Tamen, on the other hand, sounded like a gung-ho warrior. Neither gave him any confidence. "Look," he said, keen to find a role for his small outfit in such a high-profile campaign. "I'm based in Paris and would be happy to help. I don't know if it's going to fly, but if so, you can count on my office. On the other hand, we are an organization that is seen with mixed views in France."

"Mixed views" was an understatement. The Simon Wiesenthal Center is viewed with mistrust by the established French Jewish community, which treats it largely as an American transplant. Given French discomfort with the scope of American power and influence, the center was poorly placed to handle the hot-button issues of anti-Semitism in France and the country's wartime guilt. Samuels's newfound friendship with the class action lawyers hardly helped to build French confidence.

On the other hand, the lawsuit offered the ostracized Samuels a vital means of outreach to members of the community. He took his message to the air, broadcasting his position on French Jewish radio to sell the class action lawsuit to possible French claimants. Under the Alien Tort Statute, he told his new audience, you did not have to be a U.S. citizen to sue. The Simon Wiesenthal Center could help. Around 2,000 people replied in writing to make a claim, of whom 170 signed on to the class action. Frail, elderly survivors began walking into Samuels's offices for "survivors' hour" between 5:00 P.M. and 7:00 P.M. twice a week. The sessions only served to widen the rift with the French. Samuels arranged the class action lawyers' first visit to Paris, and a symposium at the Maison France-Israel, in October 1998. Attendance was poor and the French press portrayed the claimants as Americans, not French-born victims. To cap it all, Samuels dismissed the historical research efforts as a cosy cover-up between the banks and the French government. "There is something incestuous in the relationship between the banks and the state," he told reporters.

The Wiesenthal Center was not the only American Jewish group that claimed to work for Holocaust survivors. Israel Singer of the WJC flew to Paris in the spring of 1998 to harangue the French government about its independent path toward compensation. In the eighteenth-century mansion used as a staff annex to the prime minister's Matignon residence, he met Jospin's senior advisers to discuss the issue. Among them was David Kessler, a gruff-voiced former president of a Reform Jewish congregration in Paris, whose parents had survived the war in hiding. Kessler told Singer that this was not an issue for the rest of the world.

"It's not just a problem for Jews" he said. "It's a problem for France because it is part of French history. When Jacques Chirac says that France is responsible for what it did to the Jews, it is part of French history to recognize its responsibility and to see what it did at that time. So it's not a World Jewish Congress problem, it's a French problem, and we will solve it as a French problem with the French Jewish community."

An enraged Singer shot back, "It's a Jewish problem because you didn't do anything for fifty years." Singer could barely hide his contempt for the French Jewish community and its close relationship with the government officials. "They're too subservient to power," Singer told Jospin's advisers. "They have no tradition as we Americans do, of a Jewish lobby."

Whether the French liked it or not, Singer intended to turn France's problem into a concern for Jews across the world.

Americans at the Gate

T he French banks soon hunkered down into their position that there was no need for U.S. lawyers in what was a French problem to be solved by the French. Defended by the French government and the French Jewish establishment, the banks believed they had constructed a "Maginot Line" of defense. They even distributed Prime Minister Jospin's statements on the issue as if they were their own.

One of the banks took a step further by recruiting a former member of the Resistance, Theo Klein, as its legal adviser. In his early twenties he had worked in the south of France for L'Oeuvre de Secours aux Enfants, rescuing Jewish children from deportation. Later, he became one of France's Jewish leaders, as president of the CRIF umbrella group, working closely with the Mitterrand government. Now the seventy-eight-year-old lawyer, working from his offices overlooking the Champs Élysées, threw his moral authority and tough-talking spirit behind one of the banks accused of persecuting French Jews. The bank—Crédit Commercial de France (CCF)—claimed a special position, separate from its banking rivals. CCF argued that it had attempted to protect its Jewish clients, notably the Bader family, which owned the stylish Galeries Lafayette department store. When the German authorities were poised to "aryanize" the store by seizing ownership, the bank took control of the company promising to return it to the Baders at the end of the war. Although the Germans ultimately took over the Bader family shares, the bank helped to recover the company for the family at the end of the war.

Klein believed the bank's record was worth defending. He also felt—perhaps more strongly—that the Americans were overreaching and ultimately debasing the memory of the Holocaust. In editorial columns published in *Le Monde* and the *New York Times,* he launched a withering attack on the "blind and arrogant approach" of American Jewish campaigners and lawyers, who "often know nothing" about the historical facts. He also attacked the U.S. government's wartime record on turning away Jewish refugees.

"I agree that every person robbed of whatever it may be has the right to full compensation," Klein said later. "But I don't agree with the idea that you pay compensation to Jews for what they have suffered. Because what they have suffered can't in my mind be compensated by any amount of money. And I don't think I would ever allow that a *goy* could tell me one day, 'Bravo, we have settled the Holocaust, we have paid up.'

"In normal circumstances if you hurt someone in an accident and they have suffered a lot, you have to pay compensation. The Holocaust isn't like that. The idea that Jews have collected money to make amends for the Holocaust is an idea that I find deeply revolting. There was something of that in the American way of dealing with this problem. I found there was a feeling of extraordinary power from the Americans who said they were going to settle the world's problems."

In Manhattan, the WJC's Elan Steinberg was incensed. Klein had taken it upon himself to represent the banks. He could not also pretend to represent the Jewish community without suffering a huge conflict of interest. Moreover, Klein had been part of the postwar restitution effort and Steinberg believed that his comments now represented little more than a cover-up. Steinberg was convinced that Klein was betraying his transatlantic prejudice and concealing something far worse.

"It was our Brooklyn accents," says Steinberg. "It's pure anti-Americanism. It's the French. It's part of their nature. The Americans are going to come here and tell us what to do? They couldn't bear the thought.

"We would not accept as a matter of principle that world Jewry would be excluded from this process. Particularly in the case of France, where the majority of the victims were non-French. The French Jews were particularly embarrassed by this. Part of the problem was not simply that the Germans picked on the foreign Jews. The French Jewish community offered up the foreign Jews first. We knew that was part of the problem."

Klein, however, saw it differently at first hand, recalling one Jewish foreigner he knew well. "During the war I had a guy who told me that the police had come three times to his door," he recalled. "The first time they said, 'This is serious. We're coming back in twenty-four hours.' The second time they said, 'You don't know how serious this is. We're coming back in half an hour.' Two times he had the chance to escape. He didn't leave. He told me this because it was the drama of his life. He said, 'But where could I go?'" He didn't understand French very well. He didn't have much money—he was a tailor.

"So the people who spoke badly and had no money had less chance to hide themselves, compared to those with money who could count on ordinary French people."

The "Maginot Line" constructed so carefully by the banks and their lawyers was breached in December 1998, just two weeks after the defiant stance taken by the French at the State Department conference in Washington. Barclays Bank, the only British institution among those being sued, settled its case with the class action lawyers in New York. For just 335 Jewish clients at its Paris branch during the war, the bank would establish a $3.6 million fund. Any money left over would be donated to a French institution researching the Holocaust. Other non-French banks were also beginning to enter talks to settle the dispute over France. Chase Manhattan declared a day later that it was negotiating with the WJC to head off a lawsuit concerning around 100 accounts at its Paris branch during the war.

The French banks were incensed. At a stroke, Barclays had made them appear obstructive, unreasonable, and unwilling to face up to their wartime guilt. In a collective statement, the banks insisted they were "actively participating" in the French historical research and accused Barclays of undermining the process. The banks' American lawyers feared the Barclays settlement would build momentum for their opponents to argue for other settlements. "It sends a signal to a judge to the effect that if you put enough pressure on these guys, then they might come to the table," said Owen Pell, representing CCF and Chase Manhattan in the United States. "It creates momentum which goes into the public relations pressure on a bank to settle up."

However, the victims' lawyers viewed the settlement as the first ray of light. For the first time, a bank had shown "a spirit of goodwill" and established a system of paying claimants and an educational fund that would serve as a model for the bigger deal to come. In Harriet Tamen's eyes, the real reason for the Barclays settlement was simple. "They're British," she said. "I don't think they have the same issues that the French do of collaboration, obfuscation. I think they were more open. They were willing to say, yes, we did something, we'll do the research, and we kept Jewish money. In contrast, the policy of the French banks was basically scorched earth. They weren't interested."

In France, Ady Steg tried to build momentum behind a claims process in a much subtler fashion. In its interim report, published in February 1999, the Mattéoli Commission outlined the strategy that would lead to an overall settlement, in an oblique attack on Israel Singer's aggressive tactics. "The aim here is not to opt for an easy solution involving some form of emotional blackmail or other pressure to exact a price for consigning the historical events to oblivion—at the risk of purchasing false peace of mind," it noted. "But on the contrary, to give as sharp a definition as possible to the truth in order to assimilate our past history." The truth, it continued, pointed in one direction—to begin paying compensation.

In fact, little had been achieved since Prime Minister Jospin outlined the commission's goals the previous fall. Now Steg and his fellow commission members were pushing the government to move in three areas. They had already received around three hundred letters seeking compensation, and it was time to create a new claims processing panel, to be headed by Pierre Drai, the former head of the highest court in France, La Cour de Cassation. Steg also sought the creation of a general foundation, which would be funded by the government and financial companies that held on to cash and assets plundered from Jewish families. Finally, under pressure from the Nazi-hunter Serge Klarsfeld—a child survivor who lost his father in Auschwitz—they pressed the government for a fund for the orphans of foreign-born Jews, who had never received compensation.

Even as the report emerged, the WJC in New York was threatening to organize a boycott of the recalcitrant French banks. The boycott would begin by the end of March unless the French banks cooperated. Individuals would be encouraged not to trade with French banks and more threateningly, the WJC would approach Alan Hevesi, the New York City comptroller, to block any mergers involving French banks—even though such powers actually lay in the hands of state regulators, not city officials. It was just such threats that had worked miracles in the Swiss negotiations.

However, Steg wanted to avoid at all costs the American model of the $1.25 billion settlement with the Swiss banks. The sight of the public trial of the Swiss had galvanized the éminences grises of the French Jewish community—but also pushed them in a different direction. Rather than seeking to punish French businesses with large compensation claims, Steg intended to bring the truth about Vichy into the open—which required cooperation, above all else. Instead of a global settlement, the French Jewish leaders were looking for something far more specific.

"It didn't sound like justice," said Steg. "You cannot perceive justice by imposing a fine on Switzerland. We saw that by having our perspective of truth and justice, we had to proceed by truth and justice.

"But the sound, the noise around the WJC gave us ideas. It made us more cautious and more aggressive. We don't threaten people—this is completely our philosophy. We are not going to people to say, 'You will go to jail, or you have to pay one billion francs.' We wanted to know exactly what happened—to establish it, in order to be restituted."

Ultimately Steg cared as much about the truth of what happened as about the assets plundered from French Jews. It was a feeling largely shaped by his own experience as a Czech immigrant—one of the "foreign" Jews who made up the bulk of those deported and murdered in the concentration camps. "You see, I personally am a foreign Jew. My parents had nothing, really nothing. They were poor people. We owned nothing, so we had nothing to lose.

"The foreign Jews were most of the people who were deported. They didn't have the possibility of hiding. The foreign Jews had no insurance. For a Jew coming from Hungary or Poland at that time to have insurance, first of all you had to get money. In contrast the major accounts were held by French Jews, and the major accounts were totally restituted after the war."

In meetings with the French Bankers Association, Steg underlined his point. The Swiss had lied, shredded documents, and hidden information, he said. They deserved the public castigation and the demands for large, rough justice payments. In contrast, he argued, the French deserved better from their Jewish accusers. "We don't want to use the American procedure to make a global deal, not at all," he said. "We want to establish cent by cent, franc by franc, exactly the debt. Exactly."

The behind-the-scenes pressure appeared to succeed. Within a month of the historians' interim report, the banks announced they would return in full all dormant bank assets at current values. Describing themselves as "cogs in the terrible machine of the confiscation of Jewish assets," the banks also agreed to accept all decisions made by the Drai panel and to make "a significant contribution" to a general Holocaust foundation.

In reality, the banks were trying to preempt the French government in an effort to speed up the process of compensating victims in France, at the same time as they attempted to slow down their legal troubles in the United States. Prime Minister Jospin had proposed both the Drai panel and the foundation a full four months earlier, but nothing concrete had emerged since then.

The banks were also monitoring the litigation in the United States. Just a week after pledging financial support for the French compensation plans, their lawyers filed their first motion to dis-

miss the class action lawsuits in New York. With the Barclays settlement already announced, the banks needed to appear to be
ready to pay out in full. "From the outset we prompted the government to move forward as quickly as possible," said Christian
Schricke, Société Générale's secretary-general. "Throughout the
process, we felt that the government could have acted somewhat
more promptly. We wanted to show that we were fully behind the
Mattéoli Commmission, and that it was a matter of some urgency
for the government to act on its recommendations, whether those
of the first report or the final report. Because, of course, we were
concerned about possible developments in the U.S. You never
knew exactly what would happen."

In fact, some of the banks were less than committed to the
process. Jospin's office, grappling with the legal complexities of
establishing new compensation mechanisms, believed the banks
were dragging their feet to delay the U.S. lawsuits. Claire Andrieu,
the meticulous historian leading the research into the banks, found
some bankers extremely reluctant to submit to the scrutiny—
partly as a result of the lawsuits. "It was a real obstacle because the
companies who were being sued were fearful of saying anything.
Whatever they said could be used in one way or another against
them," said Andrieu. "They were afraid and the archivists who had
to work on the subject were therefore also afraid."

The banks were not the only ones to fear American intervention.
Two letters stretched the transatlantic tensions to a breaking
point. Jim Leach, chairman of the House Banking Committee in
Washington, wrote to Mattéoli to request his presence at a hearing in September 1999. Two days later, exactly the same letter
arrived from the New York City comptroller, Alan Hevesi. The
apparently simple requests created a political dilemma for the
Mattéoli Commission and the prime minister's office. Should they
accept what the commission felt was an ultimatum? Were they—as
officials appointed by the prime minister himself—allowed by
French law to appear at such a hearing? A meeting was called at
Jospin's staff office in the eighteenth century splendor of the

Matignon annex. There Steg, Mattéoli, and Andrieu met with government officials from several ministries.

Mattéoli himself was adamantly opposed to going. A Gaullist at heart, he believed in French independence and could not bear the thought of appearing to place his commission under the jurisdiction of the U.S. Congress. "We decide what we want to do," he told Jospin's advisers. "We cannot come under pressure from America." Steg, his vice chairman, vehemently disagreed. He believed the French had nothing to hide. Besides, he had traveled to America several times and his English was better than Mattéoli's. "In my experience as a surgeon and a doctor," he said, "what is explained in a meeting face-to-face is much more effective than any letter, and any press release. We should meet people."

Jospin's advisers appeared more sanguine. The prime minister had already indicated to his advisers that it was natural for the world's Jewish community to take an interest in what France was doing. Moreover, they felt that the Americans—and particularly the WJC—were portraying the French as having something to hide. The debate turned to who should represent France. Mattéoli refused to attend, citing his poor English and work pressures. The French ambassador, François Bujon de l'Estang, was ruled out because of political concerns that it could interfere with his other lobbying in Washington. So the meeting settled on Steg, who in turn insisted that he be accompanied by an expert historian—Andrieu.

For Andrieu, the Washington trip offered an invaluable opportunity to apply pressure on the most obstructive banks. While normally reluctant to force the banks to take part, she cranked up the pressure just before delivering her testimony by threatening to tell the U.S. Congress just how poorly some banks were cooperating with her research. It was the only time Andrieu would resort to a form of coercion. "We wanted to raise consciousness about Vichy in France and if we were there with a big stick threatening everyone, we would have put people in the same situation as they were in under Vichy, obeying orders. This was not a way of educating people."

The banks were not the only ones to feel the pressure of the

House Banking Committee. The Friday before the hearing, Prime Minister Jospin signed a long-delayed decree that formally created the Drai Commission to process survivors' claims. Like it or not, the American scrutiny had prompted the French to make progress.

Room 2128 of the Rayburn Office Building is an intimidatingly august space where crushingly dull proceedings play out each week. The home of the House of Representatives Banking Committee, it is far more familiar with the technical jargon of financial regulation than the compelling life stories of the Holocaust. But on September 14, 1999, its steady-handed Iowan chairman, Jim Leach, called the room to order for a clash of cultures involving American and French campaigners who all believed they were pursuing justice. In one corner sat the French bank delegation. In another sat Steg and Andrieu, representing the Mattéoli Commission, keen to appear separate from the banks. Over on the other side of the room sat representatives of the American Jewish community including the WJC's Steinberg and Rabbi Israel Miller of the Conference on Jewish Material Claims Against Germany.

Steinberg lambasted the French process for its lack of "transparency and accountability." Even the Swiss investigation, conducted by Volcker, had been more open. France, he noted, was unique in Western Europe because it offered up its own Jewish population from territory that was not directly occupied by the Germans. "The most salient fact to understand here is that the Holocaust in France took the lives of seventy-five thousand Jews," he said. "Seventy percent were non-French Jews. This point is so central, forgive me for repeating it. Seventy percent of the Jewish victims of the Holocaust in France were non-French Jews.

"We have been repeatedly told by French banks and authorities that they will not negotiate or deal with international representatives of Jewish communities and Holocaust survivors, because it is a French Jewish issue. It is indeed a French Jewish issue, and the French Jewish community must be involved. But it is also undeniably a world Jewish issue. Simply put, a Polish Jew who as a refugee was plundered in France and who currently lives in Skokie, Illinois, is not represented by French Jewry."

Steinberg continued by attacking Mattéoli for comments suggesting it was the Germans, not the French, who distinguished between Jews and non-Jews. His commission was engaged in a cover-up, Steinberg said, conducting its biased work behind closed doors. "The majority of the victims are not represented," Steinberg insisted. "More importantly, even if a new commission is put in place whereby an individual anywhere can make a claim . . . you will forgive me for using this language—the dead cannot make claims."

Steg, listening in the corner of the vast chamber, was appalled. He was himself one of those foreign-born French Jews. But what infuriated him most was the comparison with the Swiss. How could you compare the two? Switzerland, which had remained a free country during the war, held on to the Jewish assets placed in its banks for safekeeping. In contrast, France had lost the war and been terrorized by its German occupiers. Its bankers had no choice but to obey. If France had remained occupied any longer, he and the rest of the Jewish community would have died.

That afternoon he struck back. After delivering his prepared remarks, he said he wanted to add some words not as a member of the Mattéoli Commission, but as a Jew and a survivor. Steg agreed that 70 percent of the deported Jews were foreigners. But, he said, the majority of the survivors returned to France and 97 percent of them became French citizens.

"Even for the foreign Jews who had suffered in France and left France for other countries, who would better represent them than these Jews in France who lived exactly the same experience in France? Who knows better what it is to wear a yellow star? I did it. I was designated to be a victim. Who would know better what it means to walk in the street and to be anxious at every corner, because at the corner there may be a roundup by the Germans or the French police, and the same at the exit of the metro? It was terrible."

At the end of the day-long hearing, Steg was approached by someone from the other side of the room. Rabbi Israel Miller, president of the Claims Conference, walked over and thanked Steg in Hebrew.

Steg and the French delegation traveled to New York for more talks with Israel Singer and his WJC colleagues. They met for dinner at Le Marais, a kosher steak house in New York's theater district, named after the French Jewish quarter in Paris. Turning to Singer, Steg accused his American counterpart of blind arrogance. "You consider me a collaborator," Steg said. "You think we are the Jewish collaborators, that we are under the government's influence."

Singer insisted that only the WJC could truly fight for the honor and interest of Jews worldwide, but Steg interjected, "Do you know to whom you are speaking? Do you know what the French Jews have suffered and what they have done? They have rebuilt the most beautiful community in the Western world, both spiritually and intellectually—maybe it is even more important than the American one."

As the dinner wore on, the dispute died down as the two sides began to reminisce over past battles they had fought alongside each other, including the campaign to free Soviet Jews. Those memories led Steg to a more reassuring position. A compromise could be found, he was sure. Why couldn't *he* represent the WJC's interests on the board of the Holocaust foundation that was about to be created in France?

For Singer and Steinberg, however, this was totally unacceptable. They proposed instead a simple alternative. The WJC needed to be represented—by an American—on the foundation's board to oversee at least part of the French payouts. In exchange, Steinberg would take a less prominent, less strident position in the media. From that day forward, at least in the media, Steinberg became uncharacteristically quiet on the subject of France.

Singer was impressed with Steg's assurances—for the time being. "We'll give you a chance, see how you do," he said.

The following day they appeared in front of the monitoring committee run by Alan Hevesi, the man the French banks feared the most. Hevesi continued to take a tough line against the French for refusing to publish a list of names of Jewish account-holders. But under French law, he was told, that was not possible. The last people to publish a list of Jews were the Nazis, and French privacy laws now prohibited the publication of such lists. Moreover, the French insisted, such lists would be misleading. Most of those whose names were on them would have received full restitution, according to the Mattéoli Commission's research.

However, Singer confirmed his feelings from the night before. "I find Steg to be a man of high moral qualities," he told Hevesi. "I'm not saying I agree with what France is doing. But I am willing to watch how Steg deals with this question."

Hevesi also heard from the class action lawyers, who urged him to maintain pressure on the French. McCallion and Tamen accused the French of creating "one committee after another" to bury the issue. Unless people like Hevesi intervened, they said, "the French may well spend another fifty-five years establishing commissions to study history and Holocaust victims will continue to wait for justice." For Hevesi to walk away would be a disaster. "It would be seen by many of the Holocaust survivors as a betrayal of their last hope for justice."

The lawyers felt they were losing the precious momentum established by the Barclays settlement, and they staged a second trip to Paris in the hope of gaining fresh support from the community— even if its leaders snubbed them. In October, they set up a stall at the exhibition hall at Le Bourget, near Paris, where some forty thousand French Jews were meeting for a celebration of Yom Hatorah (the Day of the Torah). To their delight, the chief rabbi of France, Joseph Sitruk, gave his blessing to the Wiesenthal Center's work with the class action lawyers. The lawyers felt they at least had God on their side and the support of ordinary French Jews.

A month later, Hevesi himself traveled to Paris to attend the annual dinner of CRIF, the French Jewish community group. There he met briefly with Prime Minister Jospin, who announced that he would move ahead with both the general foundation and compensation for orphans. Hevesi later took the chance to press his case with the Jewish group's leaders. He told them there needed to be some kind of participation by international Jewish groups, such as the WJC. He was also unhappy with the way the issue of the lists of accountholder names was being handled. They needed a mechanism to allow people to check if their family names were on the list. At a meeting with the French Bankers Association, Hevesi appeared less aggressive and more understanding about why the banks could not publish a list of Jewish names—not least because of the Jewish community's opposition to such a list.

A tour of the offices of the Mattéoli Commission seemed to seal the deal for Hevesi. He and his aides marveled at the sheer number of historians and college interns working furiously in the final weeks before publication of its definitive report. Just a month later he published a summary of his findings in his regular Holocaust bulletin, *International Monitor.*

"French law bars publishing names based on ethnicity," the bulletin explained, "so this significant list of Jewish depositors cannot be legally reproduced in France." Hevesi then detailed how he was pressing for a waiver of the law but acknowledged that France had "unique circumstances." No such concessions had ever been made to the Swiss. Overall the visit "satisfied Hevesi that the French government has made a substantial commitment to researching its wartime conduct toward Jews, accepting individual claims, and establishing its own monitoring system to assure the French financial industry complies in reconciling them."

At the same time, Israel Singer and Edgar Bronfman, the leaders of the WJC, arranged a face-to-face meeting with Prime Minister Jospin in January 2000. They were all attending an international conference on Holocaust education in Stockholm. At the French embassy, they met to discuss a way of resolving the WJC's problems with the French compensation processes—and the WJC's lack of involvement. Bronfman was silent throughout, leaving Singer to speak for him in a way that surprised Jospin's advisers. "It was like the old African tribes," said David Kessler. "There was the chief and the man who says the chief's things."

Singer was in his element, advising and cajoling one of the world's leading politicians. He argued again that what happened to Jewish people in France affected Jews all over the world, so the WJC had to be associated with whatever was taking place in France. To his surprise, Jospin agreed. "We will do the right thing," Jospin said. "I promise you, Mr. Singer and Mr. Bronfman, that you will be pleased." By the end of the year, the WJC was given a seat on the board of the Holocaust memorial foundation in France.

With Hevesi and Singer out of the picture, the victims' lawyers had just lost their two biggest guns.

Rough Justice

T he last best hope for the class action lawyers was a distinctly individual federal district judge. It was not just his appearance that set apart Judge Sterling Johnson—a gray-bearded African American on a bench that was racially segregated at the end of the war. Instead of spending years at a fancy law firm, Johnson had begun his career as a New York City cop and risen to fame as the city's special prosecutor for drug-related crimes. He took a no-nonsense approach to his caseload. To underscore his strict control of his courtroom, he wrote his own set of "expectations and requirements" for trial lawyers appearing before him. Rule number one stated that trials would begin promptly. Rule number four told the lawyers to be seated and pay attention while witnesses were taking the oath. But for all his apparent orthodoxy, Johnson could also exhibit an impetuously independent streak. When judges in his Brooklyn courthouse found themselves short of space because of construction in October 1998, Johnson moved outdoors and set up his court in a park opposite. Johnson sat on one of two camping chairs he hauled out of his car, while the court stenographer sat on the other. The lawyers were perched on a park bench.

On March 15, 2000, the Holocaust lawyers gathered on more comfortable seats inside his Brooklyn courtroom to fight the French banks' attempts to dismiss their case. Johnson told the lawyers he would be forced to start late because another judge needed the courtroom. "Unless we do it in the park," he suggested wryly. When they returned to the courtroom, Johnson gave the attorneys his orders.

"What I would like to know from the plaintiffs is why they believe they are more likely to get a full accounting from this court than from the French government who is actively pursuing the same issues the plaintiffs have raised here," he said, before turning on the banks' lawyers. "What is the good faith basis for the defendant banks' claims that the banks have made substantial restitution and that the banks are actively cooperating with the government to achieve the Mattéoli Commission's goals?"

Why in Brooklyn and not in France? Ken McCallion, leading the class action lawyers, argued that the French had failed for fifty-five years to return money seized from his Jewish clients. Some 5 billion francs were taken, unaccounted for and never returned, worth $250 million in today's dollars. Moreover, the claims procedure set up in France, under the Drai Commission, was inadequate.

"The Drai Commission has never paid a dime, never paid a French franc, a French sou to anyone," he complained. "Basically these commissions are window dressing to create the illusion of activity and specifically designed to dissuade this court, among other things, to divest itself of jurisdiction." The banks failed to return cash to survivors and were failing now to hand over their documents. McCallion spoke darkly of "suspicious fires in warehouses" where archives were kept.

Fred Davis, representing almost all the French banks, dismissed the entire legal process in New York. "This suit, even if it proceeded to five years of discovery or whatever, would not end up with useful relief," he warned. "It would end up adding to discord, and disharmony." All the relevant documents were with the French government, which had filed an amicus curiae brief supporting the banks' position. Its documents would never come under the court's control.

"We fundamentally believe that a settlement here would not help," Davis concluded.

"Would not help?" asked the skeptical judge.

"Will not help," replied Davis. "The Swiss banks claimed to have settled their case two years ago. Not one penny has been disbursed.

Barclays Bank, God bless it, announced in this case in December of 1998 that they reached a settlement. Not one penny has been paid. I am willing to put my money behind it. People are going to get money out of the Drai Commission before getting any money out of the American settlement. It is just going to happen faster."

Shimon Samuels, of the Wiesenthal Center, believed they had lost their case. Judge Johnson appeared to be uninterested in McCallion's arguments. Clutching a sheaf of papers signed by French claimants, Samuels made a last-ditch appeal. "My constituents are depending on what happens in this courtroom," he said. "They believe that if America came to save Europe from the Nazi fate, today these last survivors of the Final Solution have no other recourse or trust in any other system but here to get justice and closure." As the judge adjourned the hearing to ponder his decision, a handful of survivors sitting at the back of the court rose to embrace Samuels, hoping he had saved their fifty-five-year-old claims.

A month later, in April 2000, the final Mattéoli report emerged after more than three years of historical research, political maneuvering, and behind-the-scenes pressure. From the outset, Steg and his colleagues had tried to seize the high moral ground. Now, at the point of detailing 5 billion francs of plundered property, they insisted that morality—not money—was the object of their report. Quoting one postwar French official, Emile Terroine, the report insisted that restitution should be "a labor of both justice and humanity, whose moral and political meaning far transcends the material values in question."

The researchers drew two surprising conclusions. First, the plunder of France's 300,000-strong Jewish community was far greater than previously known. The Nazis and the Vichy government "bound Jews in an inextricable lattice of crimes against human rights." It began in October 1940 when the German high command ordered a census of all Jews in the northern occupied zone of France, as a prelude to seizing their property and their lives. Around the same time, the Vichy regime—based in the southern "free" zone but claiming sovereignty over the whole country—created a new status of citizen: the Jew. Within months, both sets of authorities were competing with one another to seize as many Jewish companies as they could.

Almost every profession was caught up in the persecution. Lawyers, civil servants, politicians, and journalists all lost their jobs. As the Germans ordered the removal of all Jewish influence from the French economy, some 50,000 companies and buildings were seized and sold. Around a quarter remained unclaimed after the war, probably because the rightful owners were murdered. Property was widely stolen. More than 100,000 works of art were looted along with several million books and the contents of 38,000 apartments. Meanwhile, the banks froze 80,000 accounts from 56,000 depositors, worth around 7.25 billion francs. Part of the frozen cash was used to pay a billion-franc "fine" imposed by the Germans after Resistance attacks in 1941.

The second surprise was more encouraging. Restitution was far more widespread after the war than anyone remembered. In 1940, General Charles de Gaulle, the leader of the Free French in London, nullified all laws that had paved the way for the plunder. After France's liberation, the victims were offered broad restitution. The researchers estimated that 92 percent of cash stolen from bank accounts—to pay levies and fines to the Germans and Vichy—was returned after the war. But compensation was incomplete. Jewish families found it almost impossible to recover their apartments, especially as the new occupants were given special privileges if they were war victims. Moreover, no one could tell how much furniture the Nazis had pillaged. The postwar West German government later paid victims up to 80 percent of their apartment losses.

The historians attempted to put figures on the property that was never returned. From companies, buildings, and securities, the commission believed that as much as 477 million francs were not returned. Another 12 million francs lay dormant for thirty years in bank accounts and 133 million francs in share accounts. No one could be sure how much money was returned to Jewish bank customers from their frozen bank accounts. An estimated 2 billion francs fell into this "gray zone" of cash that could not be traced.

However, the commission also created a political gray zone of its own. Drawing a distinction without a difference, the report defined French plunder—under the laws of Vichy—as "spoliation." German plunder, on the other hand, was the far more brutal "pillaging"—perpetrated by the Germans and executed with no legal niceties. The French historians were subtly trying to place the Vichy regime in a better light than the German occupiers.

The Mattéoli team made four main recommendations. Individuals should receive compensation through the Drai claims process, if they had not already been paid. Any funds left over from dormant accounts—either in private companies or in the government's hands—should be given to the National Memory Foundation to promote education and research into the Holocaust and other genocides. Works of art in museums should be identified clearly as plundered art, and some should go on display in the Israel Museum in Jerusalem. Finally, the orphans of Jewish deportees should—wherever they lived in the world—receive new compensation such as a life annuity. "Consideration of property does not mean that Jews were exterminated merely out of greed," the report concluded, "nor that the memory of Auschwitz should be expressed in monetary terms."

The French banks seemed initially reluctant to support each of the Mattéoli report recommendations. When Ady Steg and Claire Andrieu dined with members of the French Bankers Association, shortly before their report was published, one banker accused them of inflating the figures.

Steg cut him down: "You know what you have done? You have hidden the money. You are not allowed to have it. You did nothing to publicize it for forty years."

Writing in *Le Monde* on the eve of his report's release, on April 15, 2000, Steg made the calculation explicit. The banks and the government would donate to the foundation the cash that they clung to after the war. "By their contribution to the Foundation," he wrote, "they will be settling a debt and, moreover, bearing witness by their moral approach to the tragedy of the Jews and the ordeal—which sometimes led to death—that the stripping of their assets led to. The looted money was more than money. The restituted money will be more than money."

In fact, under pressure from the American lawsuits, the banks were desperate to make some financial display of their willingness to compensate victims. In June 2000, the banks met with Jospin's advisers to press for a special envoy or ambassador to help defend their position in the United States, and the next month Jacques Andréani, the retired French ambassador to Washington, was appointed to the new post. Andréani was summoned for his granite negotiating style and his deep appreciation of the transatlantic relationship. He had just written a book on the love-hate relationship between France and America. But in his sprawling apartment in the Saint-Germain district of Paris, it looked a little more like love than hate. Above his desk, stuck to the wall, was a drawing by an American child thanking France for the gift of the Statue of Liberty.

Andréani was nevertheless infuriated by American attitudes about France's wartime record. A teenager at the time of the Liberation, he adamantly rejected American attempts to cast France as a pro-Vichy, Nazi-sympathizing country. Andréani was also convinced that American criticism of France's Vichy record was provoked by American supporters of Israel, suggesting that France was really being attacked for its pro-Arab policy in the Middle East.

In early September 2000, Andréani was embarking on his first trip to Washington to lobby the Clinton administration when the victims' fortunes turned. In the first clear legal triumph for class action lawyers in any Holocaust litigation, Judge Johnson issued a groundbreaking order. On every count, he found in favor of the French victims.

Johnson argued that he had every right to judge the case. After all, it involved possible breaches of international law, including principles established by the Nuremberg trials of Nazi war criminals. Moreover, he appeared confused and unconvinced by the Drai claims process. Citing the lack of any alternative court in France, he insisted there was no possibility that he could clash with any French law. Denying the banks' motion to dismiss, he ordered immediate discovery, opening the door for the lawyers to search through the banks' most sensitive wartime records.

The class action lawyers were overwhelmed. Harriet Tamen burst into tears on reading the judge's order, as she thought of the victims she could finally call with some good news. Even the star-studded legal teams assembled against Switzerland failed to win anything like this kind of court victory. And in France's litigation, the facts were far harder to prove than in the higher-profile lawsuits against Switzerland.

The victims' lawyers felt Judge Johnson was handing them a priceless opportunity to settle with the French banks. "I felt that the time was right," said McCallion. "I certainly felt that we had a much stronger hand than we had previously, and we would perhaps be afforded some serious respect by the French government. We had elderly plaintiffs, and it was an opportune time to resolve it. We could have tried the case two or three years from now, and I love to try cases. But who would ultimately benefit, even if we prevailed? It might be the estates of people who are still alive."

Fred Davis, representing the French banks in New York, called his clients to offer the same advice. With the Clinton administration entering its final months, Stuart Eizenstat—the administration's point man on Holocaust issues—might be leaving office.

"It's now or never," Davis told his clients. "These are the cards we have to play and the main guy to play them with—Eizenstat—is there and may not be there much longer."

In Paris, the banks were stunned at the ruling and embittered at their own government's delays in moving ahead with the Drai claims process. "We felt that the judge may not have acted that way, or he may have postponed his decision, if the government had shown earlier that it was moving in the direction of the Mattéoli recommendations," recalled Christian Schricke of Société Générale. The only alternative was to move "as quickly as possible" to settlement talks brokered by the U.S. government. At the same time, the banks wanted to slow down the legal process by opposing discovery.

The French banks had good reason to fear that the momentum was swinging against them. J. P. Morgan, one of the oldest names on Wall Street, settled its Holocaust litigation by the end of September. Although originally sued alongside the French, the banking titan lined up alongside Barclays to forge its own deal. J. P. Morgan paid $2.75 million for its collaboration with the Nazis over fewer than three hundred accounts in wartime Paris.

Andréani, the French government envoy, arrived in Washington just three days after Judge Johnson's order became public. His original idea was to ask Eizenstat to intervene with the court to dismiss the lawsuits, but he arrived too late. Now he sought to convince Eizenstat to join settlement talks—a position he was not entirely comfortable with, fearing it could compromise French control over the compensation process. In Eizenstat's Treasury office overlooking the White House, Andréani meticulously laid out what France was doing—the commissions, the historical digging, the commitment to pay claims. But he also warned of enormous diplomatic damage if the litigation went ahead. Privately he feared the litigation would lead to a separate claims process that could undermine the entire French policy of dealing with the Vichy years.

"If the lawsuits should develop fully with the procedures under the U.S. system, with discovery and all that, it would be an embarrassment for both governments," he warned Eizenstat. "We have laws which are purported to prevent such things from happening. French citizens are not supposed to cooperate with investigations by foreign jurisdictions on French territory, unless there is an agreement between the governments." If discovery went ahead, Andréani told the U.S. officials, the banks would face fines in France for complying with the American judge.

Eizenstat feigned reluctance but was flattered by the call for help. He already believed, thanks to regular updates by Steg, that the Mattéoli report was a serious and honest study of France's wartime guilt. He was impressed by Steg's history in the Resistance, by Andrieu's academic credentials, and by the support from President Chirac and Prime Minister Jospin. But the prospect of wading through another legal quagmire looked daunting—especially considering the strict deadline of the Clinton administration's end in just four months.

"Why didn't you get us involved earlier, so we wouldn't be under the gun?" Eizenstat wondered.

"We are in a special situation," replied Andréani. "I just have explained to you the dangers and the risks and what this entails for Franco-American relations."

Eizenstat laid down several conditions. He would not intervene with the court directly. And he must be allowed to bring all sides to the table, including the class action lawyers whom the French side were treating as pariahs.

"There can't be a deal without the plaintiffs' attorneys," Eizenstat stressed. "They hold the keys to legal closure. There's no such thing as an agreement that a court will accept which they are not part of. So just get over your preconceptions about it, and steel yourself to have to deal with them."

In November, as the negotiations were about to get under way, Prime Minister Jospin made his regular appearance at the CRIF annual dinner close to the Champs Élysées. There he railed against Judge Johnson's "incomprehensible" decision, which he condemned as both useless and disastrous for the French compensation process already under way.

The centerpiece of his address was the detailing for the first time of the size and scope of the fund he had announced two years earlier. The Foundation for the Memory of the Holocaust, as it was now officially called, would receive contributions from the government and companies of 2.58 billion francs, or around $370 million, more than half of which would come from the state. It would be the biggest foundation ever created in France, funding historical research and educational programs. "For many Jews who lived in France during the war, for those children who lived hidden in the fear of a roundup, I understand that the steps taken by the government might seem—in spite of their unprecedented size—insufficient," he said. "But you cannot make reparations for everything. This individual and collective suffering is, by its nature, irreparable."

In Washington, Eizenstat kept these substantial figures in mind as he met separately with both sides of the dispute before drawing up a series of settlement principles. It was an unusual scenario for the American officials. Having guided the Mattéoli members through their congressional appearance a year ago, they felt they could trust the French positions. Moreover, with the clock ticking toward the end of the Clinton administration, there was no time for recriminations and mistrust. They decided to treat the French with respect for what they had already achieved. There was more to build on than in any previous Holocaust case—an existing structure developed unilaterally by a European government. Eizenstat felt that his task was to operate inside that French structure while also dealing with the objections of the lawyers.

The two sides met face-to-face for the first time in December 2000 in Eizenstat's antique-lined conference room at the Treasury Department. There, opposite a giant brass pendulum clock topped with a wood carving of the Treasury seal, the class action lawyers felt the mighty U.S. government would at last give them a fair hearing. Their concerns focused on the French claims process, which they felt imposed too great a burden on victims.

Instead, they were stunned to find that Eizenstat had apparently made up his mind whose side he was on. After Andréani described the many procedures established by the French government, Eizenstat declared that France's conduct was almost exemplary. "This is not a case like the Swiss or the Germans or the Austrians, where we're starting from scratch," he said. "We've got a government that's very proactive here. They've created a large memory foundation. They are giving significant payments to orphans."

Looking at Michael Hausfeld, the only lawyer present at other Holocaust negotiations, he added, "You know, we have to tell these other people who've not had the pleasure of being involved in five years of negotiations, that one of the hardest things we had in all the other cases was determining where the cap should be. And then allocating the capped amount. Here we have a Drai process where there's no cap. People can get whatever the fair market value of their property is. You know this is really quite extraordinary."

Regardless of the amount of money on the table, Harriet

Tamen was outraged. Eizenstat, on behalf of the administration, was placing his trust in a foreign government's rules—the same government, she argued, that had done nothing for more than fifty years.

"You have to understand that our clients don't trust the French. They were abused in France. They ran away from France after the war. They don't trust the French to run the process fairly and they won't go to France to make their claims. We have to figure out a way around that."

Andréani visibly began to bristle at the suggestion that the Chirac government was no different than Vichy. But before he could speak, Eizenstat slapped Tamen's comments down.

"That's inappropriate," he yelled. "We're not going to have those kind of allegations here. How you could even think to equate France today with France then is unthinkable to me. This is a government which has bent over backwards to do the right thing. They don't deserve this. They don't need it, and I don't need it. You are going to have to get your clients over that. If that is your position, we have nothing to discuss. Let's get about the business of negotiating this thing without the polemics."

The intervention succeeded. At a stroke Eizenstat established his credentials with the French, even if he failed to end Tamen's emotional outbursts.

The class action lawyers attempted to refocus on the assumptions lying behind the Mattéoli report. The French researchers had detailed the blocked bank accounts as well as the amounts levied in "fines" on those accounts. But they were unsure how many of those accounts were reactivated after the war. Mattéoli assumed that 71 percent of those accounts were reclaimed, based on the number of survivors, and estimated that almost 2 billion francs fell into a "gray zone" whose fate was simply unknown.

For the victims' lawyers, that was their clients' cash—either stolen by Vichy and the Nazis or retained unlawfully by the banks. The restitution figures cited by the French were meaningless. Moreover, the American lawyers argued that there could be thousands of accounts for which there were no surviving records. As a result, they demanded a huge new "rough justice" fund to pay for so-called soft claims.

Andrieu, who had led the Mattéoli research into the banks, countered that the American lawyers were fundamentally mistaken about the gray zone. No one knew how much of the 2 billion francs belonged to those murdered in the Holocaust. And no one knew how much belonged to customers who claimed back their cash but left no record. She further argued that the idea of thousands of missing accounts was wrongheaded. Meticulous records were made of the plunder by both German and French authorities.

As the American lawyers insisted the historians had missed thousands of accounts, Eizenstat once again intervened to curtail their demands. "Where's your evidence?"

"We'll produce it," Tamen shot back.

"This is the time to do so," Eizenstat snapped. "Look, you can't tell me these guys are not honest. They've spent two and a half years at this. How is it conceivable that they would have missed this many?"

The lawyers felt caught in a trap partly of their own making. By negotiating before discovery had begun, they possessed few documents to back up their claims. All they had was an analysis of the faults they identified in the French historical methods.

In private, Eizenstat told the French they needed to find an exit route for the class action lawyers. That meant creating a rough justice fund, to cover the banks' unjust profits and undocumented soft claims, at the same time giving the lawyers something to prove they had earned their fees. The banks were appalled, claiming they were already paying twice—first for claims processed by Drai, and then to the foundation. They insisted there was no need to pay a third time to another fund.

They met again in Paris on January 8, 2001. Eizenstat began by meeting with Drai, an elderly and respected figure in the French judiciary, who did not appear to understand why he was being questioned by an American official. He seemed alternately confused and annoyed, and failed to reassure the U.S. team. After lunch with Steg and others from the foundation, Eizenstat met the prime minister at his residence, the eighteenth century mansion of L'Hôtel Matignon.

Jospin refused to negotiate with Eizenstat but he pledged his support for a deal. He also issued a clear warning to the U.S.

officials to respect their French hosts: "At the same time you must understand that we have the French law, we have our own rules, and we must stick to some principles."

From there the Americans traveled one block to begin the negotiations at the prime minister's staff offices on the rue de Babylone. They are no ordinary offices. At the back of Matignon's immaculate gardens—the largest private park in Paris—stands yet another eighteenth-century mansion. Around a thick gravel courtyard, the staff offices stretch out from a tapestry-lined lobby. At the heart of the mansion is an old oval chapel, which was long ago converted into a giant, gilded meeting room. There under the glass chandeliers, the two sides started their meeting with a guest speaker. Henri Hajdenberg, president of CRIF, the French Jewish group, told both sides he was independent. "I'm not here to defend the banks," he told the Americans, "and I will support you in the sense that you want the banks to disgorge what they might still have in their accounts. But I am not prepared to have you claim on behalf of the Jewish people."

The victims' lawyers were taken aback at what they considered an anti-American diatribe. But this time there would be no face-to-face negotiations, where they could stage an emotional out-burst. Moreover, with the Clinton administration less than two weeks away from its final day in office, there was little time for any substantive debate. Eizenstat returned to the format of proximity talks that he had first used with the Swiss, allowing him the maxi-mum leeway to fudge what both sides were saying and to push them toward an agreement. The French side based themselves in David Kessler's office, where the prime minister's cultural adviser mixed abstract modern art and black leather chairs with the eigh-teenth-century surroundings. The Americans situated themselves in an adjoining room walled with the oppressive purple marble that gave the room its name, La Salle de Marbre.

Eizenstat said he wanted to introduce some American-style "due process" to the Drai system—something an American court could readily understand in Anglo-Saxon legalese. In return, the banks wanted a government-to-government agreement to guaran-tee legal closure.

But the focus of the debate was the rough justice or soft claims fund, which the lawyers wanted to establish. Eizenstat told the banks there was no alternative to agreeing to a fund, if they really wanted to clinch the deal. What they all needed to agree was some painless way for the lawyers to have a role. "They've got to go to court and get these cases dismissed, therefore they've got to be able to show something for it—that the negotiations actually produced something," he told the bank officials. "If all they got was the process that they'd struggled with, they might as well not have brought the lawsuits."

For the French, this was something of a culture shock. Under the French system, you were master of your own lawsuit. If you wanted to withdraw it, you were free to do so. Some of the bank officials objected in principle to the rough justice fund precisely because its purpose seemed to be to justify the lawyers' fees.

In Kessler's office, the bank lawyers debated the issue with the French officials. Kessler himself was convinced the banks would have to buckle. But how could the two ideas be reconciled? The Drai process was claims-driven, with an unlimited payout. In contrast, the soft claims fund would distribute a lump sum, from a capped amount. Most of all, the French worried that if they paid too much, they would undermine the Drai process. What would be the point of making a claim under Drai if the rough justice fund—with lower standards of proof—paid out more cash?

It took until 2:00 A.M. for the banks to accept that they would have to pay into the new fund. Based on the low numbers of unrecorded accounts suggested by the historians, the banks envisaged a fund of no more than 30 million francs, or around $4.3 million. But the lawyers opened at $50 million—a dozen times the French offer. Eizenstat refused to take the first French figure to the American lawyers, claiming it was far too low. The talks broke up at 4:00 A.M. and reconvened four hours later.

Through the morning the French moved to $5 million, then $7.5 million, then $10 million, and finally $12.5 million. Shuttling between the marble room and Kessler's office, Eizenstat belittled the victims' case by pointing to their lack of facts. Then he walked to the adjoining office and warned the banks they had lost their motion to dismiss and would face a lengthy discovery process if the talks collapsed.

Eizenstat promised the French he could seal the deal at $15 million for the fund plus $3 million in attorneys' fees. He reassured them they were being treated softly compared with other companies, because they had already offered so much. These were low numbers, Eizenstat kept saying. But he returned with bad news—$15 million was unacceptable. The victims' lawyers were only coming down slowly into the high twenties. Given time, Eizenstat believed he could bring them down to $20 million for the fund and $5 million in fees.

However, Schricke of Société Générale thought the process was spiraling out of control. "We can't keep moving along like this," he said. "We have already made an effort. It's very difficult for us to accept even the principle of a lump sum payment. We cannot accept a process whereby the lump sum is going to be larger than the amount that people will get under the Drai process, because it undermines that process."

Eizenstat was delighted that he had pushed the French into double figures, and agreed to call a temporary halt to the talks. He left for Vienna that morning for other Holocaust settlement talks with the Austrian government. There would be one final chance to settle the French talks in Washington, just hours before he left office. Speaking to reporters outside, Eizenstat declared they were "on the verge of an historic agreement."

They gathered at the State Department knowing there would be no more meetings with Eizenstat. This was the last week of the Clinton administration, and the streets of the capital city were lined with inauguration day seating for President-elect George W. Bush. Government offices, including Eizenstat's Treasury, were decked with red, white, and blue.

Inside the State Department, the new Bush administration was already making its presence felt. Just down the hall from Eizenstat's talks, the new secretary of state, Colin Powell, was readying his team to take control of U.S. foreign policy. Eizenstat even staged an encounter between the stubborn Holocaust negotiators and Powell, who made it clear that the new administration supported Eizenstat's work. Unknown to the French and American lawyers, Eizenstat had won Powell's support for his remaining involved in the talks even after the new administration took power. Eizenstat kept secret his ongoing role, fearing the talks would drag on for months without an artificial deadline.

Eizenstat made one last push on the numbers. "France has done so much, it ought not to be dragged through the courts as if it has done nothing," he told the bankers. "For a very minimal, additional amount—considering how much you have already put into these different funds—you could take care of a whole set of issues. It is penny wise, pound foolish to have put this much money in, and still have the lawsuits."

"I don't have the luxury of another round of talks," he added, saying that he was going on vacation with his wife at the end of the week. "This is it."

The French remained dug in at $12.5 million while the victims' lawyers had locked in at more than double that figure. Eizenstat promised the banks he could finally end the bidding at $20 million—the figure he floated in Paris—by capitalizing on the internal conflicts between the victims' lawyers. The French reluctantly agreed, believing that would mark the end of the road.

But Eizenstat returned empty-handed. The French bankers erupted in anger, feeling once again that they'd been duped into bidding against themselves. Desperate to hold the talks together, Eizenstat assured the French a deal could be clinched at $22.5 million. It was already 2:00 A.M. and both sides were exhausted and embittered. Eizenstat suggested the talks were close enough to a deal and left for home, leaving behind a small committee to draft an agreement. The talks would resume at 9:00 A.M.

Over a bland hotel breakfast of scrambled eggs and bacon, the French banks feared the worst. Would any amount close the deal? Or would the class action lawyers keep coming back for more? Their lawyers said there was only a fifty-fifty chance of reaching a deal and they decided to harden their position. They would refuse to bid again unless Eizenstat could provide a cast-iron guarantee that he could close the bidding. They also refused to waste more time on any face-to-face sessions with the other side. If their opponents refused to settle, the French wanted the incoming Bush administration to intervene in court to help them overturn Judge Johnson's ruling.

They delivered their demands to Eizenstat at the opening session in the State Department that morning. Eizenstat went into a huddle with other U.S. officials in a corner of the room for fifteen minutes. "You're right," he said. "I don't think you should bid again because now you are bidding against yourselves. I'm going to go in and tell them that I've told you not to bid again unless the deal closes at certain numbers.

"What I am going to tell them is they are screwing their own clients. There is a deal to be had here. It's a fair deal and the ones who are holding out for no deal don't have any trial experience, don't know what they are talking about, and are only going to hurt people. I will be very strong with them. But I'm not prepared to say I'm going to recommend a change in policy to an incoming administration."

However, Eizenstat had lost credibility with the hard-liners among the victims' lawyers. Michael Hausfeld, the highest-profile attorney of the team, had seen the bargaining in the Swiss case and sensed the French talks were about to unravel. In a long walk around the halls of the State Department, he conferred with Owen Pell, the American lawyer for Crédit Commercial de France.

For Pell, the pace of these negotiations broke the usual rules of how big settlements were done. "There is too much mistrust," he said. "We're never going to get to a comfort zone where all the plaintiffs' lawyers will buy into the process. It's all happening too quickly."

"You're right," said Hausfeld. "There is a problem. There is a small group on our side which is not convinced that it makes sense to settle. In the other deals there were certainly people who sort of felt that way but over time we got those people into line. Here you don't have any room for assuaging bruised egos."

Eizenstat went to the victims' lawyers—who were still insisting on $25 million for the fund and $8 million in fees—to tell them he didn't care for their arguments. The people who would be covered by the soft claims fund stood no chance of winning in court. Moreover, he didn't care if they ever obtained any fees. The only priority was getting the deal done.

Two hours later, he returned into the French banks' room and said, "We have a deal."

Davis turned to his clients to give them one last chance to back out. "You guys don't have to sign this."

"We understand that," they replied. "We're making a business decision on whether we want this behind us. We won't sign it unless we're happy."

Among the victims' lawyers, emotions were mixed. "I don't mind French cynicism about this," said Richard Weisberg, the law professor whose book had inspired the lawsuits. "We, at least, can feel that every single one of our clients, and every single Jew whose family was alive on French soil at the time of these terrible events, is going to get some monetary restitution from the French. I think that's very important."

But for Harriet Tamen the deal was simply the worst she had ever signed. "I don't have the moral courage I thought I had," she said two months later. "If anyone would have refused to sign with me, I would never have signed. I won't talk to the plaintiffs. I can't, yet."

The French succeeded in limiting the damage. The rough justice fund would pay $1,500 for each claimant based on minimal evidence, such as a sworn affidavit. If there was any cash left over, that payment would rise to $3,000—well below the Drai Commission's typical minimum payment of $5,000. They also succeeded in stopping any supervision of the Drai process by the Americans.

For the historians in Paris, the settlement was a sign of things to come, particularly in the United States, where African Americans were only just beginning to raise the issue of compensation for racial persecution. The campaign to rewrite the history books would surely return to haunt America itself. "I see this as a spiral which will return more and more," said Claire Andrieu. "I think societies all over the world will have to pay the costs of the past because people are living longer and because it's in their minds now. People think that if they were discriminated against, thirty years ago, then the state today must pay me back. I think it's a problem for governments. It's difficult to manage the past and the present. When will we have to deal with slavery?"

But in the State Department's United Nations–style auditorium, Eizenstat was thinking more about European than American history. With little understanding of French culture or the French debate over its past, Eizenstat believed he had overturned decades of reluctance to confront the past in the space of a few frantic weeks. Using the full persuasive powers of the world's only superpower, Eizenstat set his sights on something far bigger than a pot of cash.

"What we've now agreed to adds a lustrous chapter to French history," he said, "and helps in some small way to remove the cloud which had existed over French history because of the Vichy period."

His grandiose rhetoric revealed the deep-seated beliefs driving his work at the peak of his career. Eizenstat felt the French talks—just like the Swiss deal before them—were a defining moment both for Europe and for himself. It was not the first time that Stuart Eizenstat believed he had personally helped to reshape Europe's history.

To Start a War

S tuart Eizenstat keeps a single vial of earth inside his suburban home in Chevy Chase, Maryland. Scooped from a mass grave site in Lithuania, it holds a handful of all that remains of a Jewish community that thrived for 250 years. It also represents the most tangible answer to why a coolly methodical U.S. official broke all the rules of diplomacy to embark on an emotional four-year crusade across Europe.

In the fall of 1998, soon after his failure to resolve the Swiss Holocaust lawsuits, Eizenstat visited his ancestral village of Ukmerge, known in Yiddish as Vilkomir. There the tall, lean, fifty-five-year-old diplomat pieced together the story of several unknown members of his grandparents' family and their ultimate fate. It was not his first attempt to trace his family roots in Lithuania. In the mid-1990s, as the U.S. ambassador to the European Union, he traveled to the small Baltic state on business and found his great-grandfather's family mentioned in an 1895 census. There he discovered the names of two missing sisters alongside that of his grandfather, who was then just thirteen years old.

But it was his second trip in 1998 that breathed new life into his forgotten family story. This time Eizenstat checked prewar marriage records and discovered the wedding of a third missing sister, Sonia Medintz. When his tour guide glanced at the marriage certificate, he recognized the name of the wedding day witness. The witness had once employed the guide as a store apprentice. "It was the first time it really personalized the situation," Eizenstat recalled.

The tour group traveled on to the state museum, where Eizenstat asked the whereabouts of Castle Street—the street where his family had lived at the time of the 1895 census. To his surprise, the museum itself stood on the corner of the same street. Eizenstat walked outside and gazed at the street sign, taking a photograph for his family back home. On his return to the United States, he sought out an elderly cousin at a family reunion in Chicago. He asked if she had kept any letters from her relatives in Lithuania. "No," she replied. "But I wrote so many letters for my mother I can remember the street name very well." It was Castle Street.

On September 18, 1941, the town's thriving Jewish community—including what remained of his grandparents' family—was taken to a nearby forest and massacred by the Nazis. When Eizenstat visited the site of the massacre on a rainy autumnal day almost six decades later, his tour guide scraped up some mud, placed it in a plastic bag, and handed it to the undersecretary of state.

Eizenstat's interest in the Holocaust did not begin with his efforts to trace his family roots in the 1990s. Although he grew up in the distinctly Holocaust-free world of Atlanta, Georgia, he had been fascinated by the war for at least thirty years. In 1968 he was working as research director on Hubert Humphrey's ill-fated presidential campaign, when he met a former TV producer, Arthur Morse. Morse left the campaign early to work on a seminal book, *While Six Million Died,* detailing how American apathy blocked the escape of European Jews from the Nazi onslaught.

A decade later, as chief domestic policy adviser to President Jimmy Carter, Eizenstat was one of the driving forces behind the creation of the U.S. Holocaust Memorial Museum in Washington. Carter was struggling to repair relations with the Jewish community after endorsing the idea of a Palestinian homeland and agreeing to the sale of F-15 fighter planes to Saudi Arabia. Along with a handful of Jewish officials in the White House, Eizenstat persuaded Carter to accept the idea of a Holocaust museum, which he announced at a meeting of rabbis in the Rose Garden. The decision came just a few weeks after the broadcast of *Holocaust,* the hugely popular NBC television miniseries which was credited with reawakening U.S. and European interest in the Nazis' genocide of the Jews.

In the Clinton administration, like other old hands of the Carter years, Eizenstat was largely passed over. As the relatively obscure ambassador to the European Union, he dealt with the arcane issues of transatlantic trade disputes in Brussels. But in 1995 Richard Holbrooke, then heading European affairs at the State Department, called with a suggestion: would he be willing to take up Jewish issues in Eastern Europe? Eizenstat could not resist the call, in spite of his own staff's opposition. His new brief was to examine the intractable issue of communal property—seized by the Nazis and taken over by the Communists—and how to return it to fledgling Jewish communities.

Eizenstat's curiously cold public persona masked the intensity of his feelings for the Holocaust and its victims. His professional performance was that of a passionless public servant. Meticulous about technical details, he stuck so rigidly to his briefing papers that some of his staff called him "the tightest sphincter in town." That style proved invaluable as he plotted a course through the international minefields of the Kyoto global warming treaty, and sanctions against Cuba, Libya, and Iran. But it also gave the impression that he was a governmental android. Famed for speed-reading documents with his finger running across each line, Eizenstat could be seen on long-haul flights falling asleep at his papers only to wake up and continue scanning his finger across the page. Some staffers claimed he could doze off in briefings and wake to ask the most piercing question, as if he had never drifted into slumber. Driven by an almost obsessive determination to find a deal, he would work through the night, return to his desk at dawn, and interrupt vacations with an incessant flow of meetings, briefings, calls, and memos. Moreover, he expected all those around him to follow suit. For the lawyers he often bullied into submission, his zeal seemed almost Germanic: "deal *über alles*," as one of them wryly called it. For some European officials, he was little short of a maniac.

How could such a man ever hope to broker a compensation package with any European countries? Eizenstat was so commit-ted to life as a practicing Jew that he raised thousands of dollars to refurbish the Brussels embassy to make the kitchen kosher. Yet, for all his deep attachment to Holocaust victims, Eizenstat maintained the façade of being an independent "facilitator" in compensation talks. With this in mind, his ties to the Jewish community lent him a distinct advantage. He could effectively belittle the demands of the Jewish lawyers and organizations, without being accused of anti-Semitism. At the same time, he embodied the Jewish side's best chance of success. Who else would better represent their interests than a committed American Jew?

Despite his passion for Holocaust causes, Eizenstat felt conflicted about the groundbreaking settlement with Switzerland. He had broken the conventional rules of diplomacy by publishing his inflammatory historical report about Switzerland's wartime record. Then he broke the rules again by staging a government intervention to settle a series of private lawsuits. He and his State Department officials devoted months of heartache to crafting a complex peace deal between the warring parties—only to find their bragging rights snatched away by a federal judge and a Republican senator from New York. Of course he was happy for the survivors and the Jewish groups, and he could claim some credit for structuring the agreement. He could also blame any number of other people for the failure of his talks—the belligerent lawyers, the hostile Swiss government, the pigheaded banks. But the nagging feeling remained.

Within days of the Swiss settlement, a far more substantial opportunity emerged. Pumped up by their recent triumph, the same lawyers who settled with the Swiss were filing fresh Holocaust lawsuits almost as fast as they could write them. Only this time the enemy was far more affluent and—in the public's eyes—far more guilty. He could afford to lose Switzerland. But Eizenstat knew that Germany was simply too big to fail.

"While Switzerland is a significant trading partner," recalled Eizenstat, "Germany's importance in our bilateral relationship makes the Swiss relationship pale by comparison. We are dealing with a major NATO ally, a major trading partner, a major force in

Europe. Knowing the whole Swiss scene—the threats, boycotts, and so forth—the potential fallout from a foreign policy standpoint with respect to Germany was so much bigger."

Eizenstat was not the only one inside the State Department with serious misgivings about taking the battle from Switzerland to Germany. The career diplomats who specialized in Europe were deeply troubled by the way Eizenstat had burned the administration's bridges with the Swiss. Faced with a new legal threat, the diplomats were determined to avoid destroying good relations with the Germans.

J. D. Bindenagel had just returned from Bonn and was appalled by what he saw as the Swiss debacle. He had served as acting U.S. ambassador in Germany after its reunification, and deputy ambassador to East Germany when the Berlin Wall fell. When Eizenstat asked him to become the administration's special envoy for Holocaust issues, his first reaction was to say no.

"Because of what had happened with Switzerland," Bindenagel recalled, "I didn't want to be part of an effort that would cut to the core of our relationship with Germany and put it at risk. The response to me was, 'If that's the way you feel, then you have no choice but to come in here and make sure that doesn't happen.' "

Back in Washington he was determined to protect the Germans from the vilification that the Swiss had endured. Bindenagel wanted to avoid using U.S. wartime records—which he saw as "uncorroborated and unhelpful"—to condemn any more European countries. Starting with the Washington conference on Holocaust assets in December 1998, he was at pains to tone down the U.S. position on wartime atrocities.

"These are difficult questions in any case, but to do this with a moral absolutism on top of that is impossible," he said. "This is going back to the 1920s to condemn groups of countries. You can deal with the Swiss on that basis, but you cannot deal with the whole of Europe on that basis.

"What we did with the Swiss case was we opened a Pandora's box. The reaction from the Swiss was 'We can afford it.' Then it went on to the Germans and people said, 'Wait a minute, be careful of what forces you are unleashing—the right-wing forces of the past, the ethnic complexes, the nationalist complexes.' "

———◆·———

It started with a trickle of legal papers. The first class action law-suit on behalf of forced laborers in Nazi Germany came in March 1998, while the Swiss talks were still far from completion. Its target was not even a German company. Ford Motor Company, the quintessential American automaker, was being sued for its German subsidiary's wartime use of forced laborers. Ford had been such an enthusiastic employer of forced workers that the captives constituted half of its workforce by 1943. Among those forced workers was Elsa Iwanowa, a Russian teenager at the time, who was abducted and deported by the German army when it invaded her hometown of Rostov. Along with around 2,000 other Rostov children, she was forced by Ford Werke to toil in its truck plant in Cologne. For three years she was housed in a wooden hut, without heat, water, or sewage facilities, living on two meals a day. She performed heavy labor, drilling holes into the motor blocks of engines, for no wages. Anyone who became ill or attempted escape was transferred to Buchenwald concentration camp. Those who failed to meet their quotas were beaten with rubber truncheons. Iwanowa was just one of an esti-mated 7.5 million deportees who were forced to work inside Germany's war machine.

Ford was a perfect target for Mel Weiss and the other class action attorneys: an American company with a privileged place in the Nazi regime. Unlike other enemy-owned companies, Ford Werke remained under American control during the war thanks in large part to Henry Ford's friendship with Adolf Hitler. Ford sent annual birthday gifts to Hitler, who admired Ford's anti-Semitic pamphlet "The International Jew, a Worldwide Problem."

It was also a perfect test case for one attorney, sitting high above New York's Penn Station in the offices of America's largest class action law firm. Deborah Sturman, a pugnacious young attorney working for Mel Weiss, had noticed how the German courts had been grappling with a historical anomaly since the country's reunification in 1990. Under the 1953 London Debt Agreement, Germany had been temporarily exempted from reparation payments and individual claims, pending its economic reconstruction. Now Sturman seized on a recent decision in the German courts, which had ended the moratorium and allowed compensation to resume.

Sturman was also motivated by something more personal and political. A former professional French horn player for the West German Broadcasting Orchestra, she had lived for more than a decade in Germany and had campaigned on Holocaust issues with the Jewish students union. When she returned to the United States and retrained as a lawyer, she specialized in helping Holocaust survivors obtain compensation from Germany and sell restituted property. One of her vivid childhood memories was hearing her uncle's horror stories as a *Sonderkommando* in Auschwitz. He had worked in the most grisly unit of all, dragging bodies from the gas chambers to the furnaces. In one of the piles of corpses he had discovered his mother and baby brother.

Sturman's case against Ford languished alone until the Swiss deal was settled. Then the class action floodgates opened. Just two and a half weeks after the Swiss agreement, two rival sets of lawyers beat a path to the courts. Ed Fagan, derided by the more established class action attorneys, was in such a hurry to be the first to sue that he filed his lawsuit on a Sunday—and was forced to amend it two days later. Suing more than ten industrial giants—including Daimler-Benz, Volkswagen, Siemens, and Krupp—Fagan predicted his case would attract "millions of people." Fagan was aided by the Munich lawyer Michael Witti, who at least understood existing German compensation laws. But Fagan was so rushed that he failed to check the identity of one of his targets. One of the companies named in his original lawsuit, Eicon Technology, was actually a Montreal-based business founded in 1984. Eicon's only fault was having purchased a German software company called Diehl—a common German name that it unfortunately shared with the wartime ammunitions manufacturer. To make matters even more embarrassing, Eicon was founded by the children of Holocaust survivors.

Mel Weiss and Deborah Sturman, leading the competing team of class action lawyers, filed a day later, on Monday. They sued just one carmaker—Volkswagen—but it was the first of many. Within a month they also sued Krupp and Siemens, like Fagan instituting more than ten lawsuits against German industrial companies. The flow would not slow until the following May.

The competition rapidly led to a bitter rift between the most powerful class action lawyers in the Holocaust litigation. Relations between Mel Weiss in New York and Michael Hausfeld in Washington had always been cordially cooperative rather than close. But simmering tensions over who was leading the Holocaust litigation boiled over within days of the German lawsuits being filed. To Hausfeld, who had largely led the Swiss litigation, the new lawsuits seemed hurried and poorly planned.

"Once it became evident that Switzerland was settling, it was like wild horses on the loose," he recalled. "You couldn't hold the group back from wanting to file the next case. I kept urging, 'Look, there's a lot of closure that we need with Switzerland. Slave labor claims can wait another month or two.' But Mel was insistent that he was not going to be outdone by Fagan.

"It was a difference in strategic philosophy. Slave labor was extremely complicated. The term had become synonymous with just Jewish concentration camp laborers. But if you really were going to do slave and forced labor as the Germans understood it, you weren't talking about just five hundred thousand Jews. You're talking fourteen million people."

Hausfeld and his co-counsel Martin Mendelsohn took matters into their own hands. Believing the issue required a government-to-government solution, they approached Eizenstat to broker a deal. Hausfeld envisaged an international conference of executives, lawyers, and government officials—and made overtures to both German and Eastern European officials.

Weiss was furious. A major Democratic donor, he wrote to President Clinton insisting that Eizenstat and the State Department back off the case.

"This is the same folly that was attempted by the Swiss," he wrote. "It failed." The pressures of international diplomacy imposed "an unfair burden to the victims," he added. The only way to resolve the issue was with the representatives of the victims—their lawyers and the victims' organizations.

Eizenstat replied for the administration, admonishing Weiss for failing to check his facts with his fellow attorneys. The international talks were the brainchild of Hausfeld and Mendelsohn—not the U.S. government.

At Weiss's Manhattan offices, they were convinced Hausfeld's problem was simply one of ego. "In the Swiss case Michael came to me and invited me in, which I've never made any secret about," Weiss said. "I've always paid deference to him. When I filed the Ford case he wasn't at all involved in the preparations of it. We put his name on the complaint out of courtesy. Then what he did with Mendelsohn was to go to the Eastern European countries without even consulting me. I just felt that if you are a partner with someone you keep them informed. But that was not what they did. That created a lot of tension.

"That's Michael's modus operandi. He does this all the time in all the cases that we are in with him. He's a loner. He doesn't consult. Apparently he thinks he's smarter than other people, and it's a very uncomfortable situation."

The German companies themselves were splitting in opposite directions as the lawsuits landed in September. First Volkswagen, then Siemens created their own 20-million-deutsche-mark funds to compensate survivors who had worked as forced laborers during the war, taking substantial political and legal risks in the process. First, their actions appeared to acknowledge the force of the lawsuits. Second, their decisions came in the final weeks of a bitterly fought general election campaign. It was a particularly sensitive move for Volkswagen. The company had enjoyed a unique relationship with the Nazi regime, born from Hitler's dream of placing a car ("the people's car") in every worker's hands—more automobiles than even existed in the United States. But the company also had a unique relationship with the election's front-runner, Gerhard Schröder, the charismatic candidate of the left-of-center Social Democrats. Schröder had served for years on the automaker's supervisory board in Lower Saxony, where he was the state premier.

Schröder broached the idea of a national foundation for former forced laborers early in his campaign. In June, some three months before his election as German chancellor, he proposed that all companies that had used Nazi forced labor should pay into a central fund—and do so quickly, before the survivors died. The remarks represented more of a political signal than a coherent strategy. Schröder was broadcasting his ability to solve business problems, in spite of his left-of-center credentials. He was also telegraphing his readiness to confront the war in a way that his aging rival, Chancellor Helmut Kohl, had rejected. The issue of the slave and forced laborers could cement Schröder's image as a leader who was fourteen years younger than Kohl and could tackle Germany's problems with the confidence of a new political generation.

Ludwig Stiegler, deputy chairman of the Social Democratic parliamentary group, recalled there was significant public opposition to Schröder's initiative. "In our discussions in our constituencies, people said, 'Stop it. We have paid so much.' It was not only a right-wing issue. I think about seventy-five percent of the people said, 'That's enough and we should stop because it's really difficult to find an answer.'

"But Chancellor Schröder placed it in our campaign because there was a very tough contest about economic competence. People looked to see if the Social Democrats could cooperate with big business. His message was, 'I can work together with the industry to solve a very hard problem.'"

Schröder's economic rationale represented a split from his moralistic allies in the Green Party, who were ready to form a coalition government with him. The Greens were the most vocal proponents of Germany's moral duty to address the issue, and had long cultivated a relationship with Holocaust victims' groups. It was a Green priority to place the issue in the agreement that served as the basis of Schröder's Red-Green coalition. Two weeks before election day, Volker Beck, the Greens' legal spokesman, seized on Schröder's support to press for a joint foundation including both government and industry. Schröder responded a week later by insisting there was no need for the federal government to make a financial contribution. All it would offer was an organizational helping hand.

Kohl was not opposed to the issue simply because of money, although he did voice concerns to his advisers about the prospect of a long line of claimants pressing for cash. Instead, he felt the issue had been resolved at reunification, when his government had paid 1.5 billion deutsche marks to establish foundations for former forced laborers in Poland, Russia, Belarus, and the Ukraine. In exchange, the Eastern European governments agreed to renounce all wartime claims against Germany. When the issue arose during the election, Kohl rejected the notion that the government should pay a pfennig more. His spokesman suggested it was up to the German companies to pay into the existing foundations.

Wolfgang Gibowski, head of Kohl's press and information office, said that Kohl believed he had already resolved the issue for the government. "He always refused to pay more from the side of the state," Gibowski recalled. "He is a historian, and he thought that German industry should do it. That was his intention, and if he had won the election in 1998 we would not be having this discussion. As chancellor of Germany for sixteen years he would have forced the Americans to behave in a different way."

The compensation demands were hardly new for someone of Kohl's generation. The first restitution law was enacted in November 1947 by the U.S. military government; it was followed a decade later by comprehensive restitution laws for all property seized by the Nazis on West German territory. Through the 1950s, the West German government agreed to start a series of compensation payments to the victims of Nazi crimes. Under the so-called BEG law (*Bundesentschädigungsgesetz*), victims received a basic payment for each month they endured in captivity. Later laws, including Germany's unification treaty, allowed payments and pensions to Holocaust victims suffering financial hardship. By the end of 1997, the German government had paid nearly $96 billion in claims.

The compensation process in Germany was also familiar to the Jewish side. Nahum Goldmann, the founder and president of the World Jewish Congress, had created the Conference on Jewish Material Claims against Germany in 1951 to lead compensation talks with the German chancellor Konrad Adenauer. An umbrella group of twenty-three organizations representing Jews across the world, it led the talks for decades. By the 1990s, the Claims Conference, operating from a small suite of offices in New York, had become a dusty bureaucracy. Hated by many survivors for its perceived incompetence, it was ill prepared for a sudden reopening of the issue of wartime reparations, and was still led by Goldmann's original appointees.

In 1998, as the new struggle for restitution with Germany loomed, Israel Singer engineered a purge of the Claims Conference's senior staff, and deliberately skipped a generation with new appointments. The new executive vice president, in day-to-day control of the organization, was Gideon Taylor, an Oxford-educated Irishman in his thirties. The son of a prominent member of the Irish parliament, he still spoke with a broad Irish accent despite years in New York. Taylor had an energetic personality and galvanized the sleepy organization into long-overdue reforms.

Its history made the Claims Conference the natural body to negotiate further compensation with Germany, and it provided the vehicle to enable Israel Singer to take a leading role. He would lead the conference's negotiating team, assisted on the details by Taylor, and given moral guidance by a group of Holocaust survivors who would also serve as negotiators. He would try to reawaken the organization's founding spirit, seeking a fresh round of restitution for the last elderly survivors.

Despite all the compensation the Germans had already paid, Singer and the Claims Conference pointed out, much was still missing. For Eastern Europeans, there was no compensation during the Communist years, when payments from West to East were blocked by governments on both sides of the Iron Curtain. Even for Jews in the West, the compensation payments were lacking. Broad in scope but relatively small in individual amounts, the German payments were inadequate to cover all property losses. They were also morally flawed, as the companies that had actually profited from the labor had mostly escaped having to make payments. A handful of large companies—like Krupp, Siemens, and

I. G. Farben—reluctantly agreed to paltry settlements in the late 1950s and early 1960s. Some avoided payments altogether, such as the convicted war criminal Friedrich Flick, whose holdings included Daimler-Benz. Thousands of smaller companies also had paid nothing, claiming that the government had compensated Nazi victims on behalf of the whole country.

The Claims Conference estimated that seven hundred thousand concentration camp prisoners were employed in German industry during the war. They were, in the words of Benjamin Ferencz, one of the Nuremberg prosecutors, less than slaves. The diabolical project began in the ghettos of occupied Poland in 1940, when several thousand Jews were forced to build fortifications along the new border with the Soviet Union. By 1942 the Nazis had developed the policy of *Vernichtung durch Arbeit*—extermination through labor—as part of the Final Solution. The Nazi leadership realized at the Wannsee conference on the "Jewish question" that the task of killing eleven million Jews would take time. While waiting, Jews who were able to work would be spared death temporarily. However, under hard labor, starvation, and torture, all would die after a brief period. Industrial companies competed with one another to obtain concentration camp slaves. I. G. Farben, a huge chemicals company, located a factory next to the camps at Auschwitz.

It was there that Primo Levi, the Italian chemist and Holocaust survivor, toiled in the "Buna" synthetic rubber factory. The Buna was "the negation of beauty," he wrote.

> Within its bounds not a blade of grass grows, and the soil is impregnated with the poisonous saps of coal and petroleum, and the only things alive are machines and slaves—and the former are more alive than the latter.
>
> The Buna is as large as a city; besides the managers and German technicians, forty thousand foreigners work there and fifteen to twenty languages are spoken. All the foreigners live in different Lagers which surround the Buna: the Lager of the English prisoners-of-war, the Lager of the Ukrainian women, the Lager of the French volunteers and others we do not know. Our Lager (*Judenlager, Vernichtungslager, Kazett*) by itself provides ten thousand work-

ers who come from all the nations of Europe. We are the slaves of
the slaves, whom all can give orders to, and our name is the number which we carry tattoed on our arm and sewn on our jacket.

Even before he was formally installed as chancellor, Schröder
pressed ahead to defuse the threat of the American lawsuits and
tackle Germany's wartime guilt. After meeting with President
Clinton at the White House, Schröder called Henning Schulte-
Noelle, chairman of the giant German insurer Allianz, to ask for
his help in gathering a group of executives. Just three weeks after
his historic victory, Schröder met with industry leaders—including his old Volkswagen friend, Ferdinand Piech—in Hanover to
lead the talks on wartime forced laborers. Schröder had already
told reporters that he was committed to setting up foundations
for the "forgotten victims" of the Nazis, in partnership with German industry. In fact, he was so committed that his own chief of
staff, Bodo Hombach, would lead the task, and both sides agreed
to work together to settle the issue. Word leaked that the new
government was considering two foundations—one for general
victims of Nazism such as Jews and Gypsies, the other for forced
laborers. The Jewish campaigners were overjoyed. The new round
of compensation would focus not merely on those non-Jewish
Eastern Europeans who were forced into working for German
industry. The new foundations would also offer compensation to
Jewish slave laborers—concentration camp victims who survived
the Nazi scheme to literally work them to death.

Hombach hoped to declare the outline of the compensation
foundations by mid-December 1998. A smooth and gregarious
confidant of the new chancellor, Hombach was the government's
leading spin-doctor, a master of political campaigns. But as the
lawsuits flooded in, the talks proved far more complex than
expected. The new government and the industrial companies
could not agree on a formula for resolving the issue. At the heart
of the dispute was the insistence by DaimlerChrysler that Germany's insurers and banks—recently targeted by a fresh wave of
lawsuits—should be excluded.

Manfred Gentz, Daimler's chief financial officer, led the opposition. Gentz feared the negotiations would become excessively complicated—and costly—by involving banking issues that were unrelated to the industrial laborers. He also believed, immodestly, that his expertise on Holocaust compensation could lead the way for the entire German business community. More than a decade earlier, Gentz had been selected to oversee Daimler's first attempt at compensation payments for forced and slave laborers in the mid-1980s, at the 100th anniversary of the automobile. At the time, the company paid 30 million deutsche marks to the Claims Conference and charities in the Communist bloc. An intellectually rigorous executive, Gentz would become the strategic brains behind German industry's collective response to the lawsuits and the compensation talks.

Gentz had met with some twenty other industrial executives in August 1998, at the headquarters of the chemical giant Bayer in Leverkusen. Despite their differing histories and approaches to compensation, they agreed on several issues. "We settled that we should perhaps do something and that we then have to find a way to get rid of all these unpredictable and uncalculated claims of the American lawsuits," recalled Gentz. Another priority had been to involve for the first time Eastern European forced laborers—the non-Jewish workers who were not destined for extermination. But when some executives approached the Kohl government to see if the chancellor might intervene to seek legal peace with the United States, the reaction was a definitive no. In contrast, the Schröder government seemed only too willing to support the industry's moves.

In his first meeting with Hombach in November, Gentz insisted on a wide-ranging settlement. "If we do something," he said, "we have to include the Eastern Europeans because the number of surviving forced laborers is much bigger in Eastern Europe than in the Jewish world." Hombach was cautious, unwilling to combine contributions from the government and industry. In any case, both men believed that the eventual settlement would be low, citing reassurance from the U.S. ambassador to Germany, John Kornblum. Gentz and German officials claim Kornblum said a deal could be reached for as little as 3 billion deutsche marks—a charge Kornblum strongly denies. Whatever the source, the figure became fixed in their minds as they began to plot their strategy.

In Washington, Eizenstat took heart from these developments, and he gladly agreed to take a role when lawyers from both the German and the victims' sides approached him that fall. "The companies had a broader vision than in the Swiss case of what should happen. They wanted to cover all the claims against Germany, and they wanted to benefit a little," he recalled. "Secondly, we had a government which was going to be a partner with the private sector. It was a very, very different situation from the Swiss case."

Eizenstat had convinced himself there were just two reasons why the Swiss talks had collapsed. The first was money. The second was the sheer degree of animosity on both sides. In Germany's case, Eizenstat was determined to invite as many people as he could to the table. "If this was going to succeed, on an infinitely more complicated scale, then we couldn't have that kind of situation," recalled Eizenstat. "Everybody had to be willing to sit together, negotiate together."

The tensions between government and industry were not the only ones simmering in Germany that fall. The emotional wounds of the Holocaust were reopened by the German writer Martin Walser, as he accepted the top prize at the Frankfurt Book Fair. In an apparent reference to the compensation claims, Walser condemned the "exploitation of our disgrace" and "the permanent presentation of our shame" in the media. "Auschwitz is not suited to becoming a routine threat, a tool of intimidation that can be used any time, a moral stick or merely a compulsory exercise," he said.

Walser's comments prompted an indignant backlash from Germany's small Jewish community. Ignatz Bubis, president of the Central Council of Jews in Germany, chose the sixtieth anniversary of Kristallnacht—the Nazis' infamous night of destruction of Jewish property—to respond. Bubis attacked the "spreading intellectual nationalism" in German life and accused Walser of "moral arson" for talking about the exploitation of Auschwitz.

As Germany indulged in its recurring debate over its war guilt, Israel Singer prepared for battle. A friend of Bubis, he would never indulge in tactics as crude as a routine threat or the exploitation of the Holocaust. But he was only too ready to brandish the moral stick of Jewish suffering if it would help those who had suffered at Germany's hands half a century earlier.

Doomed to Succeed

Israel Singer traveled to the steely, towering headquarters of Deutsche Bank in Frankfurt in January 1999 to deliver a blunt warning. Sitting beside him in the bank's boardroom, overlooking the city's financial high-rises, was a small, aging colleague from the Claims Conference. Saul Kagan was the last survivor of the Jewish negotiating team that had won the first postwar compensation payments from Germany to Holocaust victims. He also probably knew more about Deutsche Bank's wartime past than anyone in the building. In the immediate aftermath of the war, Kagan had served as head of financial intelligence for the U.S. military government in Germany. In 1946, he issued a damning report that found that the bank was so intertwined with the Nazis that it should be liquidated, while its leading officials should be indicted as war criminals. Deutsche's board, his report stated, "fairly bulged with strong party men and sympathetic fellow travelers," and the bank had profited hugely by "aryanizing" companies in occupied Europe. Each year the bank had contributed 300,000 reichsmarks to the Nazi party's Adolf Hitler Fund, as well as 75,000 reichsmarks a year for the personal use of Heinrich Himmler, who controlled Auschwitz as head of the Gestapo and SS.

Sitting across the boardroom table, Rolf Breuer, the bank's chairman, faced a stark choice. Either he could confront his bank's Nazi history, or he could abandon his planned $10 billion acquisition of Bankers Trust, one of New York's best-known investment banks—which he had announced only weeks earlier. Without some form of mea culpa, Deutsche's global strategy would be hijacked by the same forces that held hostage the merger of two Swiss banks.

"I'm not going to bother you or anything," said Singer, who knew that the Bankers Trust acquisition was only part of Deutsche's grandiose ambition to become a global investment bank. "I don't want to stand in the way of your plans. But I want you to be understanding of my position. I just wanted to resolve a small discreet issue of Jewish bank accounts in the Holocaust."

To underline his point, Singer had earlier told the *Financial Times* that he intended to lobby to block the bank deal, but would delay taking any direct measures for the time being. However, after their meeting in Frankfurt, Breuer failed to respond to Singer for several weeks. Singer then issued a new threat through the media—to use documents from newly opened Austrian archives to attack Deutsche. Breuer swiftly tracked Singer down to a hotel room in Zurich at 3:00 A.M. to resolve the issue.

The next day he hastily called a press conference at Deutsche's headquarters, where the bank's historian released a series of documents detailing Deutsche's complicity in the construction of Auschwitz. Through the bank's Katowice branch in occupied Poland, Deutsche had issued credits and loans to at least ten companies in connection with Auschwitz. Some had built the concentration camp walls. Some, like I. G. Farben, were linchpins in the entire killing machine. The bank also revealed evidence of secret SS accounts used to transfer money stolen from murdered Jews. Moreover, Deutsche conceded that its staff in the Katowice branch knew what was happening at the camp.

Breuer's lawyers were desperate to prove their willingness to confess the bank's crimes and become full members of the new Holocaust foundations. They feared the American acquisition would become a bargaining chip in the Holocaust compensation talks, and their concerns appeared well founded. Alan Hevesi, New York City's comptroller, said the banks' merger should not be allowed until "all claims against Deutsche on Holocaust-related issues are dealt with and resolved." Although Hevesi did not actually wield the power to block the deal—that lay in the hands of the state's banking department—his threats were taken seriously in Frankfurt.

Within a week Breuer was traveling to the United States at the forefront of a group representing Germany's latest compensation efforts, alongside Bodo Hombach, Chancellor Schröder's special envoy on Holocaust compensation. For Hombach the trip was a brief chance to calm the waters before the chancellor himself arrived in Washington to meet with President Bill Clinton. But it was an inauspicious time to seek an agreement with the Clinton administration. The president was just days away from the Senate vote in his impeachment trial in the Monica Lewinsky scandal.

Deep inside the State Department, Stuart Eizenstat was grappling with a radically different set of moral and legal problems. He had invited the class action lawyers to meet Hombach for their first face-to-face session with a German official, and more than a dozen turned up. His cramped conference room—where the failed Swiss talks had taken place—could only seat a handful of lawyers alongside the government officials. The overwhelming presence of the class action lawyers only compounded Eizenstat's bigger problem with the attorneys. Neither the German nor the Jewish negotiators wanted to see them at the table.

For Singer, the lawyers had crossed a moral line by seeking fees. No longer were some of them working for free, as they had in the Swiss case. Elan Steinberg, his executive director at the WJC, contemptuously described the lawyers' pro bono appearance in the Swiss case as a "loss leader"—a costly way to gain future profits.

For the German officials, the lawyers undermined everything they envisaged from the deal. They wanted nothing less than a new treaty with the United States—an agreement negotiated among diplomats to resolve the issue forever. "This is a government-to-government affair to be settled between governments," said Michael Geier, the leading official on Holocaust compensation inside the German foreign ministry. "What kind of role would American lawyers have in that?"

The answer was simple. There was no earthly chance the U.S. Senate would vote to ratify a treaty that restricted the legal claims of Holocaust survivors. That left the courts—and American lawyers—in charge of the lawsuits. Eizenstat began by inviting the lawyers to hear Hombach's views, as a first step toward securing their place at the negotiating table. "It is not my job to save money for these companies," Hombach reassured the five lawyers in front of him. "My job is to protect their reputation. We want a material sign of reconciliation." All sectors of the economy would be involved, including state-owned companies, and there would be a separate federal foundation.

Mel Weiss, still smarting at the involvement of government officials, warned that survivors would not accept a "unilateral fund" dictated by the Germans. Not to worry, said Hombach. "We do think of options," he soothed. "The government can be flexible. Not as much as the Mediterraneans, but more than the Prussians."

Hombach was on a whirlwind tour of Holocaust diplomacy in the early weeks of the new year, traveling to Jerusalem to win Israeli support for the Holocaust talks. There he asked Prime Minister Benjamin Netanyahu to send an Israeli team to join the talks and met for the first time with Netanyahu's envoy on diaspora and Holocaust issues, Bobby Brown. Hombach told Brown of his intense relationship with Israel. Saying that he had a friend who lived in the town of Ramat Gan, he recounted an anecdote about the Gulf war, when he had heard that a Scud missile had landed on his friend's street. He had called and learned that his friend was unhurt but that his house had been hit. A little later, he received an intelligence report in Germany stating that the Scud's guidance systems had been built in a town close to Hombach's home. "He said to me he felt like Germany was again participating in the wanton murder of Jews," Brown recalled. "To me it was a statement that came from the heart." Hombach was so committed to Israeli participation that he invited Brown to join the German team in America. Brown, the son of two German Jewish refugees, declined. He already felt compromised by making his first trip to Germany and flying with Hombach on a government plane which bore the word "Luftwaffe."

By mid-February, the German government believed it had found a solution to the Holocaust lawsuits. Standing alongside Breuer, Chancellor Schröder announced plans to establish a foundation—called Remembrance, Responsibility, and the Future—to compensate victims and promote education about Nazi terror. There was no question now of excluding financial companies, as DaimlerChrysler had wanted. The fund, to be financed by large German companies, would amount to around 3 billion deutsche marks (some $1.5 billion) according to hints from German officials. Schröder insisted the fund would not only redress the crimes of the past but also "counter lawsuits and especially class action lawsuits." The WJC welcomed the announcement as "a historic step" and a starting point for talks. It looked like the kind of political solution Singer had always wanted.

But Schröder's comments angered the class action lawyers. In New York, Mel Weiss felt the unilateral announcement by the Germans confirmed his worst fears about the government-led talks. More than ever, he believed that only a U.S. judge could resolve such negotiations on terms remotely acceptable to the victims' lawyers. "As far as I'm concerned, this is just another Swiss-type attempt to get out of this for less money than they should pay," he said. "These two governments had 50 years to find a remedy for these people and they never did until litigation was started. Who can trust this process?"

When they met again in March, at the Chancellery in Bonn, Hombach confirmed that the Germans were focusing on legal issues more than moral ones. In the last month, he said, there had been several legal developments. "What once may have been considered only as moral obligations, are now being judged as legal responsibilities," he noted. "The time is now to resolve them— together." Working toward a September deadline—the sixtieth anniversary of Hitler's invasion of Poland—he said they would first agree on a structure for the compensation funds. Once that was resolved, they could deal with the delicate question of money. "There will be no knocking on tables," he warned the class action lawyers and Jewish groups.

Eizenstat and Hombach pressed the Jewish negotiators to allow another party to the table—the Eastern Europeans. Germany did not want to damage its foreign policy by excluding them, while the United States wanted the political cover of the Polish government signing up to the process. Polish officials had already issued stark warnings to Bonn about their continued exclusion, claiming that Poland's exclusion could lead to increasing anti-Semitism.

Eizenstat spoke of four "windows" to the fund—Jewish slave labor, non-Jewish Eastern European forced labor, financial issues, and a so-called Future Fund for educational projects. All sides agreed there should be a differential between the Jewish and non-Jewish payments. After all, forced laborers were deported, beaten, and incarcerated, but slave laborers were victims of attempted murder. As Hombach said, there was a "clear-cut" difference between them. Besides, Germany "could not afford to pay the same" to both types of laborers.

The only dissent came from Manfred Gentz of Daimler-Chrysler, the leading executive among the German companies, who seethed that Eizenstat appeared to take the business community for granted. Among several working groups established to deal with the various "windows," there were no industry representatives. "I think you are misunderstanding the initiative," Gentz told Eizenstat bluntly. "It's the initiative of the economy, not of the government." Gentz realized they were being squeezed out and risked having no influence over where their money would be spent. "The German economy was seen from his point of view only in the role of paying out," recalled Gentz. "Nothing else."

In Washington, Michael Hausfeld identified what he saw as a gaping hole in the attorneys' work—nobody was representing the Central and Eastern Europeans, who had accounted for the bulk of the Nazis' laborers. As the Germans prepared to unveil the structure of their compensation fund, he filed a new lawsuit on behalf of all Polish forced laborers. At the same time, in talks with Polish diplomats at their embassy in Washington, he urged the Poles to organize a negotiating team to unify the demands of the forced laborers across Europe.

The Polish government welcomed Hausfeld's approach with enthusiasm. Poland dearly wanted to claim compensation for thousands of former forced laborers, but was constrained by its own diplomatic blunders. Under Communist control in the 1950s, then under democratic government in 1991, Poland had twice agreed to forgo any compensation claims against Germany. The Polish government was unable to pursue any legal action against German companies, but Hausfeld appeared to offer a way around those agreements. He would officially represent private Polish citizens, not the government. Meanwhile, behind the scenes, the Polish government was effectively organizing its neighbors—and overcoming historic tensions with Russia—to allow the former Soviet bloc countries to speak with one voice.

But to his fellow lawyers, Hausfeld was engaged in an opportunistic grab for new clients. The man who had led the Swiss litigation on behalf of Jewish victims of the Holocaust was now filing lawsuits for non-Jewish forced laborers. Hausfeld and his close friend Martin Mendelsohn believed their inclusion of those laborers would increase the size of the pot for everyone—including Jewish slave laborers. "Not only did it increase the amount that each would get, but it increased the liability because you then went beyond those companies that used Jewish laborers," Hausfeld said.

In New York, Professor Burt Neuborne attempted to paper over the cracks between the lawyers and the Jewish groups, just as he had in the Swiss banks case. He drew up an agreement stating that they would negotiate as a single team, advising one another if there were separate talks. "All signatories will work toward a public perception, and a functioning reality, of close cooperation among members of the negotiating team." The agreement was doomed before anyone put pen to paper.

When they met for their first plenary session in Washington, the number of negotiators had swelled to include five Central and Eastern European governments and the State of Israel, alongside U.S. and German diplomats and legions of lawyers. "Reaching the stage of today's meeting and getting everybody under one tent required a great deal of work and flexibility on everyone's part," Eizenstat told reporters at the State Department. "The participation of all those who attended is a significant accomplishment in moving the process toward closure." It threatened to be the only achievement of the meeting. The Polish delegation was already furious that the Jewish victims were heading for preferential treatment, and realized they were being frozen out of the highest-level talks. "Polish victims fear that once again they could become the subject of unequal treatment," they wrote in a briefing paper.

The Germans thought it a curious selection of European governments. They could understand the inclusion of Poland and the former Soviet states—after all, Germany had established reconciliation foundations with those countries as part of its reunification. But why did the Americans include the Czechs and not their Slovak counterparts? Some German officials suspected the Czechs were included because Secretary of State Madeleine Albright was of Czech Jewish origin. "Numerous governments came up and said they wanted to be included and we always said it was the Americans who told us who should be included and who should not," Michael Geier recalled. "The Baltic states, France, Holland, and a whole lot of other countries would have dearly loved to participate."

If Germany was suspicious of the proceedings, the American lawyers were downright hostile. Hausfeld took offense at a bizarre joke Hombach told about a pet cat being twirled in the air, saying he found it "deeply disturbing." "I referred to it as the tale of the tormented cat," the hard-bitten attorney wrote on his website. "The story of a living thing that was subjected to continuous acts of thoughtless, ruthless cruelty. It was a tale reminiscent of the horrors experienced by the slave and forced laborers in the German economy under the Third Reich."

To compound the ill feelings as the talks began, the U.S. government had failed to invite one crucial party: German industry. For all Eizenstat's talk of inclusion, Manfred Gentz—by now the official representative of the German executives—was never invited. Instead, he flew to Washington and turned up on his own initiative. There he was horrified at the size of the gathering. "We had at that first meeting more than one hundred people," Gentz said. "It was terrible. We cannot really negotiate in a group of one hundred people. That is absolutely impossible, but it was

Eizenstat's arrangement. He always needs huge groups so he can try to play games."

Gentz had his own vision for the foundation. During his vacation in May, he wrote a detailed outline of how to limit the number of people eligible for payment and target the cash to those who needed it most. Gentz was convinced that the category of forced labor included people who had barely suffered. "We have a very broad spectrum of conditions under which forced laborers had to work in order to live," he said.

"In our company we had people coming from the western part of Europe living in small hotels, or even living within families. They were treated quite well and they also got some money for the work they had to do. In our plants further south on the Bodensee, we even had a form of forced laborers returning every year for their vacation. They tell us it was the nicest time of their life.

"We also had the worst opposite of that, what you can really call slave labor coming out of concentration camps—living under very, very bad hygienic conditions without any medical support, without sufficient food, in working conditions which were very bad. That's why we decided rather early that we should define who should get some money."

Under his proposals, people in concentration camps or closed camps would receive compensation. Those living in better conditions would be excluded, along with agricultural workers who could at least eat adequately during the war. "It is almost impossible to try to compensate everybody," Gentz concluded.

Gentz proposed to limit the fund to those who worked at least six months in forced labor. He also proposed screening claimants for those who really were in financial need, and adjusting payments according to the cost of living in different countries. "The reason is very simple," said Gentz. "If a Jewish survivor in the United States, for example, has become a rich man for whatever reasons, he has a lot of money. If you offer him five hundred deutsche marks as compensation now, it is ridiculous because he doesn't need that. Whereas there are many people in Eastern Europe and also partially in the United States who really need money and financial support."

Gentz's plans were shot down. A Claims Conference represen-tative criticized the ideas at Gentz's press conference before any-one had a chance to read them. The leading class action lawyers condemned his plan for "the presumptuous and unilateral man-ner in which it was released." The lawyers were also offended by the German companies' demands for legal peace from a direct agreement between the two governments, not through the U.S. courts. In a joint statement they later attacked every single one of Gentz's suggestions. The requirement of a minimum six months' labor would be unacceptable to any court. Assessing victims' needs would undermine the desire for equal treatment in com-pensation payments. Changing payments according to living stan-dards was "arbitrary and unfair" and contrary to "humanitarian principles." In short, the lawyers said the proposals stank.

Gentz was disappointed but not dissuaded of the righteousness of his stand. A month later, in July, he traveled to New York to begin fresh talks on property issues involving German banks and insurers. For the Holocaust victims, represented by Israel Singer and the Claims Conference, this was an indisputably Jewish area of compensation. Singer pressed the banks for compensation for their involvement in the "aryanization" of Jewish property. While restitution laws had ordered the full return of such property after the war, the reality was limited in scope and inadequate in size. The banks themselves had failed to return their extensive profits from the aryanization process.

Ignoring the moral pressure, Gentz simply refused to accept their logic. "What are you claiming?" he asked. "If there is a trans-action of property and the bank is doing a job like an investment bank today, the banker normally gets a fee. Are you claiming that fee or an excess fee?"

When Gentz heard that the Jewish groups were claiming the entire unjust enrichment, he was exasperated. "Say a Jew goes to a bakery and buys some bagels. The baker normally makes a profit margin on his bagel. Do you really want to say that the profit mar-gin of the baker has to be given to you?"

Gideon Taylor, the young executive vice president of the Claims Conference, could not believe what he heard. The Germans were engaging in technical obfuscation. "That's an outrage and unacceptable," he said. "This is a moral argument. What the banks did was fundamentally immoral."

Neither side accepted the other's position. The banks rejected the notion of unjust enrichment, and the Claims Conference never attempted to quantify what the unjust profits might amount to. "Our concept was that it was more of a philosophical and moral issue," said Taylor. "There should be recognition of it, rather than a traceable asset. This was a moral claim."

That month the German compensation talks faced a far more immediate challenge. Chancellor Schröder dispatched Bodo Hombach to Brussels to lead the European Union's reconstruction package in the Balkans, and there was no one to take his place. For Eizenstat, Hombach's departure was a disappointment but also a relief. Hombach was spread too thin across his different responsibilities, with little time to spare for the complex details of the talks. Meanwhile, for the German foreign ministry officials, it was a blessing in disguise. Hombach kept them out of the loop, and liked to claim he had struck secret deals. He even asserted he had secured Eizenstat's agreement to a 3 billion deutsche mark settlement in a private conversation on a car journey in Washington. There were no witnesses to the agreement, and Eizenstat strongly disputed having struck any kind of deal.

In Hombach's absence, the negotiators made critical progress at their third plenary talks in Washington. Eizenstat agreed that the Clinton administration would issue a statement of interest in court, supporting the dismissal of the class action lawsuits. Dreamt up by Roger Witten—the German companies' Washington lawyer, who had also defended the Swiss—it was an unprecedented legal commitment that compelled all future administrations to help block further lawsuits. For the class action lawyers, the statement was an unhappy compromise. It took power away from the courts, but their lawsuits faced serious obstacles and could take years to resolve. For the German companies, the statement was less powerful than the agreement they wanted, but its promise of legal peace was a prerequisite for any deal.

The biggest risk was faced by the Clinton administration, which was walking a political tightrope. Eizenstat knew that the U.S. Senate would never ratify a treaty blocking the legal claims of Holocaust victims. He chose to gamble instead that he could convince the White House to take that political risk—in exchange for a substantial settlement under President Clinton's watch. It was a calculated risk. Eizenstat had just been promoted by the president to the number two position at Treasury. In a Rose Garden announcement, Clinton heaped more praise on Eizenstat than the new Treasury secretary, Lawrence Summers. Clinton enthusiastically cited Eizenstat's work on Holocaust issues, saying "not just Jewish Americans" but all Americans should be grateful for his contribution. Inside Treasury, Eizenstat would come to spend more time on Holocaust issues than any financial or economic policy.

The contrast between Hombach and his replacement was stark in almost every respect. Otto Graf Lambsdorff represented a different generation and a different political philosophy. He was old enough to have joined the German army as a teenager at the end of the war, when he lost a leg in combat with American troops. Where Hombach was a confidant of the left-of-center chancellor, Lambsdorff was a leader of the pro-business Free Democratic Party and a former economics minister. Where Hombach was known for his smooth personal style, Lambsdorff was gruff, uncompromising, and direct.

His strengths, however, were in great demand. Lambsdorff enjoyed extensive links with business, serving on several boards including Volkswagen's, where he sat alongside Schröder for seven years. Although they were often on opposite sides of disputes—Schröder backed the workers while Lambsdorff represented the small shareholders—they developed a mutual respect. Now Lambsdorff gave Schröder a political buffer against attacks from the right, effectively defusing the political debate. Lambs-dorff also enjoyed extensive contacts among America's political elite, counting himself a personal friend of Henry Kissinger and Lawrence Eagleburger, the former secretaries of state. Among the many U.S. officials he had cultivated over the years was Stuart Eizenstat, whom he first met in the Carter White House. Even after Lambsdorff left the German parliament, Eizenstat would stop by Lambsdorff's office in Bonn to chat about arcane trade disputes and the world economy. For Eizenstat, his new negotiating partner was a gift. "We had a lot of affection and mutual respect," he recalled. "That turned out to be crucial, because the issue of trust was absolutely seminal here. I had complete trust in him, and I think the feeling was reciprocated."

That was not the feeling among the Jewish representatives. Lambsdorff accepted the need to pay Eastern European forced laborers, but felt the Jewish claims were "overdone." On his first tour of New York as the lead German negotiator, Lambsdorff met Roman Kent, the former Auschwitz inmate who chaired the American Gathering of Jewish Holocaust Survivors. In an attempt to tone down Kent's demands, Lambsdorff echoed one of Eizenstat's most oft-repeated warnings. The compensation talks could prompt a new wave of anti-Semitism if most of the money went to Jews. Coming from a Jewish official, the threat was only just acceptable. But coming from a former German soldier, Kent felt grossly insulted. "Lambsdorff pointed his finger at me and told me: 'You are creating anti-Semitism.' It was not a very pleasant memory for me to deal with him," Kent recalled. Like other Jewish negotiators, Kent argued that anti-Semitism was the fault of anti-Semites, not Jews.

That did not stop Lambsdorff. "My reaction to that is, unfortunately this underlying anti-Semitism does exist, and it's unrealistic to close your eyes," he said. "It does exist in Poland, in Russia, and unfortunately it does exist in Germany. If we allowed the impression to grow that this was an overwhelmingly Jewish compensation negotiation, it would give nurture and food to those who wanted to reawaken anti-Semitism. And that should not happen."

———— ·•·· ————

Lambsdorff's first plenary, at the German foreign ministry in Bonn, was little short of a disaster. With the legal issues apparently settled, the lawyers pushed to discuss money and dropped a financial bombshell. For $30 billion they were prepared to settle their lawsuits. That was itself a compromise, they said, from their original idea of $40 billion. Even Singer and the Claims Conference, pursuing compensation for just the Jewish survivors, found the lawyers' demands excessive.

Gentz was aghast. For months he had assumed an agreement could be reached at around $1.5 billion—not much more than the Swiss settlement. Now the lawyers were demanding twenty times that figure. The Germans felt it was time to abandon the talks. Why not just fight it through the courts, while working with the existing forced labor foundations in the East?

Eizenstat had struggled with the issue of money for weeks. Under intense pressure from the class action lawyers, he knew that the financial haggling could demolish the elaborate negotiating structure he had so carefully constructed. Fearing a repeat of the collapse of the Swiss talks, he began to test out his own numbers. He already realized that his large plenary sessions would not resolve anything. There could be no face-to-face negotiations between the Germans and the lawyers. The lawyers would only end with a display of machismo that would drive the numbers up instead of down. If they could not or would not settle on a number, Eizenstat would do it for them—and hope that he could push all sides toward it by sheer force of character.

"It was sort of like scientifically based intuition. It's a little bit of an oxymoron but it was based on real discussions with both sides," Eizenstat recalled. "I had to come up with a number that was way above where the Germans were, but not so far above that they would walk out of the talks. It was just my instinct that it had to be something in the middle. It had to be a double-digit figure for the lawyers, but if it was anything much above the lower double-digit numbers, I could never sell it to the Germans."

As both sides prepared to leave, Eizenstat cornered Gentz and Lambsdorff for a private conversation. How about 10 billion deutsche marks? Only with such a large number—worth around $5 billion—could they make a convincing argument in public that this was a fair settlement.

"Impossible," said Gentz. "I cannot commit to that. It's far too much, given the ideas we have discussed earlier, which were confirmed by Hombach and Kornblum." Eizenstat had one more chance to bridge the gap. The German government was toying with the idea of making its own financial contribution. How about combining contributions from the German government and private businesses? At least that way the overall numbers might seem bigger—even if the two sides were actually no closer to a deal. Gentz agreed. It was an idea he had originally backed months ago, as a way to deal with the government's role in Nazi crimes.

Both sides left Bonn with an overwhelming sense of failure. They had missed the symbolic deadline of the anniversary of Poland's invasion. In truth, they knew they remained continents apart. Far from bridging the philosophical and financial divide, they seemed increasingly hostile toward one another. "There is tremendous time pressure," Eizenstat told journalists. "The biological clock is ticking. Ten percent of survivors die each year."

Lambsdorff himself was even gloomier. Closing the Bonn conference, he intoned, "We are doomed to succeed. Fate demands it."

FIFTEEN

The Magic Number

Fate hangs heavy over today's reconstructed Berlin, where even the buildings have a schizophrenic relationship with the past. Old edifices—their facades riddled with bullet holes—have been gutted and turned into postmodern marvels. New buildings seem desperate to evoke a long-lost past. Step inside the new luxury Four Seasons Hotel, and you find yourself in a mock nineteenth century mansion. It was there that Chancellor Schröder was based temporarily in the fall of 1999, while his new Chancellery offices were being completed. The German government had only just made the historic move from its postwar home in provincial Bonn. Now, in the hotel's wood-paneled salon, lit by two huge chandeliers, Schröder sat at a long dining table ready to revisit the last time the German government called Berlin its home.

Seated around him were the corporate leaders of the Holocaust compensation initiative alongside the political linchpins, including his Holocaust envoy Otto Graf Lambsdorff and his finance minister Hans Eichel. From here, the compensation fund would be a pooling of finances by the government and businesses. However, even by combining their cash piles they could never come close to the unexpectedly high demands of the class action lawyers and the U.S. government. So how could they respond in a realistic way that would keep the international talks alive?

First they talked about hard cash. The U.S. officials were now suggesting a compromise figure of 8 billion deutsche marks, but the businessmen wanted to bid far closer to where they had left off, at about 3 billion deutsche marks ($1.5 billion). For Schröder and Lambsdorff, that was impossibly low. Both believed the figure needed to be significantly higher, and certainly more than 5 billion deutsche marks. Schröder pressed the business leaders to commit themselves to the absolute limit of what they thought they could raise. After all, this compensation package was meant to come from the companies that had only paid small amounts to survivors since the war.

"We will not raise this number any higher," said Daimler-Chrysler's Manfred Gentz, "but we can say four billion deutsche marks."

"If you can say four billion," replied Schröder, "I can say two billion."

Eichel agreed to the new 6 billion deutsche mark offer on one condition—contributions from privatized companies such as Deutsche Telekom would be counted as government cash. The government was facing tight budget constraints and there was no room to find a few extra billion. When some of the executives demurred, Eichel pointed out that the business contributions could be written off against tax. "Four billion from you is really two billion from us because of the taxes," he said.

"Mr. Eichel—what you're saying is that our taxes are too high," retorted Wolfgang Gibowski, the industry group's spokesman whose previous job was head of press to former Chancellor Kohl.

The debate moved on and Eichel emerged victorious. It would prove a costly concession for German industry as it struggled to raise the cash it had promised. At the end of the meeting, both sides promised to defend the 6 billion deutsche mark figure as strongly as they could. The companies already feared it would be impossible to raise their contribution any further.

Exhausted by the complexity of the discussions, Schröder began to sympathize with Kohl's refusal to reopen talks on Holocaust compensation. "I didn't understand why my honorable predecessor didn't want to touch this issue," he told the executives. "Now I'm beginning to understand."

It was not just American pressure that forced the Germans to double their offer. A new set of numbers from the German government's historian altered the course of the talks forever. Professor Lutz Niethammer, teaching at universities in Jena and Florence, painstakingly examined the numbers of surviving slave and forced laborers. At workshops first in Buchenwald concentration camp in July, then in Florence in early September, Niethammer estimated there were around 240,000 mostly Jewish slave laborers still alive. These were the few who had survived the Nazi plan to work Jews to death through starvation and exhaustion in German factories, which were often sited close to concentration camps.

Niethammer also estimated there were around 1.25 million surviving forced laborers from Central and Eastern Europe. These were mostly the Slavs whom the Nazis had treated as an inferior race, deporting and conscripting them into similar factories but feeding them a minimum ration, which kept them alive in often brutal conditions. The professor believed there were another 800,000 forced laborers who had toiled on farms and were considered to have suffered less than others. They had mostly escaped the worst beatings and could at least find their own food.

With such high numbers of survivors, there was no way the German side could offer such low levels of compensation. If there really were so many survivors, the original offer of $1.5 billion meant they would each receive less than $700 on average.

In Florence, Niethammer tackled for the first time the ratio between slave laborers who worked for government-controlled companies, and those who worked for private sector businesses. In large numbers, he chalked up on a blackboard: "50/50." If accepted, the impact would be huge—the German government would end up paying as much as the companies. The delegates felt it was so impressive that one took a photograph of the blackboard. On the final evening, Niethammer invited all the participants to his home for drinks and a final review of the numbers. They had worked hard, without interpreters, suffering the poor English spoken by the delegates from Russia, Ukraine, and Belarus. At the professor's home, Michael Hausfeld, the only attorney present and the prime mover behind the meeting, spent the evening drinking vodka shots with the Eastern Europeans. They had good reason to celebrate Hausfeld's involvement. By defending a high level of Eastern European survivors, he was raising the ultimate compensation they would receive. Their united front—in spite of the traditional hostilities between them—would prove invaluable in later negotiations.

Few in Germany or America accepted Niethammer's numbers. From the class action lawyers to German officials, like Michael Geier in the German foreign ministry, most believed the Eastern Europeans had artificially inflated their figures to extract more cash. "Everybody knew that the figures were at least dubious," said Geier. "I'm deeply convinced that the numbers of the Central and Eastern Europeans are not entirely credible. But it helped to write down proportions which were eventually accepted by everybody. The question of how many survivors are alive is unsolvable."

A week after they had settled on 6 billion deutsche marks, the Germans scored a double victory in the U.S. courts. Two New Jersey judges dismissed five lawsuits against companies for their use of slave and forced labor, including the original case against Ford. In a 120-page opinion, Judge Joseph Greenaway tore apart the class action lawyers' arguments piece by piece. Their cases were filed too late, beyond the statute of limitations. The court could not trample over U.S. foreign policy. The court would not undermine the executive branch of government. The court refused to interfere with Germany's legal rulings. Most damning of all, Greenaway decided that "too much time had passed" since the war. Proceeding with the case raised "the specter of adjudicating thousands of claims arising out of a war that took place more than 50 years ago."

In a separate ruling Judge Dickinson Debevoise kicked out the cases involving Siemens and Degussa, which manufactured the deadly Zyklon B used in the gas chambers. The claims fell under the category of war reparations and international treaties, he said. "Every human instinct yearns to remediate in some way the immeasurable wrongs inflicted upon so many millions of people by Nazi Germany so many years ago," wrote Debevoise, "wrongs in which corporate Germany unquestionably participated." But, he argued, the court had no power and no means to do so. "By what conceivable standard could a single court arrive at a fair allocation of resources among all the deserving groups? By what practical means could a single court acquire the information needed to fashion such a standard?"

For the class action lawyers it was a devastating intervention. In Burt Neuborne's eyes, the New Jersey judges failed to realize what Judge Korman in the Swiss case understood so well. "Deciding these cases isn't what these things are about," Neuborne said. "It was using them as a matrix for a larger negotiation that was important. I think we would have settled it for five billion deutsche marks more if they had just kept their mouths shut. I made a number of noises about appeals. But the dice were rolled. If we had won you can be sure there would have been a small army of class action lawyers dressed as locusts."

The normally mild-mannered Neuborne grew uncharacteristically aggressive. In Washington the day after the cases were dismissed, Neuborne addressed the House Banking Committee. Sitting at a modest wooden desk before the ranks of representatives, Neuborne promised to play hardball with the German companies. A moral gesture would not be enough. In fact, it would only lead to "increased bitterness and calls for reprisals," he warned. What he wanted was "a reasonable counter-offer" from the Germans to the lawyers' $20 billion demands.

"Those of us who have devoted the past several years to an effort to provide Holocaust survivors with a modicum of justice will not give up the struggle," he pledged. "If the courts can provide relief, we will seek justice in court. If government sanctions can obtain relief, we will seek government sanctions against corporations that fail to disgorge unjust enrichment. If popular disapproval can stimulate just behavior, we will conduct a public education campaign designed to acquaint our fellow citizens with the facts. We will exhaust every lawful avenue open to us in a search for justice for the victims of the Holocaust."

Some of the lawyers were so upset by the dismissals that they turned their fire on Eizenstat. Martin Mendelsohn claimed he saw a Justice Department memo urging the administration to file a brief stating why the courts' opinions were wrong. The memo said Eizenstat had requested that no intervention be made by the U.S. government for three months because it would upset the German talks.

Others, like Mel Weiss, made good on the threat to educate the public. In a series of full-page ads in the *New York Times,* Weiss cranked up the pressure on the German negotiators as they arrived in Washington to make their counteroffer. The ads were uncompromising. Sponsored by B'nai B'rith and other Jewish and Polish groups, they targeted Daimler-Benz, Ford, and Bayer with pictures of slave laborers and Nazi officials. The Daimler ad contained a picture of Hitler underneath the Mercedes three-point star. Bayer was linked to Josef Mengele, the infamous doctor who conducted experiments on human beings in Auschwitz. The Ford ad carried the headline "The Assembly Lines Ford Would Like You to Forget" under a photo of concentration camp prisoners toiling over metal components. Never mind that the slave laborers were assembling V-2 rockets, which were not among Ford's wartime output. The ad's small print said: "Workers like these were used by Ford Werke and other leading German companies."

"These companies built their billion-dollar businesses on the backs of these slave laborers," Weiss told journalists in Washington. "They've had the benefit of the money for 55 years and can readily afford to reasonably compensate these remaining survivors they so brutally exploited."

Eizenstat, too, was fretting about the impending German offer. In the days before the German negotiators returned to Washington, he urged President Clinton to intervene. In a highly confidential briefing, Eizenstat explained how many problems had been overcome, but the burning issue of money remained.

Eizenstat wanted Clinton to push the 10 billion deutsche mark figure on Schröder, and to threaten him with the prospect of sanctions if the talks collapsed. "We cannot guarantee that this would resolve the matter," Clinton told Schröder. "But we would press hard for settlement at that amount."

Without the 10 billion deutsche marks, the United States could not stop the public campaign vilifying Germany, nor provide the legal peace the Germans so ardently desired. "If these negotiations break down," Clinton said, "I fear that there could be a negative public reaction in the United States, with threats of state and local sanctions against German companies, as well as negative reactions among Germany's neighbors in Central and Eastern Europe. I want to reiterate that, to ensure the moral and legal closure that Germany seeks, the German government and companies need to ultimately offer 10 billion deutsche marks, if necessary, to settle this matter."

In the United Nations–style auditorium inside the State Department, lined with the flags of the world, the German offer of 6 billion deutsche marks came as a diplomatic slap across the face. Weiss restrained himself by merely trashing it in public as "disgusting." Although he pledged not to walk out of the talks, he promised to strike back by calling on his allies on Capitol Hill. "I told the German delegation they have done more harm to the German government and German people than they can ever imagine," he warned.

Eizenstat attempted to hold the talks together by being evenhanded, although he sounded unconvinced. The 6 billion deutsche mark offer was "much higher" than the earlier German offers and was at least "a basis for serious discussion." Summoning his best diplomatic powers of understatement, he added: "The other parties have not accepted the German offer. Their responses have varied widely among them. The other parties should now step forward with a reasoned response."

However, it was Lambsdorff himself who inflicted the most damaging blow to his own side. Speaking to journalists inside the State Department's amphitheater, he strongly hinted that he never believed that 6 billion deutsche marks were enough to reach a settlement. It was, he suggested, only a starting point. "When I told Stuart Eizenstat last Monday that the German enterprises and the German government were planning to endow the foundation with 6 billion deutsche marks, I was aware that I could not expect spontaneous agreement, and that is what happened,"

Lambsdorff revealed. He told how the German government and companies agreed on a figure in September to meet Germany's moral responsibility. "They stated at the time that was a respectful, creditable amount," he explained halfheartedly.

The companies were furious, accusing Lambsdorff of selling them out by suggesting the offer was only a temporary negotiating position. It was a breach of their agreement to defend the joint offer in the Four Seasons Hotel a month earlier. "Lambsdorff's speech made it clear to everybody that was not the last offer, and that nobody could depend seriously on six billion deutsche marks," said Gentz. "Lambsdorff didn't stick to the rules of the game. He was of the opinion that he wouldn't achieve agreement with the American government. But he was completely undermining our position." Gentz immediately confronted Lambsdorff, who promised that the government would increase its contribution.

It was not only Gentz who was angry with Lambsdorff. In spite of his much-vaunted ties to the business community, Lambsdorff had lost the confidence of Germany's industrial leaders. "The CEOs are very angry with Lambsdorff because he negotiated very badly," said Wolfgang Gibowski, the spokesman for German industry. "It was a game for Eizenstat to deal with him. Eizenstat is a much better negotiator than him. Gentz was very close to killing Lambsdorff because he was playing around with the billions. He never pushed the other side down and he was telling us through the media that our offer was not enough."

Lambsdorff was unrepentant. He knew that Weiss's rage had killed the 6 billion deutsche mark figure and he wanted to force the numbers higher. "I did know of course it was a kind of disappointment to the business people because many of them thought I was their guy and I would do the business," Lambsdorff recalled. "But from my experience, without some public pressure, I would not have been ready to move them up from six billion deutsche marks to a higher amount.

"My job was to come to a result. In that context it was necessary to move the numbers up. Of course, the German business community thought that was the last offer, but Stu Eizenstat said a negotiation never begins with the last offer. When I saw the reactions, it was clear to me that six billion deutsche marks was not going to do it."

Lambsdorff already knew of Eizenstat's chosen figure of 10 billion deutsche marks, even if he didn't agree at the time it was first floated. But he came to his own assessment that it would take a similar number to settle the talks. In private conversations, he and Eizenstat reached a tacit understanding that they needed to go into double digits. "I had a feeling that a double-digits number would do the business," said Lambsdorff. "Stu and I were partners and at the same time we were opponents. It was a difficult role to play for both of us but I think we did it quite well."

Lambsdorff returned to Germany and met with Schröder. "We can't come to a defendable agreement—let alone an agreement at all—on the basis of four or six," he told the chancellor. Schröder agreed. The government's contribution would rise by 1 billion to make a total of 7 billion deutsche marks.

Although he was reluctant to increase his offer, Gentz had no choice but to promise that the companies would make their "best efforts" to raise another 1 billion. The Germans could return with 8 billion deutsche marks, a figure Gentz was convinced could settle the talks once and for all—but only if everyone stood firm.

As the lawyers and companies prepared for another heavyweight contest in Bonn in November, Weiss delivered on his promise to strike back by using his political contacts. A prodigious Democratic donor, Weiss called on some of his best friends in the U.S. Senate. Standing on the Senate swamp, a patch of grass in front of the Capitol Building, Weiss appeared alongside Senators Charles Schumer of New York and Robert Torricelli of New Jersey, who were introducing legislation to overturn the New Jersey dismissals. The bill would extend the statute of limitations for Holocaust claims against Germany to 2010 and would explicitly empower U.S. courts to rule on those claims. "This bill shows that Congress is serious about this issue and serious about compensation for survivors," Schumer told journalists. "It is a way of making sure that these companies atone for one of the worst sins of this century."

However, Weiss and his senators did not represent the entire Jewish community. Some, like Abe Foxman, the national director of the Anti-Defamation League, grew increasingly agitated. Foxman had been the most pointed Jewish critic of the World Jewish Congress in the Swiss talks, claiming they were reducing the Holocaust to a dispute over money. Now, speaking at a New York dinner honoring Lufthansa, the German airline, Foxman turned his fire on the German negotiations. "Return of rightful property to owners and heirs is an unequivocal moral obligation, which as far as I know has never been questioned," he said. "But if in pursuit of that objective we lose our sense of reason, we then run the risk of exploiting the Holocaust and the memory of its victims. The Jewish community, beginning with the ADL, must bear the responsibility of reining in those few people who have been blinded and carried away by their own rhetoric, as well intentioned as they may be."

After the debacle of Washington, the November meeting in Bonn was a make-or-break event. Eizenstat knew that without real signs of progress, the talks might fall apart completely, just as they had in the Swiss negotiations. The lawyers were ready to compromise too, bringing their demands far down from $20 billion. Hausfeld wrote to Lambsdorff suggesting $12 billion as a compromise, which was rejected out of hand. Now they were prepared to halve that demand and switch to similar figures in deutsche marks. While Weiss insisted on 15 billion deutsche marks (around $7.5 billion), a group of rival plaintiffs' lawyers led by Ed Fagan and Bob Swift was keen to settle quickly at 10 billion deutsche marks—Eizenstat's magic number.

As the meeting started, Lambsdorff told Gentz he doubted whether 8 billion could do it. "Fine," said Gentz. "But we have to negotiate very hard to show we can succeed." When Gentz stood up in the final conference session to increase his side's offer, he said he did not think he could go above 8 billion. He explained it would be a struggle to raise the new contribution of 5 billion deutsche marks from German industry.

Eizenstat seized on Gentz's difficulties and stretched the truth to breaking point. The U.S. official suggested that Gentz was hinting at something more. In talks with the lawyers and at the press conference that ended the session, Eizenstat claimed the German side had made an offer in the range of 6 to 10 billion deutsche marks. Miraculously, that now "touched" the range offered by the lawyers of 10 to 15 billion. The world's media faithfully reported that a compromise was within reach at 10 billion deutsche marks. "A negotiated settlement now seems attainable," said Eizenstat, ignoring the fact that the German side never negotiated in ranges. Gentz had offered a specific figure, well below even the lowest demand from the class action lawyers. The number was 8 billion and Gentz insisted it could "not be raised any higher."

The class action lawyers, led by Neuborne, continued to hold out for more and settled on a strategy of escalating the legal threats facing the Germans—including new legislation in Congress and an appeal to the Supreme Court. "Most of us will vote to terminate the talks rather than accept a 10 billion deutsche mark resolution," he wrote to his cocounsel.

But Lambsdorff stood his ground on the 8 billion offer. "My very strong feeling is that we have to cease bidding against ourselves," he wrote to one of the lawyers who complained he had been misled.

Eizenstat urged the Central and Eastern European governments to accept 10 billion deutsche marks, promising them "a just distribution" of the cash. He also staged a series of conference calls with the class action lawyers to break them apart. If one group agreed to his terms, the others would be forced to follow suit. With just one week left before the final conference in Berlin—the last Holocaust talks before the turn of the century—Eizenstat spent a day on the phone beating the class action lawyers into submission.

Hausfeld, Neuborne, and Mendelsohn were crunching through numbers in Hausfeld's gray Washington office. Sitting under framed newspaper articles depicting Hausfeld's past legal triumphs, they dashed through the most vital calculations. How much would each type of survivor actually receive from an 11.5 billion or a 13.5 billion deutsche mark fund? Churning out computer spreadsheets, they calculated and recalculated their numbers. Eizenstat called. How about 10 billion? They said no. Someone tried to reach Mel Weiss, but failed. Again they reworked the numbers, calling Warsaw, Prague, Moscow, Kiev, and Minsk, searching for a bare-minimum figure they could all agree to. Someone finally tracked down Mel Weiss on the phone, and Weiss promptly pointed out that their math was wrong. The three lawyers had missed half a billion in their calculations. Eizenstat called once more. It was 6:00 P.M. What was their number? They were down to the wire. Their final minimum number: 10.5 billion from the Germans and another 1 billion deutsche marks from American companies such as Ford.

Eizenstat was cool. "I've already talked to Fagan, Swift, and Whinston," he said. "They've agreed to ten."

Swift was annoyed to find himself excluded from his fellow attorneys' discussions. He claimed that Hausfeld had misled him by urging him to wait until the following week before making a final offer. When he heard of the talks with Eizenstat, Swift was determined to undercut his fellow attorneys. "The truth was that we probably would not get more than ten," he said. "What I simply didn't appreciate was Hausfeld telling me one thing and then doing another. He just wanted to do something himself. I was not going to play along with that game."

Hausfeld and his allies were stunned. What had been the point of the whole negotiation? It felt as if the air had been sucked out of the room.

"Who the hell cares anyway," Weiss told Hausfeld on the speakerphone. "The extra money is only going to the non-Jews. You and your Poles are going to get what you want."

"That's not fair," said Hausfeld.

"They're all a bunch of anti-Semites," Weiss snapped back. "And you're no better than the rest of them."

Hausfeld burst into tears and tore out of his office. It would mark a definitive breach between the most powerful action lawyers on the Holocaust compensation deals.

Their falling out was futile. With the class action lawyers in his pocket at last, Eizenstat brought the curtain down on the talks the following week with a simple letter from President Clinton to Chancellor Schröder. "Deputy Secretary Eizenstat was intensively engaged this past week with the plaintiffs' attorneys," wrote Clinton, "to move them closer to the German offer." Eizenstat had won the agreement of the lawyers, the Claims Conference, and all the governments, to settle at 10 billion deutsche marks. "This is a tremendous step to finally settle all claims we have been discussing. It will establish for the first time a flat sum and ceiling agreed by all participants in this process."

Lambsdorff had already told Schröder there would be no deal, and no legal peace, unless the German government stepped in to bridge the gap. The cost: another 2 billion deutsche marks from the government's coffers. Schröder was determined to make good on his commitment to solving the problem for German businesses and U.S.-German relations. "I cannot deny that this decision was preceded by intensive discussion," Schröder replied to Clinton, whose centrist Third Way politics he deeply admired. "After considering all aspects, we decided to increase the federal foundation's financial resources to a total of 10 billion deutsche marks."

Schröder justified stumping up so much extra cash—at a time of budgetary cuts in Germany—with two reasons. The first was legal peace for German companies in the United States: the Clinton administration had pledged to intervene in all current and future lawsuits to support their dismissal.

The second reason was the irresistible symbolism of drawing a line under the Nazi era before the dawn of a new millennium. "More than anything else," wrote Schröder, "the understanding reached on the federal foundation is a significant humane gesture of our responsibility towards Nazi victims at the close of this century. The German government has done its utmost to achieve this. It will therefore firmly reject any further claims."

Clinton summoned reporters to hear a brief statement on the White House driveway outside the Oval Office on a chilly mid-December afternoon. "We close the 20th century with an extraordinary achievement that will bring an added measure of material and moral justice to the victims of this century's most terrible crime," he said. "It will help us start a new millennium on higher ground."

———◆———

Two days later they met to rubber-stamp the deal in Berlin. At a brief ceremony in the new Grand Hyatt Hotel overlooking the ultramodern Potsdamer Platz, the cold-blooded Eizenstat could not contain himself. He walked up to Lambsdorff and bear-hugged him. Lambsdorff—and the rest of the room—was taken aback. "That is not a normal gesture for Eizenstat," said Lambs-dorff. "Neither for me, by the way. We are not open to such gestures."

Secretary of State Madeleine Albright—by chance in Berlin on other diplomatic business—led the praise. Unwittingly, she also pointed forward to the bitter argument to come: how to divide the huge compensation fund?

"Nothing we could do now would provide more than a small fraction of real justice. But in this searing context, even small fractions matter a great deal," she said. "Of course, in circumstances so unique and now distant, there is no scientific method that will guide us in determining what is reasonable and fair. Any decision must be subjective. At the same time, the settlement figure was not simply plucked out of thin air."

Not out of thin air, maybe. But out of the stubborn mind of Stuart Eizenstat.

The group moved on to the Schloss Bellevue, the eighteenth century palace that was once the guest house for the Third Reich, and is now the official residence of the German head of state. In the palace's long white dining room, lit by grand windows overlooking the palace gardens, the class action lawyers sat alongside German business executives and officials from five European governments.

Israel Singer and the Claims Conference, reduced to the role of spectators as the class action lawyers bickered over money, had always insisted on one extra price. Germany must apologize. Without a fulsome apology, history suggested they would not be able to sell the deal to survivors.

At the prompting of Singer and his colleagues, President Johannes Rau—in office as the German head of state for just seven months—agreed to address the morality behind the compensation. A craggy, chain-smoking politician, Rau wanted to mark an end to the months of hard-nosed haggling over money. "This compensation comes too late for all of those who lost their lives back then, just as it is for all those who have died in the intervening years," he said. "It is now therefore even more important that all survivors receive, as soon as possible, the humanitarian payment agreed today.

"I know that for many it is not really money that matters. What they want is for their suffering to be recognized as suffering and for the injustice done to them to be named injustice.

"I pay tribute to all those who were subjected to slave and forced labor under German rule and, in the name of the German people, beg forgiveness. We will not forget their suffering."

Roman Kent, one of the few elderly Holocaust survivors in the room, could not hold back. Striding up to the microphone uninvited, he spoke without notes but with palpable passion. "I wonder why I am here," he started nervously. "I have said before, maybe I am here because I have received a degree from Lodz ghetto, from Auschwitz, Flossenburg, and others. The Nazis killed—no, brutally murdered—one and a half million children. I am one of the lucky ones that survived. Because sixty years ago, I was a child."

Quoting from the prayers of Yom Kippur, the Jewish day of atonement, he acknowledged that Rau had atoned. "*Slach-lanu*— forgive us," President Rau said. *Shachah-tanu*—because we have sinned, President Rau said. These two words are what we, and the world at large, should remember. These words should reverberate with us for now and forever so the Holocaust would never, never happen again to us or to any other people."

A Piece of Raw Meat

The dignified words of reconciliation at the presidential palace were soon forgotten. Two months later, in February 2000, Eizenstat called together the Jewish and Eastern European representatives in Berlin to try to carve up the 10 billion deutsche marks. Agreeing on the overall size of the pot had been emotional enough. But the task of sharing the cash among rival groups of victims was fraught with memories of war, grief, and persecution. Who had suffered the most at the hands of the Nazis? Which set of victims was more deserving of compensation? And who would have the wisdom and power to decide between them?

They met at the U.S. embassy in the former East Berlin—a crumbling building surrounded by a six-foot-high security fence, which looked and felt like a decaying leftover of the cold war. Inside the 1970s-style conference room—complete with beige leather chairs, strip lighting, and the seals of every government department in the embassy—Stuart Eizenstat hoped to find common ground between the two competing groups of survivors. Instead, they began tearing each other apart, pitting Jew against gentile.

At the outset, Eizenstat attempted to assert his authority with the Jewish negotiators and class action lawyers. He warned they were stirring up anti-Semitism in Eastern Europe by making aggressive demands for Jewish survivors at the expense of non-Jewish laborers. Israel Singer cut in. "Stuart, what is wrong with you? You think all the Czechs will hate the dead Jews in cemeteries? What the hell are you talking about? There are fifteen hundred Jews in the Czech Republic and there are maybe three thousand Jews in all of Poland who are actually Jews.

"We have been accused of causing anti-Semitism since the first blood libels that go back two thousand years. There is no reason in the world why the more recent blood libels should not blame Jews for claiming restitution. It's a non sequitur from the very outset.

"I understood from the beginning that the Poles need to get paid. I just didn't want them paid out of my coin."

Everybody agreed that the other side deserved something, but nobody could agree how much. When Michael Hausfeld began making the case for his Eastern European clients, his rival class action attorneys began firing from all sides. Mel Weiss took umbrage at his very presence in a meeting supposedly addressing Jewish interests. Weiss suspected that Hausfeld had helped the Eastern Europeans inflate the numbers of their survivors at the Florence historical meeting, without telling anyone whom he was really representing. Hausfeld could not be an attorney for both Jews and non-Jews, he insisted. It was a classic conflict of interest. Hausfeld had sold out his Jewish clients and his Jewish background. "You're a traitor," Weiss said.

Hausfeld relished the chance to strike back. "You know, there are Jews in Central and Eastern Europe—a significant number—and they express nothing but gratitude for the positions I'm taking," he said to Weiss. "And I represent as many individual Jewish people outside Central and Eastern Europe as you or any other lawyer. Besides, you filed the first case on behalf of a non-Jew, Elsa Iwanowa."

Hausfeld's spirited self-defense only embittered those around him. Roman Kent, whose words seemed to sum up the sorrowful mood in December, fired off a furious tirade at Hausfeld for arguing that slave and forced laborers should receive a bigger share of the funds. "You are a disgrace to the memory of the Holocaust and your father," Kent said. "You are equating slave and forced labor. You should be ashamed of yourself."

Neuborne agreed. He had already written to Hausfeld accusing him of arrogant deceit. Who did he think he was, deciding which Europeans should get what? "For heaven's sake, Michael," he said, "stop acting as if the German negotiations were your personal property."

The tension was not just about how to divide the laborers' compensation between Jews and non-Jews. Another round of squabbling was starting over property claims. The Eastern Europeans claimed they had a right to share the property payments, because their homes had been destroyed by Nazi troops. The Germans were seeking an end to all legal claims for property, and the Eastern Europeans wanted compensation if they were to renounce their claims forever. Besides, a high level of Jewish property claims would only take cash away from forced laborers.

For the Jewish groups, that argument was nothing less than offensive. Their property claims were based on racially motivated plunder—the so-called aryanization of Jewish businesses and financial assets. Of course the Eastern Europeans had lost property, but their homes were destroyed as part of the wider war—just as British homes were flattened by German air raids. Their argument only stirred up the Jewish side's barely concealed belief that Eastern Europeans were anti-Semites at heart and had actively participated in the Holocaust.

"I refuse to watch you behave like my little children when they were in prekindergarten," Singer told Hausfeld. "All prekindergarten children have an important rule with regard to property—what's mine is mine and what's yours is mine too."

"Well, fine," replied Hausfeld. "Get the Germans to drop the demand that they need a release from all property claims, whether aryanized or not."

As the argument raged, Eizenstat hammered the table repeatedly in an attempt to regain control. Nobody was listening. The meeting with the Jewish side was running late. Outside, in a cramped hallway, the Eastern Europeans grew agitated and the head of the Polish delegation stormed out in disgust. Eizenstat responded by yelling at the remainder of the Polish team that the talks were too important for anyone to walk out.

The arrival of the Eastern Europeans in the oppressive, airless conference room only made matters worse. Now it was a free-for-all as everyone claimed all the money for themselves.

Singer started by staking a claim to higher payments for Jewish slaves. "In all other cases in history, slaves were protected by all people in all countries in all of history, including the United States, where we had slaves," he began. "But the Germans were the first to take Jewish slaves and kill them. It goes against every capitalist principle. It was a first. For this reason these slave laborers should be treated differently from the other forced laborers."

When Singer began claiming the entire share of property compensation, tempers flared once again. Eizenstat attempted to calm the dispute. "It doesn't make any sense to make excessive demands," he urged. "You've got a capped amount." But the Eastern Europeans mistrusted Eizenstat and believed he merely represented American Jewish interests. They too had suffered in the war and demanded the lion's share of the cash, not least because they represented far more survivors.

"This is not about solving the problems of the war," said Gideon Taylor of the Claims Conference. "It's about trying to do some justice for the survivors of the Holocaust—not for all the people who lost something in the war. We're dealing with the implications of the Holocaust."

The American lawyers poured scorn on the property claims of the Eastern Europeans. "It's a different class of action," said Mel Weiss. "Go file your own suit."

Frustrated and appalled by the street brawl in front of him, Eizenstat could only watch as his talks degenerated. "You are on U.S. soil right now," he yelled. "We are not going to continue if this is going to be your attitude."

Nobody was listening. Weiss remained implacable over the very presence of the Eastern Europeans. "I don't see why any of your people should be included in any part of the resolution even if they were in concentration camps," he told the diplomats from Poland, Russia, Ukraine, Belarus, and the Czech Republic. "Because if they weren't in concentration camps, they would have all been Nazis."

Hausfeld could not stomach Weiss any longer. "Your judgment

is as poor as the words you chose," he said. "There were atrocities committed against great numbers of people. Those in concentration camps cannot be punished because of guilt by association or the wrongs of others."

Israel Singer left the discussions feeling ashamed at the outbursts, and sought out the Polish side for a private meeting that night at their hotel, where he promised such disputes would never happen again. But he also felt hurt at what he saw as a German attempt to create internal strife between the victims and to blame Jews for the infighting. By postponing the discussion over allocation, the unedifying haggling over money had only became more emotional. In an interview with the *Berliner Zeitung* newspaper, Singer vented his spleen on the German government. "We have the impression the terms under which the money is supposed to be made available are not just or moral," he said. "It is about business and putting an end to the past. And if this is the case they should keep their money.

"Germany cannot want to have two groups of victims fighting at the negotiating table like hungry dogs over a piece of raw meat."

Neither the Germans nor the Americans wanted a dogfight. But in their haste to seal the deal at 10 billion deutsche marks, they left both sides with a greater appetite than could possibly be fed. The Central and Eastern Europeans had already agreed among themselves, on Hausfeld's encouragement, to divide the spoils down to two decimal places. At a meeting in Prague in early December, they decided that forced and slave laborers would take 88.39 percent of the cash, or 8.84 billion deutsche marks. Of that, Jewish survivors would receive twice as much per person as non-Jewish survivors. That was in stark contrast to the German proposal, aired the day after the embassy bust-up, which suggested 7.7 billion deutsche marks for labor claims—more than a billion lower than the figures drawn up by the Central and Eastern Europeans.

The Eastern Europeans were making impossibly high demands, which Eizenstat and Hausfeld failed to bring down to earth. In

fact, Eizenstat's negotiating style positively encouraged such wish-
ful thinking. It was a sleight of hand that could only work in proximity talks—where Eizenstat was the central figure, shuttling back
and forth among all sides, leaving everyone else in the dark as he
edged closer to a deal. "In classic Eizenstat mode, everyone had
agreed to the ten billion on a certain understanding, which was
actually incompatible," said one U.S. official. "The Poles wanted a
two to one proportion between slave and forced laborers. Whereas
the Jewish groups wanted five to one. I don't think Eizenstat ever
said yes or no to those breakdowns. It was one issue at a time, even
if one issue encroached on another."

Unfortunately for Eizenstat, the truth would eventually
emerge—to both sides' fury. At that point, only one tactic
remained—brute force. At a plenary meeting in the State Department two weeks after the dogfight in Berlin, the Polish delegation
clung to its demands of around 9 billion deutsche marks for labor
alone. Jerzy Kranz, the Polish ambassador to Germany, refused to
budge, arguing that the Central and Eastern Europeans had only
received 1 percent of German compensation since the war. A frazzled Eizenstat unleashed his most undiplomatic attack: "Fine," he
yelled. "You've had it. Have a nice life. We'll go on without you."

Eizenstat stormed out of the small caucus room, followed by
the Central and Eastern Europeans. Within ten minutes he was
fretting about how to bring the Poles back to the table. But his tactics had worked. Hausfeld told his clients to compromise, fearing
that the Jewish groups and their lawyers might cut their own deal.

The Poles were not the only ones overheating at the early
March session in Washington. The Jewish negotiators had finally
come to the point of dickering over the details of their property
claims. They had a varied shopping list of issues to discuss—banking, insurance, individual claims, and general humanitarian payments. But there was no clear idea of what the Claims Conference
was demanding, and no agreement between the two sides over
the validity of the claims. The Jewish negotiators did not even submit a formal demand on paper for an insurance settlement. In a
side meeting inside the State Department, the German negotiators offered a derisory amount to settle the insurance claims, at
around 50 million deutsche marks ($25 million).

Herbert Hansmeyer, the stolid head of the American operations of the insurer Allianz, was deeply entrenched in the notion
that there were no valid claims against his company. During the
1960s he had worked in the German embassy in Paris as an intern,
dealing with Holocaust survivors' claims, and he was now convinced that the entire issue was settled. Even though companies
had not contributed toward that compensation, Hansmeyer
believed Germany had fulfilled its obligations to the survivors.
Now the insurance executive—whose avuncular face belied a
hardened core—believed the Jewish side's tactics were just short
of blackmail. His hostility may have been heightened by his experience living in Los Angeles for several years, where he was dismayed by the level of anti-German feeling among Americans. He
remembered bitterly how Jewish neighbors banned their children
from talking to his family, saying they were Nazis. That impression
was only reinforced when he went to America to find a legal team
to defend Allianz against the class action lawsuits. Much like Generali's executives before him, Hansmeyer interviewed twenty
firms, including several that had previously represented Allianz.
None would touch the case.

To cover itself against litigation, Allianz set up hotlines for
potential claimants in the U.S., Israel, and Europe. After three
years the insurer received around thirty-six hundred inquiries. Of
those, Allianz made offers to just eighty people, including cases
where the insurer believed that the policy was either restituted or
cashed in. For Hansmeyer the exercise confirmed his gut feelings.
"This was basically a nonissue, as far as Germany is concerned," he
said.

Instead, he considered the claims just another round in the
never-ending demands pressed on Germany by Jewish groups. He
would joke to Singer that he was keeping a good set of files in case
the door was not entirely closed on another round of talks. "I'm
writing my memoirs," he said, "so that my son and my grandson
can use those notes to be better prepared for the next round."

The latest round was now locked into a claustrophobic State
Department meeting room, complete with interpreters' boxes
staring down on the proceedings. The view from the window was
just another gray concrete State Department wall, less than two

feet away. The only respite from the bleak scene was an inexplicable watercolor of red, green, and orange chili peppers.

There the Claims Conference focused far less on German insurance policies than on Allianz's exposure in Eastern Europe, through the Italian insurer Riunione Adriatica di Sicurtà (RAS), which it had acquired a few years earlier. The Jewish side considered RAS one of the leading culprits in the plunder of Jewish insurance policies, with a prewar market share among Eastern European Jews second only to that of Generali. Like Generali, RAS was founded in Trieste, and the two companies followed the same expansionary path throughout the Jewish communities of Austria-Hungary. But Hansmeyer adamantly opposed the idea of paying for RAS's claims. RAS's business in Eastern Europe had been nationalized by Communist governments. There were no assets left and no paper records available to figure out how much had been seized by the Nazis. The company said it had destroyed virtually all its records when it moved its headquarters from Trieste to Milan. All that was left of its entire Nazi-era archives now fitted into two filing cabinets.

While the rest of the delegates met in the auditorium across the State Department hallway, Eizenstat proposed a relatively low settlement of the property questions: 250 million deutsche marks for insurance, plus 50 million deutsche marks for individual claims and another 50 million deutsche marks kept in an escrow account to be used only if there was a large number of insurance claims. As tension mounted, Israel Singer and Gideon Taylor let off steam by walking around the State Department's outdoor atrium to thrash out the numbers among themselves in the spring sunshine. They chewed over a single question: what figure could they sell to the U.S. officials?

They returned to demand a bigger escrow account to pay for the claims, fearing there would not be enough money to meet the claims of victims and their families. After all, a year earlier, they had refused to allow Generali to cap its liability at $100 million. Now they were being offered one-fourth of that amount for companies including RAS, which they believed would face similar levels of claims in its own right.

However, the Germans again rejected the very existence of any claims and insisted they would not agree to any cash outside the total of 10 billion deutsche marks. "Fine," said Taylor. "You say there's a small number of claims. In that case you have nothing to fear from an escrow account. Let's take it from inside the ten billion. Let's take it from the Future Fund."

Gentz could not contain his anger. The Future Fund, earmarked for 1 billion deutsche marks, was his prized project: a chance to educate future generations about the Holocaust and Nazi crimes. He had already seen its importance whittled down from half of the foundation's cash to just 10 percent. Now it was being raided once more. Support for the Future Fund was eroding on all sides. Alongside the Eastern Europeans, even members of the German Bundestag were critical of the resources committed to it.

At the heart of the problem for both Singer and Hansmeyer was the failure of the process they had themselves helped to design to settle the complex insurance claims. Lawrence Eagleburger's international commission, intended to negotiate an insurance settlement through consensus, was deadlocked. Eagleburger had sunk into a morass of technical details, while the companies footing the bill grew ever angrier about what they saw as excessive expenses. Hansmeyer wanted to use the German talks to push the insurance issue forward—with or without the agreement of Eagleburger's commission. Any deal in the German talks would undermine the insurance commission, which was arduously building a costly system to handle individual claims, no matter how many there might be. By contrast, the German talks were now discussing how to limit the cost with a capped sum of cash, regardless of what the claims were worth.

The gap between Singer and Hansmeyer was so wide that the debate grew personal. They had been sniping at each other for more than a year and now neither man could abide the other's positions.

Desperate for a solution, Eizenstat and Lambsdorff needed help from one man more than any other—they needed Eagleburger's blessing to bypass his own commission. After negotiating late into the evening, the State Department's J.D. Bindenagel called Eagleburger to see if he would agree to meet both sides.

Early the next day, Eagleburger called in to say he had the flu and was too sick to travel to the State Department in Foggy Bottom. Instead, the negotiators hopped in their cars and drove to Eagleburger's apartment across the Potomac River in Arlington.

Eagleburger was sitting in his bathrobe when the door opened to Singer, Hansmeyer, Gentz, and a gaggle of German and U.S. officials. Among them was Lambsdorff, who knew that there was no chance of raising the 10 billion deutsche marks without Allianz's support. Lambsdorff was also close to the German insurance companies, as a board member of the insurer Victoria zu Berlin—a company that the Jewish side ranked third in prewar Eastern Europe, after Generali and RAS.

Eagleburger coughed. "Tell me what this is all about."

"We have a proposal on insurance and you are the only one to help," replied Bindenagel. As the negotiators explained how they were ready to undermine more than a year of his work on his insurance commission, Eagleburger's illness appeared to improve.

"I tried everything to get a capped amount," he finally told the bizarre gathering. "But I found it impossible. If you can miraculously get to a number, I'll defend it and respect it. I don't like it, but I'll agree."

They left the details of the deal to one final meeting before the last big plenary conference in Berlin. But with so little time in their busy schedules before the Berlin meeting, there was no convenient time or place for them to talk. On a Friday at the end of March, Singer flew from New York overnight while Hansmeyer and Gentz were traveling in opposite directions. The only location where they would overlap was at an airport—the Concorde lounge at Paris's Charles de Gaulle Airport. There, in front of the exclusive supersonic jet's passengers, they had just one hour to resolve one of the most intractable problems of any compensation negotiation. Singer was rushing to return before Shabbat began in New York, where his newest grandchild was to have a formal naming ceremony.

Singer did most of the talking. Normally he would remind Hansmeyer that he and his boss, Edgar Bronfman, were Allianz policyholders. But this time his usually garrulous style seemed more edgy. Fresh from a trip to Israel, where he had met with Israeli members of Eagleburger's insurance commission, he claimed he held a mandate for his positions. Hansmeyer was skeptical about the mandate he claimed. A mandate to do what? From whom?

At the center of the dispute, threatening the entire deal, was RAS. Hansmeyer insisted that claims against RAS had to be included under the umbrella of legal peace as an Allianz subsidiary. Singer was astounded. RAS was not a German company and was not even part of the German insurer during the war. "Why don't you buy some new companies now and get closure for them," he thundered. "Why don't you buy some exposure from Jews in the Arab world and put them in the German foundation? You bought that company long after these events. You only absorbed that company in the last years. You've no right to include that."

Hansmeyer again insisted there were no legal claims against his company. Everything was settled by postwar compensation payments. Every part of Allianz must be included in the deal or there would be no agreement.

"Go fuck yourselves," retorted Singer. "I'm going home now. Good Shabbos to both of you."

Gentz insisted Singer stay. The price: another raid on his precious Future Fund. Determined to take credit for breaking the logjam, Gentz conceded 200 million deutsche marks to cover the Eastern European claims against companies such as RAS. The deal included an innovative twist—a further 50 million deutsche marks would be added from interest earned on the foundation's cash reserves. Through brinkmanship and bravado, Singer had more than doubled the cash available for individual claims. Singer took his supersonic flight back home confident that he had struck a hard bargain for the victims' families who had waited so long for the insurers to pay up. All that remained was a final battle over the forced laborers in Berlin.

SEVENTEEN

The Spiderweb

They gathered inside Hitler's newly renovated Reichsbank in Berlin in March 2000 for what they hoped would be their final talks on how to divide up the 10 billion deutsche marks. It was hard to imagine a more jarring location—the former central bank where so much looted Nazi gold was hauled from conquered countries and concentration camp victims. Now the building forms half of the new German foreign ministry, its central banking hall converted into a giant conference room known as the Weltsaal—the World Auditorium. The Holocaust compensation negotiators were the first to use the brand-new hall, dominated by its vast doorways—nineteen wooden double-doors in all, each four inches thick, stretching around three sides of the auditorium. "You can consider these doors locked," said Eizenstat. "We are not leaving this room, and we are not going to stop, until we reach an agreement. I don't care how late it gets. We're through with posturing, we're through with demands. We're going to settle this right now."

He meant it. When reasoned debate failed, and when emotional outbursts failed, Eizenstat resorted to a peculiarly psychological form of pressure: the sheer mental and physical exhaustion of an all-night meeting. There would be no bathroom breaks, no sandwich breaks, and no sleep. Eizenstat knew that tempers were still running high—particularly among the Poles and Czechs—after the torrent of insults at the U.S. embassy in January. For Eizenstat it was the make-or-break session.

If these talks collapsed or ended without agreement, he was staring at another Swiss-style failure. The cases would head to court and the companies would establish their own private funds. Moreover, a court-ordered solution would not have included German government cash at all. "The German government would not have accepted it—period," said Michael Geier of Germany's foreign ministry. "It was a big threat that a U.S. court would run the ten billion deutsche mark foundation. Nobody in Germany would give a U.S. judge billions of deutsche marks of tax money to do whatever they wanted to do with it. The example of the Swiss settlement is bad enough."

First came the issue of labor. Even Eizenstat, the acknowledged master of complex international talks, found it "excruciating." The haggling over money focused on the number of survivors each group claimed was alive in each of the several categories of slave and forced labor. "It was like a spiderweb," said Eizenstat. "Each item was connected to another. Pull one thread, and the entire lattice could collapse. The levels of complexity were just staggering."

Using windowless breakout rooms beside the giant auditorium, Eizenstat shuffled among the German companies, the Central and Eastern Europeans, and the class action lawyers. As the talks dragged on into the night, no one knew where Eizenstat was in the old Reichsbank or whom he was speaking to. "Nobody exactly knew what happened except him," recalled Stephan Keller, of Germany's foreign ministry. "These proximity talks had a kind of confessional style. Eizenstat was very, very familiar with all the details you can imagine, and that gave him a tremendous grip on the negotiations.

"He never slept and he expected his delegation never to sleep. He kept people awake until four A.M. and after physical exhaustion he would get some concessions. He also tried to bully people. America is the only remaining superpower and you knew that behind him he had President Clinton and the whole administration. He told us if we wanted legal peace, we had to accept his terms."

Managing the weblike allocation were J. D. Bindenagel and his assistant Jody Manning of the State Department. On Manning's laptop computer, they set up a spreadsheet to calculate and recalculate the negotiated numbers as they were tweaked and retweaked. Soon no one knew what factors had gone into the numbers that were distributed on photocopied sheets. So many versions were in circulation that few people—other than Eizenstat—knew which spreadsheet was the latest proposal. Eventually, by chance, Manning and Bindenagel stumbled into a solution. As they played with the concept of sharing the huge interest earned on the funds, the number "1.812 billion" appeared twice on their chart—once beside the Claims Conference, the other time beside the Poles. "Stop right there," said Bindenagel. "Let's think about what we did."

It was a symbolic resolution of the bitter arguments in the U.S. embassy a month earlier about who had suffered more—the Jews or the Poles. Equal treatment was the Polish delegation's bottom line for agreeing to the deal. An equal number was the only political solution possible.

The one missing party as the talks began was the Claims Conference. Israel Singer and Gideon Taylor wanted to push their case for a bigger share of the labor claims. In particular, they wanted to argue that their claims included not just 129,000 slave laborers but another 28,000 Jewish forced laborers mostly from countries occupied late in the war—such as Hungary, Romania, and Bulgaria.

But they were fogbound inside London's Heathrow Airport, where all flights into the Continent were delayed or canceled. As they sat inside a terminal thick with cigarette smoke, the talks began between Eizenstat and their Claims Conference colleagues in Berlin. They could only stare outside at the fog and shout instructions down their cell phones. Eizenstat said there was not enough money for the extra 28,000 claims. Couldn't they just be flexible? A jet-lagged Taylor gasped at his colleague Karen Heilig in Berlin. "Don't budge an inch," he insisted. "Under no circumstances."

As soon as their plane touched down in Berlin at 11:00 P.M., they resumed the telephone talks. When Singer and Taylor staggered into the Hilton Hotel a few blocks from the German foreign ministry, Eizenstat walked in behind them. He was so driven to conclude the talks that he had left the foreign ministry and wanted to start right there in the hotel lobby, beside the mock granite waterfall, the artificial stream, the dismal bar, and the black cabaret piano. Instead, they walked up a floor to a claustrophobic corporate meeting room complete with a whiteboard and overhead projector.

Eizenstat, clutching his trademark sheaf of yellow notepapers, sat at the head of the table and ripped into Singer. Threatening to abandon him, Eizenstat said the Jewish side was holding up the negotiations on all fronts. "We are not going to let you guys spoil this. We've come so far. We'll settle without you. There are enough people. There are millions of people waiting for this. People are going to die without payments because of you, and you're going to be blamed."

Singer replied by saying he would not budge on the issue of Jewish forced laborers. "We didn't create a racist category of slave laborer and we are not going to create a racial distinction with regard to forced laborers," he insisted.

After midnight, Eizenstat cut a secret deal—the first of several concessions that would remain hidden from other parties who might object. Desperate to win Singer's approval for the labor deal, Eizenstat promised to divert 260 million deutsche marks from laborers in another category—labeled "the rest of the world"—to cover the extra Jewish forced workers. "I don't care if it came out of your grandmother's inheritance, or if you took it out of your pension plan," Singer told Eizenstat.

The headline number of 1.812 billion deutsche marks would still look the same as the Polish figure. But you would only know the truth if you read all the footnotes to the final allocation charts—and those footnotes were not widely circulated that night. Amid all the confusion, few people knew which chart was the latest version of events, and the crucial footnotes were not included in the official chart handed to the media the next day.

It was not the only secret side agreement that Eizenstat cooked up that night. Unknown to the Jewish negotiators, Eizenstat also promised to boost the Polish figures, only this time it was with American—not German—cash. The amount was far less, at just $10 million. But it was an extraordinary concession by the U.S.

government, using cash appropriated by Congress for an international fund for Nazi victims. The United States was effectively paying a share of a compensation package for the wartime guilt of German companies. It was the clearest possible sign of how much Eizenstat and the Clinton administration had taken control of the compensation deal—and how much political capital they had staked on its success.

The Polish deal was sealed without a lawyer present. Hausfeld, representing the Central and Eastern Europeans, was not in Berlin, citing a family commitment. His team sent the Poles a fax with instructions: "Be strong."

The Jewish talks continued in the airless room until almost 3:00 A.M., focusing on insurance and property. Hansmeyer reopened the entire Concorde lounge agreement, while Singer was exasperated—this was a tactic he used to wear down the other side by constantly renegotiating. "That's my line," Singer exclaimed. "What the fuck are you doing? What's wrong with you? You are supposed to be a straitlaced German! You're behaving like a Jew. You're trying to nickel-and-dime us at every turn." Eventually they settled back down to the Concorde terms.

Eizenstat, too, was at his wits' end with the Germans. Turning toward Lambsdorff, the German mediator sitting beside him, he blurted out, "For God's sake, man, don't just sit there like a bump on a log."

For their part, the German bank officials were so uninterested in the talks that they spent the night dining and drinking in a nearby restaurant on the historic Gendarmenmarkt Square. The contrast with the Jewish negotiators could hardly have been more stark. As the Hilton talks ended, Taylor and Heilig of the Claims Conference started fixing the terms of their agreements in writing, printing letters on hotel notepaper.

A sleep-deprived Eizenstat stood up the next day in the Weltsaal to declare victory in front of the world's media. "This is a great day," he began, after seventeen hours of talks. "We have achieved a consensus agreement on the allocation of the 10 billion deutsche

marks in the German foundation to which all parties have agreed."
The slave and forced laborers would receive 81 percent of the cash.
Property would be allocated another 10 percent. The once-mighty
Future Fund, for memorials and educational projects, would take
just 7 percent. Administrative costs, including lawyers' fees, would
be less than 150 million deutsche marks, or around $75 million.

Eizenstat's joy was not shared in Israel. There, news of the deal
was received with contempt at the low figures involved. Slave laborers, who had survived Nazi attempts to work them to death, would
be paid just 15,000 deutsche marks, or $7,500, for their years of
misery. The *Jerusalem Post* condemned the deal as "neither humanitarian nor just compensation." "It reflects the triumph of practi-
cality," the editorial said. "The longer victims' advocates held out
for benefits, the fewer survivors there would be to collect them."

If the deal was struck quickly in a rush to pay survivors, no one
told the German side. Within days of declaring victory in Berlin,
the Clinton administration was bogged down in a legal quagmire.
In his drive to clinch agreement on dividing the 10 billion
deutsche marks, Eizenstat suggested he could deliver something
approaching definitive legal peace for the German government
and companies. The Germans expected more than Eizenstat could
deliver, and Eizenstat had promised more than he could reasonably achieve. So began the bitter wrangling between the two government mediators themselves—Eizenstat and Lambsdorff.

Within two weeks, German officials accused their U.S. counterparts of seeking to hold the door open to a new set of claims. Only
this time, they argued, it was the administration itself that was
keeping alive the possibility of seeking more money from Germany. The German side demanded to know if the United States
would rule out the notion of reparations for a forgotten group of
forced laborers—American prisoners of war. As the U.S. presidential elections loomed in six months, the Germans suggested that
Clinton was unwilling to alienate the war veterans' vote.

For U.S. officials, the reparations issue was a red herring. They
had not raised it in talks and believed it had no place in the

discussions. Instead, they felt the Germans were trying to push them toward a new legal structure similar to the Iran-U.S. claims tribunal. The Iranian process, based in The Hague, was agreed on as part of a solution to the 1980 hostage crisis, which had helped bring down the Carter administration. For the current administration, the Nazi-era claims were far different. There was no hostage crisis to justify such a drastic move against wartime claims. Eventually the Clinton administration agreed to a compromise. Reparations claims might exist, but the United States would not raise them against Germany.

The Germans feared that Eizenstat had welshed on his deal to file a strong statement of interest to end all current and future lawsuits. "You need a really strong wording so that the judge will have a legal reason—not a political reason—to stop the litigation against a company," said Wolfgang Gibowski, the spokesman for the German companies. "If we don't get rid of the reparations issue, the French will come and the Greeks will come. This is a deal breaker. It's a matter of what the American side is willing to give us for the ten billion deutsche marks."

In Washington, the U.S. officials claimed that their German counterparts were attempting to push them into an unconstitutional position of interfering with the judicial branch of government. At heart this was a culture clash, they suggested, between the Anglo-Saxon legal system and the German civil code.

"They don't understand the system," complained a frustrated J. D. Bindenagel, of the State Department. "In layman's terms, this is a very simple proposition. The system we have here is good Anglo-Saxon case law with an independent judiciary. Under the civil code, it would be nice to ban all future cases. But we cannot do that, and we cannot waive the rights of American citizens to sue. That is something that is anathema to us and is politically very difficult."

The class action lawyers suspected a darker motive on the part of the Germans. The German companies were encountering problems raising the cash they had promised. At each stage, the Germans argued that more companies would sign on just as soon as an agreement was reached. First it was the size of the deal, then it was the allocation of the cash. Now—with less than half of their 5 billion deutsche mark contribution in hand—they argued it was because businesses were waiting for legal closure.

The executives leading the foundation pressed their colleagues and competitors. First they sent mass mailings to more than two hundred thousand companies, arguing that German industry needed to display its solidarity and stand together. It was irrelevant whether the company had employed forced or slave laborers—or even existed during the war. This argument scored some high-profile successes, including SAP, Europe's largest software company. But the foundation also struggled enormously with companies such as Porsche, the luxury automaker. Porsche enjoyed a special relationship with Hitler, as its founder helped to design the Führer's original Volkswagen. Still, the company claimed it was a small engineering outfit during the Nazi era and had used less than twenty forced laborers, whom it could compensate individually. It would take several letters and personal phone calls before Gentz could get Porsche to join the foundation—not because of its wartime record but out of German solidarity.

The foundation encountered even greater problems with foreign-owned companies. Hewlett-Packard became the only company in Germany with a turnover in the tens of millions of deutsche marks to refuse to participate. Others took part under pressure from their own workers. John Deere, the tractor maker, agreed to contribute after its workers' council took up the cause. Deere was an American company but had established itself in Germany by taking over the German producer Heinrich Lanz in the 1950s.

Such companies were crucial to the German fund-raising effort. While Eizenstat had pledged to seek 1 billion deutsche marks from American companies involved in wartime trade with Germany, the German negotiators took a different view. They wanted an end to litigation for all companies with any kind of presence in Germany before the war. In spite of vociferous objections by the class action lawyers, that definition would eventually pass into German law. The substantial American contributions promised by Eizenstat would never materialize.

Ultimately the German fund-raising drive failed to raise the full 5 billion deutsche marks, in spite of Gentz's best efforts. It would be another ten months before the original founding companies agreed to increase their contributions to pay for their free-riding friends in the German business community.

Without the legal agreement, the companies argued they had been hoodwinked into confirming they would contribute 5 billion deutsche marks. They insisted the only reason they had signed the deal was that President Clinton had promised legal peace in his letter to Chancellor Schröder in December.

The argument boiled down to one detail: Would the U.S. government merely *support* dismissal of the cases? Or would it go one step further and *recommend* their dismissal? The choice of word represented the frontline where political arguments clashed with legal ones. Eizenstat had assured the Germans that the Clinton administration would recommend the dismissal of the cases in the interest of U.S. foreign policy. For the Justice Department lawyers, however, that represented an unacceptable commitment to intervening in every case, regardless of its merits. For the State Department diplomats, it was the only way to avert unending conflict with Germany. As the Justice Department dug in its heels, Lambsdorff demanded that Eizenstat go over the head of the attorney general by appealing directly to Clinton.

The solution was an agreement to recommend dismissal on any valid legal ground. It was ultimately a political statement cloaked in legal language, complete with a list of reasons why the cases should be dismissed.

"It was like negotiating a marriage contract with an unwilling bride and groom," recalled Eizenstat. "The prenuptial agreement had to be very precise. And that's not really an exaggeration. The level of detail—every word, every comma, every phrase—was argued. Because they were trying to push us as close as possible to a legal position, and we recognized that and we tried to make it clear this was a policy position. It was a matter of almost unbelievable difficulty."

———•◆•———

They met in Berlin for one last time in July. It was ten days after the German parliament had created the new Holocaust foundation in a historic vote, which saw the right-of-center Christian Democrats voting alongside the formerly communist Democratic Socialists. The class action lawyers arrived secure in the knowledge that they had just secured 125 million deutsche marks in fees—a small percentage of the overall amount, but a large sum in hard cash. Mel Weiss would later be awarded 15 million deutsche marks in fees, worth around $7.5 million. Michael Hausfeld was not far behind at around $6 million. Even Burt Neuborne, the law professor who publicly insisted he was not receiving a penny for his work, received some $5 million. That compared with a maximum payment for each slave laborer—who had toiled in the factories next to the concentration camps—of just $7,500.

Among them the happiest was perhaps Ed Fagan, whose personal financial difficulties seemed to be drawing to an end. Fagan was more than just hyped about the prospect of receiving around $4 million. Unknown to Eizenstat, he was traveling with a camera crew from ABC television, which was filming a documentary of his finest hour.

Fagan staged a last-minute dispute with Eizenstat while the ABC cameras trailed his every move inside the German foreign ministry. After weeks of detailed negotiations between the lawyers and government officials, Fagan decided to object to the agreement on fees. What he did not know was that the cameras were preparing a *20/20* documentary exposing him for neglecting his clients and failing to return their phone calls. As officials waited inside the Weltsaal, the microphone pinned to his tie picked up Fagan boasting about having raised his legal fees. The documentary described him as "an obscure New Jersey lawyer" who would soon become a multimillionaire.

When Eizenstat heard that Fagan was making no less than eight demands, he erupted in anger, unaware that ABC television was recording their cell phone conversation. "What the hell are you doing?" shouted Eizenstat. "We are going to sign this. What do you mean you have demands? There are no demands."

"I have taken a lot of shit from a lot of people and a lot of my clients are getting screwed in this deal," Fagan yelled back.

The bust-up threatened to break apart the entire deal. As the German foreign minister, Joschka Fischer, waited for the signing ceremony to begin, Manfred Gentz demanded to know if the U.S. officials had really obtained legal peace. Fagan finally agreed to sign, in the mistaken belief that he had secured Eizenstat's agreement to raise the legal fees.

Eizenstat was so taken aback that he could hardly trust his eyes at the signing. "I didn't believe it until everybody literally walked up and signed," he recalls. "And then I went to make sure it wasn't signed in disappearing ink."

His speech that day was more generous. Describing the Holocaust as "history's greatest robbery," he hailed the historic deal as the last of its kind—before recognizing the lawyers who brought the German side to the negotiating table. "We must be frank," he told the gathered negotiators. "It was the American lawyers, through the lawsuits they brought in U.S. courts, who placed the long-forgotten wrongs by German companies during the Nazi era on the international agenda. Without question, we would not be here without them."

The Claims Conference, representing Jewish victims, agreed that the deal was historic. Roman Kent, who had spoken after President Rau's apology six months earlier, said the foundation was "the moral recognition for past wrongs," even if it was a token gesture sixty years late. "We survivors take it as such," he said. To Kent, the deal represented "the conscience of a new generation." Germany had entered a new era, when "the new generation born after the war realized the magnitude of the destruction brought forth by their forefathers."

Such noble words did not represent the reality of the talks. At the end of the negotiations, both sides appeared more embittered and less reconciled with one another than they had been at the outset. It was as if the long hours of face-to-face talks had merely reinforced the clash of historical views, entrenching both sides in a war of words that no one could win.

At Deutsche Bank, Klaus Kohler, the bank's general counsel,

remained unreconciled to the notion that there were any valid claims against his bank. "Clearly we know that we were all involved in what was going on during the Nazi dictatorship," he said. "Nobody could escape that, and that's why we are accepting our responsibility. But that's not a legal responsibility. And that's not always understood."

If there were no justifiable claims, why did the Germans pay out so much? The unspoken feeling was that they were simply paying blood money to settle the country's never-ending guilt over its Nazi past. Herbert Hansmeyer of Allianz began by believing the insurance claims against his company were either settled or unjustified. By the end of the talks, after agreeing to pay around 200 million deutsche marks to the foundation, he declared that his position was unchanged. When asked if he thought he had been the subject of emotional blackmail, he said, "I never called it blackmail." But he conceded that did not reflect how he felt. "Sometimes I had to leave out my feelings."

Even within the German government, there was resentment at what was considered an exaggeration of the nation's guilt. "People always said there were billions and billions taken, it was the greatest theft in history, and they talked about the forgotten victims," said Michael Geier, at the foreign ministry. "It's really crap. You know that ninety percent of the so-called forgotten victims have already got compensation from German public money? There is a common feeling in Germany that it wasn't enough. But the idea they were forgotten is purely American rhetoric."

The German negotiators only seemed to be displaying what Wolfgang Gibowski, spokesman for the German foundation and one of the country's leading opinion pollsters, called Germany's ambivalence toward the Holocaust.

"My opinion is that people are not interested in it," he said. "The public doesn't take a lead on this issue. They don't demand that the companies should participate. The German population is just behaving politically correctly. They agree to what is done, they accept what is done. But my impression is that you can't win over the German population on this issue. They are much more trained than the Swiss population or the Austrian population. They know what is right but they are not enthusiastic."

EIGHTEEN

Claims by Committee

Lawrence Eagleburger launched his insurance commission in late 1998 with high hopes of success. He enjoyed the support of some of Europe's largest insurers as well as several governments, and he believed everything was in place for a sweeping resolution by the end of 2000. But in the time it took Germany to negotiate its $5 billion deal with Holocaust victims around the world, Eagleburger's optimism faded rapidly. In his long and distinguished career in government, the former secretary of state had witnessed some of Europe's most convulsive events—the collapse of the Soviet bloc and the brutal civil war in Yugoslavia. Yet nothing prepared him for the sense of bitterness, injustice, and downright stubbornness that would deadlock his work on wartime insurance.

Unlike the reluctant Paul Volcker before him, who never enjoyed the task of auditing the Swiss banks, Eagleburger hurled himself into the investigation of Europe's insurers with almost missionary zeal. He even surrendered several lucrative posts to take the job, at a time when his physical strength was failing. At sixty-eight, and overweight, he did not enjoy good health and walked only with the aid of canes.

Nevertheless, for Eagleburger the chance of achieving some kind of justice for Holocaust survivors was almost a moral duty. His feelings were shaped by observing the genocide that followed American inaction in the Balkans, and he sensed something similar had happened during World War II. Eagleburger believed that

American isolation and indifference had contributed to the deaths of European Jews attempting to flee the rise of Nazi Germany. The Holocaust was "the West's moral responsibility," he argued. "We had a moral obligation from the beginning of the Holocaust and the whole process of the rise of anti-Semitism in Nazi Germany, which we didn't fulfill," he said. "We either didn't want to hear about it or didn't much care." Now he wanted to make amends for America's mistakes, to redeem the State Department's failings. Looking in the mirror, he felt modern Westerners should say, "There but for the grace of God go we."

Eagleburger seemed the perfect man to lead the complex, international talks. As a Republican, and not Jewish himself, the insurers could hardly claim that he was part of a liberal Jewish conspiracy. He was close to politicians throughout Europe, but he also enjoyed the trust of the Jewish side, counting Edgar Bronfman, a neighbor in Charlottesville, Virginia, among his personal friends. Israelis regarded him as a staunch ally during his time as secretary of state.

However, settling the issue of Holocaust insurance by committee always seemed ambitious. By far the most complicated of any of the restitution campaigns, the problem covered many different companies, and governments, in countries on both sides of the old Iron Curtain. There was no single party with whom the Jewish groups could negotiate. Furthermore, insurance itself was even more complicated than bank accounts or slave labor, with variable premiums and payouts. The chances of any sizeable group of people reaching agreement on a subject so broad and technical seemed minuscule.

But Eagleburger could only move forward with the agreement of all sides in all countries. Under the rubric establishing the International Commission on Holocaust-Era Insurance Claims (ICHEIC), every decision had to be taken by consensus, implying the need for unanimous votes. It was a requirement that almost guaranteed slow and labored progress.

Eagleburger foresaw this problem when he launched the commission and tried to counteract it by creating working groups, each dealing with one of a number of technical insurance issues, hoping this would persuade participants to treat the issues as subjects for dispassionate discussion, not moral debates. He also wanted to avoid the expensive precedent of the Volcker Commission, which had spent more money on auditing the Swiss banks than it found in deposits. Unfortunately, the questions he needed to answer were far more difficult than even those Volcker had faced with the Swiss banks.

Who would be liable for the policies of companies nationalized by the Communists? Were companies morally responsible for "blocked accounts," which they handed to the Nazis under duress? And how much were the policies worth when most were denominated in prewar currencies that collapsed when the Communists took power? Company reserves, also held in those currencies, suffered the same fall in value, arguably justifying a lower payout for claimants. Then there was the question of policies whose premiums were not fully paid. Insurers can legitimately refuse to pay the full value of a policy in this situation, but the case of Holocaust survivors raised moral questions. When incarcerated in ghettos, or shipped to the concentration camps, the victims had no choice but to stop paying premiums. Should not insurers make some allowance for this?

Separate working groups tackled each question and met frequently in the early months of 1999, but after six months of increasingly personal clashes they failed to reach agreement. Eagleburger now grasped that his commission was the result of a shotgun marriage, that the insurers did not want to be there, and that any consensus would have to be imposed by him.

He began to make a series of executive decisions. Crucially, he ruled that companies could be held liable for policies even if their Eastern European subsidiaries had been nationalized after the war. Generali, in particular, had desperately argued against this, but Eagleburger pointed out that in most cases the Communists only nationalized insurance in the late 1940s. The insurers had had a few years to seek out policyholders and make payments before the Communists took control.

On the question of valuation, which proved the most contentious, he decided that Eastern European policies should be valued as if they had been denominated in dollars. In a stroke, Eagleburger thereby canceled out the effects of the postwar collapse of Eastern European currencies. He also imposed an arbitrary minimum: many policies were worth tiny amounts, but he ruled that any justified claimant should receive at least $500.

He kept standards of proof low, and if claimants could make a good case that they had ever held a policy, the onus moved to the company to prove that they had paid out. Although his decisions generally favored the victims over the insurers, the consensus held and no companies chose to leave. But Eagleburger realized that he had very few ways to keep the companies in line, other than threatening to quit—a warning he repeatedly issued to the warring parties inside his commission.

Frustration with Eagleburger's lumbering pace was only worsened by the mounting costs of the whole operation, even though Eagleburger had intended to avoid the excessive costs of the earlier Volcker inquiry into the Swiss banks. The insurers agreed to make a $90 million "good faith" payment before joining, and a first installment of $30 million was placed in a Bermuda trust account, where it started to accumulate interest. The money was meant to show the companies' willingness to pay claims, but within a year, it looked like the commission's own administrative costs would soak it all up.

The companies refused to base any claims-processing center in the United States, even though Eagleburger had set up the commission's headquarters in Washington. They felt this would protect them against U.S. lawsuits and the risk that lawyers would be granted powers of discovery by the courts. So Eagleburger was forced to set up a second office in London, adding fourteen staff to a burgeoning bureaucracy that included a fifteen-strong workforce in Washington and a roster of twenty-four consultants.

Eagleburger's system of working groups required frequent meetings, which took place in different cities, reflecting the international nature of his task. Always behind closed doors, the full commission would meet like a small but subdued United Nations, with rings of seats surrounding the desk where Eagleburger sat. In successive months during 1999, the commission met in good hotels in London, Jerusalem, and Washington. The Westin Fairfax was the favorite haunt in Washington, while in London the commission checked into the Conrad International, a luxury hotel in the Chelsea district. Bills for travel and salaries mounted, as Eagleburger flew first-class between meetings. Observers and alternates, particularly from Israel, swelled the total at each gathering to sixty or seventy people—a hideously expensive undertaking, particularly as many meetings only took two days.

Martin Stern, still doggedly pursuing Generali for his grandfather's insurance policy, watched aghast as dozens of delegates filed into one of the British capital's most expensive hotels. Deeply distrustful as ever, Stern found out the number of Israel Singer's room and sent him a fax from his office, wishing him a good night in his $1,200-a-night suite. In fact Singer, whose expenses were met by his employer Edgar Bronfman, did not claim any money from the commission.

Internal financial documents, however, confirm a picture of excessive spending. From its inception at the end of 1998 to the end of August 31, 2000, the commission spent $571,727 on members' travel. Staff spent a further $645,248 on travel over the same period, while the expense of arranging meetings came to $387,653. Travel to press conferences around the world to unveil the process for policyholders to make claims consumed more than $100,000 in further expenses. The commission spent $8.9 million on an international outreach campaign to publicize its work to potential claimants, including press conferences in Argentina, South Africa, and Australia, and advertising in seventy countries.

Divisions in the Jewish delegation, far different from the group of Israel Singer's loyalists on Volcker's committee, intensified the difficulties. Bobby Brown, adviser to Benjamin Netanyahu, represented the government of Israel, while Holocaust survivors—notable by their absence on the Volcker committee—took the two other Jewish seats. Roman Kent represented the World Jewish Restitution Organization, the umbrella group largely led by the World Jewish Congress that had been set up in the early 1990s to coordinate restitution efforts in Eastern Europe. Moshe Sanbar, who survived Dachau to become the treasurer of the Claims Conference, took the third seat. Stubborn and tough, Sanbar had an intellectual grasp unweakened by advancing years—he was already over seventy when asked to take part in the commission—and refused to follow Israel Singer's line. Sanbar's grasp of the details could intimidate people who tried to negotiate with him, and his position was strengthened by Israel's troubled politics.

Raised in Hungary before the war, Sanbar was seventeen when he entered the camps but survived to emigrate to Israel, where he was wounded during the battle of Latrun in the War of Independence. Both his parents perished in the Holocaust. An unusual figure among Israel's socialist Zionist founders, Sanbar built a career as a banker, running the Bank of Israel, the nation's central bank, in the late 1970s before taking over as chief executive of Bank Leumi, Israel's biggest commercial bank. He now lived a comfortable retirement in a Tel Aviv apartment, surrounded by a collection of carvings of elephants—a sign of his prosperous career.

Sanbar's steely personality revealed itself in a refusal to give any quarter on issues that mattered to him. Disgusted that the Swiss National Bank had escaped without paying anything in the Swiss settlement, he refused to allow any insurer to do the same. "How did these insurance companies become so big?" he asked. "Because they didn't pay back to the owners of the deposits and insurance policies the payments they had to pay."

His career in global finance qualified him to rake through the insurers' books, while his life experiences left him disinclined to trust anyone. For him, the Memorandum of Understanding that founded the commission was a "constitution," which must be followed to the letter. For Sanbar, the measure of Eagleburger's success would be the publication of the names of policyholders who had died in the Holocaust. "Without lists there are no claims," he said. "That means companies have to publish lists of unpaid policies."

Sanbar's personal experience showed why the commission needed to publish lists. His father had been a successful exporter before the war, holding his insurance policies in the family's safe deposit box. But when his older brother escaped the camps and returned home, he found the box had been looted. With no idea which company had insured his father, Sanbar could not press any claim unless a company first published his father's name in a list of unpaid policies.

Also representing survivors' interests on the commission were Chuck Quackenbush and Bill Nelson, the insurance commissioners of California and Florida, respectively. The huge survivor communities in their states pushed for names to be published. In spite of Eagleburger's opposition, both men wrote laws giving them the power to revoke the licenses of European insurers that refused to join the commission or publish names. Eagleburger firmly believed that companies joining his commission deserved "safe harbor" protection from such laws, and he resented the aggressive attitude taken by politicians on both sides of the political divide in California. "I am more than slightly irritated by what I consider to be pure political posturing," he complained. "It irritates me most because I don't know of a better way to get these people paid."

Quackenbush's career on the commission terminated in controversial circumstances in June 2000 when he resigned as California's insurance commissioner under threat of impeachment. He was alleged to have diverted millions of dollars paid by insurers to settle complaints after the 1994 Northridge earthquake into nonprofit foundations that spent much of their money furthering Quackenbush's personal cause. In one case, disbursements had been made to a football camp attended by his children. European insurers noted that Quackenbush had suggested to them that they could make their own separate settlements with California, and the incident did nothing to raise the commission's credibility. Meanwhile, Quackenbush went into exile in Hawaii.

Neil Levin, the insurance superintendent of New York and the Eagleburger Commission's chief architect, had envisaged a lean organization that would make a top-down investigation, assess in broad numbers the total liability of the insurers, and wind up its activities swiftly. But this vision foundered on the determination of the Israeli delegates and his fellow commissioners to investigate from the bottom up, publishing names and examining claims one by one. "We were supposed to take a balanced approach," he said. "We weren't supposed to spend an inordinate amount of money on creating lists. That changed."

Deborah Senn of Washington State, who had clashed with him during the drawn-out campaign that led to the commission's founding, thought Levin's position self-contradictory. "Neil used to talk incessantly about a top-down process," she said, "and I hope I spoke as incessantly about the publication of names. Because if you don't do a bottom-up process, how do you find where the claims are?"

When Levin pointed to the huge fees paid to auditors in the Volcker process, or the risks of letting money seep out in legal fees, Senn would reply, "I agree. I didn't want the money to go to accounting firms any more than to Ed Fagan. But you do have to spend money auditing them to find out what's there."

Herbert Hansmeyer of Allianz sharply disagreed with the notion of creating lists and auditing archives and feared that Eagleburger's work would never finish because of what he dismissed as "the conflict of constituencies making a living out of the process." Like Neil Levin, he had expected the commission to broker a swift "top-down" humanitarian settlement. He said, "If you have people who want to drive meaningful claims processes for the next fifty years, then of course they can make a nice living. They have wonderful reasons to take trips around the world, spend time in expensive hotels, and talk to victims' agencies instead of addressing any issues."

While harboring this underlying contempt, Hansmeyer met with Israel Singer at the Concorde lounge in the Paris airport and made what he thought was a deal with his Jewish opponents. However, once the deal had been signed as part of the slave labor talks in Berlin, he found that Singer could not and did not speak for all his Jewish colleagues.

Moshe Sanbar barely noticed the total of 400 million deutsche marks that German insurers agreed to pay, caring much more about the amounts earmarked for paying claims. The amount paid for Allianz's Italian subsidiary RAS, he said, came to 50 million deutsche marks (about $25 million). The German deal also covered the Eastern European subsidiaries of other German insurers, including Victoria zu Berlin, which was almost as big as RAS and Generali before the war. "RAS and Victoria are between them fifty percent bigger than Generali," fumed Sanbar, who noted that Otto Graf Lambsdorff, the chief German negotiator, was a director of Victoria. Two years earlier, by comparison, Generali had offered $100 million, and it had been held to be insufficient by restitution advocates in Israel. Sanbar bitterly complained that insurance had been "held hostage," as the Jews could not object to the insurance agreement at Berlin without toppling the much larger slave labor deal.

Worse still, Hansmeyer effectively negotiated for all the other German insurers, which had not joined the Eagleburger Commission, to establish their own claims process free from the threat of class action lawsuits. The deal between Singer and Hansmeyer left for later the details of how this would be done, and there was no guarantee that the new German process would even follow Eagleburger's guidelines. No claims could be paid before the Eagleburger process was merged with the new German system, and late in 2001, more than eighteen months after the Berlin settlement, negotiations to bring them together had made no progress.

Other companies now tried to strike their own deals, while efforts to publish names virtually ceased. Only Generali appeared to make a serious attempt to publicize the people who might have a claim against them, publishing almost ten times as many names as the other companies combined. The Jewish side did not believe the other companies were even trying, and so the commission's researchers resorted to scouring state archives in Germany and Austria looking for inventories of names to publish. Thanks to efficient Nazi documentation, they found lists of policies that had been surrendered.

Even this action provoked discord within the commission. In early 2001, Danny Kadden, an aide to Deborah Senn and the son of Holocaust survivors, found his grandfather's name, Hermann Motulsky, on the Eagleburger Web site. It was among some twenty thousand names of Nazi victims discovered by Eagleburger's researchers in German public archives recording stolen insurance policies. Kadden personally obtained his grandfather's files from Hamburg, which included official property declarations required of Jews facing deportation or emigration before the war, and found that Motulsky had reported three insurance policies in early 1938. Later that year, in July, his grandfather was arrested on political charges and imprisoned in the Sachsenhausen concentration camp, prior to Kristallnacht.

On his release in August, Motulsky was given three weeks to put his affairs in order and leave the country, and he surrendered the three policies to pay the required confiscatory flight tax before emigration. Kadden grimly noted that all his actions at this time were under extreme duress as he prepared to abandon his wife and children to save his own life.

Motulsky kept good records and survived the war in Cuba and the United States. His family could find no evidence that he ever received benefits from these policies, and there was no mention of insurance in his application for money from Germany's postwar compensation program. However, just a few weeks after Kadden discovered his grandfather's name on the Eagleburger website, it promptly disappeared. He learned that Allianz had matched the names with German compensation records. It had then successfully lobbied the Eagleburger Commission to remove the names of five thousand people, claiming that the policies were effectively "paid" if the holder had received any government compensation.

But in April, the commission changed course again, deciding it would no longer remove names without evidence that their policies had been specifically compensated by the government. Kadden's grandfather's name was among more than two thousand names restored to the website.

The incident was symptomatic of the Eagleburger Commission's fundamental weakness. Handicapped by the need to secure everyone's agreement, the commission could not compel companies to publish their own names. Deborah Senn found her worst fears confirmed. "To me what's been so astonishing about this process is that the commission has spent money researching Austrian archives to get lists of names of policyholders as opposed to spending time auditing companies and making them disgorge the names," she said. "That's astonishing."

Processing claims also proved maddeningly difficult. Generali, the company most affected, employed more than twenty people full time to check each claim in its "policy information center." Bottlenecks in the commission's London bureaucracy slowed the flow, but by the spring of 2001, they would send about seventy new case files each day to Generali's head office in Trieste, each containing a thick dossier of information about the claimant. By April 2001, Generali's center had a waiting time of three months, mostly due to the difficulty of matching names to their records of policyholders. Generali had typed all the names from the prewar policyholders onto computers, but first and last names—and even place names—might take different spellings. For example, if a claimant named Isaac came forward, Generali's software would search for eighteen different spellings of the name—a tiny subset of the 1,398 variations of the spelling recorded in the archives at the Yad Vashem museum in Jerusalem. Generali policies had been filled out in several languages, and this could affect the way the policyholder's name was spelled.

The company's records detailed the fate of every policy by number, showing when premiums had ceased coming in, and whether a sum had been paid out. But current employees did not know how to use the old ledgers, so Generali rehired a retired actuary to match names to numbers. Every detail could be crucial. For example, if a claimant said she was an only child, and the policy listed a son and daughter as beneficiaries, the claim would be regarded as false.

As time passed, commission officials began to suspect the companies of deliberately ignoring the "relaxed" standards of proof they had negotiated. In one case, the claimant produced a note their mother had handwritten during the war, containing the name of the insurer, currency, policy value, and the dates when the policy started and when premiums ended. The claimant did not, however, have a policy document. The claim was rejected for failing to meet "minimum written evidence." One New York claimant produced a seven-page letter written by the policyholder shortly before they were deported, listing all his assets, including his policies, only to be rejected.

Even well-informed claimants seldom had enough information to find their policy. When Sanbar's form arrived in Tel Aviv, he realized that even he, a bank president who had stayed with his family until the relatively advanced age of seventeen, did not know enough about his family to answer the questions on his own form.

Not surprisingly, the results satisfied nobody. In the first week of 2001, the date when Eagleburger had hoped to disband his commission, Deborah Senn published a damning progress report.

For her, the publication of names was the yardstick. Approximately 40,000 names appeared on Eagleburger's website, more than 30,000 of them culled from German and Austrian state archives. Generali provided 8,740 names and sent far more to Yad Vashem to be matched against the names of known Holocaust survivors and victims. Zurich Group published 20. Winterthur published four. Allianz's RAS published just one name.

Worse still, even those claimants whose family names were published had still not been paid. Seventy percent of "fast-track" claims—a process designed only for those with good documentation—had been denied, as had 95 percent of regular claims. Generali was by now dispensing a steady stream of checks to survivors, as was RAS, albeit to a much lesser extent. But Allianz's record appeared insulting—it had paid no claims at all.

As the delays dragged on, anger with Allianz only intensified, and any appearance of consensus vanished. Herbert Hansmeyer himself, appalled by the infighting among the Jewish delegates, lost any desire to dissemble about his opinions. In May 2001, he said what he thought in an interview in *Forbes* magazine. "Ultimately it is an act of public appeasement," he said. "I cannot become very emotional about insurance claims that are sixty years old."

One of the biggest obstacles to agreement was the question of who would pick up the bill for the whole exercise. Allianz, covered by its separate deal through the German foundation, proved the most difficult problem. In June 2001, Eagleburger received a draft proposal from the German foundation, suggesting that all the expenses that Allianz had ever incurred as part of its membership of his commission should be deducted from the money it had agreed to in Berlin to pay claims. This would reduce the available money from $100 million to just $49 million.

Eagleburger, already exasperated by the insurers' failure to pay claims, thought the German foundation was trying to "dictate" to him, an attitude that he found "arrogant as hell." He refused to accept any of the 400 million deutsche marks the foundation was prepared to pay his commission until the issue was resolved—an attitude that stunned the Germans. It even looked as though the issue might be delivered to the lawyers once more, as they prepared to reopen their litigation against Allianz.

Eagleburger's patience snapped. Having avoided almost any public comment for thirty months, he erupted at a special event to commemorate the fiftieth anniversary of the Claims Conference in Washington in July 2001.

Eagleburger walked laboriously to the podium on his two sticks and started the way he meant to go on. "I should say to you all that this is probably not the best time for me to be appearing before you," he warned, speaking without notes. "You are looking at a person who is so thoroughly frustrated by the activity of the last two years of trying to get some justice done sixty years too late that I am likely to put my foot in my mouth before the day is over here. What the hell?

"I have negotiated at one point or other in my life with the North Vietnamese, with the Soviet Union; you name it, I've met with them. I don't think I found any of them any more difficult or frustrating than have been the companies."

Then he reviewed the claims paying records of the leading insurers which were members of his international commission, before focusing on just one company.

"I told you that Allianz has received 8,473 claims," he said. "How many have they paid as of the third of July? A great big fat zero. Nothing! From the largest German insurance company and the German insurance company that has largely led the way amongst these insurance companies as they have dealt with this issue."

He defended the commission's expenses from the attacks of "pipsqueak journalists" before treating his audience to a fresh insight about the insurance industry.

"I found during this exercise that—I think it's part of their character—insurance companies just don't like to pay claims. I hadn't really thought that before. I sure as hell think that now."

In the Crossfire

W hile most of the European insurance industry attracted the ire of Lawrence Eagleburger and the Jewish groups, one insurer largely escaped reproach. Generali, the first to prompt public attacks for its failure to pay the debts of the Holocaust, had set about changing the script. While once it had treated its accusers with legalistic disdain, now it took the lead in paying families of Holocaust victims, going out of its way to cooperate with Eagleburger's process for settling claims.

The man responsible for Generali's new respectability was one of its most senior executives, Giovanni Perissinotto. Tapped to handle the Holocaust scandal after the collapse of the company's first settlement with the class action lawyers, Perissinotto soon recognized that Generali could no longer treat its problem as a legal one. "I wanted simply to prove that even such thorny issues could be solved with goodwill," Perissinotto said. "I forgot as much as I could about the legalistic approaches."

Perissinotto threw his company into the work of the Eagleburger Commission, where it soon established a reputation as the company that published the most names, provided the most help to claimants, and paid out the most money. But he also launched a series of parallel negotiations with the company's other critics in the Jewish world—a daunting diplomatic challenge for a career insurance executive. A small and unassuming man in his forties who had spent his entire career at Generali, Perissinotto looked much younger than his age. With a disarming charm and a deceptively sharp business brain, he set about tacking a new course for Generali. He strongly believed in his company's presence in Israel after spending months there negotiating the acquisition of Migdal, Israel's largest insurer, and impressed almost all of the Jewish leaders who met him with his calm and open demeanor. But he lacked powerful friends—while Allianz had the German government fighting for its interests, the Italian government never took a significant role.

Perissinotto looked elsewhere for allies and soon found one in the shape of a New York lawyer: Kenneth Bialkin, senior partner at the powerful Manhattan legal firm of Skadden, Arps, Slate, Meagher and Flom. A Wall Street heavyweight who sat on the board of Citigroup, the world's largest financial company, Bialkin had engineered a series of huge mergers and acquisitions. More important, he counted several former Israeli prime ministers among his friends and had served as head of both the Anti-Defamation League and the Conference of Presidents of Leading American Jewish Organizations, giving him credentials as a Jewish leader as strong as Edgar Bronfman's. Bialkin feared that Bronfman and Singer's aggressive campaign for restitution, complete with sanctions and boycott threats, reduced the Holocaust to a "billing exercise." A small and dapper gray-haired man in his sixties, Bialkin cultivated a reserved charm that he used with equal success on Wall Street financiers and Zionist leaders. His decision to help Generali created shock waves on the Jewish side.

"We want to do this because our name is on those policies and we want to look ourselves and our children in the eye," Perissinotto told Bialkin. Reassured, Bialkin studied the facts and grew more hawkish than his client.

"The more I got into it," Bialkin said, "the more I felt that Generali and others were being pressed and tarred with the anathema of the Holocaust and asked to pay money which they didn't owe, in amounts which bore no relationship to what was fair. I saw there was a kind of terror in the community. All you had to do was accuse someone of some peripheral involvement in World War II and they bring their attitude toward the Holocaust to anyone who is so accused."

He thought that by agreeing to be bound by Eagleburger,

Generali showed that it would make payments as a moral gesture and that the time had come for careful and detailed compromises over technical issues like valuation. Instead, as Bialkin recounted, he was received with outrage. His erstwhile Israeli colleagues would respond, "How can you say that when all of these people died in concentration camps?"

Bialkin grew increasingly angered. "These people weren't treated badly by Axa, Generali, or Allianz," he said. "They were badly treated by the forces of the Third Reich. I went to some of those early meetings with some of these executives from Generali and other companies, many of whom weren't even born when the war ended, and some of my colleagues were addressing them as though it was 1943."

Unlike the other companies, Generali also had a problem outside the Eagleburger process: the indefatigable Martin Stern, who ambushed Bialkin when negotiators on Eagleburger's commission visited Yad Vashem, Israel's main Holocaust museum. Stern, who lived within walking distance, had already been ordered out of Yad Vashem's lecture hall when he tried to attend the commission's meeting there. Stern felt that Generali would never have agreed to make payments without his own efforts and angrily took refuge in the Hall of Remembrance, a virtually holy spot where an eternal flame burns for Holocaust victims and visitors are required to cover their heads. As Yad Vashem's staff approached, he reassured them, "Even I wouldn't make a scene here. My grandparents were killed."

Instead he lay in wait for Bialkin at the cavernous opening of the children's memorial, possibly the most moving site within Yad Vashem, where visitors walk out of the Jerusalem sunshine into a submerged tunnel. Multiple mirrors give a visitor the impression of being surrounded by candle flames and photographs of children who perished. The effect can be overwhelming by the time visitors reemerge into dazzling sunlight.

Hanging on the edge of the group as it entered the tunnel, Stern positioned himself at Bialkin's shoulder. As they reached the sunlight, Stern cleared his throat. "Mr. Bialkin, that was very moving, wasn't it?" he said. Bialkin nodded.

Then Stern offered his hand. "And my name's Martin Stern."

Bialkin, who had realized that Stern was on his shoulder, paled and nodded. The two did not shake hands.

Stern did not confine himself to the public confrontation of a face-to-face encounter. To their campaign of media invective, the Stern family added legal punch in California. In early 1998, Stern's sister-in-law Lisa, a California attorney, joined Bill Shernoff, one of the best-known insurance lawyers in California, in filing suit against Generali, calling for a jury trial and demanding $135 million damages. The lawsuit recited in relentless detail the company's acrimonious correspondence with the Sterns and Guido Pastori's initial denial that the company had any record of Mor Stern's policy.

To strengthen the case's chances, Shernoff also helped draft a law in the California legislature—the Holocaust Victims Insurance Act—to extend the statute of limitations to allow individuals to bring Holocaust-related insurance claims until the year 2010. Marvin Hier, dean of the Los Angeles–based Simon Wiesenthal Center and a friend of the Sterns, maintained the pressure on the state's politicians, still led at the time by Republican insurance commissioner Chuck Quackenbush, and the bill was soon passed into law.

Shernoff had grown rich suing insurance companies in "bad faith" lawsuits, using the California statutes under which extra damages could be extracted from insurers if they had shown bad faith in declining to pay a claim. He sued Generali on four counts: breach of good faith and fair dealing, breach of contract, unfair competition, and spoliation of evidence. Shernoff asked for $10 million to cover the value of Mor Stern's policy and $125 million in punitive and exemplary damages, including treble punitive damages for the three Holocaust survivors who were still alive— Adolf, Edith, and Celia.

Bialkin knew that this was lethal. It was far more deadly than the class action lawsuit Ed Fagan had launched on the other coast, which lacked hard evidence and was governed by relatively lenient New York law. A California jury could easily award $100 million in damages and set a precedent for other claimants. Privately Bialkin harbored doubts about the strength of the Sterns' case. The Nazis had taken control of Generali's offices in occupied territories when Italy left the war, so whoever was running the Prague office at the time, it was not Generali. Added to that, Mor Stern's policy clearly stated that there would be no payout until 1949, twenty years after he had started paying the premiums, even if he died before then. Even if Adolf Stern had produced his father's death certificate on his famous trip to Prague, the insurers would have told him to go away for four years.

But these doubts were irrelevant in the reality of California in 1999. Bialkin knew he could never let this lawsuit reach court and had to negotiate a settlement. A few legal maneuvers removed the judge slated to adjudicate the case, but it was hard to find someone who negotiated for the Sterns, as Martin Stern and his family's lawyer were not on the same page.

Martin Stern had so far enjoyed running what was virtually a one-man campaign against Generali. Before his sister-in-law teamed up with Bill Shernoff, he had asked for the advice of Sam Dubbin, an attorney who worked for survivor groups in Miami, about a possible lawsuit there. Southern Florida, where Martin's Uncle Adolf kept a winter home among a large community of Holocaust survivors, would have made an attractive legal venue. Martin was taken aback when Shernoff brought suit on his behalf and was surprised when Shernoff found extra plaintiffs in California with similar complaints against Generali. Stern dismissed them as "hitchhikers."

Moreover, Stern could not stomach the 40 percent legal fees that Shernoff was proposing to charge. After tentative talks with Bank Leumi officials in Israel, he agreed to meet directly with Generali's Giovanni Perissinotto. When the Eagleburger Commission rolled in to Jerusalem for a meeting in the summer of 1999, Stern went to meet Perissinotto in the foyer of the Jerusalem Hilton, a sweeping, modern glass-walled hotel offering a serene view over Jerusalem's Old City.

The two men instantly struck up a rapport, and Perissinotto succeeded in charming his company's most obdurate adversary. Their talk lasted longer than planned, while Generali officials stalked nearby looking at their watches. After exchanging telephone numbers, Perissinotto closed proceedings with a wink, and said, "You can see my associates are looking at me, because the clock is against us."

Both gladly excluded Shernoff from their discussions, and a deal took shape swiftly over a series of telephone conversations: the Stern family would receive $1.25 million in return for promising that the amount would remain confidential. Perissinotto assured Stern that the company would publish the names of any new unclaimed policies it found, and added his most important condition—that Stern would shut up. Martin Stern had become the greatest public relations nightmare in the company's history and $1.25 million was a small price to pay for his silence. The three elders of the family, as he requested, would receive the most.

Stern was letting off Generali very lightly given the scale of the damages that might have been awarded by a California jury. But he felt that holding out for the maximum possible settlement would set a bad precedent for future claimants. To push for more would make it harder for anybody else—with less well documented claims—to get a hearing from an insurance company.

Martin Stern enjoyed dealing with Perissinotto and was soon on first-name terms with him and other Generali managers, even helping them to plan their vacations. But he still found Shernoff's contingency fees unsightly and asked if the case could be settled without reference to his lawyers. Bialkin patiently explained to him that in the American system, any legal settlement needed a lawyer to sign it. Stern then tried to persuade Shernoff to give the money to charity and after this suggestion was laughed down, returned to Perissinotto to negotiate a 20 percent fee for his lawyer. According to Shernoff, California courts commonly award contingency fees of 33 to 40 percent in bad-faith cases. At the same time, Generali agreed to settle with the other California plaintiffs Shernoff had found, for which he received his normal contingency fee.

Shernoff alerted other members of the Stern family that if they were prepared to wait months or years they could win much more, but they preferred not to wait. "I told him that it's already too late and too little," Edith Stern said. "I'm seventy-two years old and I'm not the healthiest person. It's better to have a bird in the basket than ten in the tree."

Adolf Stern, whose story had sparked the lawsuit, had similar reasoning. "I have had a heart attack," he said. "I don't want to be aggravated all my life."

While Perissinotto's charm succeeded in calming the voluble Martin Stern, he still had to fashion an accommodation for Generali with the broader Jewish establishment, and for this he leaned heavily on the doughty Kenneth Bialkin. Once the German insurers made their own separate peace in Berlin, Bialkin decided the best way to cut through the warring factions on the Eagleburger Commission was to deal directly with Edgar Bronfman and Israel Singer, who were happy to talk to him. Bialkin, relying on Bronfman's political clout, prepared a grand meeting.

In June 2000, Bronfman hosted Perissinotto for dinner in his private dining room at the Seagram Building, where they dined under the profound stare of abstract paintings by Mark Rothko. Bronfman sat at the center of one side of the table, flanked as ever by Israel Singer. Perissinotto sat alongside a retinue of fellow managers from Trieste, along with Bialkin. They were accompanied by the ailing seventy-four-year-old Dov Levin, who chaired the Generali Trust in Israel, charged with distributing the $12 million the company had offered to Holocaust survivors three years earlier.

The discussion was cordial and businesslike. Overruling Bialkin's lower offer, Perissinotto proposed paying $100 million to settle the issue—exactly the sum Generali had offered to settle the class action lawsuit in New York two years earlier. That would be on top of the $12 million the company paid into the Generali Trust in Israel. They would continue to do whatever the Eagleburger Commission asked of them and would pay the money through the Generali Trust. The symbolism of giving control over the claims to a Jewish-controlled body in Jerusalem overseen by Levin—an Israeli supreme court judge—appealed to Bronfman and his friends.

Sensing a rare opportunity to make a Holocaust settlement with goodwill on both sides, Bronfman decided not to bargain hard. "We would have lost the moral high ground if we had kept on haggling. And the moral high ground is so important," he commented later.

All they needed now was to win over Lawrence Eagleburger. When the commission met in London the following month, they gained his approval "subject to the consent" of the other commissioners. It looked as though Generali had at last cut the Gordian knot of the Eagleburger Commission and found a way to settle its debts. They still needed to dress up the deal correctly, however. By adding the $100 million to the expenses Generali had already paid, and to the $12 million in the Generali Trust, they could label it a $150 million settlement.

With this, Elan Steinberg of the World Jewish Congress emerged from a side meeting room to announce the breakthrough. Generali had agreed to pay $150 million to settle its Holocaust debts, he said. The State Department would be asked to file a statement with the U.S. courts, similar to the document recently filed in the German deal, stating that this settlement was the "exclusive legal remedy" for all Holocaust-era insurance claims against the company.

But once Kenneth Bialkin circulated a draft of the agreement, a new bout of warfare opened between the Jewish factions on Eagleburger's commission. In Tel Aviv, Moshe Sanbar vowed not to allow Generali to escape the same way that Allianz had done. He had refused to attend the dinner in Bronfman's private dining room as it clashed with a ceremony in which he would receive an honorary doctorate from Bar-Ilan University, and nothing—not even Singer's offer of a private jet to shuttle him to New York and back—would dissuade him.

Bialkin's draft agreement made him see red. Sanbar found the agreement vague and empty of detail. The lack of definition meant that Generali could escape its obligations by exploiting legal loopholes. Sanbar rallied all the Israelis on the commission behind him.

Once more, Generali was caught in the crossfire between the American and Israeli Jewish communities. Following the election

of Ehud Barak, diaspora affairs were in the hands of Michael Melchior, a left-wing Orthodox rabbi and friend of Edgar Bronfman.
He also had problems with the settlement as it was presented, not
least because the Generali Trust had discredited itself in Israel. Its
managers, appointed by Avraham Ravitz, the ultra-Orthodox
chair of the Knesset finance committee, were themselves mostly
ultra-Orthodox. The Israeli press feasted on the discovery that the
trust had chosen to advertise its humanitarian services only by a
mikvah, or ceremonial bath, in Bnei Barak, an ultra-Orthodox
community outside Tel Aviv. It readily handed out money for dental treatment to ultra-Orthodox claimants born years after the war
but was painfully slow to handle claims from survivors, with its five
trustees meeting only once every two months. By the beginning of
2000, the Generali Trust had dealt with 72 claimants on insurance
policies, out of 1,250 it had received. Meanwhile, it had made 271
"humanitarian" payments, often for dental work. Ironically,
Israeli lawyers pushing the claims of survivors had more faith in
Generali's own operation in Trieste than they did in the Israeli-
run operation in Jerusalem.

Arie Zuckerman, the twenty-nine-year-old lawyer Melchior
appointed to monitor the insurance commission, suspected that
paying through the Generali Trust was a way to allow Generali to
walk away from the problem. Under Eagleburger's system, the
trust did not process any claims but merely passed them on to Trieste, where researchers had access to the company's full archives.
Zuckerman turned against the trust: "Just to have Jews give
refusals to Jews isn't the idea that we wanted."

Legal peace posed a further problem. Bialkin wanted the same
protection for Generali from the American courts that had previously been extended to German industry and proposed that the
Eagleburger Commission, alongside the Clinton administration,
should recommend dismissal of future lawsuits. A year later, Sanbar was still fuming at the temerity of this request: "Generali said
they wanted that we should protect them in the courts, *against survivors.* Against claimants! We could not do that. We could not go
to court against Jewish people and defend Generali, especially if
the agreement was wrong."

Sanbar rallied his forces, and Perissinotto was summoned to a meeting in Jerusalem with a group of Israeli leaders, which ended with a draft compromise. Then Perissinotto signed a contract enshrining his version of the settlement with Bronfman, Singer, and Eagleburger, prompting an angry Melchior to tell his friends in the United States that they had no right to sign an agreement on behalf of the Jewish people without involving the State of Israel.

At the demand of Sanbar and the Israelis, the Jewish negotiators wrote Perissinotto a letter to say that their settlement would not stand. Even an embarrassed Israel Singer, the creator of the settlement, was obliged to sign it, as it became obvious that he could not win around his Israeli allies, including Moshe Sanbar. Singer, accustomed to the world of U.S. business where negotiators would shake hands and sort out the details later, found the episode deeply embarrassing. He later commented, "When you agree that you have settled you try to make it work, and the war is over even if you don't like the settlement. That's the thing my colleagues didn't understand."

Bialkin knew all about the fragmentation of Jewish politics, but the scale of the internecine warfare astonished him. Bemused, he tried to remonstrate with Sanbar: "How can you delay? You saw that Singer said okay."

Sanbar, the seasoned businessman now in control of the situation, replied, "You know better than I do. This is a parliament. You have to deal with all of us."

Sanbar and Zuckerman came to form an unlikely but effective team: Zuckerman, a religious man representing a socialist government, was young enough to be the grandson of Sanbar, the survivor of Dachau and former international banker, who became his mentor. With the Israeli delegates plainly representing the strongest opposition to Generali's proposed settlement, Zuckerman decided to go early to November's meeting of the Eagleburger Commission in Rome, taking Sanbar with him. In a Rome hotel, the two Israelis negotiated with a team of six Italians, led by Giovanni Perissinotto. Both sides arrived with draft agreements, and Sanbar characteristically refused to yield on the details that mattered to him. Zuckerman let Sanbar do most of the talking but persistently argued that $100 million was less than the sum Jews were owed as policyholders.

Perissinotto shot back with a fundamental point: "You know and I know that the claims won't reach more than $25 million," he said. "That means I'm giving you $75 million for humanitarian purposes. If you don't cut a deal here, you lose $75 million because I'll never give that much for humanitarian purposes."

He was, however, prepared to make a further concession: if claims exceeded $100 million, Generali would pay the extra. Perissinotto thought this would never happen, but he needed a fixed amount to report to shareholders and insisted that it did not appear in the signed agreement. The Jewish side could now sign the agreement confident that they would never have to turn away a claimant.

Late in the evening, they shook hands. Once more, Perissinotto thought he had reached a deal. The headline of $100 million was the same, but Sanbar had ensured that they filled in far more details, to his satisfaction. Zuckerman and Sanbar retired to bed, while Perissinotto phoned Kenneth Bialkin, six time zones away in New York. After the call, Perissinotto phoned Zuckerman in his room to tell him the news was still bad: Bialkin could not get the legal peace he wanted and the deal could not be finalized.

The next day, however, the final details fell into place. Singer, predictably apoplectic to hear the Israelis had held talks without him, arrived to watch Moshe Sanbar resolve the final issues—covering Generali's contribution to the expenses of the commission—to his satisfaction. Generali at last had a settlement approved by the commission. Bronfman signed it on behalf of global Jewry.

This was now the fifth separate time the company believed it had settled with its accusers since 1997. It appeared that Giovanni Perissinotto's new approach of attempting to win his accusers over with goodwill had finally worked.

Any such hopes were soon dashed. Instead, the settlement merely provided a new target for those critics of Generali who had not been involved in signing it. Martin Stern may have settled with the company himself, but he still had no intention of meekly accepting any agreement signed by Edgar Bronfman. Convinced that the Jewish *machers* he always distrusted had taken advantage of his campaign to enrich themselves, he renewed his stream of invective against the Generali Trust, and he even persuaded his friend in the Knesset, Michael Kleiner, to hold a new hearing reexamining Generali's latest settlement. Held on September 12, 2001, the day after the destruction of the World Trade Center, the meeting failed to gain the oxygen of publicity, but it showed that Generali still had committed critics in Israel.

More dangerous for Generali was the prospect of renewed legal action. Ever since the setting up of the Eagleburger Commission in late 1998, lawyers had effectively been frozen out of the action. But the lawsuit *Cornell v Generali*, filed by Ed Fagan four years earlier, had still not been dismissed. Unnoticed by the press, the commission had compensated Marta Cornell, Fagan's lead plaintiff, by paying her $75,000 for her father's policy. Nevertheless, Generali remained at risk of legal action until Judge Mukasey, presiding over the case in Manhattan, could be persuaded to dismiss the suit.

The class action lawyers, believing that politicians had squeezed them out of the process only to set up an inferior body, had no intention of letting Generali off the hook. As one lawyer put it: "We're certainly not going to roll over and say we'll accept a deal negotiated by Edgar Bronfman." They particularly disliked the idea that any money not used to pay claims could be left to the discretion of Jewish organizations. Bob Swift, one of the leading attorneys, made the aims clear: "What we want is to maximize the amount of money that gets into the hands of beneficiaries and heirs, as opposed to some discretionary fund for insurance commissioners and NGOs to decide how it should be distributed."

At the same time, the Sterns' California lawyer, Bill Shernoff, launched his own new lawsuit. *Haberfeld v Generali* sued Generali for inducing claimants to accept payouts under the Eagleburger formula when they could have won more in the California courts.

Suing on behalf of an elderly Holocaust survivor who had been offered $500, Shernoff's true target was the Eagleburger Commission itself, which he considered "little more than a trade association for European insurers."

"To date," he said, "[the commission] has spent more than $30 million on administrative expenses, and requested another $60 million, while paying out only about $3 million through its claims process."

For Shernoff, the legal point was clear: Generali could not use the Eagleburger Commission to force claimants to sign away their rights to sue in U.S. courts. Shernoff called Generali's offer "unreasonably low" because it failed to tell his client that under California law, she could sue in addition for emotional distress and punitive damages. The commission's bureaucracy did not help by sending his client, Felicia Haberfeld, a letter wrongly stating: "The company you named in your claim form [Generali] is unfamiliar to us."

Martin Stern had now come full circle. As the complaint fed out of his fax machine in the small hours of the Jerusalem morning, he resolved to defend Generali and did not retire to bed until he had found ten points on which he could challenge his former lawyer. He was further enraged to discover that Shernoff had hired Michael Ovitz—the Hollywood "superagent" who was once president of Walt Disney—to sell the rights for a movie based on the Holocaust litigation.

Not that Stern had any sympathy for Eagleburger's commission. Recalling how its members shuffled in and out of exclusive hotels in London, he said, "It's only because of these people's greed that Shernoff has a chance to get back into this."

Stern, pilloried by the Jewish establishment for his bizarre antics and outspoken attacks, still had every reason to be pleased with the impact of his campaign. "Lunacy works," he said. By keeping up the volume of his attacks, he had helped force the company into going much further than most of its peers in helping Holocaust survivors.

Generali's harassed executives could only agree up to a point. Stern's campaign of invective had pushed the company onto the defensive, but now it seemed as if nobody could bring themselves to end the ceaseless negotiations. Whether driven by animosity or avarice, Generali's accusers showed no sign of reconciliation after five years of negotiations.

One Generali manager laughed when he stumbled across a comment by William Sloane Coffin, the former dean of the Yale Divinity School. His words seemed to fit Generali's experience perfectly: "No good deed goes unpunished."

Freedom Fighting

For Israel Singer, one country stood out among the European nations that had failed to settle the debts of the Holocaust. Austria—the homeland of his parents—was a burning symbol of the Europe he sorely wanted to confront. Singer had grown up hearing tales of the anti-Semitic mob that had humiliated his parents on the streets of Vienna and had celebrated as German soldiers swept across the country in March 1938. Two generations later, Singer felt the searing experience almost as keenly as if he had been forced to flee himself. With Austria, it was not merely a question of compensation for historic crimes. At the start of the new millennium, the nation was flirting with the far right once again in the form of Jörg Haider, the demagogic leader of the Freedom Party. This time, Singer felt driven to pursue not only the sins of the past but also the sins of the present day.

"Austria, the home of my parents, has a special place in my heart," Singer told a congregation of Holocaust survivors in a Manhattan synagogue in early 2000. "I always felt uniquely warmly toward that country which made my father clean the streets. Those who do not take the election of Haider seriously are people who do not understand what it is that we have been dealing with.

"We are in an educational process that has been going on for fifty years. Only because of our failure have they been able to elect someone like that. It's because we didn't speak up in the 1950s or the 1960s because of the cold war, or in the 1980s because of the Soviet Jews. The only way to treat anti-Semites is to unmask them.

The Holocaust is not over as long as the truth is not told. This is about the truth."

With Switzerland and France, Singer had struggled to turn the war years into a contemporary political battle. But with Austria, the world's leaders were ready to launch an offensive of their own. In January 2000, on a typically deep-frozen winter's day in Sweden, Singer sat alongside some of Europe's most respected leaders at an ambitious conference on Holocaust remembrance and education. The audience—including Chancellor Gerhard Schröder of Germany and President Václav Havel of the Czech Republic—was gathered inside Stockholm's conference hall when news broke of the imminent collapse of Austria's government and Haider's role in forming a new coalition to take power.

The conference opened with a stark monologue by a child Holocaust survivor, before the burly Swedish Prime Minister Göran Persson strode to a steel-encased podium. Raising a smooth stone in his right hand, he explained he was holding a memento from the Holocaust museum in Washington. Inscribed on the stone was a single word: "Remember." Persson then held aloft another stone in his left hand. This stone was rough and sharp. It was collected by a friend near some old railroad tracks, close to a transit camp in Poland—a stopping point on the way to Sobibor or Belzec.

"Have you seen the neo-Nazis marching, the symbols of hatred on jackets and walls? Have you realized what evil view of humanity guides some of the new political parties now gaining ground? Have you noticed how the Holocaust deniers are spreading their lies?

"I know you have."

Persson's message about Haider was unmistakable. The sight of one of Europe's extreme right-wing parties entering power raised the specter of January 30, 1933, when Adolf Hitler was sworn in as chancellor of Germany.

Haider was no Hitler. But he had earned international notoriety in 1991 for endorsing the Nazis' labor policies and lavishing praise on Hitler's war veterans, including members of the SS, four years later. He described the Mauthausen concentration camp as a "punishment camp," suggesting that its victims were criminals.

He later apologized for his remarks, saying that Nazism was not part of his personal values. Nevertheless, his appeal in Austria stemmed from his nakedly nationalistic agenda, including vocal attacks on immigrants. His party also possessed a long record as a natural home for former Nazis. In 1975, the Austrian Nazi-hunter Simon Wiesenthal uncovered the party's leader, Friedrich Peter, as a member of an SS extermination squad responsible for widespread civilian killings in Poland and Russia. The fresh-faced Haider, the son of proud Nazi parents, rebuilt his party with a new appeal—to shake up the moribund "grand coalition" of parties from the left and right that had held on to power for most of the postwar years.

News of the Freedom Party's elevation to government electrified the somber Stockholm conference. Hours before the opening ceremony, the Israeli and Swedish prime ministers sat together for a press conference in almost identical dark funereal suits. After ten minutes of questions about the Middle East peace process, they took a question from an Israeli television reporter about Haider's party joining the Austrian government.

"The European Union is a union consisting of values—values about tolerance and human rights. The program that is the foundation for this party in Austria is not aligned with those values," Persson began, warning that it was a challenge not just for Austria but also the European Union. "It's serious and we are very much, very much worried."

The Israeli prime minister added that Austria was not the only country where the far right was making electoral gains. "We see it as highly relevant to the conference today," said Ehud Barak. "I believe that for every Jew in the world, and of course for every Israeli, it's a highly disturbing signal. It touches every one of us. It will influence our position toward Austria and we will not be able to ignore it."

Their warnings helped to shape an extraordinary reaction by Europe's leaders to Vienna's political turmoil. As they gathered in Stockholm, they decided the new Austrian government would be tested as much by its attitudes to the country's past as by its policies for the present. Toward the end of the conference's first day, Austria's outgoing Social Democratic chancellor, Viktor Klima, delivered a heavy-hearted speech. Lifting his reading glasses to his head, he wagged his finger as he admonished his fellow Austrian leaders back home.

"The Holocaust is not only the worst crime of the twentieth century; it is one of the most monstrous crimes in the whole history of mankind. As an Austrian politician, especially in these days when we have fought very hard to avoid a government including the Freedom Party of Mr. Haider, I want to underline this sentence. Anyone who does not say this clearly and unambiguously is unsuitable to be entrusted with any responsible public position, either national or international.

"One of the standards by which the next Austrian federal government will be judged internationally is how sensitively and fittingly it addresses these difficult and painful questions of Austria's Nazi past."

The following week, the European Union took the unprecedented step of seeking to block the formation of one of its own democratically elected governments. If the Freedom Party joined the Austrian government, the EU would adopt diplomatic sanctions by ending bilateral relations with Vienna.

A day later, the Freedom Party entered the new government led by Wolfgang Schüssel of the conservative People's Party. Haider remained outside the government, but his party colleagues held the ministries of finance, defense, justice, and social affairs. Israel promptly withdrew its ambassador from Vienna. The United States was more cautious, temporarily recalling its ambassador and limiting contacts with Austrian officials. Secretary of State Madeleine Albright condemned any party that failed to "distance itself clearly from the atrocities of the Nazi era and the politics of hate."

In Austria, the reaction to the world's condemnation was as righteously indignant as the European Union's. Schüssel professed to be baffled by the EU's failure to consult with Austria before threatening sanctions. After all, the EU had not acted against the Italian government in 1994 when it included the far-right Northern League, led by the populist Umberto Bossi whose anti-immigrant outbursts arguably exceeded Haider's. The parliamentary leader of Schüssel's party, Andreas Khol, argued that the sanctions were a humiliating insult. "We are treated like a colony," said Khol. "France would never accept such treatment. Italy, never. Spain, never. Germany, maybe."

As for Haider himself, the rabble-rouser's reaction sounded muted by comparison. Most observers predicted that any new round of elections would catapult his party to the top. "I am somewhat horrified how lightly one takes democracy in a country such as Austria," he noted.

Inside the new chancellor's office in Ballhausplatz across the street from the Habsburgs' sprawling palace, Schüssel was deep in talks with his foreign policy advisers. Hans Winkler, legal adviser to the foreign ministry, had accompanied Schüssel's predecessor to the Stockholm conference and realized that the new government needed to stanch the bleeding quickly. Other countries had already tackled their failure to compensate Holocaust victims fully. Austria must soon follow suit. Here was the chance for the new government to build some degree of trust by accepting Jewish demands to compensate Holocaust victims. Winkler offered Schüssel's government a relatively painless solution.

"It will really help if this government shows immediately that it cares about these questions," he said. "We should say that we not only seek a long-term process of negotiations but will do something immediately for the surviving victims."

Schüssel seized the moment enthusiastically. Within hours of his swearing in, he dashed off a letter to Israel Singer and the Claims Conference in New York. Enclosing a copy of the new government's principles, he promised rapid "interim" payments to needy Holocaust survivors, well before the full findings of Austria's historical commission. The letter was so rushed that it was sent before the chancellor's stationery, with his official government letterhead, had yet been printed.

"The federal government works for an Austria in which xenophobia, anti-Semitism and racism have no place," the new government declared. "Austria accepts her responsibility arising out of the tragic history of the 20th century and the horrendous crimes of the National Socialist regime."

Israel Singer was unimpressed. "They want to pay the Jews now. But there should be no arrangement of legal closure as long as this government is in power," he said. "Even if it's more money, who cares? This government could last for three years. It's a corrupt place and they're corrupt people."

It all felt unnervingly familiar in Austria—the international condemnation, the dark talk about its Nazi past, and the knee-jerk response to foreign meddling. Fourteen years earlier, almost to the day, the *New York Times* ran a front-page story about the wartime record of a candidate for the Austrian presidency. Kurt Waldheim, former secretary-general of the United Nations, had served in German army units responsible for brutal campaigns against Yugoslav partisans and the mass deportation of Greek Jews. Waldheim, running in a close race against a socialist rival, had concealed his wartime service, for which he was decorated by Croatia's puppet fascist regime. He also claimed he knew nothing of the deportations, despite working for General Alexander Lohr, an Austrian executed as a war criminal in Belgrade in 1947. While Waldheim was not accused of taking part in atrocities, he was charged with working as an intelligence agent and interpreter, where he knew the full scale of the war crimes taking place around him. The *Times* based its story on archival documents unearthed by the World Jewish Congress and quoted Edgar Bronfman saying Waldheim would never have risen to the top of the UN if his full war record had been known.

The Waldheim affair prompted a worldwide scandal. Within six weeks, the small Nazi-hunting office inside the Reagan administration's Justice Department recommended barring Waldheim from entering the United States. Its recommendations were based on findings after the war by both the Yugoslav and UN war crimes commissions that Waldheim should face charges as a war criminal.

The West German chancellor, Helmut Kohl, rode to Waldheim's defense. He castigated an arrogant younger generation for tarring the name of his "old personal friend" and warmly endorsed his presidential campaign. Waldheim even won limited support from the most unexpected quarter. Simon Wiesenthal condemned the World Jewish Congress for meddling in Austrian politics, having concluded that Waldheim had lied about his war record but was no war criminal. When Waldheim won the presidential election in June 1986, his opponent blamed the World Jewish Congress for creating a nationalist backlash that had led directly to his defeat.

That was not the end of the Waldheim affair. Almost a year later, the Reagan administration accepted the recommendation of its Nazi-hunting office and placed Waldheim on a list barring him from entering the United States—the first head of state in the world on a watch list at America's borders. In his 1996 autobiography, Waldheim blamed the campaign against him on a conspiracy involving American Jews.

For Austrians, the Waldheim affair was a shameful intrusion into its domestic politics by foreign elements, particularly in America. But it was also a cathartic moment that would reshape its self-styled image of the war years. Martin Eichtinger had just joined the Austrian Foreign Ministry when news of Waldheim's past broke. Several months before Waldheim left office in 1992, Eichtinger arrived in Washington as head of the Austrian embassy's information service.

"I think it was an enormous disappointment to all Austrians and to me, as well," he recalled. "In Austria after the war, we owed so much to the U.S.—our freedom and protection during the cold war, as well as the Marshall Plan and the whole reconstruction of Austria. Austrians had an extremely favorable attitude toward the U.S.

"But it was also a defining moment for Austria because it really began the most incredible, profound treatment and analysis of Austria's role in the Nazi regime."

For Ernst Sucharipa, director of Vienna's diplomatic academy, the Waldheim affair also shaped Austria's foreign policy for decades to come. Sucharipa had worked with Waldheim at the UN in the late 1970s and returned there after the crisis ended in the early 1990s. "It became very clear to me that this was one of— if not the major issue for Austrian foreign policy in general and for the repeated 'image crises' we seemed to be incurring.

"It would have happened without Waldheim. But the fact is that Waldheim triggered a soul-searching exercise among official Austrians."

Once Waldheim left office in 1992, Austria's official reevaluation of its wartime past began in earnest. As the fiftieth anniversary of the end of the war approached, Waldheim's successor, Thomas Klestil, visited the Israeli parliament to demolish the myth of Austria's war years.

"We know full well that all too often we have only spoken of Austria as the first state to have lost its freedom and independence to National Socialism, and far too seldom of the fact that many of the worst henchmen in the Nazi dictatorship were Austrians," he said in Jerusalem in November 1994. "And no word of apology can ever expunge the agony of the Holocaust. On behalf of the Republic of Austria, I bow my head with deep respect and profound emotion in front of the victims."

As for compensation, Klestil promised a new fund for Nazi victims, which would become Austria's National Fund, paying lump sums of up to 210,000 schillings to Nazi victims.

"We know full well that for far too long we have not done enough, and not always the right thing, to alleviate the plight of the survivors of the Jewish tragedy and the victims' descendants. And we know that for far too long we have neglected those Jewish Austrians who were forced to leave their native land, humiliated and embittered."

Austria's wartime attitude to its Jewish population was indisputably atrocious. It was not just that both Hitler and Adolf Eichmann, the architect of the Final Solution, were Austrian. When German troops streamed into Austria on March 12, 1938, Hitler received a delirious welcome in every town he visited. "I have in the course of my struggle won much love from my people," Hitler said, "but when I crossed the former frontier there met me such a stream of love as I have never experienced."

Before the Anschluss, when Germany annexed Austria, Viennese

Jews owned three-quarters of the city's newspapers, banks, and textile firms. More than half the country's attorneys, physicians, and dentists were Jewish. In Vienna alone, the Jewish community represented almost 10 percent of the population. But the night before Hitler's army took control of the city, the British journalist G. E. R. Gedye reported a mob of thousands of Viennese rampaging through the Jewish quarter of Leopoldstadt, clubbing and beating Jews. In the weeks following the Anschluss, as the Nazis rounded up their political enemies, Vienna began "an orgy of sadism." Jewish men and women—the parents of Israel Singer among them—were forced on their hands and knees to scrub anti-Nazi slogans off the sidewalk or clean gutters and latrines. Moritz Fleischmann, a senior representative of the Viennese Jewish community, told at Eichmann's trial how he was given a bucket of boiling water and forced to clean steps. The bucket was in fact filled with acid. Austria's seventy-year-old chief rabbi joined him, scrubbing the sidewalks on his stomach while still wearing his prayer shawl. The SS looted Jewish homes, and Germans flocked to Austria to buy Jewish businesses at knock-down prices. It was, in the words of one historian, as if medieval pogroms had reappeared in modern dress. Within eighteen months, around two-thirds of Austria's 191,000-strong community had fled the country. The remainder was sent to the death camps to be murdered.

Between 1938 and 1943, the Nazi Party in Austria was enormously popular, enrolling more members as a proportion of the population than their counterparts in the old German territory. Austrians represented only 8 percent of people living in greater Germany but made up 14 percent of the SS by the end of the war. Some 40 percent of those involved in extermination programs, including Auschwitz, were Austrian.

It would be easy to dismiss Austria's postwar blindness about its Nazi past as an indication of its guilt. But that blindness was deepened by a single document drawn up by the Allied powers. In October 1943, the governments of the United States, United Kingdom, Soviet Union, and China signed the Moscow Declaration, which described Austria as "the first free country to fall a victim to Hitlerite aggression." After liberation, Austria seized the declaration as proof that it was Hitler's "first victim," largely ignoring the end of the Allied statement on Austria: "Austria is reminded, however, that she has a responsibility, which she cannot evade, for participation in the war at the side of Hitlerite Germany."

For Singer, the notion of Austria as a victim of Nazism was a sick distortion of the truth. "The Austrians were very willing participants," he said. "They aren't the first victims, they are the first participants."

After the war Austria was divided into four zones, controlled by the United States, France, the United Kingdom, and the Soviet Union. It would take a decade before the country's sovereignty was restored in the Austrian State Treaty of May 1955. After a long list of Austrian property to be seized by the Soviet Union, the treaty declared that Austria would either return all property seized from persecuted minorities or pay full compensation. Austria in fact passed seven restitution laws between 1946 and 1949, but they were seriously flawed. Lawyers representing Jewish victims in the United States reported to the State Department numerous difficulties in obtaining the cooperation of the Austrian authorities. Austria denied compensation for cash, bank accounts, and securities and refused to repay the punitive flight taxes imposed on fleeing Jews.

The Austrian government of the day knew it was not enough. As it negotiated the terms of the state treaty, it needed to prove its willingness to compensate victims who did not or could not claim their property back. Just before staging an official visit to New York in November 1954, Chancellor Julius Raab summoned an American Jewish lawyer to Vienna. Seymour Rubin was a former State Department official who was then representing Jewish groups in the United States, including the Claims Conference and the American Jewish Committee. In talks for the last two years, he had been frustrated by the buck-passing between the Germans and Austrians, as both countries blamed each other for the Nazi atrocities on Austrian soil. Rubin traveled to Vienna to find Chancellor Raab and most of the Austrian cabinet waiting for him in the Ballhausplatz palace. Sitting on one side of a long table was Raab and his entourage. Seated on the other side, alone, was Rubin.

"This was not a negotiation which I had anticipated," he recalled. "I had no backup or anything of that sort. I think because the state treaty was about to be signed, the Austrians decided they had better settle this damned business of Jewish claims. I think they really anticipated the possibility they might arrive, parade down Fifth Avenue with the Austrian chancellor there, and rocks would be thrown at them, and anti-Austrian slogans would be shouted by every Jew in New York."

The Austrians said they were ready to do something. They acknowledged they bore some responsibility for the plunder and murder of the Jews but insisted that the real responsibility lay with the Germans who had occupied Austria. The result was the creation of the Austrian *Hilfsfond,* or Assistance Fund, with 550 million schillings. Rubin was delighted with his achievement, but he returned to New York to find his Jewish clients appalled at the low settlement.

"That amount, which was worth $50 million, was not regarded by anybody on the outside as being a very adequate amount," he said. "I came out of the negotiation, having been conditioned by absolute resistance to any statement of liability whatsoever. I thought I'd made a pretty good deal, considering back in those early days, it was before the class action suits, before Stuart Eizenstat and others began to get in on the act. You have to remember the U.S. government was standing way off to one side on all of this. There was no help whatsoever."

Victims found the Austrian restitution efforts insulting. Nazi-controlled businesses in Austria had profited from their slave and forced labor in the Mauthausen concentration camp. After the war, those businesses reverted to Austrian control. Simon Wiesenthal was one of those concentration camp laborers in Mauthausen. Among his survivor friends, only "one or two" ever received compensation from Austria.

"After the war, I could get only compensation from Germany and not from Austria," Wiesenthal observed. "People were working here in Austrian industry. Even when it was a German institution like Hermann Göring Werke, this was in Austria and after the war, it was changed into an Austrian institution."

Less than two months after filing his first lawsuit against German industry, on October 16, 1998, Ed Fagan fired off another against Austrian industry for their use of slave and forced labor. It would take another six months before the companies named in the litigation—Voest-Alpine Stahl and Steyr-Daimler-Puch—were served with a copy of the lawsuit. Voest-Alpine, the giant steelmaker, was the direct descendent of Hermann Göring Werke, controlled by Hitler's deputy and the leader of the Third Reich's economy. Much of Göring's steel interests in Austria passed into his hands as a ransom paid by Baron Louis de Rothschild, the head of the Jewish banking dynasty in Central Europe, to buy his own freedom. Such companies profited enormously from the Anschluss, as the Nazis invested in energy sources and raw materials for their war machine. National Socialism modernized Austria, transforming its largely agricultural economy into a manufacturing one.

The victims' lawyers could have targeted almost any industrial company in Austria, as the use of forced labor was widespread. However, they faced a particularly Austrian difficulty. Unlike the West German economy, many of Austria's leading companies were nationalized after the war, in part to save their machines from being dismantled and carted away by Soviet troops. Voest-Alpine and Steyr-Daimler-Puch, the vehicle maker, were two of the largest nationalized companies. Now many of those state-owned companies had been reorganized and privatized. Austrian officials believed that made suing them, as the legal successors to wartime Nazi-run operations, almost impossible.

The class action lawyers were not the only ones pressing the Austrians for compensation that fall. The most unlikely victims emerged in the shape of two octogenarian archdukes. Felix and Carl Ludwig Habsburg-Lothringen, the sons of the last Austrian emperor, Karl I, claimed they too were Hitler's victims. Now living in Mexico and Belgium, the archdukes were not seeking to regain the Habsburg dynasty's palaces and treasures. They merely wanted the return of several thousand hectares of forests and

buildings, worth around $3 million in the late 1930s. The broth-
ers were exiled, along with their parents, to Switzerland at the end
of World War I, when their father signed away the family's five-
century-old powers. Archduke Felix spent the prewar years tour-
ing America to warn about the imminent threats posed by Nazi
Germany, and later served in the U.S. Army. Now they hoped to
convince the international community to broaden its investigations from Jewish assets to all Nazi victims. Their only problem
was the point-blank refusal of the Austrian government to sit
down and talk.

"They lost their property and they should be compensated or
repaid for that," Archduke Felix said of the Jewish campaign in
December 1998. "We feel that we also have a right, since it was
taken away by the same enemy, to our own compensation."

The Austrian government's response to the slave labor lawsuits
was only slightly less negative than its response to the Habsburgs.
Viktor Klima, then chancellor, told the companies that the problem of Nazi forced labor was the responsibility of the companies
involved, not the state. It would be another year before the companies approached the Austrian government for help, just as Eastern European governments were pressing Austria to follow
Germany's lead and open compensation talks for the Nazis' laborers. With an election looming in October 1999, no one wanted to
place the issue before the Austrian voters. But for a new government that included Jörg Haider's party, the task of dealing with
the Nazi years would become Austria's political priority.

First Victims First

To those on the other side of the table, she was Austria's Margaret Thatcher. Her bouffant hairstyle, swept over the top and curled at the sides, was perhaps more tightly controlled than the Iron Lady's. But Maria Schaumayer's politics—as well as her personal style—bore more than a passing resemblance to the former British prime minister's. Schaumayer, a former president of Austria's central bank, was held in the highest esteem in the close-knit world of business and political leaders. Once a conservative member of Vienna's city council, her corporate career reached the boardroom of OMV, the formerly state-owned oil and gas group, where she was chief financial officer. This mixture of business and conservative politics made her perfect for the job Chancellor Schüssel had in mind.

It was not just her résumé that drew her out of retirement in February 2000. Schaumayer could make middle-aged men go weak at the knees. Her way of doing business proved irresistible for the almost entirely male politicians and bureaucrats she encountered. With her curled eyebrow and wry smile, she appeared almost grandmotherly in her concern for those around her. But when it came to business, her style was all poker. Both a keen smoker and a tennis player, she won every round by being smarter and harder than the rest.

"She's the toughest negotiator I've ever met," said Hans Peter Manz, foreign affairs adviser to the chancellor. "You feel that after more than twenty years of diplomatic service, you're quite able to stand up to just about everybody, but she takes you in. She's a complete professional. She comes looking sort of like a homely housewife with chitchat and things like that. Then suddenly the hook is there."

Chancellor Schüssel was so in awe of Schaumayer that he was prepared to make the most extraordinary political sacrifice. Knowing the controversial nature of his coalition with the far-right Freedom Party, he feared he lacked the political strength to lead such a government. With his trademark bow tie, Schüssel was seen as being too intellectual to be truly popular. He turned to Schaumayer and asked her to become chancellor. She refused, but the chancellor's respect and admiration endured.

Schüssel had in mind another tough assignment for the former central banker. Schaumayer's credentials were so strong that she was the only person who could cleanse his government's tainted international image. Her task was to resolve the issue of wartime compensation and demonstrate that Austria had turned its back on its Nazi past forever.

Schaumayer was unimpeachable on both sides of the political divide in Austria. From the left, she earned enormous respect because her family had been opponents of the Nazis. Aged seven at the time of the Anschluss, she could remember her father losing his job as an agricultural school director in the province of Styria for his openly anti-Nazi opinions. For those on the right and in business, she had a similarly high stature for her tight control of the nation's money. No one could accuse her of wasting resources on anything.

"Maria," said Schüssel, "you have carte blanche. We are committed to solving this issue, and I have absolute confidence in you. So you tell me what you need and what you want to do. I want to see this issue settled."

Schaumayer publicly accepted her new mission on February 16, 2000, in the eighteenth-century Kongresssaal inside the Chancellery. It was the same room where the political map of Europe was redrawn during the Congress of Vienna of 1814 and 1815, following the defeat of Napoleon Bonaparte.

Sitting beside the chancellor, Schaumayer laid down the ground rules of the task she was about tackle. First, this would be a purely Austrian initiative. Any suggestion of a joint compensation package with German industry was to be set aside. Austria needed to take responsibility for its own conduct.

Second, she would only deal with the question of forced laborers. It was essential to make payments to the neediest, most neglected victims as soon as possible. The far more complex questions about Jewish property would have to wait for another special envoy and another round of talks.

Third, this was a voluntary exercise. Austria had no obligation under the state treaty to resolve claims from its period of Nazi rule.

But one question dogged Schaumayer. Was she just a fig leaf for the new government—an attempt to cover up its embarrassing inclusion of Jörg Haider's Freedom Party? "This is my personal interest because I think that Austria needs to do this," she replied. "If there is a side effect for the Austrian government—fine, so be it. But it will also be of tremendous importance for Austria, regardless of the political situation. It is one of the chapters that we have to close in our wartime history."

Schaumayer started work the next day, across the narrow Viennese street in an empty office inside the Hofburg palace.

The chancellor made a similar moral and political calculation. Compensation could naturally help his government's rehabilitation in Europe, but it was also simply the right thing to do. Schüssel was not merely attempting to prove his coalition's commitment to human rights and undertake an honest appraisal of its Nazi past. At the same time, he was keen to demonstrate his personal conviction that something needed to be done quickly to help Austria's Nazi victims.

"Schüssel can be an extremely cool character," said Hans Winkler, legal adviser to the foreign ministry. "But he really has a certain moral conviction that this is the right thing to do. Not only that it was good for him and his party, but that he really believed it.

"We were born in the same year, 1945. This is a generation that grew up believing that Austria was Hitler's first victim. We believed we didn't do anything wrong, but nevertheless we did everything we should have done after the war to restitute and compensate everything. Then we suddenly found out this was not the single truth. And I think intelligent people—and Schüssel is certainly one of them—began to think that maybe the story was not so black-and-white."

Inside the chancellor's office, Schüssel was actually helped by the European Union's imposition of sanctions. Now he could curtail criticism from the right and left over the new round of compensation by portraying the debate as an issue of national unity.

"Given the European sanctions and the need for this government to establish itself very quickly, it certainly made it easier for the chancellor to pursue this issue without having a large debate," said Hans Peter Manz, the chancellor's foreign policy adviser. "Who could argue against it?"

Schaumayer began by tackling her toughest opponents face-to-face. Within a week of taking office, she called meetings with the leading class action lawyers. Among them was Ed Fagan, who had struck an earlier settlement with Bank Austria, the nation's largest bank, over property restitution. Schaumayer was determined to restrict the meeting to a getting-to-know-you session, and refused to start the negotiations immediately. However, she was appalled by Fagan's obsessive desire to talk to the media, watching aghast as he staged press conferences before and after their meeting. Schaumayer considered his public comments an impossible breach of confidence. She was also taken aback by his insistence that she should deal with all areas of compensation—both forced labor and property claims—in spite of her refusal to do so.

She faced an even tougher challenge from Israel Singer and the Claims Conference. In mid-March, the Jewish side formalized its opposition to Schüssel's ruling coalition by refusing to negotiate "with the present government of Austria." Singer was disgusted by the Austrian idea that the country was Hitler's "first victim" and appalled by the inclusion of Haider's party in government. He told Austrian officials that he would never travel to Vienna to acknowledge Schüssel: "Why should I go to Austria and talk to your chancellor? To give him a chance to hand me money in public? So that he could make himself laundered in the eyes of the rest of Europe? For whatever the hell reason? Your people are not paying enough to get yourselves laundered for what you did fifty years ago, much less for what you're doing today."

Singer demanded to negotiate with the Austrian head of state—President Klestil—instead of the chancellor, but the distinction was a legal impossibility for the Austrians. The president was a ceremonial figure who had no negotiating power and could not muster a majority in parliament. Eventually, Singer and the Claims Conference were unable to maintain their promise not to talk to the Austrian government. Instead, Singer hatched an awkward compromise: he and his Claims Conference negotiators refused to travel to Vienna but talked frequently with Austrian officials over the telephone and with their diplomats in the United States.

Just four days after the Jewish negotiators refused to deal with her, Schaumayer was sitting inside Stuart Eizenstat's office in Washington, next door to the White House. In his huge second-floor office, lined with photos of Eizenstat standing next to sundry presidents and world leaders, the deputy Treasury secretary delivered a thinly veiled warning. The United States had chosen not to join the European Union in imposing sanctions, but it was limiting itself to dealing with Austria's lower-ranking officials. If Austria wanted to restore full contact with the Clinton administration, its chances would depend in part on how it handled Holocaust issues. The Holocaust was now a benchmark in assessing the Austrian government. This was a message underlined by Secretary of State Madeleine Albright in talks with Chancellor Schüssel— the Austrian government was on probation. Eizenstat invoked Albright's authority in issuing his warning, underlining how his work with the new Austrian government was supported at the highest levels.

If Schaumayer failed to charm the lawyers and Jewish groups, she worked wonders with the U.S. government. Eizenstat's tough message was almost drowned in the chemistry between the grandmotherly Austrian and the normally ice-cold American. Eizenstat knew he was being charmed and loved it. After the acrimony of the German talks, Schaumayer was a breath of sweet, fresh air.

"Schaumayer is a delightful, wonderful person," Eizenstat said.

"She's a happy person, she's an upbeat person, she's a positive person. She speaks beautiful English and—what was most important—she was really committed to help get this done. She believed in it. She believed Austria had a responsibility for it. You couldn't help but be attracted to her."

Those feelings were not requited. To Austrian officials, Eizenstat appeared jaded and misinformed. They were offended by his initial position that the Austrians had done "nothing" on restitution, and Schaumayer set about correcting his ignorance, citing the seven restitution laws in Austria. Now her government was willing to offer a generous deal that more than matched the German settlement. In the German deal, payments were limited by the size of the overall pot of cash. If too many survivors emerged, each would receive less than the headline figure. In contrast, the Austrians were guaranteeing a fixed amount of compensation to all forced workers. Moreover, Schaumayer promised to include any Jewish victims omitted from the German settlement—specifically some fifteen thousand Hungarian Jews who were kept in dismal concentration camp–like conditions and worked as forced laborers. But she maintained the Austrian position that Germany was responsible for the concentration camps on Austrian soil, such as Mauthausen.

Eizenstat was pleasantly surprised and said he was ready to accept the Austrian plan to deal with labor issues first. Worn out by the mammoth German plenary sessions, Eizenstat wanted no repeat of the recriminations over how to carve up the German fund. Now he was eager to hold direct talks with just the government officials.

"I don't want to do this ever again," said Eizenstat. "I don't want to sit in a room for months with a hundred other people haggling with each other about the distribution of the funds. With you Austrians I want to do it differently. Let's do one after the other—labor then property."

Ed Fagan opened the bidding. Filing a new lawsuit in mid-April 2000, the lawyer sued 100 unnamed Austrian banks and another

100 unnamed Austrian companies. Fagan now claimed to have filed "the most comprehensive global complaint against Austria and Austrian industry." But it was the cash figure that attracted most attention in Austria: $18 billion, covering both labor and property. Around four times the size of the German deal, his demand represented almost 10 percent of Austria's annual economic output. It was met with incredulity in Vienna. Schaumayer said the figure would "bankrupt the Austrian state," while Chancellor Schüssel dismissed it as "ridiculous."

Two weeks later, Eizenstat convened a Washington meeting of the class action lawyers for talks with Hans Winkler, representing the Austrian government. Both made it clear they would not talk about property claims until the labor issues were resolved.

"We will not repeat the mistakes of the German process where everything gets lumped into one fund," said Eizenstat.

To the lawyers, it looked like the only beneficiaries from the first round of Austrian talks would be the Central and Eastern European laborers, represented by Michael Hausfeld. Michael Witti, the Munich-based member of Ed Fagan's team, wheeled around to Hausfeld. "Your people are getting exactly what they want," he said. "Will they help us out on aryanized property?"

That weekend Schaumayer turned up at the studios of Austrian television's Sunday talk show *Pressestunde*. There she was asked a simple but as yet unresolved question. Did she have any idea how much money the compensation deal could be worth? In private with her government advisers, Schaumayer was grappling with figures ranging from 4 billion to 10 billion schillings. But in front of a national TV audience, Schaumayer ended the debate in a stroke.

"Well, I think 6 billion schillings should do it."

The chancellor, along with the rest of his government, was shell-shocked. Surely the figure, worth around $400 million, was too high? Schaumayer stuck to her figure and forced everyone else to follow. Based on recent historical studies, she believed there were at most 239,000 survivors from the 1 million laborers forced to work in Austria during the war. Many of those would be covered by German compensation, but the figures were not yet fixed. Schaumayer simply made an educated guess at an overall figure. It was high enough to cover all costs as well as any excessive numbers of claims.

Schaumayer enjoyed a relatively free hand. While the German government was hampered by the reluctance of its business leaders, the Austrian government was guaranteeing Schaumayer's cash. The chancellor had identified a huge surplus in a government-managed insolvency fund designed to aid Austrian businesses in financial distress. The fund had rarely been called upon in recent years and was overflowing with cash raised from business taxes. It was a perfect source for the compensation payments—a onetime surplus originally funded by business but entirely controlled by the government. While Austrian business leaders complained they were losing the source of promised tax cuts, their position was weak. Austrian industry was far from reaching the half-share collected by its German counterpart, donating 1.8 billion schillings, or around $120 million—less than a third of the overall total.

In mid-May, Eizenstat and a small team of U.S. officials prepared to travel to Vienna for what the Austrians called their Reconciliation Conference. It would be the first high-level contact between the Clinton administration and Freedom Party members of the Austrian government. Before setting out from Washington, Eizenstat issued an unusual written statement under pressure from Israel Singer and the Claims Conference. Now was the time not just to press ahead with compensation for forced workers but also to begin talks on settling the property claims against Austria. Noting the coalition government's stated commitment to human rights and democracy, Eizenstat warned: "We are watching developments in Austria closely to ensure that the government lives up to its promises. We will look at what the government does, as well as what it says. One important benchmark in this regard is how the new government will deal with unresolved Holocaust issues."

In Vienna, Eizenstat met Chancellor Schüssel for direct talks in his expansive light-filled office, surrounded by the chancellor's striking selection of abstract art and modern furniture. Schüssel had turned down the traditional, dark wood-paneled office used by chancellors for decades in favor of the bright, high-ceilinged room overlooking a peaceful park next to the Hofburg palace. The only distraction was the sound of horse-drawn carriages ferrying tourists round Vienna's historic streets.

"I'm here to help do justice for these people," said Eizenstat. "But I'm also here because I believe the relationship between our two countries is important. I can help with that relationship, and with Austria's place in history."

Eizenstat delivered a similar message to two Freedom Party ministers—Vice-Chancellor Susanne Riess-Passer and Finance Minister Karl-Heinz Grasser. He urged them all to move ahead rapidly with the more sensitive issue of Jewish property claims by appointing a special envoy as soon as possible.

Across the street from Schüssel's office, inside the Hofburg's Marmorsaal, its marble-lined conference room, the forced labor negotiators met for a marathon session. Over the course of eight hours, fed by a lavish kosher buffet, Schaumayer and Eizenstat pinned down the Central and Eastern Europeans to some hard numbers. They settled on an overall figure of 150,000 surviving forced laborers. Even with a generous margin of error, that would leave more than enough cash to spare from the 6 billion schillings—some 1 billion schillings (around $66 million) to cover additional administrative costs. Everyone realized the labor issue was effectively over. A day later, Schüssel named a new special envoy on property issues— Ernst Sucharipa, the director of Vienna's diplomatic academy.

Schaumayer claimed the talks "were guided by the spirit of reconciliation," while Eizenstat showered the Austrian government with the international praise it was longing for. "They have acted with great alacrity, great courage, and shown leadership—not just in Austria, but leadership to the rest of Europe and to the world about how one can reconcile with one's past, and how one can heal wounds even many decades later."

The wounds reopened less than two weeks later. In pursuing a swift settlement of the labor issues with the Central and Eastern

Europeans, the Austrian and U.S. mediators had sidelined the class action lawyers representing Jewish victims. Several had turned up in Vienna for the Reconciliation Conference only to find there was no invitation for anyone other than government officials. Now those lawyers threatened a repeat of the hand-to-hand combat in the German talks earlier in the year. Mel Weiss filed a new lawsuit against the Austrian government and the Dorotheum auction house, which had sold off the most valuable property stolen from wealthy Jewish families. The lawsuit drove a wedge into efforts to close the talks on labor. There would be no legal peace until all claims—Jewish and non-Jewish alike—were resolved.

Michael Hausfeld and the Eastern Europeans were alarmed. They thought their deal would be a quick win for thousands of needy victims. Now Hausfeld—firmly established as an enemy of Mel Weiss after the German talks—accused his fellow attorneys of abusing one group of clients in favor of another.

The bickering worsened inside the State Department as the lawyers met with Austrian diplomats at the start of June. They were meant to be addressing the technical issue of legal closure and the wording of the agreements to end all litigation. But when the Austrians insisted on following the German settlement, the attorneys lashed out.

"I don't trust the German process anymore," said Weiss, disgusted by recent delays in agreeing to the terms of the deal with Germany. For once, he was backed by Fagan's team. Larry Kill, an attorney siding with Fagan, chimed in, "Once we agree on labor, we do not have leverage for property."

Eizenstat's frustration reached boiling point. First the German deal was halted by the issue of legal peace. Now the rapid agreement with Austria seemed to be slipping between his fingers.

"We need to pay these people while they are still alive," he exclaimed. "You cannot hold the Eastern Europeans hostage, no! This needs to get through parliament and payments need to be made. If this does not occur it will be a tragedy."

——•◆•——

It was not just the lawyers who were drawing parallels with the German talks. The Austrians themselves were modeling their work on their counterparts' efforts in Berlin. They copied not only the amounts paid to survivors but also the hard-fought agreement for legal peace. Germany and Austria attempted to frame their new laws so that they interlocked, overlapping nowhere and leaving no gaps between them. Around 5 percent of forced laborers had worked on both sides of the German Reich, in present-day Austria and Germany. Neither government wanted to pay survivors twice, nor did they want to be accused of ignoring any one group of survivors.

Nowhere was the cooperation clearer than on the emotional issue of the Mauthausen concentration camp. Sited in Austria, Mauthausen was a key concern of Israel Singer and the class action lawyers. Eager to prove Austrian complicity in Nazi war crimes, they believed that Mauthausen survivors needed compensation directly from Austria. Such a deal would also help lift the strain on the German fund, which they argued would soon be overburdened with survivors.

For the Austrians, Mauthausen was entirely off the table. They were no more responsible for the camp than the Poles were responsible for Auschwitz. Their one exception was the Hungarian slave laborers working in Mauthausen's subcamps. In March 1944—just three months before the Allied landings in Normandy—Adolf Eichmann formulated a deportation plan for Hungary's 750,000 Jews, who had largely escaped the worst Nazi terror. Within two months, the SS was deporting more than 10,000 Hungarian Jews a day. In negotiations with the SS, the Budapest community managed to save some 15,000 of its own people by convincing the Germans they could be exchanged as future hostages for war materiel. Those so-called exchange Jews were sent to work in Austria while waiting for the ransom to be paid.

Now they were again pawns in a new set of negotiations. Israel Singer and the Claims Conference sought $15 million for handling the claims of its Hungarian survivors and to supplement any unexpectedly low payments from Germany to Mauthausen survivors in general. At first the Austrians adamantly refused to agree to such a high cash figure and to any suggestion of paying for Mauthausen, but they buckled under intense pressure from Eizenstat. Both the United States and Austria needed to secure Jewish backing to establish legal peace.

"It was a deal breaker," admitted Hans Winkler.

For Israel Singer and the Claims Conference it was a matter of principle rather than money. "At the end of the day that $15 million undermines the argument that Austria was a victim of Nazism," said Gideon Taylor. "It says the fact that a concentration camp was located in Austria was not just a coincidence. There was a profit by Austrian companies from the use of slave labor."

The deal with the Claims Conference was given little publicity. Instead, Austria received the absolution it was seeking in mid-June when Otto Graf Lambsdorff came to Vienna. At a press conference Lambsdorff, leading the German government negotiations, was asked for his opinion on Austria paying for Mauthausen. "Why should they? It's the responsibility of Germany and German compensation laws," he fired back.

It would be hard to find a starker contrast to Maria Schaumayer than Ernst Sucharipa, Austria's point man on property claims. Where Schaumayer was tough talking, Sucharipa would swallow his words. Where Schaumayer softened her subjects with the personal touch, Sucharipa seemed coldly intellectual. Above all, Schaumayer had the freedom to operate as she pleased, as a leading conservative with the full trust of the chancellor. But Sucharipa, as a left-of-center Social Democrat with no prior relationship to the chancellor, was on a short leash. Sucharipa was never given the same official title—government representative— as Schaumayer. His brief, as a special envoy, was to scope out how agreement could be reached in the murky area of Jewish property. He did possess one advantage, however—his partly Jewish family. With two Jewish grandparents, one on each side of his family, he was at least sensitized to the issue of anti-Semitism in Austria from an early age. With his prior experience working at the

United Nations in New York, he had developed close contact with American Jewish leaders—among them, Israel Singer.

Sucharipa knew his task was harder than Schaumayer's. "It's particularly difficult in the Austrian case," he recalled. "We had to establish the line that we as Austrians needed to acknowledge that past measures were not sufficient. But at the same time we also needed to get the principle accepted that—even though they were insufficient—the past measures must be taken into account. This was much more difficult than the issue of labor, where there was nothing in the past."

Sucharipa was further frustrated by the battle fatigue of those on the other side of the table. Israel Singer and the class action lawyers were embittered by the Austrian talks so far, which had only concentrated on labor claims by non-Jews in Eastern Europe. Now they were holding up the labor deal to force progress in the property talks. Moreover, Sucharipa was flying blind, with no historical report by Austria's official panel of historians to map the task before him. The historians would need at least another two years to report their findings, and no one—except Sucharipa—was prepared to wait that long.

Some property issues were easy to identify among the gaping holes in Austria's seven restitution laws since the war. Apartments seized by the Nazis stood at the top of the list, particularly long-term leases on such apartments—the most common form of home ownership in Vienna. An earlier restitution law identified the apartments as deserving compensation but left the issue to later legislation which never materialized. Another area was liquidated businesses—companies bought by Aryan rivals and closed down or simply driven out of business by the destruction of their Jewish clientele.

Sucharipa's first trip to the United States was destined to fail. With no authority to negotiate and no cash in hand, he performed far below expectations, bitterly disappointing Eizenstat. All Sucharipa could do was reiterate vaguely the need to do more, while insisting that Austria had already restituted a lot. With such fuzzy talk, there was no chance to break the logjam on the labor deal any time soon. In a clear warning sign to the Austrian government, the power brokers in other Holocaust deals intervened. Alan Hevesi warned that Austria needed to "fully participate" in compensation talks.

Israel Singer, who was dismayed by Austria's failure to begin talks on its property claims, backed Hevesi's warning. The Austrian government was supposed to be dealing with Holocaust issues to prove its mettle against any pro-Nazi sympathizers within the Freedom Party. But it had singularly failed to address Jewish claims. Now it had just passed a law creating a fund for forced laborers that was almost entirely dedicated to non-Jewish survivors. Singer's reply was simple: there would be no legal closure for Austria until there was a deal on Jewish property.

In July, Eizenstat stepped in with his own framework for tackling the property claims. He proposed an immediate payment of $150 million to cover a first round of property claims. Nearly all the surviving twenty-one thousand Jewish victims from Austria would receive cash from such a fund, which could be handled by the Austrian National Fund established on the fiftieth anniversary of the war to pay compensation to Austria's Nazi victims.

Over the summer Eizenstat came under intense pressure from all sides. For the Central and Eastern Europeans, the wait was impossibly long. They had already agreed to a settlement for their forced laborers. Why should they wait any longer? "The victims waited for this solution for a long time," several Polish negotiators complained to Eizenstat in writing. "It needs to be emphasized that compensation for slave and forced labor is important mainly to survivors, while the property issue [is important] to heirs."

In mid-September, four months after the agreement on compensation for forced laborers, Eizenstat presented a draft agreement to the class action lawyers based on concessions by the Austrians. It was a classic piece of horse-trading. The lawyers would agree to legal closure on labor, based on the compensation fund of 6 billion schillings. In exchange, the Austrian government would make a $150 million "advance payment" against a larger capped fund to fill the "gaps and deficiencies" in previous Austrian restitution laws. Most important for the small Viennese Jewish community, talks would start on returning specific property that had been seized by the Nazis and remained in government hands. The talks about the size and scope of the property fund would begin immediately after signing the labor deal.

For Schüssel, the strategy of proving his government's credentials was working more successfully than anyone had hoped. As he began to address the issue of Jewish property in the late summer of 2000, the European Union prepared to lift its sanctions against Austria. A panel of experts found that Austria enjoyed a better human rights record than many other European countries and that sanctions were merely generating "nationalist sentiments" in Austria. By mid-September, the sanctions were lifted. Schüssel found himself in the strongest negotiating position of his brief career as chancellor, just as he began to confront his Jewish antagonists.

TWENTY-TWO

The Last Waltz

S tuart Eizenstat was in Vilnius, Lithuania, close to his ancestral home, when he received the call from Chancellor
Schüssel. It was not good news. Schüssel would only agree to
the $150 million down payment on Jewish property if it closed the
debate on several types of claims. He was particularly unhappy
with the notion that the $150 million would merely cover the
claims of Holocaust survivors for their lost apartment leases.

Eizenstat was increasingly frustrated with the Austrian negotiations. With little more than a month before the U.S. presidential
election—and what looked like the end of the Democratic hold
on the White House—there was no time left for protracted talks.
It was bad enough that the American lawyers and Jewish groups
were blocking the labor deal. Now the Austrian side was holding
up the long-agreed settlement.

Sitting beside him in the VIP lounge in the Vilnius airport was
Hans Winkler, the eternally optimistic Austrian foreign ministry
official. They had both attended a forum on Nazi-looted art and
were heading on to Vienna. Eizenstat turned to Winkler to ask
some advice. How could he bring the chancellor back on board?

"How about two or three categories?" replied Winkler.

"What do you have in mind?"

"Well, we could have valuables, the contents of apartments, and
personal effects. Then Schüssel can say he gets three categories
out of the way."

When they reached Vienna, Schüssel agreed. In a stroke, the

claims of Jewish survivors to their lost possessions would be wiped clean. But the chancellor wanted something more for his $150 million. He wanted to settle not just the claims of survivors but also of their heirs—representing a far higher number than those of the elderly Holocaust victims themselves. From Schüssel's office, Eizenstat placed a conference call to Israel Singer and Gideon Taylor in their respective offices in New York. Singer was still so hostile to what he called Austria's "shitty government" that he refused to conduct face-to-face talks. But Eizenstat desperately needed his agreement to clear the path for the long-delayed deal on Eastern European forced laborers and to move on to the bigger debate about Jewish property.

Singer adamantly, passionately could not accept the $150 million as compensation for the heirs of Austria's Jewish victims. As the son of Austrian refugees, Singer was determined to guarantee a $7,000 payment to each of the elderly survivors. Large numbers of heirs would simply shrink the payments to survivors. If Schüssel wanted to include the heirs, he would have to pay more.

The negotiation was not helped by the hopeless speakerphone in the chancellor's office. Over a faint and crackling line, Schüssel and Eizenstat huddled together to bellow their positions down the three-way call. Schüssel refused point-blank to consider paying any additional compensation for the heirs of Austrian Jews. Taylor could not hear the chancellor's insistence. Singer shouted it back to him.

"Payment to the twenty thousand living survivors cannot give closure to the one hundred eighty thousand who died," shouted Taylor. "It's not just the money. It's the principle of it."

Eizenstat insisted they needed to agree to full closure. This was cash that would be paid immediately. Why hold things up any more?

"You are not going to get closure if you don't include all the Jewish claims against Austria," shouted Singer. "It's very simple. And by the way, it doesn't mean that we are just not going to approve. We are going to oppose closure because you are trying to make a deal for everyone except Jews."

"Are you crazy? What about all this money for all these people? I have got you $150 million," exclaimed Eizenstat. "Even if nothing else happens on property, it's free money. It's your $150 million. This is a down payment. Give them closure on this piece."

"Fine, for God's sake," yelled Singer. "I'll give them closure on any piece. But we want restitution and we want the discussions to start immediately."

It was almost midnight in Vienna when they ended the call. Although they had just agreed to a new round of property talks, they felt a crashing sense of relief at reaching the critical breakthrough on the labor issue.

"Are you hungry?" asked Schüssel.

"Not really," said Eizenstat, notorious for his light appetite.

"We are," piped up several officials in the chancellor's office. Schüssel told the Americans there was a fine Italian restaurant near his office. He could call down for a delivery of pizza.

"I don't eat pizza," said Eizenstat. "Can I have a cheese sandwich?"

When the pizza came, the Austrians and Americans opened a couple of beers and poured a few shots of schnapps. As they chatted past 1:00 A.M., even Eizenstat and Schüssel kicked back as though they thought the end was in sight.

Eizenstat had developed a curious bond with the Austrian chancellor. Both men were supremely tough negotiators, both prided themselves on keeping a cool professional front, and both relished the task of solving the complex puzzle before them.

"On the chancellor's side, there was huge respect for the way Eizenstat approaches his job," recalled Hans Peter Manz, foreign affairs adviser to Schüssel. "I think the chancellor accepted the challenge with some sort of relish at going up against someone who was clearly a superior negotiator. He very much appreciates the man, in the sense that boxing champions have respect for each other. It's the sort of relationship between fierce competitors who appreciate the other's straightness and fairness and skill. I think in a perverse way, it was fun for both of them to do this."

They gathered again in the Kongresssaal for the long-delayed ceremony to conclude the forced-labor settlement—five months after it was first agreed on. Even the normally frigid Eizenstat sounded impressed by how much they had achieved. Gone was the dark talk about the Austrian government's commitment to human rights and the presence of the far-right Freedom Party. Instead, Eizenstat hailed the deal as a sign of the two countries' shared values.

The officials then trooped across the street to the Hofburg palace to see President Klestil. There, Eizenstat struck a historic note as he claimed that the Holocaust deal represented more than a wartime issue.

"The recent efforts to assist survivors are part of a new stirring of the moral conscience of the world," he said, "evident not just regarding Holocaust issues and other crimes of World War II, but to human rights violations everywhere—in the Balkans, Rwanda, East Timor, or Iraq. As long as crimes against humanity continue, remembrance of the Holocaust and other injustices and suffering perpetrated by the Nazis is essential."

As soon as the ceremonies were over, they began talks on how to resolve Jewish property issues in the Austria Center, Vienna's huge conference site. Everyone admitted the issues were both ill-defined and sweeping. With no report by Austria's official historians, both sides thrashed out their competing views of history in talks lasting until 11:00 P.M.

On one basic point, the two sides could agree: Austria's compensation and restitution laws were inadequate. Liquidated Jewish businesses, for instance, were excluded from previous restitution. Some businesses had closed down as their Jewish clientele escaped or were murdered. Others were intentionally closed by non-Jewish rivals, who had bought them under Nazi aryanization laws. Of the more than thirty-three thousand Jewish businesses that had once existed, the former owners were only able to claim for some four thousand. Moreover, the burden of proof lay with the victim, who was required to show that the transfer was the result of persecution. In contrast, German law assumed such transfers took place under duress.

On the details of exactly how the laws had failed, bitter disputes remained. For instance, the two sides disagreed over how to handle property taxes and flight taxes imposed on Jews applying to emigrate. The bill for both Nazi taxes amounted to around half of the Jewish assets, and businesses were often sold simply to pay the flight taxes. If the businesses were reclaimed after the war, the former Jewish owner was required to pay back the total amount they had received—including the money spent on Nazi taxes. It was as if the survivors were being forced to pay the Nazi taxes twice.

Martin Mendelsohn, the class action lawyer who also acted as Simon Wiesenthal's personal attorney in the United States, admitted he could not put a figure on the Jewish property claims. "I still don't have a firm grasp of the dimension of the problem," he said later. "Access to archives is limited in Europe. All of us were dealing with estimates because we had very little hard information. Both sides were stumbling, trying to come up with something that made sense."

To compound the problems, Ed Fagan continued to agitate for more compensation for stolen property. Within hours of the signing ceremony, he told the Austrian press that he was ready to pull out of the labor agreement if the property settlement proved inadequate. Eizenstat could barely contain his anger at the sight of Fagan repudiating the deal that all the lawyers had just signed.

"Mr. Fagan's statements are wholly, completely and totally inaccurate," he told reporters at Vienna's airport as he prepared to leave Austria. "The labor agreement stands on its own, and the attorneys who signed it, including Mr. Fagan, have to understand . . . that we expect all of the attorneys, and anticipate all the attorneys, will abide by its terms and will dismiss their claims as soon as possible."

The property talks did not just suffer from historical uncertainty and legal brinkmanship. They were also seriously hampered by the Freedom Party. At the very moment when the Austrian government was rehabilitated in the international community—as European sanctions were lifted—the far-right party began to flex its muscles. The young finance minister, Karl-Heinz Grasser, led the Freedom Party's charge against further Holocaust compensation, insisting "not a cent more" of federal funds be spent on the issue. His resistance to the ongoing talks with Jewish groups squeezed Schüssel into searching for creative solutions. Eizenstat asked for a token gesture from the Austrian government to add to a property settlement, but Schüssel held fast to the line that not a cent more could be taken from the federal budget. Instead, the chancellor pressed the banks for contributions and took funds from peripheral government sources, including $60 million from the profits of the Austrian National Bank.

Instead of hard cash, the talks focused on a package to meet each Jewish interest group. For the Claims Conference, the most pressing option was to expand Austria's generous social security benefits to Holocaust victims abroad. Jewish survivors already received pensions and a limited amount of *Pflegegeld,* or medical benefits, under existing compensation laws. But the Claims Conference knew that for very elderly survivors, social security could be more valuable than a single lump sum of cash. For those with disabilities, the payments could rise to $1,000 a month. The Jewish negotiators also wanted to expand the scope of Austria's pension payments to survivors who escaped Austria as very young children. Under current rules, payments were limited to those aged six and over in 1938.

Unlike a cash settlement, the social benefits were limited only by the ultimate death of the survivors. "The costs of this go way beyond what is available in a capped fund," said Gideon Taylor of the Claims Conference. "You don't know what the real cost implications are. They receive it until the very last."

That prospect alarmed many in the Austrian government, who strongly resisted the uncosted expense of paying foreign residents throughout the course of their lives.

"That was very tough," said Hans Peter Manz, "because that is potentially the most expensive part of the deal. We asked the Ministry of Social Affairs to come up with some projections but I think we came up with three different projections before the end. People might live ten years longer—we just don't know."

When the Austrians sat down for talks with the class action lawyers in Vienna at the start of December, they were as far apart as ever.

At stake was the size of a new fund for individual property claims, but the sums discussed were far beyond anything the Schüssel government was prepared to pay. On their own, Jewish-owned businesses liquidated during the war were worth around $1.3 billion in today's dollars. When the attorneys opened the bidding, their demands ranged from $750 million to $1 billion. The Austrians refused to consider such figures, prompting Fagan to threaten to pull out of the previous labor deal once again. The American negotiators left Vienna with no end in sight.

Within a month, the lawyers' demands more than halved to $300 million, as the Austrians made clear there was only some $250 million on the table. Besides the cash, the two sides agreed on a procedure to return former Jewish property that was currently in public hands, such as buildings and art. As a concrete measure, the negotiators quickly settled the long-running dispute over the Jewish Hakoah sports ground in Vienna. The city offered $8 million to build a new facility near to the original property seized during the Nazi years.

In January 2001, a week before Eizenstat was due to leave office with the rest of the Clinton administration, the negotiators met for their last talks in the Austrian Chancellery. Eizenstat carried a message of support from the new secretary of state, Colin Powell, pledging that the Bush administration would continue the talks if they could not be completed in time.

For the attorneys as well as the Austrian officials, the prospect of talks under Bush was not attractive. "The Bush administration is not going to do anything for us," said Deborah Sturman, negotiating on behalf of Mel Weiss's clients. "Bush didn't get any Jewish votes and this administration is just giving up on it. That was bearing down on us and we had to make these deals fast."

Schüssel too was determined to reach an agreement before his sparring partner left government. While there were still details to be settled, Schüssel announced the final sum he could raise from Austrian industry—$210 million. In addition to the 6 billion schilling labor deal and the $150 million for Jewish property leases and household goods, Schüssel felt he had more than proved himself in office.

"In all, we have come close to one of the major goals of my

government. In less than one year we solved two extremely important issues of dealing with our past—i.e., forced labor compensation and restitution. I think that we have achieved a lot," he told reporters in the Chancellery. "This is a great national effort, considering the sums that must be paid in times when there are massive budget cuts in Austria. I will add quite frankly that only one who deals with one's past now, in the present, can act freely in the future."

The final obstacle to a settlement emerged not in America but in Vienna. Ariel Muzicant, a Viennese property developer leading Austria's Jewish community, was determined to press hard for substantial restitution to rebuild the country's Jewish infrastructure. Faced with a small surviving community and a large influx of Jewish immigrants from Eastern Europe, Austria's Jewish institutions were in dire financial need and saddled with debts of more than 700 million schillings, or around $46 million. Muzicant identified the Holocaust talks as his best chance of rebuilding his community's finances.

Claiming "millions and millions" of schillings in Jewish property that was never restituted, Muzicant's demands appeared outlandish to the Austrian officials. Muzicant sought either the full return of Jewish property—both private homes and community buildings such as synagogues—or adequate compensation. But his credibility was undercut when he identified a palace on Schmitgasse in central Vienna, now used by U.S. diplomats, as unrestituted Jewish property. On investigation, the Austrian government found it had been returned after the war to its rightful owner, who later sold it. It was, they said, "an exemplary case of compensation."

"These restitution issues are not supposed to be negotiations about political subsidies for the Jewish community, which we have done throughout the years," said Ernst Sucharipa, Austria's negotiator on restitution issues. "Everyone agrees it's in Austria's interest to have a thriving Jewish community, and there is a big case for more financial aid to do that. But that is separate from restitution issues."

Muzicant's ambitious agenda was not advanced by his choice of attorney. After a dispute with his previous lawyer, Muzicant retained Charles Moerdler, whose family had escaped from Germany just before the war. Moerdler identified passionately with Holocaust victims and still kept his transit pass bearing official Nazi stamps. As the senior litigator at the powerful Manhattan law firm of Stroock, Stroock and Lavan, he was closely connected with Republican politics and made Muzicant's battle far more credible in the United States.

Moerdler had represented Austrian banks in an earlier settlement with Holocaust survivors, and his fellow American attorneys were appalled at his apparent conflict of interest. Some of them believed that his acting for Austrian survivors was a way of atoning for his sins. Moerdler himself commented that perhaps they were right. However, Muzicant preferred to see his new lawyer as a great negotiator rather than a turncoat. Even Eizenstat could scarcely accept his presence at the negotiations, limiting Moerdler to observing but not taking part in the talks. Moerdler believed that Austria had never faced up to its wartime sins and needed to be held to a full accounting. When he attempted to interject in one session, Eizenstat was swift with a one-line put-down.

"I hear the voice of Jacob, but I see the face of Esau."

Moerdler entered the talks with disdain for his fellow negotiators and what they had already agreed to. In particular he loathed the labor settlement, which he condemned as "an absolute travesty" for committing $15 million to Jewish survivors, to be handled by the Claims Conference. Moerdler would argue incessantly with Muzicant over how to proceed with the negotiations. But he was prepared to work for Muzicant for free, in part because the Austrian Jewish leader was living, breathing proof that Israel Singer could not speak for the world's entire Jewish population.

It took until the last days of the Clinton administration to finalize the Austrian settlement. In Washington, the State Department's corridors were bustling with the Bush transition team. Colin Powell, based in an office down the hall, bumped into the Austrian and U.S. negotiators and cheerily encouraged Eizenstat to keep up the good work.

His work on Austria was not complete, though. An agreement on the social benefits package was still elusive in the final hours of the talks. Sucharipa insisted that Austria was not prepared to extend its pension payments to survivors who were younger than six years old in 1938, arguing that they were too young to have truly suffered. The Jewish negotiators were appalled. Gideon Eckhaus, chairman of the Austrian Jewish Committee in Israel and a child refugee in 1938, delivered an impassioned moral condemnation of the Austrian position.

"I don't know how you can turn this down," said a frustrated Eizenstat. "People will die and you have this responsibility to help them."

The Jewish negotiators were dismayed—Eckhaus was himself one of those elderly survivors. They returned to their hotel convinced the agreement would collapse. Eizenstat sensed their defiant opposition and called Schüssel the next morning to extract a final, vital concession—all child survivors would be able to claim an Austrian pension. For Israel Singer, this was a critical, personal victory. "It could have applied to me if I had been born a couple of years earlier," he said. "People born in March 1938 in Vienna actually spent most of the war dragging through Europe and not getting an education. They should be pensioned."

Even as they prepared to sign the deal, the tensions among the negotiators, sitting far apart from one another inside the State Department's auditorium, were barely concealed. Several—including Muzicant—left before the signing was over, claiming they needed to catch planes. After a short speech, Eizenstat called the lawyers to the dais one by one to sign the deal. Hausfeld signed and gave the deputy Treasury secretary a bear hug. Fagan walked up to the podium, remonstrated with Eizenstat, and walked away.

Eizenstat called Fagan back to sign the deal last of all. "Ed, thank you for your great contributions," he said, prompting several in the room to burst into laughter.

Trailed by two television cameras, Fagan was the only lawyer to deliver a speech after signing the settlement. "For those of you who may not know me, my name is Ed Fagan," he said to his fellow negotiators. "I brought the first lawsuit together with my colleagues. It related to each and every one of the settlements that we ultimately achieved over the last few years.

"It's not the total sum of money that people should be looking at, it's whether they have the ability to make a claim. So it isn't perfect. It wasn't meant to be perfect. And it never could be perfect. But at the end, a lot of people will have an opportunity to make claims that they never could have made. And I tell you that I have never been so concerned about a settlement as this one, nor have we ever gotten as many concessions as we got from the other side, meaning the Austrians, as we got in this one. They bent over backwards. But there has never been a settlement like this when we have changed Austrian law, we have created a system, and we have done a measure of justice, not perfection. Thank you."

He was right that it was not a perfect agreement. Before rushing out to catch his plane, Muzicant scribbled a note to Eizenstat explaining that "subject to review and discussion, as needed, essential concepts of the proposal are acceptable in principle." But on his return to Vienna, Muzicant lobbied the Austrian government for more. He felt duped as he discovered two weeks later that the other negotiators had extracted separate concessions in side letters to the main agreement.

Muzicant now insisted on "a declaration" that the government would guarantee his community's survival by returning around 10 percent of the Jewish assets stolen or destroyed under Nazi rule. He also demanded the return of all Jewish property in public hands— not just the federal government, but local governments too. Muzicant estimated that 200 billion schillings were stolen, worth around $13.3 billion, of which only 40 percent was returned. Without both concessions, the Jewish community could not give up its right to sue forever. It would be tantamount to agreeing to its own liquidation.

For the chancellor and his aides, Muzicant could not have made his demands at a worse time. Schüssel wanted to force through the law enacting the property deal in only ten days—an unprecedented effort in Austrian legislation, requiring his officials to work without sleep for three nights. The deadline was so tight that parliamentarians had no time to read the legislation before voting it through the committee stage. Above all, Schüssel insisted that the law must be passed swiftly enough to prevent it becoming a political football in the forthcoming municipal elections in Vienna at the end of March.

Just hours before parliament voted, Muzicant declared he would not agree to the deal—even though he had initialed it. "The state is holding on to wealth from which Jewish blood is dripping," he told reporters.

Within a month, a group of Holocaust victims who rejected the Austrian deal filed a new lawsuit in Los Angeles against the Austrian government and the country's leading businesses. Herbert Fenster, the survivors' attorney, said the settlement was "pulled out of the air" and was "deeply flawed."

Muzicant's demands prompted the first public intervention by Jörg Haider, the effective leader of the Freedom Party, who attacked the settlement on Jewish property. "There must be an end at one point," he told a Freedom Party meeting in Vienna. He condemned Chancellor Schüssel's desire for a deal as a "treacherous hope" that he could win "overwhelming applause from the East Coast"—Haider's shorthand for Jews in New York and Washington. He also attacked Muzicant for demanding that Austria should pick up his own community's debts. Haider placed the Jewish question at the center of the upcoming elections as a way of targeting the city's Social Democratic mayor, Michael Häupl. To illustrate the choice Austrians faced, he cited the name of the mayor's election consultant—Stan Greenberg, the Democratic pollster who advised the Clinton White House and Ehud Barak, the Israeli prime minister.

"Häupl has a campaign strategist whose name is Greenberg," Haider said, to laughter from the crowd. "He had him flown in from the East Coast. Dear friends, you have the choice, between the spin-doctor Greenberg from the East Coast and the Heart of Vienna."

On Ash Wednesday, at a Freedom Party rally of more than two thousand supporters, Haider was in similar rabble-rousing form. In a pun on a brand of soap powder, he suggested that Muzicant was hiding a scandalous past. "I don't understand how someone called Ariel can have such dirty hands," he taunted the Jewish leader, echoing the "dirty Jew" propaganda of the Nazi regime.

Haider's tactics failed in the Viennese elections. His Freedom Party won around 20 percent of the vote, down from 27 percent in the national elections, which had taken them into the coalition government. Haider blamed the party's defeat on his political ally Chancellor Schüssel, arguing that he needed to introduce "more heart in his policies" and more concern for the common man.

Schüssel's government appeared to have traveled full circle. The chancellor seized on Holocaust compensation in part to inoculate himself against public criticism of his partnership with Haider's party. Once the compensation deals were settled, Haider reemerged to poison Austria's political debate and further tarnish his country's image around the world. Schüssel succeeded in securing an international Holocaust settlement, but there were few signs of reconciliation at home.

For Austrian government officials, the rancorous dispute over the Holocaust deal—and the ensuing political controversy—was squarely Muzicant's responsibility. "There was a real consensus," lamented one official. "The only thing that was unpleasant was the Jewish community, which Schüssel will never forgive them for. Muzicant threatened to use his international contacts against this country, which doesn't go over well with the government. When Schüssel hears the word Muzicant now, everything shuts down."

Muzicant remained unrepentant: "Yes, I fought this government. Yes, I was outspoken. I fought Schüssel because he is responsible for the government and not Haider. It was Schüssel who made Haider possible. I am not going to keep quiet. It increased anti-Semitism, but this is not my personal decision. This is overwhelmingly the opinion of the Austrian Jewish community."

Israel Singer saw Muzicant's vocal campaign as proof that his long struggle against European governments and companies had succeeded. Instead of relying on American Jews to confront their opponents, European Jews were now fighting for themselves. "Two years ago, Jews were afraid in Europe," Singer said. "Now they are speaking up themselves. We no longer have to act the way we did in the Waldheim case. We should be proud of the fact that we gave them the courage to behave in a way which is different.

That's why the governments are behaving in an aggressive way. They don't see the Jews cowering and cringing."

Other Jews, however, were neither cowering nor fighting. Simon Wiesenthal, the Nazi-hunter and survivor of Mauthausen, bitterly opposed the compensation payments. "Look, I am a survivor," he said in his dusty Vienna office, heaving with books, archives, and index cards. "I come to the office every day for two or three hours because this is part of my life. If we close this office, I will sit at home and wait for death. Do you understand me? When I am in the office, and friends come and they talk about this, no one is satisfied by the situation. The laws have a nice name, but when you look at them and what people receive, it is nothing.

"Survivors my age, they need nothing. Every law is coming too late, and a law too late doesn't make sense. This makes me sick talking about this."

TWENTY-THREE

Assigning Guilt

To American eyes, the signing of the Austrian settlement appeared to mark the end of the Holocaust restitution campaign of the 1990s, completing the journey that Israel Singer had begun five and a half years earlier. The deal came within twenty-four hours of the French agreement, on January 18, 2001, during a last session of intense all-night negotiations in Washington. As President Clinton left the White House at the end of the week, Stuart Eizenstat left office and the battle seemed to be over. The German foundation was ready to start paying former slave laborers, waiting only for a handful of U.S. judges to dismiss the class action lawsuits against German companies. Under the deal signed in Berlin, lawyers on all sides had agreed to seek the dismissal of their own cases in exchange for 10 billion deutsche marks of compensation. With the support of the lawyers and governments on both sides, dismissal appeared to be a mere formality.

Two federal judges had already fallen into line. Judge William Bassler of New Jersey dismissed the slave labor lawsuit in November 2000. The following month, Judge Michael Mukasey of Manhattan dismissed the insurance lawsuit, praising the lawyers' fine work. After sparsely attended public hearings, both judges found the cases so clear-cut that they took the unusual step of issuing immediate rulings from the bench, without taking time to deliberate.

Only Judge Shirley Wohl Kram of Manhattan remained. She was expected to dismiss the litigation against the German banks, and she scheduled her own hearing on Wednesday, January 24, six days after the Austrian government made its peace in Washington. The fate of the entire $5 billion German compensation package—destined for hundreds of thousands of Holocaust survivors and former forced laborers—rested with her.

As 10:30 approached, spectators packed into her courtroom on the sixth floor of the Southern District of New York's grand copper-spired courthouse in downtown Manhattan. German news outlets worked on the assumption that Kram would dismiss the case there and then, and German journalists occupied a whole row of seats in the courtroom, hoping for a dismissal in time for the evening news bulletins back home. So many lawyers were clustered around the table before the judge's bench that some had to take their seats on the press benches. Professor Burt Neuborne was one of them: looking like a man about to see a dentist, he crossed his arms and folded them defensively high across his chest.

Neuborne was now the effective leader of the fractious plaintiffs' lawyers. As "settlement counsel," he was responsible for ensuring that the agreement was enacted and held a seat on the board of the German foundation. He believed he could persuade the Germans to accept a dismissal from Judge Kram as legal peace, triggering immediate payments to survivors.

However, Shirley Kram was a notorious wild card. A seventy-eight-year-old widow who retained great energy, she was a controversial figure among the attorneys in New York's Southern District, many of whom disliked her condescending manner in court. Kram owed her elevation to the bench almost twenty years earlier to Al D'Amato. The New York senator had plucked her from her career as a children's court judge to name her in his first federal judicial recommendation after winning his seat in the U.S. Senate. Kram subsequently returned the favor by naming D'Amato her special master in the Holocaust litigation, giving him the power to mediate a settlement within weeks of his election defeat in November 1998.

Neuborne recalled Judge Kram's performance two years earlier in a much smaller lawsuit, the Holocaust litigation against Bank Austria. In that case, originally part of the litigation against the

German banks, she had accepted a $40 million settlement over strong objections from Neuborne and Israel Singer, who considered it far too low. Kram overruled them largely because of a substantial sweetener that Bank Austria had added to its cash payment. Bank Austria claimed that Deutsche and Dresdner, the largest German banks, had looted it during the Anschluss, and it reserved the right to sue for damages. The Austrian bank's attorneys offered the victims the chance to sue the German banks on its behalf, suggesting its claims could be worth a huge amount. Any money they extracted could then be used to swell the pot for Austrian survivors.

The dark-robed judge finally arrived more than half an hour late, carrying a black leather pocketbook. A bustling figure with neatly trimmed gray hair and glasses perching low on her nose, she had the bearing of a bad-tempered high school principal and looked younger than her age. Without apologizing for her lateness, she launched into a brief explanation of the case for the audience, making clear that it could only be dismissed with her approval: "This is to ensure that the settlement hasn't been contrived for the benefit of lawyers or named plaintiffs," she said.

Then she called on Burt Neuborne, who was not prepared to address the court. He gasped, then stood and strode to the lectern, speaking without notes. He started to explain that he was there both as counsel for plaintiffs and as a trustee of the new German foundation, when Kram interrupted to say he only had ten minutes to speak.

She interrupted him a few more times as he explained the legal principles that underlay the baroque architecture of the German compact. The plaintiffs had opted to dismiss the case voluntarily. Under U.S. laws of procedure, this stripped her of any discretion to rule whether the settlement was fair or adequate. Instead, she had merely to decide whether there was collusion between the lawyers—a laughable possibility given the well-known acrimony of the negotiations—and whether there was prejudice to possible plaintiffs who had not yet joined the action.

When Neuborne finished, Kram stared at him from the bench and asked if there was an appeals process for people whose applications for compensation were rejected.

"The short answer is no. We are committed to . . ."

"I know," interrupted Kram. "But you don't presently have an apparatus set up."

Then she asked if the German foundation had set up an auditing system. Neuborne started to tell her that the German ministry of finance would monitor payments, when Kram interrupted again. "So there will be no outside independent auditing?"

She said she had thought a large accounting firm would do the auditing.

"That's an enormously expensive proposition," protested Neuborne. "That money has to come from somewhere. The balance between the best possible audit and the most possible money to victims is a difficult one."

Kram interjected to insist on strict accounting and then called Larry Kill, who usually worked in tandem with Bob Swift. As Swift was on a fly-fishing vacation, it fell to Kill to explain how aggressive the negotiations had been. Kram interrupted to ask if he had been present for all the negotiations.

When Kill said yes, she posed another question: "Are there any agreements or understandings that may affect the funding of the foundation that haven't been presented to the court?"

Kill, looking startled, said there were none to his knowledge.

"You say you were present for *all* the negotiations?"

Kill said that all the agreements had been disclosed.

She continued her barrage of questions and summoned up the ghost of the settlement with Bank Austria and the transfer of its claims against the German banks. She had vivid recollections of the evidence she had heard from Bob Swift, who suggested their value could be as much as $300 million.

"Part of the reason that a $40 million figure was considered adequate was because supposedly these assigned claims had value," she said. Now she wanted to know why "nothing was ever done" about them. Why had they been ignored?

"I would like to know whether there wasn't a conflict of interest."

As Kill told how the assigned claims had become a bargaining chip in the negotiations, Deborah Sturman left her seat and leaned over to Neuborne, asking if she should intervene.

Neuborne shook his head vigorously. "There's no talking to her," he said. "There's no point."

Larry Kill's ordeal continued for several more minutes before Kram motioned for him to sit. Kill turned from the lectern with a visible shrug. "I know I asked you a lot of questions," said Judge Kram with a sweet smile as he walked, "but you really have to try to get some answers. Thank you."

Neuborne's face grew longer as the hearing continued. A succession of lawyers spoke, and all received the same imperious treatment. Kram repeatedly asked whether any secret deals had been left undisclosed, her obvious skepticism unpunctured by any of the lawyers' arguments.

Then she turned to Jack Dweck, a friend who had represented her personally in two real estate transactions and ran a small law firm out of offices in Manhattan's Helmsley Building. Kram had tapped him to lead the pursuit of the Austrian banks' assigned claims. Dweck pled with the judge not to dismiss the case. "It's our belief," he said, "that the claim on behalf of the Austrian banks that was assigned probably involves billions of dollars." Fifteen months earlier, when she cleared the Bank Austria settlement, Judge Kram had heard that they were worth only $300 million. Now the price was rising.

Dweck added, "I have taken it upon myself, with the mandate I had from this court, to file a complaint."

In other words, Judge Kram herself had asked him to sue German companies for the wrongs they had done to the Austrian banks during the Anschluss. The "assigned claims," thrown into the $40 million Austrian deal almost two years earlier, now stood as a serious obstacle to the $5 billion German foundation.

The German journalists, who had come to see the final declaration of peace, instead bore witness to the launch of yet another lawsuit. The legal war was not over.

Kram announced that she was reserving her decision—a hammer blow to confidence in Germany after the swift decisions other judges had made to dismiss the cases before them. "It's a tough decision in many ways," she said. "I am well aware that time is of the essence. It's very important. But as I indicated earlier, I'm not just sitting here to take up room."

With that she swept out of the room, leaving the lawyers below her to exhale deeply. Neuborne rose slowly. He knew that the delay and the new lawsuit would strike at the core of the German compact—the hard-fought notion that the Clinton administration's intervention would persuade judges to dismiss the cases.

The other lawyers huddled, gazing with intense embarrassment at the row of German journalists. "You know," confided one, "I think that was even more embarrassing for American justice than the Supreme Court and Florida."

At the center of the impasse was Charles Moerdler, the lawyer who had represented the Austrian Jewish community in the Austrian talks. Still speaking with a noticeable British accent, the legacy of a childhood spent in England after his family's flight from Germany, Moerdler professed to dislike Germans. He also had a strong sense of Jewish identity. He served as an overseer of the Jewish Theological Seminary, keeper of the flame of conservative Judaism in the United States, and Rabbi Israel Miller, chairman of the Claims Conference, had officiated at his wedding.

With a history like this, Moerdler seemed a natural friend and ally for the class action lawyers. But instead, his hardball tactics on behalf of Bank Austria aroused bitter resentment. An aggressive negotiator, by turns charming and then rude and bullying, he had a track record as a political "fixer" for Austrian banks. So it was natural that Gerhard Randa, Bank Austria's chief executive, turned to Moerdler in 1998 after reading a report about Deutsche Bank's gold transactions during the war. Compiled by a team of historians Deutsche had assembled, the report noted that the transit agent for Deutsche's gold shipments from Berlin to Istanbul was the Austrian bank Creditanstalt.

Bank Austria had just merged with Creditanstalt and was running scared. While only a minnow of European banking, it was by far the biggest bank in Austria and its offices in New York opened it to the risk of class actions in U.S. courts. It was also the successor to Creditanstalt and Länderbank—both of which had been controlled by the giant German banks Deutsche and Dresdner during the war. With nothing to gain from protracted litigation, Randa wanted to settle swiftly with his Jewish accusers.

Moerdler disliked the idea of litigating against Holocaust survivors and told Randa that he would in no circumstances take the case to court. Rather, he would negotiate a settlement, justifying his involvement by securing payments for survivors faster than anyone else. He also insisted that any historical records uncovered should be put on the public record. Luckily, he knew Judge Kram well. She was a personal friend of his wife, and Moerdler had often worked as Kram's special master on technical cases.

Nobody had yet sued Bank Austria, but Moerdler approached Ed Fagan to tell him Bank Austria wanted to settle if sued. Fagan was only too ready to oblige. By adding the Austrian banks to his slim complaint against the German banks, he and his colleagues Bob Swift and Larry Kill gained a tidy jump on the rival faction of plaintiff lawyers led by Michael Hausfeld and Mel Weiss. Still bloodied by their disagreements over the Swiss case, the two factions now attacked each other in open court. Swift's faction accused Hausfeld and Weiss of attempting to lure away lawyers from their team and even enticing away their plaintiffs. Kram described the affair as "disgraceful" in court, which appeared to strengthen the position of Swift and Fagan.

Conditions were ideal for Moerdler to secure a good deal for the banks. He held what was in effect a "reverse auction," talking to the two factions and asking each of them how much they would accept in settlement. The lowest bidder would win—a contest in which Mel Weiss, who expected at least $100 million, had no hope. Bob Swift, however, would settle for far less, and Moerdler thrashed out $40 million as a fair compromise with him.

Accompanied by Al D'Amato, Moerdler also held talks with Israel Singer who had not become involved to this point. Moerdler held out a bait for him. In return for legal peace, he could open the banks' archives to inspection. With any luck, that would yield the incriminating documents needed to force more money out of Deutsche and Dresdner banks, the true villains of the piece in his mind.

Israel Singer liked the concept, while Elan Steinberg briefed the press that the Austrian settlement would allow pursuers to get at the truth about the German banks. Moerdler sent a team of more than thirty Bank Austria employees to look through the bank's well-ordered archives. Describing himself as "ever distrustful of certain Teutonic tribes," he appointed John Rees, an English management consultant, to supervise them. The researchers combed the archives, cellars, and boiler rooms of the banks going through seventy different locations, spreading from Vienna itself into Poland, Russia, and Germany, delving through about two thousand boxes of documents.

Moerdler needed to bring at least one member of the rival faction of plaintiff lawyers on board and turned to Michael Hausfeld, who had wanted to settle at $75 million but realized a deal was in hand at almost half that amount. Attempting to salvage what he could, Hausfeld suggested part of the cash could be allocated to cover the costs of archiving the material from the banks. He proposed that $2 million should go to the U.S. Holocaust Memorial Museum in Washington, and Moerdler happily agreed.

Hausfeld was already planning how to spend the money with the Holocaust museum when his rival attorneys discovered the deal and informed the museum's directors, telling them the museum was effectively taking cash away from needy survivors. If the money was not spent on archives, it would otherwise go to Holocaust victims. Hausfeld insisted that the museum funds were negotiated separately from the rest of the deal, but it was too late. The Holocaust museum found the controversy embarrassing and pulled out.

By the end of January 1999, after several weeks of negotiations with Singer, Moerdler drafted an outline settlement. Bank Austria would pay $30 million into a settlement fund, which would be disbursed by the Claims Conference. A further $10 million would cover any claims made before the settlement was cleared, along with administrative, legal, and archiving expenses.

D'Amato arranged a signing ceremony in the grandeur of Claridge's Hotel in London, a conveniently neutral location. Singer arrived, read the memorandum, asked for a few changes, and signed. However, confusion reigned over exactly what Singer agreed to. The typed paper he signed includes two passages that have been crudely scratched out with a pen.

Even with the agreement, Moerdler felt something was missing. The $40 million deal looked tiny after the $1.25 billion paid by the Swiss banks, and nobody had researched how many claims might be outstanding. Moerdler therefore decided to add the assigned claims that would later create so much controversy. He said the survivors' attorneys could take over the right to sue the German banks for looting during the Anschluss, making the $40 million headline number more palatable. Even though the Austrian banks had never sued Deutsche or Dresdner, Moerdler believed the Germans should pay. It would not cost his clients a penny.

Swift accepted the idea, and they had a deal to take to Judge Kram. In March 1998, she accepted it on the advice of Moerdler and D'Amato, despite furious opposition from Israel Singer and Mel Weiss, who thought $40 million far too little. Kram ignored them and set November 1 as the date for a "fairness hearing," where claimants could make objections.

An outraged Singer formed the impression that both D'Amato and Kram would do whatever Moerdler asked them. It had not even occurred to him that a judge could clear a settlement to which he objected. He argued that the papers he signed at Claridge's were only a draft and claimed he never accepted that $40 million was enough. Further, the documentation coming out of Bank Austria turned out, to his disappointment, not to add much to the public record about Deutsche Bank. Singer told D'Amato that he wanted more money for his colleagues at the Claims Conference.

Moerdler complained that he had already taken the settlement to the bank's board, which had approved it. Singer was disavowing his own signature. He eventually snapped, "Fine, we'll go without you."

Now Moerdler told Judge Kram that Singer was looking for more money. After Kram verified this with D'Amato, she said, "They are out. They get nothing." The WJC and the Claims Conference, previously guaranteed a role in deciding how to divide the money and administer claims, were now excluded altogether.

This provoked Elan Steinberg, Israel Singer's colleague at the

WJC, to launch a six-month publicity campaign against Bank Austria, using tactics honed in the Swiss battle, such as threats of boycotts from Alan Hevesi. Moerdler finally agreed to make an extra payment of $5 million to the Claims Conference. Singer also wanted a formal apology from the Austrian banks, but Moerdler refused—unless it was balanced by an apology from Elan Steinberg for his public criticisms of the Austrians. Steinberg, rarely at a loss for words, was struck dumb by the notion that his aggressive brand of public relations campaigning was morally equivalent to stealing from Holocaust victims, and refused.

Unnoticed amid the recriminations, Moerdler and Swift drew up a crucial addendum about the assigned claims, which they added to the settlement agreement in May 1999. Couched in thick legalese, Moerdler attested that "no warranties shall be deemed to have been expressed or implied by the Austrian banks." In other words, the Austrian banks were not guaranteeing that their claims against the German banks were worth anything.

The names of neither Mel Weiss nor Burt Neuborne appeared on the list of signatories to this addendum, and when the final settlement came before the judge, they refused to sign it, with Weiss saying that he did not oppose it but did not support it either. Moerdler ridiculed this position, saying, "Either he gets something he likes and says he's part of it, or he has an obligation to oppose it."

Both Weiss and Neuborne believed that the claims could not be worth much. Neuborne assumed they were merely "scrip" thrown in to make the settlement look more generous and win the judge's approval. If the claims had been truly valuable, he reasoned, Bank Austria would have filed suit itself some time in the last fifty years.

When Kram held her hearing on the fairness of the settlement in November 1999, Weiss, Neuborne, and Hausfeld all absented themselves, as did Israel Singer. For all the fierce arguments they had made in the judge's chambers, they would not go public with them in court. Instead, the day was left to Bob Swift, lead counsel for the plaintiffs, and Charles Moerdler. Swift spoke first, announced that he anticipated about one thousand valid claims on the settlement fund, and stated that the assigned claims against the German banks may be worth "up to $300 million."

Moerdler followed with a passionate speech about the Holocaust, which he called a "genuine mea culpa, *mea culpa maxima,* and an apology" on behalf of Bank Austria. He reserved his vitriol for the German banks. "The record demonstrates that at war's end, both Creditanstalt and Länderbank were hopelessly insolvent," he said, "the Reich and the German banks having siphoned off the hard assets of these Austrian banks during the course of the war and largely replaced them with valueless paper."

D'Amato set great store by the assigned claims, which he said had been discussed in the negotiations with Germany. "Plaintiffs' counsel have raised the matter of this assignment in the ongoing negotiations with the German bank defendants," he said. "I believe that they are very valuable and will, at the very least, aid in a settlement of that outstanding matter."

In support, Swift called John Rees, the English management consultant Moerdler had hired to oversee the search of Bank Austria's archives. Rees testified that he and his team had looked closely at the securities that were taken from the bank during 1938 and 1939 and transferred to Hermann Göring Werke and other German companies. He estimated their value at $300 million "in today's dollars." Swift only asked him one question about the claims, and nobody apart from Moerdler cross-examined him. No more witnesses were called, and no one said anything about the Austrian banks' refusal to guarantee that the claims were worth anything.

Instead, Judge Kram heard a series of impassioned pleas from Austrian survivors and their heirs who felt that the settlement was by no means enough. Several pointed out that eleven thousand claims had already been sent in, far swamping the one thousand that Swift estimated.

Moerdler concluded by promising to help "realize the maximum potential" of the assigned claims, "for it is true beyond words that these wrongs must, to the maximum extent that law and justice permit, be righted."

Judge Kram cleared the settlement, saying that she believed the assignment of the Austrian banks' claims would ensure that the final amount paid would fall "well within the range of reasonableness." She ended the hearing in classic schoolteacher style by thanking her friend Al D'Amato, "certainly a special master who gets a special star."

The assigned claims met a painful fate in the German negotiations. When they came up in discussions, the German negotiators produced a passage from the treaty establishing the state of Austria in 1955. It explicitly waived all claims by Austrian nationals against Germany for any losses during the Anschluss. The treaty was not some obscure, forgotten legal tract but one of the centerpieces of cold war geopolitics, agreed to by the Soviet Union and the West, recreating Austria as an independent nation outside both NATO and the Warsaw Pact. But nobody had mentioned it to Judge Kram in 1999.

Once the treaty was revealed, no middle ground remained between the rival factions of lawyers. Neuborne and his colleagues believed that the value of the assigned claims had been deliberately exaggerated before Judge Kram in a bid to make her accept an inadequate settlement. They held Moerdler responsible.

Moerdler, meanwhile, believed the plaintiffs' lawyers should have pointed out any reservations about the value of the claims to Judge Kram before she cleared the Bank Austria settlement. His view was that the treaty did not necessarily void claims by one financial institution against another.

Whatever the rival attorneys thought, the lawyers for the German banks thought it obvious that the treaty voided all claims by the Austrian banks. Neuborne and the other plaintiffs' lawyers agreed. Bob Swift and Larry Kill, colead counsels in the Bank Austria settlement, were the only exceptions. They persisted in arguing that some money should be earmarked for their Austrian claimants, giving up their efforts only on March 23, 2000, as Stuart Eizenstat forced through his settlement in Berlin.

Kram showed her disapproval of the German agreement even before it had been signed. On May 17, 2000, Al D'Amato, acting as her special master, called a meeting of all the lawyers in the case. D'Amato complained to them that the German deal took no account of the Austrian banks. The judge had approved the $40 million settlement because she believed the assigned claims were worth between $300 million and $350 million. D'Amato warned that the Berlin agreements were not binding on Judge Kram. "I think that what might very well take place is a Herculean effort involving thousands of hours being wiped out because you didn't pay attention to the fact that you are going to have to get this court to agree."

Instead, in July 2000, the German defense lawyers joined with most of their opponents in going to the Multi-District Panel, a group of judges who allocated cases across state boundaries. Nervous about the risk of cantankerous behavior by Judge Kram, they proposed that the banks case should be moved to the New Jersey court of Judge Bassler, who also adjudicated the slave labor cases. However, Bob Swift wanted to leave the cases with Kram, prompting the suspicion among his fellow lawyers that he was hoping any extra money from the assigned claims would allow him to claim a bigger fee. The judges on the Multi-District Panel let her keep the case.

D'Amato told the banks' lawyers that they could buy Kram's approval by making an extra payment to Austrian survivors, but he received no response. After the marathon negotiations leading to the German deal, the chances that anyone in Germany would produce more money were zero. When Charles Stillman, another of Kram's special masters, later examined the issue, he sided not with D'Amato but with the Germans and emphatically advised Judge Kram to dismiss the lawsuits without delay. But her demeanor on January 24 left no room for doubt—she was convinced that the Austrian survivors had been treated unjustly.

———•◆•———

On the afternoon of January 26, 2001, two days after Kram's hearing on the German settlement, Burt Neuborne arrived back in his office at New York University. In the intervening forty-eight hours he had made a whirlwind trip to Berlin, where he had attempted to convince skeptical colleagues on the board of the German foundation that he could deliver legal peace. He hoped that Kram would dismiss the German suits but suspected he needed to ready himself for a long legal battle.

A devotee of British comedy, Neuborne found an analogy in Monty Python. Like the bellicose knight in *Monty Python and the Holy Grail,* he might have lost both his arms and legs in combat. But he was still game for a fight.

Legal Peace?

Itook only twenty-six pages of understated legal argument for
Judge Kram to stop the German settlement in its tracks. On
March 7, 2001, she issued a memorandum, opinion, and
order refusing to dismiss the cases before her and left the $5 bil-
lion German settlement floating in a legal limbo—all for the sake
of the earlier, far smaller deal with Austria.

Kram savaged the German deal for failing to take the Austrian
settlement into account. She argued that the plaintiffs' attorneys
suffered a conflict of interest which led them to give up the fight
for Austrian claimants in favor of more money for other survivors.
Furthermore, she tore into the Clinton administration's "statement of interest," saying it impinged on the separation of powers
between the executive and judicial branches of government.
Kram argued that the administration's statement was so powerful
that she represented the claimants' last hope in court.

Kram's move also undermined German public confidence in
the settlement, making it look as though the U.S. government
could not deliver the legal peace it had promised. Would another
willful judge tear up the settlement and start all over again?

Israel Singer reacted with moral outrage. "Any person, be they
a judicial person or a normal person, who delays closure is delaying payments to survivors, who are dying," he boomed. "They
should remember that and have it on their conscience." But
Singer was virtually powerless, as were politicians on both sides of

the Atlantic. The only arena that mattered now was the U.S. court in the Southern District of New York.

Judge Kram attacked the German companies for failing to fund the foundation fully. In spite of massive mailings, widespread advertising, and behind-the-scenes pressure, thousands of small companies were refusing to take part. Germany's largest companies represented by far the biggest contributors among the six thousand businesses that signed up to the deal by the end of 2000. Overall, German industry was more than 1 billion deutsche marks short of its promised 5 billion contribution.

The delays looked terrible to the survivors. At Warsaw's State Jewish Theatre, eight elderly Poles dropped coins into a collection box marked "Voluntary Contributions for German Industry," in an attempt to embarrass the German companies. Rather than blame the obscure judge in New York, the survivors accused German companies of hiding behind the legal technicalities. Privately, the German industrialists worried that the delays were sapping public support for their agreement.

Within a week of Kram's ruling, the German companies pieced together a financial guarantee for the 5 billion deutsche marks. If necessary, the seventeen founding companies would raise their contributions to close the gap. Judge Kram had succeeded in forcing their hand and was hailed as a hero in Germany. Several German newspapers ran editorials thanking her for shaming German companies into doing the right thing and saving the nation from embarrassment—the *Berliner Morgenpost* even anointed her "A Judge with Courage."

Kram was not the only person to undermine German confidence in their negotiated deal. Three weeks earlier, on Saturday, February 10, Burt Neuborne entertained Michael Hausfeld at his apartment in Manhattan. He liked Hausfeld despite their disagreements during the German case, and it was good to meet his wife for the first time. Neuborne confided that he was near the end of his tether with the German case and wanted the whole saga to end.

He was an expert in election law, the nation had just suffered the
Florida presidential recount, and he was itching to get back to his
life's work. He just hoped that nobody would bring any more lawsuits because with the skittish mood in Germany, fresh legal
action might torpedo the deal for good.

Hausfeld was uncomfortable with the discussion and preferred
to concentrate on social chitchat, wanting to spare his long-
suffering wife from inside-baseball analysis of their legal battles.
When Neuborne suggested things were tense in Germany, Hausfeld looked askance and replied, "I think it's going to get even
more tense."

The next day's *Washington Post* published extracts from a sensa-
tionalist new book, *IBM and the Holocaust*, which alleged that IBM
had sold the Nazis punch card technology to help them organize
deportations and mass murders. Then the Internet hummed with
another story: a lawsuit had been filed against IBM on Saturday
morning in the federal district court in Brooklyn. Monday
brought news that Hausfeld was leading the lawsuit, just as the
book went on sale in forty different countries, including Germany. The German press portrayed the lawsuit as a fresh American legal attack over Nazi crimes.

Hausfeld's characteristically eloquent complaint accused IBM's
employees of entering concentration camps to fix card-sorting
machines and therefore knowingly helping the Nazis to execute
the Holocaust. But Neuborne knew nothing about it, and he felt
undermined by Hausfeld's unilateral actions.

Hausfeld claimed he was partly pursuing the promise of a 1 billion deutsche mark contribution by U.S. companies with a presence in the Third Reich. He also spoke of plans to sue 100
different American corporations that had profited from Nazi
Germany. But whatever his justifications, Hausfeld had clearly
broken the spirit, if not the letter, of the Berlin agreement, which
expressly committed the lawyers to dismiss all Holocaust litigation against Germany. He was forced to write a letter of explanation to his Eastern European clients, arguing that his actions did
not threaten legal peace, and within weeks he withdrew the suit,
without opening negotiations with IBM or serving them with a
writ.

Hausfeld claimed his interest in the case was satisfied by IBM's agreement to open its wartime archives—an action they had taken months before his lawsuit—and quietly dropped his demands for the disgorgement of IBM's ill-gotten profits. The incident left the impression that he had piggybacked on the book's publicity to raise his own profile.

Kram, and her defense of the Bank Austria claimants, remained the biggest obstacle to legal peace. Without resolving the problem, the German foundation was dead. The stymied lawyers on all sides could choose among three options. One was to persuade the judge to change her mind. Another was to convince the German banks to pay more in settlement of the claims. The final option was to ask the appeals court to force her to dismiss. This would require a little used legal maneuver called a writ of mandamus, which appeals courts only use for overturning blatantly erroneous decisions.

Neuborne, in his element when it came to legal theorizing, and enraged by Kram's behavior, could not wait to see her in court. After a few days studying precedents in the New York University library, he was sure he could not only defeat but humiliate Judge Kram. The drawback was that the appeals process would likely take some months.

On Tuesday, March 20, Neuborne filed his papers calling for a mandamus with the appeals court. To do this Neuborne, alongside the defense lawyers, tried to prove that Kram had prejudged that the assigned Austrian claims were worth something. After all, she had only cleared the Austrian banks settlement on the basis that the claims would add to its value, and she risked looking foolish if they turned out to be worthless.

Neuborne's papers showed a fine legal mind in overdrive. Citing fifty-five cases and twelve statutes, he said that Kram's decision was a "gross usurpation and abuse" of her limited powers—the kind of strong language needed to sway appeals court judges into the extreme step of forcing a lower district judge to change her decision. But Neuborne's prose also dripped with personal contempt for Kram. He variously condemned her course of action as "completely indefensible" and her reasoning as "inexplicable." He accused her of "taking money out of the pockets of some Holocaust victims to put it into the pockets of victims who enjoy the patronage of the District Court." And he savaged her for acting with a reckless disregard for the victims. "In order to protect Holocaust victims against a non-existent possibility of future harm, the District Court has condemned them to an indefinite delay in receiving long overdue compensation."

Neuborne did not apologize for the colorful language, which he saw as a trademark of his advocacy. "This was a mandamus petition, not a tea party," he said. On the same day, Judge Kram issued a statement continuing her refusal to dismiss the case and rebutting arguments Bob Swift had made to her in an attempt to make her change her mind. The fate of the settlement now lay with the appeals court, which could not hold a hearing until May. Money for survivors was now delayed by at least five months.

Within a week of Neuborne filing his appeal, Judge Kram hired trial lawyer David Boies to represent her, signaling that she would not give up easily. In the preceding two years, Boies had arguably become the nation's best-known lawyer, representing Vice President Al Gore in his fight to win the Florida recount in the 2000 presidential elections as well as leading the U.S. government's antitrust case against Microsoft. Dressed in a series of identical cheap Sears catalog suits and sporting black Reebok shoes, he did not look the part of the hotshot lawyer. But Boies cultivated his everyman image to mask his talent as a legal tactician. Famed for his near-photographic memory, Boies once fancied his chances as a professional blackjack player and now loved the craps table. In litigation he liked to assess the odds of winning each case and enjoyed narrowing his opponents' chances of success. For Boies, hard work and meticulous planning were far more effective than the rhetorical grandstanding of flashier attorneys.

However, he was unfamiliar with the Holocaust compensation campaign—the years of feuding and the endless hours of complex and emotional talks. He knew most of the leading lawyers involved and even claimed that Stuart Eizenstat had introduced him to his wife, Mary, when they had worked together in the Carter White House. But he had never taken a personal interest in the Nazi-era lawsuits, in spite of the best efforts of Swift and Fagan to add his name to their first German lawsuit. When the call came from Kram's chambers, Boies jumped at the high-profile job.

Others were appalled. Weiss and Eizenstat urged him to drop the case, saying it was vital to dismiss the lawsuits quickly. But it was too late for Boies to pull out. Reading Kram's opinion, he felt that she had taken a principled stand to defend the apparently voiceless victims of the Austrian banks when everyone else wanted to drive the settlement through, no matter what the harm to the Austrian victims' claims.

"Nobody lightly wants to step in front of this locomotive," recalled Boies. "On the other hand, I thought that the judge's decision was right. I thought that even if the hydraulics of the situation were such that she was going to get run over, it was the right thing to represent her."

Boies agreed with Kram that the lawyers suffered a substantial conflict of interest. Nobody was representing the Austrian bank claims, and it was no good saying those claims were worthless now, when nobody had told her at the time she agreed to the Austrian bank deal.

"There was nothing in the record that justified giving substantial amounts to everyone but the Austrian bank assigned claims," Boies contended, as he read the transcript of Kram's fairness hearing. "You had a negotiation in which lawyers who were representing multiple classes of plaintiffs were in effect trading off one group of plaintiffs' claims in favor of another. The way it came down, you had a very troubling situation."

For Michael Hausfeld, Boies's arrival was a golden opportunity to break the deadlock. He had worked closely with Boies in a recent $1 billion settlement of a class action case against a worldwide vitamins cartel. Here was a priceless chance to reestablish himself as a leader in the Nazi litigation and redeem himself after his IBM escapade.

"I understand a lot of people would like you to resign," Hausfeld told Boies on the phone. "I personally think it's almost better with you in there because you can understand what the situation is and you have the persona to recommend a resolution."

Boies began by seeking a lump sum of around $25 million to settle the assigned claims, but Hausfeld flatly ruled out extra cash. "The Germans aren't going to give you any," he said. "The Central and Eastern Europeans don't have any. And you certainly can't expect any from the victims. You have no source of your money."

Racing against the date of the impending appeals court hearing, Hausfeld regrouped his coalition of European governments. By the end of April, he drew up a series of options to settle the dispute, starting with an offer by the Central and Eastern European diplomats to "urge and support" the German foundation to change its rules to allow compensation for the Austrian claims. They could do nothing more than promise to advocate the rule change, as they were outnumbered on the German foundation board.

On the first Monday in May, they met for talks in Hausfeld's newly opened New York office. Boies flew in that morning from Lake Maggiore in Italy, where he had been speaking at a conference. Feeling relaxed after his weekend by the picturesque northern Italian lake, Boies was impressed by Hausfeld's offer. In addition to the attempt to change the foundation's rules, Hausfeld even volunteered to sweeten the deal by waiving his legal fees in the Austrian settlement and also offered to hand over more than $2 million set aside for the archiving of bank records. Boies was unaware that the archival funds were unwanted by their initial recipient—the U.S. Holocaust Memorial Museum in Washington.

After hearing the pleas of the Central and Eastern Europeans, Boies agreed to the deal. Impressed by Hausfeld's selfless decision to waive his fees, he stepped out to call Judge Kram.

"We think there could be a meeting of minds," he said on his return. "I'm going to the court and we're just going to explain it in person."

An elated Hausfeld filed a declaration in court within forty-eight hours, detailing how Kram could save face and dismiss the cases. He believed he had struck a historic deal.

The next day—only five days before the appeals court hearing was scheduled—Judge Kram called a hasty public hearing. That morning David Boies was shambling down the courthouse corridor toward the courtroom when he bumped into Mel Weiss and Burt Neuborne. Neuborne was highly mistrustful of Boies's intervention, warning Hausfeld that the high-profile lawyer was setting "a trap" to scuttle his mandamus in the appeals court. Now he wanted to know what Boies understood by the commitment to "urge" the German foundation to change its rules.

"Urging is urging," said Boies. "I know it's not a guarantee."

The discussion grew heated as Weiss pressed Boies not to oversell the deal to the judge, while Neuborne threatened to walk out. Weiss grabbed hold of him and told him, "Don't blow your cork." Neuborne left the corridor and sat gulping coffee on his own in the courthouse cafeteria. The dustup left Boies with the impression that Neuborne, a director of the foundation, would never change its rules to help the Austrian claimants.

Kram was already sitting at the head of the court when the attorneys shuffled in. Hausfeld, glowing with anticipated triumph, began by introducing diplomats from Poland, the Czech Republic, Belarus, Ukraine, and Russia to the judge. Then he outlined his plan. They would urge their colleagues on the board of the German foundation to change the rules.

Kram greeted his presentation in customary school-principal style. "Mr. Hausfeld," she said, "I have to say, I am very impressed. You are a resourceful and creative lawyer."

She did, however, want to know about the chances that Hausfeld's bright idea might actually be implemented.

Hausfeld reassured her: "You have the delegations of five respected and influential Central and Eastern European countries who by themselves represent the vast majority of the survivors, for example, of the labor fund. Over a million and a half people reside really in the votes of those five countries."

Hausfeld said they would be "extremely powerful and influential" on the board. Judge Kram looked satisfied and asked the defendants' lawyers if they wished to speak.

Neuborne, thoroughly alarmed by what he had just heard, jumped to his feet. He thought Hausfeld had spoken far too positively about the chance the foundation would change its rules. "The last thing I would want is for any suggestion to be made that the court was misled this morning," he said. "So I wish to be as candid with the court as I can about what I think will happen now."

"Are you about to tell me bad news?" asked Judge Kram, almost threateningly.

Neuborne said that he hoped not, and that he could guarantee that the proposal would "receive serious, unbiased and intense attention. We will listen. You could not get a more sympathetic set of people." But, he ended, "what I cannot represent to you is what the result of that consideration will be."

"I understand that," said Kram, "but I have great confidence in Mr. Hausfeld and his reputation for honesty and fairness."

Lawyer after lawyer, representing both banks and survivors, followed Neuborne to point out that the Central and Eastern Europeans only had five votes out of twenty-seven on the board of trustees. They stressed that a vote of the full Bundestag, over whom neither Hausfeld nor Kram had any power, would also be required to ratify the changes. Kram said she had faith and confidence in Hausfeld's creativity. With that, she ruled from the bench to dismiss the case. Her written order would be available the next day.

Outside, a beaming Michael Hausfeld told television interviewers about the tough diplomacy needed to make the deal happen, then kissed Burt Neuborne on the cheek.

That evening, the two lawyers celebrated by going to Fanelli's, one of SoHo's classic pubs, renowned for its pasta sauces from nearby Little Italy. By chance, sitting at the next booth, was none other than Judge Kram. Neuborne plucked up the courage to stroll over to her, offering to shake hands and make up.

"I am sorry that this has been a contentious experience," Neuborne ventured, "but I am delighted it has ended well."

"I too am glad it is over," the judge replied in a bittersweet tone. "You are considered one of the most important academic figures in the New York legal community. So many of your students look to you for guidance. In fact, two of my clerks are ex-students of yours. It was inappropriate for you to submit papers with such extreme language in light of your standing in the academic community."

Neuborne was taken aback by the judge's rebuff. "I am very sorry you feel that," he gasped. "In the future," he said with tongue firmly in cheek, "I will try to remember your example."

They exchanged brief, awkward smiles and returned to their meals.

Early the next afternoon, Judge Kram released her order. Her office sent it out by fax—a lengthy process, given the dozens of legal firms involved. As the afternoon wore on, lawyers around New York and Washington read anxiously through the seven-page document, finding that on the last page she ordered clearly enough that "all claims against all German defendants . . . are dismissed."

Above it appeared an apparently innocuous sentence. Plaintiffs could move to vacate her order "in the event the eligibility criteria of the German Foundation and/or Austrian Foundation are not revised as contemplated in the Hausfeld Declaration."

This meant that the order was not dependent merely on the Eastern European governments *urging* the rules to be changed. Rather, Kram had made her dismissal conditional on the rules actually being changed. That was too much for the banks. Late that Friday afternoon, they issued a hurried, one-paragraph press statement. The order, they said, "is conditional on matters beyond our control and we must view it as an obstacle to closure." Therefore, they would continue with their appeal before the Second Circuit the next week.

"Why?" Hausfeld asked out loud, as he read the fax. "Why did she have to do that?"

Hausfeld called Neuborne, but his old friend was too angry to speak to him. Then he issued a statement venting his anger on the Germans for refusing to begin payments to victims. "The German actions are like stopping a tank on a clear road for a dead ant lying in the way," he said. "There is no reason to stop! This is a poor excuse by Germany for avoiding their moral commitment to provide just and speedy compensation to the remaining survivors."

Other lawyers, including Mel Weiss's team, were more annoyed with Hausfeld. "Boies outsmarted him," Deborah Sturman snorted angrily.

Hausfeld called Boies in a frantic attempt to lobby him to change the judge's language. Boies had told him the judge wanted to wash her hands of the case, so why tear up their deal and cause so much grief?

"You guys are nuts. Why are you leaving this in there? Tell her to change the language. It doesn't add anything."

Boies shrugged off the criticism, convinced that the judge's opponents were intentionally misreading her words. "I think there were some people who had fallen into a very unfortunate rhetorical act," he recalled. "They were so offended that this federal judge had the temerity to disagree with them that they were on the attack."

Boies also believed the judge's order was essentially no different from any other dismissal of a Holocaust lawsuit. Judges always stated that settlements could be reopened, Boies suggested. But his opponents, acting for both the victims and the banks, found this argument ludicrous. The dismissals by Judges Bassler and Mukasey were conditional on the Germans doing what they said they would do in Berlin—if the 10 billion deutsche marks were not forthcoming, they could be hauled back before the court. By contrast, Judge Kram's dismissal was conditional on the Germans doing something they had already rejected in the Berlin negotiations—a totally different proposition.

Hausfeld believed that weekend was fruitless because the dispute between Neuborne and Boies had become personal. "David wasn't going to budge because Burt had demeaned or defamed the judge," he says. "Burt wasn't going to move because he thought the judge was so off the wall that the Second Circuit was going to wipe the floor with her."

For Neuborne, the disappointment merely confirmed his original fears. Boies' deal seemed like a ruse to muddy the waters for the appeals court. Armed with a dismissal of the case, Boies could argue that the issue was now moot. Neuborne drew up yet another blistering legal memorandum, which he delivered to the appeals court on Monday afternoon. His exasperation seeped through the legal prose. Judge Kram was holding the German foundation hostage, he argued. "In the absence of textual support for its exercise of raw power," he wrote, "the District Court's behavior is a classic usurpation of power."

The Second Circuit heard the appeal in room 1512, nine floors above the courtroom where Judge Kram had apparently dismissed the cases five days earlier. They chose a more elegant courtroom, with dark wooden paneling and thick blue carpets, but it was far too small and almost a hundred people stood at the sides of the room.

Before the three judges sat the lawyers. David Boies, looking disheveled in his familiar cheap blue suit, sat on the judges' left. A small crowd of lawyers sat to the right of the lectern. Neuborne, Swift, and Stephen Whinston, as the official lead counsels for the three lawsuits against the banks, would each take a turn as would Jeffrey Barist for the banks and a lawyer for the U.S. government. They worried they would not have the time to develop a coherent argument. Michael Hausfeld, who had no right to speak, sat bolt upright in the back corner of the court, his face set in a fixed smile.

Neuborne spoke first, and the judges quickly interrupted to ask him about the Austrian claims and the German settlement. Neuborne tore in with relish, saying the 1955 treaty was obviously intended "to end these claims once and for all."

Jeffrey Barist, waiting to speak, noted that the judges questioned Neuborne for twenty minutes, far beyond the eight minutes they had allotted him, and never once asked if the question was moot. By the time he stood to speak, Barist believed that the mandamus would be granted, and he started to lay waste Judge Kram's order. "The fundamental error by the district court was to believe that its extremely limited powers somehow gave her the power to require the rewriting of international agreements and also to give instruction to the parliament of a sovereign nation," he said.

One of the judges, Jose Cabranes—a legal heavyweight who had been touted as a future Democratic nominee to the Supreme Court—began to sink his teeth into the compromise of the week before. Teasing information out of Barist about Hausfeld's declaration, he mused out loud. "This Hausfeld declaration appears to be simply a fig leaf of some sort," he said. "It sounds like a bit of a con quite frankly. It doesn't sound authentic."

A devastated Hausfeld sank rapidly into his seat at the back of the court but maintained his fixed smile. "Here I was being called a con artist by an appellate court," he recalled, "when all we tried to do was find a way to resolve a complicated issue and basically save some face for a federal judge."

Barist explained once more how the two teams of lawyers had come to decide that the claims were worthless.

"So the only purpose of this must have been to provide some limb for Judge Kram to come on to," mused Judge Cabranes, "and it backfired. Because she then lo and behold took it seriously."

"I think she took it two steps further than he was prepared to go," confirmed Barist with a slight grin as he finished his presentation and made for his seat.

David Boies seemed muted by comparison. To the incredulity of the lawyers for the plaintiffs and defendants sitting just to his left, Boies abandoned his defense of the judge's language. Under questioning from the judges, he conceded that he would accept removal of the offending sentences from Kram's order.

"I didn't think the changes made any difference in the substance of it. And I don't think it made any difference to the judge either," Boies said afterward.

The judges' ruling seemed certain by the time the hearing ended, and only two days later they unanimously decided to issue the mandamus, forcing Judge Kram to strike the offending sentences from her order. Burt Neuborne appeared to have been vindicated. The next week, a chastened Judge Kram held a sparsely attended hearing in which she dismissed *Gutman v Deutsche Bank*, the case she herself had ordered to pursue the Austrian claims. Within a week the Germans declared legal peace and within a month the Bundestag had voted the foundation into being. Shirley Kram's well-intentioned attempt to defend the Austrian survivors won them no extra money but held up payments to all other survivors by five months.

After the appeals court hearing, a cast of now familiar characters ran the gauntlet of TV cameras in burning sunshine. Many interviewees enjoyed their moment in the sunlight. Burt Neuborne, looking younger than he had in months, turned to make the short trip to his office at New York University where a mountain of student papers in need of marking awaited him.

But one small and graying man, speaking with a strong Polish accent, could not force his face into a smile. More than a year had passed since Roman Kent had made his impromptu and impassioned speech before Germany's President Rau in Berlin. Then he had believed the Germans had made a great moral gesture. Now he was dismayed by the persistent German refusal to pay anything to his brethren during the months of legal wrangling. He believed a tenth of the survivors had already died since the signing in Berlin.

"This moral gesture amounts to words, and words only," he said, his eyes moistening. "This is the best proof of what morality means for them. For them it's strictly business. Cold-blooded business."

The Judgment of Judah

T he slave laborers were not the only ones trapped in a legal labyrinth. The Holocaust survivors who started the whole restitution campaign—the families with Swiss bank accounts—appeared to have settled their case once and for all in Brooklyn in August 1998. But three years after the banks agreed to their historic $1.25 billion payment, no survivor had yet received a penny. To the survivors, the agonizing delays seemed inexplicable and inexcusable.

Their chance to vent their anger came on November 20, 2000, when Judge Edward Korman held a hearing on a plan for distributing the money among hundreds of thousands of applicants. Gizella Weisshaus, the first survivor to sue the Swiss, spoke first, followed by fellow survivor Greta Beer, once Senator D'Amato's star witness. The two women who first gave a human face to the misdeeds of the Swiss banks now sadly symbolized the intractable difficulty of finding a just resolution.

Wearing a somber fur hat atop an auburn Orthodox wig and an incongruous bright blue patterned cardigan, Weisshaus could not control her anger. As she stood to speak before the overflowing courtroom, Korman sat with lips pursed, the tips of his fingers pressed tight. Members of a Russian survivors group, all wearing large yellow stars, lined the back of the room.

"This is justice here?" Weisshaus wailed. "This is robbery!"

Out of disgust, she had withdrawn her name from the suit and sued Ed Fagan, her former lawyer, accusing him of "racketeering." Weisshaus had grown angry that Fagan had involved several non-Jewish plaintiffs, particularly Romani Gypsies, and had utterly failed to keep her informed of the tortuous moves toward a settlement with which she did not agree. She had written a series of complaints accusing Fagan of "unethical" behavior. Weisshaus no longer stood to benefit from any settlement and had even booked time on a Manhattan public access cable channel to attack what she called "Jew.org embezzlement." She believed the Jewish organizations, the lawyers, and even the judge were just as bad as the Swiss banks. In a letter to Justice Ruth Bader Ginsburg of the U.S. Supreme Court, she asked that Korman be "disciplined for the harm that he has maliciously inflicted upon me, my fellow survivors, and on the judicial process."

"I started this case because of people like my father who deposited money in Switzerland in good faith," she shouted to Judge Korman. "Who benefited? Nobody. Nothing went to any Holocaust survivors. . . . How can you fight these people? It's unbelievable. We have no rights. No survivors were involved in this."

Her arguments wandered among allegations of conspiracy, denunciations of American justice, complaints that her legal papers had been destroyed, and passionate evocations of the wrongs done her family.

She called for a Nuremberg trial for people who were "unjust to Holocaust survivors" and inveighed against letting any Swiss money go toward Holocaust museums. "My parents and my whole family are not represented in the Holocaust museum. They didn't ask for a museum. They didn't ask for thievery and money. It's a shame what you are doing here."

At this Korman cleared his throat to tell her that her five minutes had already elapsed. Weisshaus stared at him balefully and stalked to the press box to distribute press releases.

Greta Beer rose next. An elegant figure, wearing her favorite Hermes scarf and a long coat, she showed none of Weisshaus's fury. "For the first time in my life," she said, "I am at a loss for words. The lines behind me are getting shorter by the day."

Indeed, the continuing delays meant fewer Holocaust survivors would live long enough to see any payment. Beer struggled to understand how the best intentions of so many good men had led to such delay and disappointment. She had stayed in close contact with almost all of the case's leading actors, inspiring their affection. While Weisshaus wrote ever angrier legal memos to the judge, Beer made new friends. She treated the Swiss ambassador in Washington, Albert Defago, as family. She sent New Year's cards to lawyers, and she felt especially fond of the staff in Alan Hevesi's office. Eric Wollman, Hevesi's legal adviser, held her hand before she rose to speak.

Beer read her statement in a careful whisper, made crisper by her lingering East European accent, while looking straight into the eyes of Judge Korman.

"Please have a heart. We have great trust in you. You have our lives in your hands," she pleaded. "The banks have come forward with money, which is now in your hands. Don't procrastinate— our voices are getting so much quieter."

Judge Korman's voice softened noticeably as he thanked her for her contribution, and the hearing continued.

Sadly for Greta Beer, Gizella Weisshaus, and thousands of others, the sheer complexity of the case prevented rapid payments. In two sweaty days in Brooklyn more than two years earlier, the lawyers had agreed that $1.25 billion would cover all the banks' liabilities, to be split among five different groups with separate grievances against the Swiss. The headline deal on money left the most awkward details for later, and resolving them took years.

In addition to dormant accountholders like Beer and Weisshaus, the money would compensate four other groups of victims. Anyone whose possessions were looted by the Nazis held a claim, because the Swiss banks laundered the proceeds. Then there were the laborers for thirty-six Swiss companies (including Nestlé and Novartis) that admitted using slave labor in Germany during the war. Another much larger group of victims held a claim because they labored as slaves for companies that banked in Switzerland.

Finally, the settlement covered refugees who were turned back at the border as well as those who crossed the border only to find themselves working in Swiss labor camps. German Jews had long resented Swiss border officials for asking the Nazis to stamp their passports with a large letter *J*.

Like so many extra bargaining chips, these extra classes had been included in August 1998 to help reach a settlement. But they added tens of thousands of claimants, and dividing the fund fairly was an immense task.

Moreover, the requirements of U.S. justice forced proceedings to slow to a snail's pace. Class action law requires lawyers to make every effort to find all claimants, even after fifty years. Any claimant has the right to appeal the settlement, and a series of appeals slowed down the workings of justice. Many Jewish leaders yearned instead for the simplicity of a handshake and the setting up of a big humanitarian fund.

The first legal dispute broke out within weeks of the agreement on $1.25 billion over the definition of "Nazi persecutee." The executive committee of ten plaintiff lawyers had to decide on whose behalf they had sued. Deborah Sturman, working with Mel Weiss, suggested using Adolf Hitler's own racial definitions from the Nuremberg Race Laws of 1935. This added Sinti and Romani Gypsies as well as Jehovah's Witnesses to the Jews. With little dissent, the lawyers then agreed to add two other groups who had suffered much the same treatment as Jews: homosexuals and the disabled.

Bob Swift, the only gentile on the committee, argued for the inclusion of political prisoners—a larger survivor group than homosexuals, the disabled, or Jehovah's Witnesses. "In human rights, it's the political dissidents who are usually the first arrested and who bear the brunt of reprisals and when they are gone, then the weak and the helpless can be preyed upon," Swift said. His colleagues responded, Swift said, by saying, "Some of them might be German." "My reaction was so what? They stood up against Hitler. Think of the Jews who didn't stand up against Hitler. They were the weak who suffered because of the reprisals against the dissidents."

Roger Witten, the Swiss banks' lawyer, also favored including people who were persecuted because of their national origin, such as Poles. Doing so would reduce the risk of future lawsuits against the Swiss from those who were excluded.

The plaintiffs' lawyers objected. "It was too many people," said Burt Neuborne. "We thought that would so dilute the class that no one would receive any money." Swift, supported only by his colleague Ed Fagan, continued to push for the inclusion of political prisoners. The matter ended before the judge, who accepted Neuborne's argument that this was primarily a Jewish settlement. "Everyone knew on that August day who we were talking about," said Neuborne. "We all knew we were talking about Jews and a very small number of other people who were exactly analogous to them in the way the Nazis treated them."

By oversight, another group was excluded— "righteous gentiles" who had courageously protected Jews during the Holocaust. Neuborne admits their exclusion was a mistake. "Righteous gentiles never came up at all," he said. "If someone had said it, we would have done it."

Having narrowed the payout to five classes, the money then had to be allocated within each class. But the question remained, how big a share should each class of victim receive? This Solomonic task was too big for a busy federal judge, so Korman appointed a special master, giving the task to a former judge named Judah Gribetz. The allocation issues decided by acrimonious negotiations in the German case were to be decided in the Swiss case by just one man.

A veteran of New York politics, Gribetz served for a while as deputy mayor and as general counsel to Hugh Carey, New York's Democratic governor of the 1970s. As a trustee of New York's Holocaust Museum and a former head of the Conference of Presidents of Major American Jewish Organizations, he understood the currents within the community of survivors who would ultimately judge the allocation. He had even written a book on Holocaust history.

Gribetz found that the total number of claimants might be as high as ten million—far more than the lawyers had grasped. The precedents of class action law held that payments must not be meaninglessly small, so he had to find a fair way to exclude some survivors. He also had to assess the legal strength of the different claims.

Dormant account–holders had a stronger legal claim than the other classes since they had suffered a direct breach of contract, so Gribetz decided that all depositors must receive the full amount to which they were entitled. This meant that he could not make an allocation until Volcker's commission had finished assessing how much money was left in dormant deposits. While the lawyers in Brooklyn had been keen to settle quickly, they would now be forced to wait for the Volcker audit to grind to a close.

The Volcker process ran into trouble soon after the Brooklyn settlement. By agreeing to pay on behalf of all banks in Switzerland, UBS and Credit Suisse removed any incentive for smaller banks to cooperate with Volcker's minions. "The settlement changed the mentality and the willingness of the small banks to cooperate," one private banker said. "Suddenly the money was supposed to be there and so there was no problem anymore. We thought it would streamline the whole process and instead it had exactly the opposite effect."

The cost of the Volcker audit weighed heavier on small banks. For example, Gonet et Compagnie, a private bank in Geneva, had a total workforce of six during the war, and even in 1999 it only employed about thirty, yet it was subjected to a full audit. The Banque Cantonale de Genève flatly refused to allow the auditors onto its premises, while others grew uncooperative.

In September 1998, Roger Witten, the Swiss banks' lawyer, led a Swiss delegation including Rainer Gut and Marcel Ospel, the heads of Credit Suisse and UBS, to New York to persuade Volcker to speed up the investigation. Tired of the audit, the banks wanted the process over. Volcker found the request insulting and pressed on.

Volcker's ever-persistent right-hand man, Michael Bradfield, wanted to pin down the banks' liability with precision. The greatest bone of contention was his decision to search for closed accounts that would have remained dormant but for actions taken by the banks. "We did not know that we were also talking about closed accounts," lamented Hans Baer, the Swiss banker who sat on Volcker's commission. "We had no idea."

Sometimes, banks would close an account and add its contents straight to their profits, or they would close it by deducting excessive administrative fees. Some accounts were closed and turned over to the Nazi authorities. In such cases, people who never wanted to close their account might still be waiting for their money.

Curt Gasteyger, the Swiss historian who sat on the Volcker Commission, said the decision led Volcker, tenaciously pushed by Bradfield, into an ever more expanding investigation "to an extent which made many Swiss wonder whether they found themselves in *Alice in Wonderland.*"

Bradfield saw it differently. "They wanted the presumption to apply that if an account was closed it was closed properly in the ordinary course of business," he said. "That issue was discussed vigorously in the committee—very vigorously."

With only sketchy information about closed accounts, Bradfield adopted a meticulous methodology, starting with all the 4.1 million accounts from the prewar period whose records survived and slowly excluding those which evidently did not belong to Holocaust survivors.

Of these, 2.25 million remained after removing small savings accounts and those registered under a permanent Swiss address, which were highly unlikely to belong to Holocaust victims. Bradfield then embarked on a process of "matching" the names on these accounts with databases of Holocaust victims, a decision that created a huge windfall for Yad Vashem, the main Israeli Holocaust Museum, which received funds to upgrade its archives and transfer lists to computers. During 1998 it employed more than a thousand people to transfer millions of names to a database where they could be checked against Bradfield's database of accountholders. This exercise revealed 276,905 accounts that matched the name of a Holocaust victim.

Eventually, 53,886 were found to be "probably or possibly" Holocaust victims' accounts, of which 26,000 were "probably" Holocaust-related. Both numbers were far in excess of anything the Swiss had ever admitted before, and they were in addition to the 5,570 accounts published in 1997.

Jacques Rossier, head of the exclusive Geneva bank of Darier Hentsch, dismissed the "acrobatics" of the auditors, pointing out that 72 percent of the "probable and possible" accounts were closed. "Highly hypothetical figures," he said, "were twisted, kneaded and rearranged several times in order to produce the sum of 53,886 accounts."

Professor Gasteyger said that the Swiss side "felt obliged to admit that, yes, such accounts . . . had possibly or probably not been correctly dealt with." He added that they accepted such a "seemingly distant possibility" only grudgingly. "Once you had gone that far, you had to go all the way, however bitter and often unjustified it appeared to us."

Disagreements over the wording of Volcker's final report created another layer of delays. Both sides threatened at different times to refuse to sign or produce minority reports, actions that would call the whole expensive exercise into question. Commission members haggled over every line of the introduction to the report.

When Volcker finally published his report in November 1999, fifteen months after the banks had agreed to pay $1.25 billion in Brooklyn, reactions hinged on two paragraphs in the foreword. The Swiss took comfort from Volcker's finding that there was "no evidence of systematic destruction of records of victim accounts, organized discrimination against the accounts of victims of Nazi persecution, or concerted efforts to divert the funds of victims of Nazi persecution to improper purposes." So the Swiss were not wanton criminals. As Volcker himself put it, "While there was a lot of recalcitrance it was not part of a master plan." Others on the committee felt the entire issue of "organized discrimination" was loaded—asking a question that the Swiss were not afraid to answer. As one Volcker insider put it, there was no discrimination because "they treated everyone badly."

But in the next paragraph, Volcker found "questionable and deceitful actions"—a phrase he had insisted on. The report found a catalog of behavior designed to stall retrieval of Holocaust survivors' assets, in one case even detailing a 1949 memo from a bank's legal department telling staff to deny the existence of accounts that had in fact been turned over to the Nazis.

Banks levied fees on accounts long after any activity in them had ceased, forcing them to dwindle to zero, and in one instance an account was extinguished with a single fee of 4,761.70 Swiss francs (about $2,720). For the great survey of 1962, banks charged special "research" fees that, in sixty-two cases, erased the value of the entire account, meaning that they went uncounted.

Employees at some banks essentially treated dormant accounts as free gambling money. Volcker's auditors found an account opened in 1930 by a Russian with the stipulation that it should only be invested in low-risk bonds. Instead, the bank chose to invest the account in stocks while periodically "creaming off" the extra returns into a separate account, leaving the account itself with no profits. By 1962, the bank had transferred 488,600 Swiss francs to its own account, while actually reducing the Russian's account by 1,061.40 Swiss francs for charges and commissions.

At another bank, employees used the money from a dormant account to bet on futures and options. It was worth 65,850 Swiss francs in 1990. Four years later, the bank's disastrous trades had reduced the account to only 557 Swiss francs.

Banks also treated security boxes as their own property, periodically forcing open safes to sell enough contents to cover unpaid rental costs, even if they knew that the accountholder had likely perished in the Holocaust. At one branch, a voucher was found stating that the accountholder had died in Auschwitz in 1943 and that the heirs probably lived in Romania. It was closed in 1967.

Most damningly for the Swiss, the special investigation of dormant accounts ordered by the Swiss parliament in 1962 had given them the chance to put their houses in order thirty-seven years earlier. But the Volcker Report poured scorn on that endeavor. It found that the banks had defined their task narrowly, arbitrarily excluding accounts if no conclusive evidence of persecution could be found and excluding all accounts that were held in names that could be either Christian or Jewish. The banks had also charged fees of up to 300 Swiss francs to conduct their searches.

Volcker produced a tough document that challenged the core

institutions of Swiss banking. At great expense, it had delivered what Singer and his Jewish colleagues wanted, with conclusive evidence and unanimous approval. It would be accepted as the final word on the dormant assets issue.

Converting these findings into solid restitution, however, remained a matter of contention. Volcker proposed publishing the names of the "probable and possible" accounts and creating a database of all the 4.1 million Nazi-era accounts for which records still existed. These rules required the Bern-based Swiss Federal Banking Commission, a strong supporter of Volcker until now, to relax secrecy rules.

The banking commission was, however, a political body, and cantonal banks—controlled by local politicians—lobbied hard against Volcker's proposals. The commission pondered its decision for four months, prolonging the delays for survivors, before authorizing publication of the 26,000 "probable" accounts but not the 28,000 accounts "possibly" linked to the Holocaust. It refused to mandate the creation of a database of all the 4.1 million Nazi-era accounts, saying that Volcker had, "after a very thorough investigation, no reason to believe that these accounts were in any way related to victims of the Holocaust."

"Our fear was, and still is, that if you create a database with no documentation, you'll get matches, but there'd be no other way of judging the claim," said Urs Zulauf, chief legal counsel of the Swiss banking commission. "That would mean there would be pressure on the bank to go on investigating—our fear is that the Volcker process would go on eternally."

The cantonal banks did not even have to publish accounts "probably" linked to the Holocaust. Only about 250 of their accounts fell into that category, but the principle grated with Volcker. In April 2000, he wrote Korman recommending that he delay clearing the settlement in order to exert more leverage on the Swiss. Once more the parties descended into undignified haggling before a compromise emerged. The two big banks allowed access to the files they had already prepared for Volcker, but no new information. In addition, a "data librarian" would let plausible claimants look at any Nazi-era account with a Swiss address. The smaller banks escaped scrutiny.

It was August 2000, the second anniversary of the deal in
Brooklyn, before Korman could clear the settlement, officially
ruling that the banks could indeed limit their liability to $1.25 bil-
lion. He vented his anger at the Swiss banking commission's
behavior. "It amounts to nothing less than a replay of the conduct
that created the problems addressed in this case," he said, adding
that the cantonal banks did not feel a moral obligation to the victims of Nazi persecution.

Korman summed up by quoting Ernest Lobet, an Auschwitz
survivor:

> I don't say the settlement is fair, because fairness is a relative term.
> No amount of money could possibly be fair under these circum-
> stances. But I'm quite sure that this is the least of the evils that the
> settlement negotiators could reach. The world isn't perfect.

Korman's order finally allowed Judah Gribetz to complete his
proposal for apportioning the money. He had no shortage of
advice. In the two years following the settlement in Brooklyn,
more than thirty thousand people sent Gribetz suggestions on
how to spend the money.

Submissions to him revealed deep philosophical divisions.
Some called for the Swiss money to pay for memorials or museums.
Agudas Chasidei Chabad, the governing body of the Lubavitcher
Orthodox sect, requested money to rebuild Jewish communities
in Eastern Europe and Russia. They said it was their "614th Com-
mandment," or *mitzvah,* to "deny Hitler the posthumous victory of
silenced Jewish voices throughout Eastern Europe."

Survivors in the United States, however, felt the money should
not finance attempts to re-create a vanished way of life in Eastern
Europe and should instead be allocated on the basis of need,
funding nursing care that would provide dignity in their closing
days. "This would give us survivors some feeling of justice and
would make it easier to face our old age," an American survivor
named Agnes wrote Gribetz. "This would be much more dignified
for us than paying off the sufferings of the victims of the Holocaust

with a few hundred dollars each, and giving hundreds of thousands of dollars to [charitable] institutions which will only take us if we give them our last penny."

Survivors even argued over the definition of a "Holocaust survivor." Russian and Eastern European survivors, excluded from postwar restitution efforts because they were behind the Iron Curtain, resented the notion that money should go only to Swiss bank account–holders and those held in the camps.

Hitler's armies also forced the Jews in occupied territories into desperate escapes into Siberia. A woman named Yelizaveta, a Russian, wrote Gribetz to say that those forced into evacuating their homes suffered "equally." She had walked three hundred kilometers, she had been bombed, and she had lived in cold and poverty in Siberia until 1944. "Did we not experience the Holocaust?" she asked.

Spreading to two volumes of more than 500 pages each, Judah Gribetz's report proved even longer than Volcker's when it appeared after twenty months of work in September 2000. It was translated into twenty-one different languages, and 675,500 copies were sent to individuals and organizations.

His core recommendation that $800 million—far more than most experts had expected would be found in the banks—be earmarked for people who held accounts provoked criticism from some of the lawyers. Stephen Whinston, one of the plaintiffs' attorneys, said: "The fear I have is that we will be back in this court room in two years' time with a huge amount left in the fund, and a vastly smaller number of Holocaust survivors to distribute it to."

Gribetz, concerned primarily to produce a legally watertight allocation, remained unrepentant and pointed to a footnote in the Volcker Report that suggested that Holocaust-related accounts might contain more than the total $1.25 billion. Even his $800 million might theoretically lead to "rationing" of payments to the depositors whose claims had driven the case.

However, his decision left only $450 million for the four other classes of victims. The "looted assets" class included any Nazi victim who could prove they had been displaced during the Holocaust. It therefore affected the most people, but they had only $100 million to share among them. With so many potential claimants, Gribetz ruled that the payouts should be treated as charitable donations based on need. Claimants would not have to prove that they had been looted.

Gribetz decided to allocate $90 million to Jews, with the remaining four groups—Romani, Jehovah's Witnesses, the disabled, and homosexuals—sharing $10 million.

Slave laborers received a chunk of money based on the German settlement. Any member of the five groups of victims who qualified for labor payments under the German deal would receive an extra $1,000 from the Swiss. Refugees denied entry to Switzerland would receive up to $2,500 and no less than $1,250. Those detained and abused within Switzerland would get between $250 and $500 each.

Gribetz's huge report resulted in the same kind of round numbers that tough bargaining had produced in the German settlement, leading lawyers on both sides to question whether the effort was worth it. Morris Ratner, one of the leading plaintiff lawyers, respected Gribetz deeply but wondered if he had been unnecessarily consumed with the idea of making a historically valid distribution. "I felt, why justify this?" said Ratner. "Any inquiry shows that it's nothing but a rough justice token payment."

Despite the anger at Judge Korman's hearing, Gribetz's plan produced little organized opposition. It was sent to around 650,000 people, of whom only 1,000 replied, and only a few dozen Holocaust survivors arrived in Brooklyn to complain. Two days after the hearing, Judge Korman upheld the findings in full. The judgment of Judah appeared to have survived with surprisingly little struggle.

But still the delays continued. Volcker published a list of names of possible dormant account–holders (including people named Sigmund Freud and Albert Einstein) in early 2001 and gave survivors six months to make a claim. As accounts might attract more than one claim each, he ruled that nobody could be paid until all claims had been received, in August 2001.

Matching real life claimants to names on lists proved immensely difficult. Volcker established a Claims Resolution Tribunal in 1997 to deal with the first list of names published by the Swiss banks. The average number of claims it received on any one account was eight, with some accounts—particularly those with common German or Jewish names—attracting more than ten claims. One account attracted claims in nine different languages. Each claimant filled in a detailed form explaining the life history of the accountholder and in the event of competing claims the lawyers became genealogists, delving into long-forgotten family history.

Often, even though the accounts were still open and the accountholder might show up some day, banks knew nothing more than the holder's first and last name. This could cost them dearly. In one case, five people, all unrelated to each other, offered plausible arguments that they were descended from the same depositor, and the bank was ordered to pay the full amount to all five.

Many accounts belonged to governesses, mistresses, or illegitimate children. One account was opened by a man with a Jewish name and gave a much younger man, with a German surname, power of attorney. Swiss law does not allow for heirs to inherit a power of attorney. However, the tribunal made an exception when the son of the holder of power of attorney came forward. He said his father was the accountholder's illegitimate son, by a German woman. To keep the relationship secret, the Jewish father had set up a Swiss bank account to pay for his son's school fees. The arrangement also helped the son to hide his Jewish parentage and, knowing that he was half-Jewish, he served in the Wehrmacht during the war.

Hans Baer, one of the architects of the Volcker process and Switzerland's senior Jewish banker, called the claims process "impossibly difficult." "The trouble is that you get into so many avenues once you explore," he said. "You ask me how long it will take to work off a list of twenty thousand? Ten years. Am I convinced it cannot be done in a reasonable time? Yes." In effect, Baer was predicting that the process might not end before all the survivors had died.

His gloomy prognosis appeared to be confirmed in August 2001, when the lawyers at the Claims Resolution Tribunal could finally take stock of the claims they had received. In total, about 30,000 claims arrived—a number far smaller than the 85,000 who had told Gribetz that they might have a claim to an account. The tribunal lawyers were at a loss to explain this—maybe their publicity was at fault, and maybe people were getting tired of making claims. Most likely, many of those accounts might be truly "heirless": the Holocaust had wiped out not only the depositor, but all their descendants.

More worrisome, only about 5,000 applications staked a claim to one of the "probable" account names that had been published. At least 16,000 of the 21,000 accounts published earlier in the year—and probably many more, given the likelihood of multiple claims for the same account—appeared to have gone unclaimed.

Michael Bradfield responded by deciding to look through all of the 560,000 forms that had been sent to Judah Gribetz expressing an interest in the settlement. Only about 85,000 had ticked the box saying they had a claim against the Swiss banks, but he ordered his legal staff to look through all the remaining forms to look for claims. Burdened by all these delays, it was not until November 2001—more than three years after the Swiss had agreed in his courtroom to pay $1.25 billion—that Judge Korman could authorize the first twenty-four payments to survivors. A further thirty-five received their money in January of the following year, by which time the total money awarded came to about $10 million, of which $3 million had gone to one survivor in Australia. The average award—showing just how significant the issue had been for many families—was $159,000.

But with $790 million remaining to be distributed, and 20,000 people claiming accounts that did not appear in the list of "probable accounts" published earlier in the year, the tribunal's lawyers faced an arduous task. Survivors faced yet more delays.

One thing, however, was clear: the tribunal would not find owners for all the $800 million set aside by Judah Gribetz. A residue of many hundreds of millions of dollars seemed inevitable. Deciding how to distribute that money would provoke possibly the most bitter battle of the entire campaign—pitting Holocaust survivors against those who had campaigned in their name.

Jew versus Jew

Israel Singer and the World Jewish Congress laid claim to the leftover millions at a black-tie dinner dedicated to their biggest political allies. Edgar Bronfman rented the ballroom at the Pierre Hotel, a huge turn-of-the-century institution just off Central Park, on September 11, 2000, for a dinner that represented the WJC's greatest show of strength, with President Bill Clinton booked as the keynote speaker.

The night was meant to honor the WJC's "Partners in History," who were celebrated in a large fake-leather-bound volume. Among them was First Lady Hillary Rodham Clinton, who was vying for New York's vacant U.S. Senate seat against Republican Rick Lazio. Although Lazio had served on a Bronfman commission to examine American involvement in the Holocaust, he was not honored. To their critics, it seemed as though Singer and Bronfman were paying Mrs. Clinton back for her role in introducing them to her husband, five years earlier.

Singer's most reliable friends and allies were also honored: Stuart Eizenstat, Alan Hevesi, and Knesset speaker Avraham Burg among them. Others went unrecognized. Reflecting the bitter splits among the campaigners, the honorees included no class action lawyers and none of the California politicians who had made life uncomfortable for European companies.

Greta Beer, who gave a human face to their campaign with her testimony in the Senate hearings in Washington, found out about the event only a day beforehand. Firmly believing that she had started the entire campaign, she desperately rang the WJC asking for an invitation. None was forthcoming. Christoph Meili, the Swiss watchman whose instinctive decision to rescue documents from the shredder at UBS had transformed the campaign, took his exclusion as "a kick in the teeth."

The list of paying guests read like a roll call of Singer's European opponents: Allianz, Bank Austria, Deutsche Bank, Credit Suisse, and Generali were all there, bowing to political necessity by making an appearance. Their tuxedo-clad executives listened as President Clinton extolled the glories of Holocaust restitution.

But the dinner had another purpose: to unveil a Foundation for the Jewish People to support global education initiatives. It would be funded by the residues from the different restitution settlements. As the guests continued to dine, a letter was circulated from Ehud Barak, the Israeli prime minister, saying he was "very inspired" by the foundation. In an unguarded moment two weeks before the dinner, Elan Steinberg of the WJC had told Reuters that he expected "hundreds of millions, possibly billions of dollars" to be left over once claimants had been paid. He went on to assert that "the Jewish people are the heirs of the Jewish assets."

Steinberg's words angered Leo Rechter, a man who had made a quiet living in New York as a banker with Manufacturers Hanover. As a child, he had fled from Germany to Belgium, before living out the war in concentration camps. "The Germans kept following us around," he said. After the war he moved on to displaced persons camps before going to Israel and eventually deciding to settle in the United States. Rechter believed that assets won in the name of Holocaust survivors should go to Holocaust survivors. Since retirement, he had occupied himself writing a newsletter for the National Association of Child Holocaust Survivors from his home in Flushing, Queens, and his editorial that month declared war on Singer, Bronfman, and the WJC:

HOW IS THAT AGAIN? "The Jewish people, as a whole, are the heirs of Jewish assets."??? Are we back in the dark ages when reigning religious authorities were able to lay claim to the assets of their disciples? . . . Under the terms of the German Slave-Labor agreement and of the proposed Swiss Banks apportionment, the (relatively) few children who managed to survive the Shoah, most of whom became orphaned, will not be entitled to anything. They do not "deserve anything because they survived and are alive . . ." but the Jewish people as a whole, including those that were never in any danger, ARE RIGHTFUL HEIRS? What a preposterous concept.

Rechter had uncovered a silent tragedy. Even as death thinned the ranks of Holocaust survivors, the number of those in poverty was increasing. Survivors would lose a spouse or suffer a debilitating disease and face the enormous costs of U.S. medical care. For Rechter, nobody in the WJC had the right to spend their money on anything else while survivors were still alive, their memories growing ever more vivid with the onset of old age. Some even slept on park benches. He complained that survivors had been "constantly ignored" and that the funds the Foundation intended to use "belong rightfully to Shoah victims."

Survivors in South Florida and Los Angeles expressed equal outrage. In Miami, the heart of America's second biggest population of survivors, Rositta Kenigsberg headed the Holocaust Documentation and Education Center at Florida International University. "This is a population that is justifiably the hereditary and biological heirs, if you will, to what was stolen in Europe," she said. "That this is so difficult to understand for those negotiating these settlements, in the name of these survivors, is a shocking, shocking revelation."

As Singer and Bronfman unveiled their fund to the diners inside the Pierre, Rechter and other Holocaust survivors picketed outside, bringing into the open festering divisions between survivors and the most successful advocates on their behalf.

Knesset speaker Avraham Burg, honored that night, regarded the development as close to inevitable. "You know, we did something almost impossible," he said. "We created for the first time in the history of the world a united Jewish front. It was unbelievable and I had a feeling that once the money poured in, the fight would begin."

The fight hinged on a simple philosophical division: had the funds been earned in the name of surviving Holocaust victims or the Jewish people as a whole? Most survivors took the former view. Roman Kent, who sat on the board of the Claims Conference, thought most money should go to survivors, not the wider Jewish community, "because after we are gone, they can have it all."

Singer and Bronfman, however, believed that treating the residues as a collective payment recognized that six million had died, many heirless, and that the Holocaust was a collective attack on the Jewish people and their culture. Bronfman argued that payments should first compensate needy Jews who had survived to see a new century—and also those who perished. "I've tried to put myself in the shoes of a man in Auschwitz," he said. "What would I want? It would be to have [this money] used to revive Judaism." This line of thought led to financial support for new *yeshivot* in Eastern Europe, Holocaust museums and memorials, and Jewish education.

Elan Steinberg, himself the son of Holocaust survivors, angrily dismissed Leo Rechter's logic, saying that only about 10 percent of Europe's Jews had survived and that 80 percent of those survivors had since died. "My father was a survivor but he died 30 years ago. They are saying the money belongs to the survivors who are left in 2001, and that's maybe 20 percent of all the survivors. They aren't the heirs to begin with—they're only the heirs in the same sense that the entire Jewish people are the heirs."

The furious debate showed that Judah Gribetz's painstakingly argued report had not closed the matter. Indeed, two of his most careful decisions proved to be the touchstones for further angry opposition, particularly from U.S. survivors. The first concerned his division of the $90 million of the Swiss money allocated to the Jews who had suffered looting during the Holocaust. He recommended that 75 percent should be earmarked for programs helping destitute survivors in the former Soviet Union, to be handled in part by the Claims Conference. His report detailed their meager state pensions (the average was less than $20 per month) and the lack of adequate health care. "Their situation is so dire, their number so great, and their half century of virtual exclusion from compensation programs so inequitable," Gribetz said, that the allocation was justified. Righting this historical wrong meant, however, that only minimal funds were left for needy American survivors without claims to a Swiss bank account.

Leo Rechter and his colleagues felt insulted by the priority given to survivors in the former Soviet Union and by the role given to the Claims Conference, an organization built around the belief that reparations could be paid to the Jewish people as a whole. Already, 60 percent of the conference's funds went to Israel and 15 percent to the former Soviet Union, compared with only 10 percent to the United States. Rechter also derided Claims Conference grants to causes other than Holocaust survivors, such as $1.5 million for a Yiddish theater company. Instead, he wanted money to go toward sheltered housing or health care for American survivors.

Gribetz's second controversial decision was his allocation of $800 million to cover dormant accounts. The initial poor response to Volcker's appeal for claims in August 2001 appeared to leave most of the accounts—and the cash—unclaimed. Holocaust survivors feared that large Jewish organizations would surreptitiously use the remainder for their own educational and memorial projects. Steinberg's comment that "possibly billions" could be left in residues only fueled those suspicions. A lot of Swiss money plainly remained at stake, and American survivors, who calculated that they would get a total of about $200,000 from the original allocation, wanted to make sure they got their share of the leftovers.

Leo Rechter vowed to fight the allocation, and Sam Dubbin, the Florida lawyer who had worked on the insurance cases, helped him by launching an appeal against the fairness of the entire settlement. He complained that property claims had been turned into a welfare program for overseas needs. "The American survivor community didn't have a voice in the allocation," Dubbin said, "and they didn't get a result. Their rights were extinguished and they got nothing out of it." Dubbin withdrew his appeal in May 2001 after a private meeting with Judge Korman and Burt Neuborne, but he made it clear he intended to fight hard for U.S. survivors when the issue of the unpaid accounts money finally came to court.

Despite the survivors' suspicions, most contemporary restitution settlements—including the French and Austrian agreements—were aimed exclusively at Holocaust survivors and excluded their heirs. In the German case, the WJC and the other Jewish groups actively negotiated against the Future Fund, devoted to memorials and education, in favor of giving more money directly to former slaves.

But none of this could conquer the survivors' distrust of the Claims Conference. On the day that payments to slave laborers started, Greg Schneider, the conference's head of allocations, tried to be philosophical. "I can understand that sort of suspicion and level of anxiety among the survivors," he said, "because if I had had that kind of life, who could I trust?"

Survivors made their instinctive distrust for Jewish leaders apparent to Israel Singer at a breakfast meeting hosted by Alan Hevesi in Manhattan's Lincoln Square Synagogue on the morning of Sunday, February 6, 2000. Hevesi, beginning his ultimately unsuccessful campaign in the New York City mayoralty race of 2001, invited hundreds of local survivors for bagels and coffee followed by an informal briefing on the restitution campaigns. But the setting did not lend itself to informal discussion, and with the men covering their heads, it felt more like a religious occasion.

Knowing there was a risk of hostility from the audience, Singer launched an angry diatribe against those who said they did not want the "last sound bite of the Holocaust to be about money"—a quote from Abraham Foxman of the Anti-Defamation League, whom Singer did not mention by name.

"We aren't going to stand for them saying that this is about money," Singer cried. "It's a scandal! The people who say these words and carry these thoughts within themselves and claim to be the heads of a Jewish organization should be ashamed of themselves. They should be scandalized. They should not be allowed to stand in public and claim they represent Jews. They don't!"

Then he rhapsodized about the moral component of what he and the WJC had achieved. Only recently he had persuaded President Rau of Germany to send an apology to every surviving slave laborer. Singer said this was "a small commitment to try to enter the next century with some kind of self-respect knowing that [Germany] attempted to speak to each person that's still alive that's still a victim.

"Not every one of you who receives money is someone who's participating in some kind of financial or material squeezing of countries," he said contemptuously, dismissing the arguments of those who said the entire restitution campaign was a shakedown. "You are not taking bread out of the mouths of poor children in Switzerland or food from the table of the poor farmer in Austria. You are getting an apology."

Singer, a veteran campaigner, had attacked Foxman to avert a likely attack on him from the audience. But while the audience cheered Singer's speech, Hevesi soon lost control of the meeting when he returned to the step in front of the Ark. Dozens of survivors spoke at once when he called for questions, everyone shouting to make their voice heard.

Survivors said they feared that the Germans would use the new fund as an excuse to take back money they handed out in earlier restitution programs, and they attacked the infuriating and nitpicking bureaucracy of the Claims Conference. "There are hundreds who were children during the war," one woman shouted. "We didn't qualify for anything under the laws of the Claims Conference. We didn't qualify under German laws because I was under fourteen years old. I was in the Warsaw Ghetto! How are the officers of the Jewish Claims Conference acting to disqualify these people who are under age?"

Vociferous applause showed that in this gathering, the Claims Conference was almost as unpopular as the German government. "With all due respect," Hevesi snapped, "we've spent hours, days, and years pursuing survivors." Trying not to talk down to his audience, he told them that they needed to negotiate with foreign governments "and they have big armies, and myths and legends to get through."

But all the angry people around him saw were Jewish leaders talking politely to former oppressors. All they knew was that, despite the headlines about billion-dollar settlements, they had so far received no money to alleviate their suffering. Hevesi conceded that the meeting was out of control and stalked out of the sanctuary, still wearing his yarmulke as he exited onto Amsterdam Avenue.

Singer would confront his single most outspoken critic at another venue on Manhattan's Upper West Side two months later. Norman Finkelstein, a professor at New York's Hunter College and the son of survivors of Auschwitz and Maidanek, was a passionate anti-Zionist who believed Singer had exploited the memory of the Holocaust to enrich his own organization. He embarked on a noisy campaign to attack what he called "Holocaust profiteering" with the full support of Noam Chomsky, another radically left-wing, pro-Palestinian academic.

Finkelstein finally confronted Singer in person in the restrained surroundings of a subterranean lecture theater at Columbia University's law school, a marble building in Manhattan's Morningside Heights. Singer was discussing international law in a panel jointly organized by the law school's Jewish and German students' associations, sharing the dais with the plaintiffs' lawyers Burt Neuborne and Morris Ratner. Relaxed after the Berlin deal, Singer repeatedly told his audience, "It's not about the money."

Unknown to Singer, Finkelstein was sitting uncomfortably by the aisle a few rows from the front, listening intently. He had recently finished the manuscript for his book *The Holocaust Industry*, a work he considered a rendering of his parents' legacy. His father, whose tattooed number he could still remember, had received compensation checks from the German government throughout his life while his mother, who was supposed to be compensated by the Claims Conference, received nothing.

Finkelstein believed the Claims Conference deliberately inflated the number of slave laborers to extract more money from Germany. He also accused it of downplaying Germany's record of paying compensation to slave laborers so that it could squander the funds on pet projects. In short, he wanted the German government, not the Claims Conference, to distribute the money. As a Palestinian sympathizer, Finkelstein was at odds with organized Jewry. However, his history as the Jewish son of an Auschwitz survivor gave him credibility with the world media and he was itching to confront Israel Singer.

The moderator, a Columbia law professor, asked for questions. After two students had made legal points, Finkelstein started to speak in a high and angry whine.

"My father was in the Warsaw Ghetto from 1943 and then he was in concentration camps," he shouted, wagging a finger at Singer. "I have rich personal experience on this whole matter of reparations. The truth is that it's only about money. It has nothing to do with morality and most assuredly it has nothing to do with justice for the Holocaust victims. You're with the WJRO, the Claims Conference, a dozen different hats you wear, it's all just Holocaust profiteering."

Singer, who had looked bored, with his chin lodged on his hand, looked up, his eyes coming into sharp focus. "And you are?"

"Professor Norman Finkelstein of Hunter College." Singer recognized the name and grimly crossed his arms as Finkelstein, shouting like a man possessed, launched into a fast and noisy diatribe.

"You are vice president of the Claims Conference. It received money from Germany in 1952. They received ten million dollars a year from 1953 to 1965. That money according to the agreement was explicitly supposed to go for the resettlement and rehabilitation of people. That money went not to victims but to Jewish communities in the Arab world."

Singer shrugged expressively and said he hadn't been around at the time.

"They said there were no longer any needy Jewish victims!" shrieked Finkelstein. "They didn't need the money, so you decided to use it for other purposes!"

Then he jabbed a finger in the direction of Burt Neuborne. "And you, Professor Neuborne. You were so pious there. Let me ask you something."

Finkelstein reminded him of suggestions that there were more dormant accounts of Holocaust survivors in the United States than in Switzerland. "Why pick on the Swiss banks before the American banks?"

Neuborne looked at Finkelstein with heavy-eyed bemusement. He interrupted. "I can't understand the anger," he said. "I can understand the pain."

"I am angry at your profiteering from the Holocaust."

"But I don't accept any money for what I do," Neuborne said, still looking more bemused than angry. "I have worked as a lead counsel for three years, in the most intense way, and I haven't made a dime."

That seemed to trigger something in Singer. Suddenly he sat bolt upright in his chair, face flushed and eyes glittering, and shouted at Finkelstein. "Yes, that's right, Burt here never took a dime. You can insult me, but you can't insult him. I think it's an insult for you to have even come here."

Finkelstein shouted he was the son of Holocaust victims, so Singer should be his spokesman.

"I don't want to be your spokesman. It's disgraceful. You have chutzpah to be here."

As Finkelstein kept shouting from the audience, Singer leaped from his chair and strode to the front of the dais. "You'd better be careful!" he shouted, stretching his arm and pointing directly at Finkelstein. A tall man and whippet slim, Singer suddenly seemed bigger and more threatening.

Finkelstein shouted that he wanted an answer to his question about the money that went to Israeli settlements.

"I don't want to answer your questions," Singer bellowed, "because they have been posed in an unpleasant manner. By the way, I think you should hire an attorney to stand up here because you are in difficulties. Remarkable!"

Singer had no intention of allowing the shrieking Finkelstein to draw him into a debate and did not accept that the man had any right to speak to him. Finkelstein quietened as the moderator took another question and he left before the end of the session. Afterward Singer, as relaxed and charming as ever, put a protective arm around his son-in-law, who was studying at Columbia Business School, and chatted with students as though nothing had happened.

Finkelstein, however, did not go away. His book turned out to be a commercial success, particularly in Germany, where it sold 130,000 copies within weeks. It was due for translation into sixteen languages. He used his website to continue attacking the restitution campaigners and summed up Singer and Bronfman's gala dinner at the Pierre thus: "Mass murder. Horrible plunder. Slave labor. Let's eat."

In March 2001, against the background of this deepening feud among American Jews, Avraham Hirschson, chairman of the Knesset's restitution committee and one of Singer's closest allies in Israel, proposed a new law establishing Bronfman's Foundation for the Jewish People. Voted into being by the Knesset, it would be chaired by an Israeli high court judge with overseers drawn from an appropriate range of worthy Jewish organizations in Israel and the Diaspora, including survivors' groups.

Avraham Burg presented the move as an attempt to deal with the Claims Conference's democratic deficit. "You have a group of very limited interests sitting around a table and dealing with the most volatile issues of the Jewish world today from a perspective of their constituency—self-serving interests," he said. "I was very angry at how the processes were working, no transparency, no real controlling." He thought the foundation would be transparent and accountable.

Martin Stern, an intractable opponent of the WJC and all its works, did not believe it. Instead, the proposed foundation smacked of the Generali Trust, which he believed handed out money to political and religious cronies. When the law came to debate in the Knesset in May 2001, he arranged for foreign journalists to cover it. "Your governments paid out money," he told them. "They thought it was going to survivors. This will show you what they're really going to spend it on. It's going to the Jewish pot." With several dissenters within the Knesset voicing strong criticisms of the law, it failed to make its way on to the nation's statute book.

Meanwhile, in the United States, Leo Rechter and his friends set up a rival foundation to receive the money: Holocaust Survivors' Foundation–U.S.A. Its aim was "to oppose attempts by other organizations (predominantly directed by non-survivors), including the Foundation for the Jewish People, to attain control of all unclaimed or 'residual' funds." It also aimed to prevent any portion of the funds being diverted to monument-building, rebuilding Eastern European Jewish communities, or anything that did not "directly contribute to the welfare of the survivors."

David Schaecter, a wealthy Miami businessman and survivor, agreed to chair the foundation, which staffed its board with representatives from several states and vowed to ensure an inclusive health insurance system for all survivors. The new foundation would serve as a "supervisory conduit" to existing local social service organizations, and would be staffed with unpaid volunteer survivor representatives. The leadership of every organization backing this foundation was elected. Rechter's chapter in Queens had 900 dues-paying members, while the Florida coalition of fifteen groups had more than 4,500. The foundation's big battle would be for the residue of the Swiss money, and it steeled itself to fight head-on with Singer and Bronfman's Foundation for the Jewish People, and with the Claims Conference.

Late in 2001, the battle lines between the two foundations were drawn: the organizations that had won the money in the survivors' name now faced a fight against the survivors to keep it.

Perhaps it had been inevitable, as the fissure between survivors and Jewish organizations had persisted for at least half a century. Nahum Goldmann, founder of the World Jewish Congress and the man who engineered the first reparations with Germany, knew that the issue of reparations was disputed by the majority of Jews. But he had also felt that as a Jewish leader, he had every right to ignore them—an attitude the survivors believed they could discern in Israel Singer and Edgar Bronfman.

"I have often said that if the Jewish people had unanimously agreed to the idea of negotiating for cash reparations from the Germans, I would be ashamed of being Jewish," wrote Goldmann. "The Jewish people were bound to display their opposition, but its leaders had to take no notice; that is politics."

Epilogue

Fifty years before Israel Singer clashed with American Holocaust survivors, David Ben-Gurion struggled to frame the same, painful question: how could anyone provide even a small measure of justice with money? Ben-Gurion, prime minister of the infant state of Israel, became the first Jewish leader to negotiate compensation from Germany. But the deal he struck with Konrad Adenauer, first chancellor of the new state of West Germany, provoked a furious reaction in Israel that foreshadowed the bitterness at the end of the century.

Amid rioting on the afternoon of January 7, 1952, stones shattered the windows of the Knesset's temporary headquarters on the slope of Jerusalem's King George Street. Israel's founding politicians grasped for their handkerchiefs as tear gas drifted through the broken glass. Leading the rabble was Menachem Begin, a former leader of the Irgun Zionist militia and a future prime minister, who was haranguing a huge crowd in Jerusalem's Zion Square. "For this we all are ready to give our lives and there is no sacrifice too dear," he said. "That blood which was poured out in German concentration camps gave us courage to rise and overthrow the British. . . . How shall we face the world after trading that blood for marks?"

Begin's argument left Ben-Gurion struggling for an answer. Inside the Knesset, he cited the Bible to win over a skeptical audience: "Let not the murderers of our people be also their inheritors." Ben-Gurion was invoking the story of Naboth's vineyard from the First Book of Kings. Naboth refused to surrender his vineyard to King Ahab, only to be stoned to death on the orders of Jezebel, Ahab's queen. Ahab was on his way to take possession of the vineyard, when the prophet Elijah appeared before him to ask, "Hast thou killed and also taken possession?"

Although Ben-Gurion was staunchly nonreligious, his biblical quotation helped sway the Knesset to accept reparations in a narrow vote. But when the German money was finally handed over, the signing ceremony was held in secret in Luxembourg. Nobody wanted to talk about it. Over the decades that followed, Germany continued to pay compensation to Israel, but all talk of restitution for the Holocaust fell silent: the survivors wanted to get on with rebuilding their lives, while the world's politicians were too busy fighting the cold war to think about settling the debts left by the last war. Many survivors refused to accept compensation from Germany and Austria, considering it blood money—a way for the perpetrators to buy forgiveness.

However, by the end of the century, the survivors seemed to care more about financial justice as they advanced in years. "There's a saying in medicine that time is the best medicine," said Roman Kent, a key Jewish negotiator and survivor of Auschwitz. "It may work with many people in many medical cases, but it doesn't work with survivors. We are the exception to the rule. After the war we didn't think about the Holocaust. We wanted to forget it and build our lives, and not dwell on it.

"Now we are old, the kids are gone and in many instances the spouses are dead and we are more sick and the memories of the Holocaust are more vivid than they were thirty years ago. Many of us would like to see some justice done before we are all departed."

The new attitude of the survivors was coupled with the emergence of a new generation—people like Michael Hausfeld, the lawyer who grew up in Brooklyn, and Martin Stern, the businessman brought up in the comfort of London—leading the contemporary debate over justice and money. Both Hausfeld and Stern were born after the war but descended from Holocaust victims and were passionate about their cause.

"They never wanted restitution," Hausfeld recalled of his parents and their survivor friends. "They always said that what was taken first and foremost was lives. But they felt that even after they survived, there seemed to be a willingness on the part of the world to forget. And that is something they never accepted."

Was it worth pursuing compensation and restitution more than half a century after the Nazi crimes against humanity? For the needy survivors—as the increasingly aggressive campaign by Leo Rechter and American survivor groups showed—the answer was clear. Even relatively meager payments might make a difference for elderly people in penury. That was especially true of Nazi victims in the former Soviet bloc, where compensation was denied during the cold war. For hundreds of thousands of forced laborers in Central and Eastern Europe, the compensation payments negotiated in recent years represent the first recognition of their wartime suffering.

For both the needy and the forgotten, the struggle for compensation was driven as much by the desire for recognition as it was for money. Catherine Lillie, who hunted for banking and insurance claims for New York State's Holocaust Claims Processing Office, believed that in many cases the documents brought to her by survivors "provide the last remaining link to a world that has since been lost."

"For the sole surviving daughter, the dowry policy her parents purchased for her is often the only link that remains to the world, the people, and the time in which she grew up," she said. "It carries much more than just the weight of evidence. It is hugely charged with emotion. Denying its value can amount to denying the existence and value of a world that is now lost and the people who perished."

Money represented the most important token of the recognition they longed for. Without money, the apologies and historical commissions across Europe rang hollow. But without an apology, the money seemed no more than a mercenary deal. Survivors valued the apology by President Rau of Germany as much as the compensation they received. In contrast, the Swiss settlement felt like a hollow victory in spite of the size of the deal, which the lawyers felt was the best settlement they obtained. With Switzerland there was no apology and no contrition, not least because the Swiss government refused to take part. One survivor even wrote to Judah Gribetz refusing to accept the Swiss money, saying to do so would surrender his right "to call a spade a spade, a thief a thief, and a bastard a bastard."

As the former slave laborers accepted their checks from Germany in June 2001, Israel Singer appeared almost apologetic for the money he had struggled so hard to obtain. "There's no way to make good again that which it is impossible to make good again," he said. "You can't make the dead good again. We can only take a modicum of justice—a modicum of attempting to somehow right wrongs in a small way for those who are still alive."

Maybe it was not about money. Maybe the six-year struggle for compensation was about something more than lost accounts and looted heirlooms. Like a *yahrzeit* candle lit on the anniversary of a loved one's death, maybe Singer simply wanted to keep the flame alive.

"This subject had been on the wane," he recalled at the end of his battle, in late 2001. "The last really impressive event was the creation of the U.S. Holocaust Museum in Washington. We jump-started interest in the subject again one more time. We uncovered one more issue. Now the documentation will take years for scholars to pore over and analyze. But the problem is you can't keep people's attention for too long. The issue is a moral one. But you will find one day that the moral issue will lose its urgency as well."

For Singer, the fight over money was the most immediate way to raise those moral issues one more time, before the final survivor of the Holocaust died. However, as he contemplated his long campaign, it seemed as if most of the money had missed its mark.

"It hasn't produced something lasting," he conceded. "I am proud of the fact that I got 92,500 new pensions for Eastern Europeans, where people were struggling. Those people's lives have been changed immeasurably.

"But maybe I didn't succeed in what I wanted to do. Maybe these dollars are all I got, and I didn't succeed in getting all I wanted. Just one billion dollars of the money are important, but the other five or six billion, I don't know how important they are. All we had was a small window. That's all."

Singer was not alone in speaking largely about money. Whether they were lawyers or corporate executives, Americans or Europeans, their attempts to come to terms with one of the darkest deeds in human history often looked and sounded like any other financial transaction. Business talks, however, provided an unsatisfying way to search for justice. The Jewish negotiators and class action lawyers were often frustrated by their opponents' obsession with limiting their legal liability. On the other side of the negotiating table, the business executives and their lawyers were frustrated by their opponents' obsession with an intangible moral purpose. Meanwhile, the survivors—the victims of the Nazi terror and plunder half a century ago—were eternally disillusioned by the injustice of it all.

To the hard-liners on both sides, the dispute appeared as a contest between Shylock and Hitler. But those caricatures were grossly unfair. Neither the class action lawyers nor the Jewish organizations needed cash for themselves. The American Jewish community is prosperous and endowed with many successful charitable groups. Some attorneys were already millionaires, while Edgar Bronfman is one of the richest men on earth. On the European side, none of the executives had any complicity in war crimes and many felt an overriding moral purpose. People like Manfred Gentz of DaimlerChrysler and Giovanni Perissinotto of Generali were dealing with the issue precisely because they sympathized with the victims. Gentz vividly recalls his mother's Jewish friends in postwar Berlin. Some companies—like Bank Austria or Generali—tried hard to do the right thing and were exasperated by divisions among their Jewish antagonists.

At the heart of the controversies were the tactics used by both sides. Israel Singer and his colleagues at the WJC frankly admitted that for them, the ends sometimes justified the means. "Why did it work?" asked Elan Steinberg, Singer's executive director. "Because we beat their brains out. It's like Pharaoh. This is punishment."

Many companies felt they were not simply being punished but that they were the victims of blackmail—either they paid up or faced the destruction of their reputation. That was an exaggerated response by the Europeans, because their opponents' true ability to threaten their bottom line was extremely limited. The legal cases were often weak and the campaigners had no power to haul a sovereign government into settlement talks. But for companies without government officials to protect them—like Generali or the Swiss banks—the damage to their public image could still be severe. Even after they had agreed to pay money, companies such as Allianz still fought hard to prove they were not culpable.

The controversy appears to have stigmatized companies that traded blamelessly for decades and has already passed into popular culture. In the opening scene of the James Bond movie *The World Is Not Enough,* the British spy arrives in the offices of a Swiss bank to pick up a case from a secure safe and comments sardonically on how difficult it is for anyone to get anything out of a Swiss bank. An episode of *Law and Order* features crimes committed by an Italian insurance company called Federali as it attempts to cover up its role in robbing Holocaust survivors.

However, the tactics of those being sued were also suspect. The stubborn denials of European companies and governments suggested a moral blindness. Rather than confess to their complicity in the Nazi plunder and human rights abuses, the companies variously denied responsibility, hid behind their legal counsel, or claimed to have paid adequate compensation already. Their legalistic responses made matters worse, insulting survivors by refusing to acknowledge their suffering. The executives' apparent inability to empathize with the victims often made them seem as callous as their postwar predecessors, who failed to make amends immediately after the war's end. Instead, the companies made reluctant concessions with an eye on the courts rather than history or morality. The simple truth is there would have been no compensation payments without the lawsuits and the media campaigns.

In return, the lawyers were pilloried for their work. Otto Graf Lambsdorff, the leading negotiator for the German government, looked back on their role with open disdain. "I wish to stress that none of these lawsuits, neither in Germany nor anywhere else in the world, were ever won by any claimant," he told a conference of American lawyers in Berlin.

For all the talk of reconciliation, the two sides grew farther apart as the talks progressed. For one side, searching for moral peace, the payments could never be enough to compensate for the horrors of the Holocaust. For the other, searching for legal peace, the payments would always be too much. In reaching settlements, the negotiators entirely failed to reach any personal reconciliation with their opponents. They may have fought their way to a wary legal and political cease-fire, but the emotional and cultural war rages on.

Did the compensation battle reinforce anti-Semitic prejudice? The sight of Jewish activists, backed by Jewish politicians and Jewish lawyers, prompted a revival of anti-Semitic cartoons in Switzerland. But anti-Semitism is largely a hidden prejudice in Western Europe, visible only in the desecration of cemeteries and synagogues by far-right thugs. It is impossible to establish any convincing correlation between such attacks and the compensation campaign. Israel Singer insisted that only anti-Semites were responsible for anti-Semitism—a formula first used by Nahum Goldmann, the founder of the World Jewish Congress. Besides, Singer was determined to flush anti-Semitism out in the open, where he believed it could be easily challenged.

But for the leaders of the Jewish communities in Europe, where anti-Semitic attacks on Jewish property are commonplace, that argument sounded glib. Theo Klein, a former leader of the French Jewish community, accused American Jews of failing to respect their European counterparts. "There is an important Jewish rule," he says. "The rule is that the local rabbinical court decides if meat is kosher or not. The authority is with the community and there is no superior authority which can tell the town what to do."

Even some of the most vociferous campaigners conceded that it might have been simpler for Holocaust survivors, and for the Jewish community as a whole, to have stayed quiet. Asked if the restitution campaign was good for the Jews, Rabbi Marvin Hier, dean of the Simon Wiesenthal Center, promptly answers that it was not. "I know that a lot of people don't understand it. They ask why the Jews are getting all this money. It's fifty-five years later and it's very hard for the average nonstudent of the Holocaust to figure out. But nevertheless, it's right for the Jews to do it because they've earned every penny."

Even after the major compensation claims were settled, some of the most highly charged restitution battles still remained to be fought. Poland, home to the world's largest Jewish community before the war, faced increasing pressure for property restitution. And in Israel, the Knesset set up a committee to examine dormant accounts and allegedly stolen safe deposit boxes in its commercial banks. Many of these assets traced their way back to the stormiest days of the creation of Israel, when money was sent to Palestine by Zionists who hoped to make *Aliyah* but who died in the Holocaust.

The successful fight for Holocaust compensation also cleared the way for other campaigns for historical justice. The law passed in California to allow Holocaust slave laborers to sue the Germans gave rise to lawsuits from people forced to work for the Japanese during World War II. Victims of the Armenian genocide, dating back to 1915, also won a settlement from the insurer New York Life.

By far the biggest emerging battle is over compensation for African Americans. Lawyers preparing to litigate over slavery and segregation cite the Holocaust lawsuits as a model. Some, like Johnnie Cochran—the highest-profile African American attorney in the country, and O.J. Simpson's defense attorney—have exchanged information with the Jewish plaintiffs' attorneys about how to proceed. The lawyers believe they can successfully sue companies that have remained in existence for centuries—companies such as the insurer Aetna, which has already apologized for writing policies for slave owners on the lives of their human property.

Aetna became a lightning rod for the issue of compensation for African Americans, but its apology came precisely because it prided itself on its racial diversity and community relations. "It's so ironic to us," said one Aetna executive, "because our senior management team is made up of African Americans." However, as the painful experience of Generali demonstrated, making fulsome apologies and having a close historical link to the aggrieved community was no protection against public pressure for compensation.

Some commentators have dismissed the slavery claims as being too old to be taken seriously, and the lack of surviving claimants does indeed pose enormous legal obstacles. However, many African Americans suffered economic losses at the hands of southern employers enforcing segregation far more recently. The human rights abuses may be less severe than slavery, but the victims are alive and can easily testify to the humiliation and deprivation of the Jim Crow South.

What African Americans lacked was the political will behind the Jewish campaign. Through Edgar Bronfman, the World Jewish Congress gained critical access to President Clinton. With backing from the White House and Congress, Jewish groups pursued compensation with the full support of the world's only superpower.

That helps to explain one of the critical questions surrounding wartime compensation: why did the battle for restitution only resume fifty years after the war had ended? The U.S. government, free from the dogma of the cold war, was willing and able to confront its European allies as it pursued the domestic concerns of a powerful voting and lobbying bloc. The end of the cold war also served to break the European mind-set that deferred the outstanding issues of wartime compensation until some nonexistent date in the future. With economies booming across the world in the late 1990s, there was a critical window of opportunity for settling the issue of Holocaust profits once and for all. That window appeared to close abruptly in 2001. It would be hard to envisage the United States adopting a similar stance during the war against terrorism, when it could not risk the collapse of its broad coalition of allies. European companies would have proved even more intransigent had the compensation claims arrived at a time of war and recession, when they were enduring a sharp downturn in profits.

By chance, the political support for Jewish causes coincided with the newfound readiness of American judges to allow people to sue for violations of international law. From Paraguayan police torturers to the leader of the Bosnian Serbs, a new breed of human rights litigation has emerged in U.S. courts. Holocaust lawyers realized they could sue corporations instead of governments, which could claim sovereign immunity. As corporations extend their reach across the global economy, they are increasingly open to legal challenges in the United States for their conduct elsewhere in the world. Burmese and Nigerian activists have sued oil companies for alleged complicity in human rights violations, and the Indian victims of the Bhopal chemical spill have sued Union Carbide in a Manhattan court. Some observers have dubbed this plaintiff's diplomacy—a process in which the courts, not the administration, shape foreign policy.

The potential to bring international cases like the Holocaust lawsuits seems limitless. What is to stop a former German soldier from suing a Russian company for exploiting his forced labor after the war? Or Palestinian Americans suing an Israeli bank for mortgaging a Jewish home in the occupied territories?

One fact seems incontrovertible. The victims themselves, on whose behalf the battles were fought, do not share the same sense of success that exists among the lawyers, companies, and governments who waged those fights. Jaime Rothman, receiving his German slave labor compensation in New York, voiced sentiments shared by thousands. "The point is always the same," he said. "Too little, too late. But if it had been earlier or larger, it would have been no more moral."

Those unsatisfied feelings were echoed by one of the judges required to adjudicate the historic struggle, which forced so many European companies to pay so much money, so long after the war.

In Newark, New Jersey, Judge William Bassler reached for a more meaningful citation than just another legal precedent. As he agreed to the voluntary dismissal of forty-two lawsuits against German companies, the judge said he felt compelled to make some "personal observations."

After reading the lawsuits and the public statements at the signing ceremony in Berlin, he was reminded of the words of the existentialist Danish philosopher Søren Kierkegaard. It was now, he suggested unhappily, time to move on. "Life can only be understood backwards," he quoted, "but it must be lived forwards."

Notes on Chapters

PROLOGUE
2 "We need moral and material restitution . . ." Singer's comments are taken from his speech to Cardozo Law School in New York on February 9, 1998. All other observations and quotations in the prologue are drawn from the author's notes of the event.

CHAPTER ONE: FOR WANT OF A CHAIR
7 $7 billion in Holocaust survivors' money The (questionable) mathematics behind this claim are laid out by Itamar Levin, the journalist who wrote the story, in his book *The Last Deposit* (New York: Praeger, 1999).

7 a front-page article See "Secret Legacies" by Peter Gumbel, in the *Wall Street Journal,* June 22, 1995.

7 Switzerland's bank regulators This is drawn from an interview with Urs Zulauf, chief legal counsel of the Swiss Federal Banking Commission, in Bern, April 4, 2001. He had circulated a letter to Swiss banks proposing setting up a centralized registry of dormant accounts a few months before the meeting at La Grande Société.

7 40.9 million Swiss francs, or about $24 million Throughout the book, the Swiss franc will be converted into dollars at a rate of 1.75 Swiss francs to the U.S. dollar. That was its rate in July 2001. However, it should be noted that the Swiss franc weakened over the period covered by this book, so that offers denominated in Swiss francs grew steadily less attractive to those thinking in terms of dollars. In September 1995, the exchange rate was 1.18 Swiss francs to the U.S. dollar. By the beginning of 1998 this had risen to about 1.5, and the currency worsened to about 1.75 in late 2000.

7 the red-carpeted, chandeliered splendor of La Grande Société The account of the meeting is based on the author's interviews with the following participants: Hans Baer, Zvi Barak, Rolf Bloch, Edgar Bronfman, Avraham Burg, Georg Krayer, and Israel Singer. Strongly partisan accounts of this meeting, viewed from the Jewish side, appear in Tom Bower, *Nazi Gold* (New York: Harper-Collins, 1997) (Bower gives the encounter the wrong date), and Levin, *Last Deposit.* Edgar Bronfman's *The Making of a Jew* (New York: Putnam, 1997) also briefly touches on the meeting, in which he describes the Swiss tactics as "very fresh" and claims that the Jewish contingent arrived early.

8 welcome speech   All the words attributed to Georg Krayer are taken from the text of his speech.

8 Swiss government decree   This survey was in fact far less complete than it should have been, as later research would reveal. This was mainly because the banks deliberately interpreted their obligations unnecessarily narrowly. See the Report of the Independent Committee of Eminent Persons (The Volcker Report), Annex 5, cited later. Tom Bower goes into exhaustive detail in *Nazi Gold.*

8 "Edgar, say that was a most interesting speech . . ."   Avraham Burg, then head of the Jewish Agency, was the speaker.

9 a clear image of Swiss arrogance   Bronfman's comments about a chapter title came in a speech to the Commonwealth Club in New York, while his *Time* interview appeared in March 1997. It is quoted in the letter Georg Krayer wrote to Bronfman after the *Time* piece had been published.

10 "you have to complain about the chairs . . ."   Baer made these complaints in an interview with the author at his office in Zurich, April 2, 2001.

10 "comfort the afflicted . . ."   Singer was alluding to Finley Peter Dunne's view of the role of newspapers. These comments are drawn from a startlingly personal speech Israel Singer delivered to law students at a symposium at Cardozo Law School, New York, February 9, 1998. This is also the source for his discussion on campaigning and tactics, which appears later in the chapter. A transcript of the entire speech can be found on the Internet at www.cardozo.yu.edu/cardlrev/v20n2/singer.pdf

11 "one-size-fits-all Judaism"   Singer's discussion of his religious beliefs is drawn from a brief essay in *Partners in History—A Tribute,* published by the WJC on September 11, 2000, a brochure celebrating the fruits of the restitution campaign.

11 the civil rights movement   Singer's recollections are drawn from a telephone interview with him on July 24, 2001.

11 to coordinate international efforts against Nazism   The definitive account of the establishment of the WJC is *The Jewish Paradox* by Nahum Goldmann himself, published by G&D.

12 Singer helped bring him to Judaism   Bronfman describes his early days with Singer in his own book. This also includes his admission about eating pork on Yom Kippur. Other details are drawn from an interview with Edgar Bronfman in New York, March 7, 2001, while Singer described Bronfman's importance to the campaign in a telephone interview with the author on August 28, 1998.

12 Dan Tichon   Tichon went on to be speaker of the Knesset during Benjamin Netanyahu's premiership and regretted that this promotion made it harder for him to oversee the actions of the WJC and the Jewish Agency, which he deeply distrusted. This is based on a telephone interview with Dan Tichon in Jerusalem, April 24, 2001.

12 the biggest donor of soft money   As cited by the Center for Responsive Politics in its survey of soft money donors in the 1995–1996 election cycle.

14 The banks offered precise statistics   The statistics quoted are all drawn from the Swiss Bankers Association's press release of the time. This also included their statement saying rumors were "totally unfounded."

15 "Kill them."   This memorable interchange—as well as Bronfman's initial reaction—is also reported in Levin, *Last Deposit.*

16 The guest of honor was . . . Hillary Rodham Clinton.   The account of this meeting is based on interviews with Edgar Bronfman in New York on March 7, 2001, and with Hillary Rodham Clinton in Washington on July 12, 2001.

16 Greta Beer   This material is drawn from an interview with Greta Beer in Boston, February 21, 2001.

17 "judge, jury and executioner"   See Gregg Rickman, *Swiss Banks and Jewish Souls* (Washington, D.C.: Transaction Publishers 1998), p. 50. Rickman, himself the son of Holocaust survivors, was D'Amato's legislative director and effectively in charge of the Senate investigation.

17 With a bang of the gavel   All the dialogue from the hearing is drawn from the official Senate transcript.

19 *Doctor Strangelove*   See Rickman, *Swiss Banks.*

20 The only other person in the room   This account is based on interviews with Bronfman and Singer.

20 Bronfman had a biblical analogy   He made these comments in an interview with the author in New York, March 7, 2001. Esther is the Jewish heroine who successfully frustrated the evil plot by Haman, chief minister to the King of Persia, to kill the kingdom's Jewish population.

CHAPTER TWO: THE FINAL ACCOUNTING

21 the front-page *Wall Street Journal* article   This is "Secret Legacies" by Peter Gumbel, published on June 22, 1995, already cited. Baer was at a conference when it appeared and had to endure seeing all his fellow participants reading the offending article.

22 the perfect bridge between Hans Baer and Israel Singer   In interviews with the author, both Hoxter and Singer attested to the strong confidence they had in each other. Both Singer and Baer said in interview that they assumed the other was paying Hoxter.

23 Hoxter presided over negotiations   This version of events is drawn largely from Curtis Hoxter's recollections. They are confirmed by Singer and Baer.

23 His Israeli colleagues from the mission to Bern   Avraham Burg and Zvi Barak were both more skeptical of Baer's efforts and persistently pushed Singer to be more aggressive.

24 "unfettered access"   This phraseology is drawn from the Memorandum of Understanding, which is available on the International Committee of Eminent Persons' website: www.icep-iaep.org.

24 It would prove one of the most expensive pieces of paper   Both Hans Baer and Georg Krayer say in interviews that they had no conception at this stage of the final cost of the audit.

25 Burg's father attempted to use the contacts . . . with the SS   This is based on interviews with Avraham Burg and Israel Singer.

25 "Okay, we're coming tomorrow to Bern. . . ."   This is based on the author's interview with Avraham Burg at Ramat Gan, Israel, April 18, 2001.

25 a former fighter pilot   Zvi Barak was interviewed by the author in New York, March 23, 2001. This interview forms the basis for all the subsequent quotes from Barak throughout the book.

26 He canvassed his Jewish friends   The account of the wooing of Paul Volcker is based on the author's interview with Volcker in New York, March 19, 2001 (which is also the source for the subsequent quotations from Volcker in this chapter), as well as several interviews with Curtis Hoxter and an interview with Edgar Bronfman, March 7, 2001.

26 Fritz Leutwiler   Volcker lost his most trusted Swiss confidant early the next year, when Fritz Leutwiler died suddenly. Many in Swiss banking circles believe the affair could have been cleared up much more swiftly and with less acrimony had he lived.

27 "We were naive."   This comment comes from Franz Zimmermann, legal counsel to the UBS, in an interview in Basel, April 3, 2001.

28 "This is not going to be the possible thing . . ."   This account is drawn from the interviews with Volcker and Gasteyger.

28 Rubbing salt into the wound   Michel Dérobert, secretary of the Geneva Private Banks Association, described some of his members' grievances in an interview in Geneva, April 6, 2001.

28 "extinguished by actions"   This is from the ICEP Mandate, Phase One, available on the ICEP website.

29 UBS had accumulated a pile of papers twelve kilometers long.   This comes from the interview with Georg Krayer, Basel, April 3, 2001.

29 "If you want the truth, you have to pay for it."   This comment lived in the memories of several Swiss bankers. It was mentioned in an interview with Franz Zimmermann of UBS.

30 over kiddush   Jeffrey Taufield, of the New York PR firm Kekst and Company, recounted the story of Borer's goodwill mission in an interview in New York, January 29, 2001.

30 crisis of confidence   The crisis was exacerbated by a maverick Swiss member of parliament, Jean Ziegler, who published a book attacking the Swiss war record: *The Swiss, the Gold and the Dead* (New York: Penguin, 1998).

30 Its first report would not appear until 1998.   The Bergier Commission produced a huge amount of historical research, in August 2001 bringing out ten separate reports on different aspects of Swiss economic support for the Nazis. The reports were viewed almost universally as strongly critical and impressively impartial history. Summaries of the reports, and details on obtaining them, are available on the Bergier Commission's website: *www.uek.ch.*

31 "I remember Aunt Rebecca."   Krayer's comments are drawn from his interview with the author in Basel, April 3, 2001.

32 "When demands are made not in good faith . . ."   See Reuters, December 31, 1996.

32 "This is a war which Switzerland must win . . ."   See, for example, *New York Times,* January 27, 1997.

33 The shredding room was popular   This is based on a telephone interview with Christoph Meili from his home in Orange, California, May 21, 2001. This interview is the source for all the thoughts and quotes attributed to Meili that follow in this chapter.

33 he returned to the shredding room   Meili gave this version of events in his testimony before the Senate Banking Committee, April 1997. It is available in the official transcript along with his strongly worded plea of self-justification.

34 "It was probably all a coincidence . . ."   The executive quoted is Urs Roth, who later became chief executive of the Swiss Bankers Association, in an interview in Basel, April 11, 2001.

35 "Imagine that!"   D'Amato's comments are in the official transcript of the Senate Banking Committee hearing May 6, 1997.

35 donations of more than $10,000 on the spot   See *Jewish Journal* of greater Los Angeles, April 28, 2000.

36 a gala at the Beverly Hilton   See *Jewish Bulletin* of northern California, April 2000.

36 "I told the lawyers what to do."   Meili made these claims in his telephone interview of May 21, 2001. None of the lawyers and politicians involved in the campaign for restitution would attribute anything like this much influence to him, although the importance of his story for the public relations campaign is undeniably profound.

36 "This is why Meili is so important."   Zimmermann made this comment in an interview in Basel, April 3, 2001.

CHAPTER THREE: A PRIDE OF LAWYERS

37 the eighty-first floor of the World Trade Center   Luckily for Fagan, he left the World Trade Center in 1998, three years before the building was destroyed.

37 His trip prompted complaints   See "The Sensation Hunter" by Nikos Tzermias, *Neue Zurcher Zeitung,* February 12, 1998.

38 a libel lawsuit from the movie star Sylvester Stallone   The details of *Fagan v Stallone* remain on file in the Southern District of New York.

38 a client of his named Gizella Weisshaus   The account of Fagan's decision to launch *Weisshaus v UBS* is based on telephone interviews with Ed Fagan, May 31, 2001; and Gizella Weisshaus, May 8, 2000.

39 At synagogue during Kol Nidre   Hausfeld provided details on his upbringing in an interview with the author in Washington D.C., May 19, 2000. This is the source for the subsequent quotations attributed to him in this chapter.

40 a mailing list of more than four hundred thousand donors   These details are from the Simon Wiesenthal Center's website, *www.wiesenthal.com,* which also provides information about the center's museum and plentiful historical material on the Swiss assets and other restitution campaigns.

40 which Simon Wiesenthal himself strongly opposed   For an account of this incident, see *Simon Wiesenthal* by Hella Pick, an excellent and definitive biography of the Nazi-hunter. See also Chapter 20.

40 Ratner's firm suggested another name   The source for this is Morris Ratner, interviewed in New York, January 29, 2001.

42 a huge framed account of that trial   Bob Swift was interviewed by the author in his office in Philadelphia, February 5, 2001.

43 winning an injunction against the government   This is based on a telephone interview with Burt Neuborne in New York, June 1, 2001. The details of Neuborne's personal motivations for becoming involved come from an earlier interview, March 31, 2000, which is the source for all his other comments in this chapter.

44 Bob Swift complained   He made his complaints in letters to the judge, available in the case docket in the Eastern District of New York.

45 chatting amicably in the front row This account and the ensuing dialogue is based on the official court transcript, also available in the case docket.

45 defending campaign finance laws against attacks from Neuborne   Korman, as a judge presiding over active litigation, was not available for an interview for this book. This is based on the telephone interview with Burt Neuborne of March 31, 2000.

45 financing himself with loans from factors   Fagan described this in an interview on May 31, 2001, when he had recently heard of a multimillion award from the German case that would rub out the debts and make him a millionaire.

47 Fagan also befriended Christoph Meili   The account of Fagan's relationship with Meili is based on interviews with Fagan, May 31, 2001; and Meili, May 21 and September 3, 2001.

48 secure in the conviction   Roger Witten was interviewed by the author in Washington, D.C., February 12, 2001.

49 "Did you say *billion* with a *b*?"   Roger Witten and Michael Hausfeld have almost identical recollections of this exchange.

CHAPTER FOUR: REWRITING HISTORY

51 U.S. and Allied efforts   The report's full title is *U.S. and Allied Efforts to Recover and Restore Gold and Other Assets Stolen or Hidden by Germany during World War II—Preliminary Study. Coordinated by Stuart E. Eizenstat, Prepared by William Z. Slany.* The report, along with a wealth of other information produced by the State Department during the various restitution campaigns, can be found on the following website: *www.state.gov/www/regions/eur/holocausthp.html.*

52 I trusted him"   Singer was speaking in a telephone interview on June 8, 2001.

52 "Despite repeated Swiss protestations . . ."   This and the following comments by Eizenstat are drawn from the official State Department transcript of the press conference, held May 7, 1997.

53 estimated at between $185 million and $259 million   This figure is taken from the Eizenstat Report, p. 85.

53 More than fifty years later   Countries with claims on the gold would eventually agree at a December 1999 conference in London to donate it to a special fund for needy Holocaust survivors. See Stuart Eizenstat's concluding statement, from the Washington Conference on Holocaust-Era Assets, Washington, D.C., December 3, 1998, also available on the State Department's website, and his statement at the conclusion of the London conference on Nazi Gold, December 4, 1997.

55 Freeman, an ebullient political appointee   Bennett Freeman provided his account of the writing of the report in an interview in Washington, D.C., March 16, 2000. This is the source for all subsequent quotes attributed to him in this chapter.

55 prolonging Nazi Germany's capacity to wage war   For both the offending sentences, see the Eizenstat Report, page v.

56 four-hundred-year-old neutrality For an excellent discussion of the history and applications of Swiss neutrality, see Jonathan Steinberg, *Why Switzerland?* (New York: Cambridge University Press).

56 "The morality language was important . . ." Eizenstat said this in an interview with the author in Washington, D.C., July 2000. This is also the source for his later comments on changes he could have made.

57 "Matterhorn of integrity . . ." See "Old Crimes . . ." by Jim Hoagland, *Washington Post,* May 25, 1997.

57 "Europe was a devastated area. . . ." Seymour Rubin's comments were made in an interview with the author in Washington, D.C., March 27, 2001.

57 "Wartime objectives were replaced by the new Cold War imperatives." Eizenstat said this in his speech at the State Department, May 7, 1997.

58 the report was "totally" unfair Borer was not interviewed specifically for this book, although he spoke to the author for a number of contemporaneous news reports, because he had moved on to a new position as ambassador to Germany and deemed it inappropriate to talk about the Holocaust affair. He was quoted in an excellent documentary *Swiss Jewry—An Island in the Twentieth Century,* produced by JEM/GLO Productions in New Jersey. Copies of the video are available from JEM/GLO, P.O. Box 43127, Upper Montclair, NJ 07043.

58 the Melmer account crimes These comments are taken from the transcript of the Embassy of Switzerland's Press Conference, Washington D.C., May 7, 1997.

58 Swiss newspapers lambasted the gross hypocrisy This paragraph quotes from a good example: "Who Prolonged World War II—And When?" by Professor Walter Hofer, *Neue Zurcher Zeitung,* June 7–8, 1997.

59 "righteous gentiles" See Meir Wagner, *The Righteous of Switzerland— Heroes of the Holocaust* (New York: Ktav Publishing House, 2001).

59 "The Clinton administration's assertion . . ." Jacques Rossier made these comments in a speech to the Harvard Faculty Club in Boston, May 26, 1999.

59 "a highly emotional and politicized confrontation" Professor Gasteyger made these comments to the author in Geneva, April 6, 2001.

60 "It fostered two things" Rolf Bloch was speaking to the author in Bern, April 4, 2001.

61 "Stay your hand. . . ." This account is based on an interview with Roger Witten in Washington, D.C., February 12, 2001.

61 "I hate to tell you this, Stuart . . ." This is based on Baer's recollections, from his interview in Zurich, April 2, 2001.

CHAPTER FIVE: SHOT ACROSS THE BOW

62 Singer disliked sanctions. His comments on sanctions are drawn from a telephone interview, August 28, 1998. His invocation to "just buy from the nice guys" was made during his campaign against the Dutch insurer Aegon in January 2000.

63 Hevesi would play "good cop" to Al D'Amato's "bad cop" Both Alan Hevesi and Israel Singer volunteered this description of the two men's roles in interviews in New York in August 1998.

63 Hevesi wrote discreet letters This is drawn from an interview with Alan Hevesi, August 28, 1998.

64 in a bid to avoid prying eyes   Hevesi recounted this incident in an interview with the author at his office in New York, January 18, 2001.

64 Shuttling along the scenic route   The account of Newman and Hevesi's visit to Switzerland is based on the interviews with Hevesi, already cited, and with Steve Newman in New York, January 24, 2001.

65 an interview in the *New Yorker*   The offending piece appeared in May 1997.

65 Wollman established   See the speech by Eric Wollman, Cardozo Law School, February 9, 1998.

65 He started sending them bulletins   This is based on an interview with Eric Wollman in New York, February 7, 2001.

67 cleared with the mayor, Rudolph Giuliani   At the time, Hevesi had good relations with Giuliani, but they degenerated spectacularly in the campaign for the Democratic nomination for mayor in 2001, when Giuliani launched a series of attacks on Hevesi's integrity.

68 "Sanctions and boycotts . . ."   This is taken from Eizenstat's letter to Matt Fong, October 17, 1997.

68 "like an atomic bomb . . ."   Eizenstat made these comments in an interview with the author in Washington D.C., August 1998.

68 the State Department itself used sanctions often   For a more detailed discussion, see John Authers *Boycotting the Corporation: The Power of Economic Sanctions* (Reuters Forum Journal, 2000).

70 McCaul suspected that they chose it for its large vault   Elizabeth McCaul was interviewed by the author in New York on March 9, 2001.

70 Irwin Nack, traveled down the mine shaft   He discussed the incident with the author on March 20, 2001.

70 a heavy financial toll on the banks   The figures come from Credit Suisse officials. The New York State Banking Department will not release figures on the total amount of accounts found, in respect of the accountholders' right of privacy.

71 Outside, their breath forming clouds   The description of events at the Plaza conference is based on the author's contemporaneous notes.

CHAPTER SIX: TAKE IT OR LEAVE IT

74 Mel Weiss paced his corner office   This scene is based on an interview with Melvyn Weiss in New York on December 12, 1997.

75 his share alone came to $102 million   See "Milberg May Be Short on Coverage," by Paul Elias, *The Recorder/Cal Law,* American Lawyer Media, April 15, 1999.

75 a large collection of Picasso's   Weiss wrote about his admiration for Picasso in the catalog for the Weiss Collection, at an exhibition held in Argentina in March 2001.

76 As his plane touched down   The account of Eizenstat's movements in Zurich is based on interviews with Bennett Freeman in Washington, D.C., March 16, 2000, and June 21, 2001.

76 Eizenstat was determined   This is based on the author's interviews with Bennett Freeman and other administration officials who wished to remain anonymous.

77 Credit Suisse had reserved the hotel's largest private dining room   The description of the meeting is based on participants' contemporaneous notes and subsequent interviews with Stuart Eizenstat, Bennett Freeman, Michael Hausfeld, Urs Roth, Bernhard Stettler, Robert Swift, Peter Widmer, and Roger Witten.

80 Hevesi's boardroom   The account of the meeting in Hevesi's office is based on interviews with Steve Newman, Bennett Freeman, Alan Hevesi, Israel Singer, Jeffrey Taufield, Roger Witten, and Eric Wollman.

81 Both sides, accustomed to face-to-face bargaining   The account of the talks in the State Department is based on participants' contemporaneous notes; on interviews in June–August 1998 with Stuart Eizenstat, Bennett Freeman, Michael Hausfeld, Israel Singer, Elan Steinberg, and Roger Witten; and later interviews with Robert Swift and Gideon Taylor.

83 about 300 million Swiss francs   This comes from contemporaneous briefings by Swiss bank officials.

83 Her objections to the merger remained   Elizabeth McCaul was interviewed in New York by the author, March 9, 2001. This is also the source for her later remarks.

84 "prompt and just resolution"   This letter is cited in Gregg Rickman, *Swiss Banks and Jewish Souls*. Rickman was Senator D'Amato's chief of staff. Israel Singer and Curtis Hoxter confirmed this course of events.

85 "She did as much good for survivors . . ."   The lawyer making this comment wished to remain anonymous.

85 New York's Four Seasons Hotel   The account of this meeting is based on contemporaneous notes of participants.

85 "We believed him"   Singer was speaking in an interview in New York, August 28, 1998.

85 a report in the *New York Times*   See: "Swiss Banks Said to Offer Holocaust Payment," *New York Times,* June 5, 1998.

86 "chagrined and annoyed"   Robert Swift wrote his letter to Michael Hausfeld and Melvyn Weiss, June 9, 1998.

87 "Helvetia Unter Druck"   The cartoon was provided in an interview with Eric Wollman in New York, February 7, 2001.

88 Fagan grabbed the receiver back.   The incident happened during the author's telephone interview with Ed Fagan and Gizella Weisshaus in New York, on June 19, 1998.

88 It is a disgrace for you to do so.   Letter to Stuart Eizenstat from Mel Weiss, Michael Hausfeld, and Israel Singer, June 29, 1998.

88 "The mood in Switzerland has changed in the past year . . ."   Borer was quoted in "How a Swiss Bank Gold Deal Eluded a U.S. Mediator," *New York Times,* July 11, 1998.

88 "my role in this phase of the matter closed"   This appears in the official transcript and is quoted in the letter to President Clinton from Alan Hevesi and Carl McCall, July 28, 1998.

89 the tiled Victorian corridors   The account of the second meeting in Hevesi's office is based on the author's contemporaneous notes, and interviews with Ed Fagan, Bennett Freeman, Alan Hevesi, Steve Newman, Israel Singer, Elan Steinberg, Jeffrey Taufield, and Eric Wollman.

90 "irrelevant"   Elan Steinberg said this in a contemporaneous interview.

90 "wrong both in principle and practice. . . ."   This is taken from Bennett Freeman's testimony to the Executive Monitoring Committee, July 1, 1998.

90 "crass exercise of economic leverage over us." See the testimony of Richard Capone, Executive Monitoring Committee, July 1, 1998.

92 billions of dollars' worth of Swiss shares would be sold For an analysis of the sanctions, see John Authers and William Hall, "Swiss Banks Face Phased Package of Sanctions," *Financial Times,* July 3, 1998.

92 Swiss companies planned retaliation For an account of this episode, see John Authers, William Hall, and Richard Wolffe, "Banks Pay a High Price for Putting the Past Behind Them," *Financial Times,* September 9, 1998.

93 "come off the $1.5 billion figure" The account of this press conference is based on an interview with Robert Swift, Philadelphia, February 5, 2001. The subsequent letters are in the possession of the author.

93 *outraged to be left in the dark* Gizella Weisshaus's letter to Judge Korman is in the official case docket in the Eastern District of New York. The emphasis is in the original.

CHAPTER SEVEN: THE PRICE OF PEACE

94 Gage and Tollner was not kosher. Israel Singer described the experience in New York, August 28, 1998. The account of their meeting in the steak house is also based on interviews with the following attendees: Israel Singer, Elan Steinberg, Mel Weiss, Michael Hausfeld, Roger Witten, Peter Widmer, Franz Zimmermann, Burt Neuborne, Ed Fagan, Morris Ratner, and Robert Swift.

95 "I'll give you an answer . . ." This is based on an interview with Alan Hevesi on August 28, 1998, and a supplementary interview with Steve Newman.

97 worth $13 billion in 1998 dollars These figures are taken from the confidential damage book presented by Michael Hausfeld at the meeting.

97 Ground rules These caused great amusement among the Swiss, and were recalled by several members of the Swiss legal team who were not present at the meeting.

98 "a deliberate move to defuse any feeling . . ." Weiss made this comment in an interview in New York a few days after the meeting in August 1998.

100 Swift and Fagan had sued three Swiss insurance companies The class action lawsuit against European insurers is covered in Chapter 9, "Falling like Dominoes." Fagan and Swift were in advanced talks with the Italian insurer Assicurazioni Generali at the time.

101 a settlement for Christoph Meili This was not the end of the Meili saga. A few weeks later, Meili says, Ed Fagan, his lawyer, visited the young security guard in New Jersey bringing a bottle of wine. He emerged with a letter signed by Meili agreeing to pay him $250,000. While 25 percent was a huge percentage compared with the fees the lawyers would win from the rest of the Holocaust litigations, Fagan pointed out to a dubious Meili that it was still below his usual rate of 33 percent. Three years later, Meili had still not received his money, although the lawyers had received theirs. He commented: "I'm a young man and I'm not experienced. What was I to do?"

101 Singer said he was happy to settle This is based on an interview with Israel Singer in New York on August 28, 1998. Gregg Rickman's *Swiss Banks and Jewish Souls* also mentions this conversation, although it does not include the agreement to exclude interest payments. Hausfeld and Witten also confirm this version of events.

102 Freeman grabbed Foxman's telephone   This account is based on an interview with Bennett Freeman, Washington D.C., March 16, 2000, and also with Abraham Foxman, New York, March 2, 2000. His comment on the "last sound bite," often repeated, is substantially the same as comments Foxman made to PBS's *NewsHour*, August 12, 1998. Freeman was invited to attend Hevesi's press conference on August 13, and subsequently had high praise for the city comptroller's handling of the affair. He conceded that Hevesi had behaved "with a steady hand and reasonable temperament but also with a willingness to go for the banks' jugular just when the time was right."

103 a tough reelection campaign   D'Amato in fact lost the election, heavily, to Charles Schumer, a Democrat from Brooklyn. His support in the Jewish community collapsed, despite opening his campaign with a television advertisement by Estelle Sapir, one of the best-known Holocaust survivors to claim against the Swiss banks, which ended, "God bless you, Senator D'Amato." D'Amato's failure was widely attributed to an off-the-cuff remark in which he called his opponent a "putzhead," a Yiddish vulgarism. Alan Hevesi, in his own campaign for mayor three years later, decided to be much more understated about his role in the restitution campaign, although he suffered the same fate as D'Amato, losing heavily.

105 Neither showed any contrition.   Some Jewish leaders opposed the settlement on the grounds that the SNB was allowed to get away without payment and without an apology. Raul Teitelbaum and Moshe Sanbar's *Holocaust Gold: From the Victims to Switzerland: The Paths of the Nazi Plunder* (Tel Aviv: Moreshet Publishing House, 2001) is a trenchant attack on the SNB and on the decision of Singer and the others to accept the deal.

106 "showing up and taking the credit"   Hausfeld made this comment in a contemporaneous interview with the author.

CHAPTER EIGHT: GATEWAY TO ZION

107 Mor Stern   Details of Adolf Stern's life story, his attempts to claim on his father's policy, and the early stages of the Sterns' campaign against Generali in 1996 and 1997 are drawn from the complaint *Adolf Stern et al v Assicurazioni Generali*, filed in Superior Court for the State of California for the County of Los Angeles. Some details have been corrected following an interview with Martin Stern. This complaint is also the source for all the correspondence between the Sterns and Generali cited in this chapter.

107 now in Ukraine   Uzhgorod has at different times belonged to Czechoslovakia, Hungary, and Ukraine.

109 He was deported, never to return.   Generali's website, at *www.generali. com*, includes an excellent corporate history from which many of these details are drawn. Others come from interviews with Generali officials in Trieste, April 9 and 10, 2001.

110 the incoming Nazis had targeted Jewish companies   See *Insurance in the Nazi Occupied Czech Lands* by Tomas Jelinek, a working paper drawn up by the Czech delegation to the December 1998 Washington Conference on Holocaust-Era Assets.

110 the biggest direct foreign investment   It did not hold this title for long, being eclipsed in 2000 by the $4.5 billion Lucent Technologies of the United

States paid for Clariant. That latter investment, however, was written off barely a year later as Lucent took a heavy loss.

110 When Martin Stern read   This is based on a telephone interview with Martin Stern, July 30, 2001.

113 "nobody ever died"   Martin Stern discussed this in an interview in Jerusalem, April 18, 2001.

113 a small, low-slung warehouse   This description is based on the author's tour of the warehouse in Trieste on April 10, 2001.

114 a job that took twenty people six months   Author's interviews with Alberto Tiberini and Guido Pastori in Trieste, April 9, 2001.

115 a nationalistic firebrand   Kleiner was interviewed for the book in Jerusalem, April 16, 2001.

115 Migdal had been deliberately undervalued.   Dan Tichon repeated this allegation in an interview on April 23, 2001.

116 Elisheva Ansbacher   She was interviewed in Jerusalem, April 18, 2001.

117 "So we should do better."   This is based on Scott Vayer's recollection, offered in an interview in New York, May 2000.

117 Generali would have no control   The account of the foundation of the Generali Trust is based on interviews with Avraham Hirschson, Michael Kleiner, and Martin Stern.

118 We wish to confirm as most praiseworthy   The statement was signed by Hirschson, Kleiner, and Ravitz in June 1997 and given to Generali.

Chapter Nine: Falling like Dominoes

119 Cornell said she was given no explanation.   This is drawn from the testimony of Marta Cornell, at the National Association of Insurance Commissioners hearing in Washington, D.C., September 22, 1997. This transcript, along with many others from the developing campaign over Holocaust insurance, is available on the website of the Office of the Insurance Commissioner for Washington State at *www.insurance.wa.gov.*

120 To his surprise, they were invited in.   Both Ed Fagan and Guido Pastori of Generali recounted this incident in interviews.

120 Fagan journeyed to Israel   This is based on interviews with Martin Stern and Ed Fagan.

121 *"Morte in Campo Concentramento"*   This is taken from the testimony of Scott Vayer to Congress, 1997.

121 close links to Senator D'Amato   Berman and D'Amato actually set up a lobbying business together, Park Strategies, after D'Amato lost his Senate seat.

122 "To corner public support"   Deborah Senn said this in an interview in New York on March 29, 2001. This is the source for all subsequent quotes attributed to her throughout the book, except where otherwise stated.

123 "the open hostility conveyed . . ."   Davis's letter is quoted in the transcript of the New York hearing, available at the Washington insurance commissioner's website, *www.insurance.wa.gov.* The dialogue that follows is drawn from the transcript.

128 Neil Levin   Tragically, Neil Levin was among the victims of the World Trade Center disaster on September 11, 2001. He left his job as insurance commissioner in the spring of 2001 to become executive director of the Port Authority of New York and New Jersey, the owner of the twin towers, and apparently stayed at his desk during the tragedy. He was interviewed for this book in March and February of 2001, while still insurance commissioner, and checked the quotes attributed to him in these pages during the summer of 2001. All the people quoted who comment on Levin's actions, critically or otherwise, were talking before the tragic events of September 11.

128 Fagan phoned journalists   Ed Fagan discussed this and made the other assertions attributed to him in this chapter in an interview on May 31, 2001.

129 Elie Wiesel   Bob Swift explained his hopes to the author in an interview, February 9, 2000.

129 Mukasey's courtroom   The account of the hearing is drawn from the court transcript, Southern District of New York, August 19, 1998.

130 a news conference   This is based on interviews with Deborah Senn in New York, March 29, 2001; Bobby Brown, Jerusalem, April 16, 2001; and several phone interviews with Martin Stern.

131 Fagan commented   This was stated in an interview, May 31, 2001—well before Levin's tragic death.

131 "it wasn't thought through . . ."   Singer spoke in an interview with the author, June 8, 2001.

132 "then it will not take effect"   The wording is drawn from a Generali press release, August 28, 1998.

132 Fagan implored   See the letter of Ed Fagan to Judge Mukasey, in case docket at Southern District of New York.

132 "a vehicle for plaintiffs' counsel . . ."   See the letter of Neil Levin and Glenn Pomeroy to Judge Mukasey, in the case docket at Southern District of New York.

132 "They sold out."   Morris Ratner spoke with the author on January 29, 2001.

132 Amid the crowds   The account of the meeting is based on the author's contemporaneous notes. Ed Fagan provided the text of Zentner's and Cornell's letters. The emphasis is in the original text.

CHAPTER TEN: THE LAST PRISONERS OF WAR

134 the French felt positively victimized   This passage is based on the author's interview with Ady Steg, Paris, April 4, 2001, as well as interviews with French officials who wished to remain anonymous. This is the source for all subsequent quotes from Steg, except where otherwise stated.

135 "The French museums are not jails . . ."   Steg's comments were made in his press conference on December 2, 1998.

135 a name he loathed   Steg made his feelings clear to the historian Claire Andrieu, interviewed by the author in Paris, April 4, 2001.

135 He was a teenager in Paris   Steg's account of his war years is drawn from the author's interview with him in Paris, April 4, 2001.

136 Steg could cajole   Claire Andrieu testified to Steg's negotiating skills after working closely with him on the Mattéoli Commission. She was interviewed by the author in Paris, April 4, 2001.

136 Untold by the exhibition   The true story was first published in the *Boston Globe*, November 30, 1998.

137 In the custody of the French government   The MNR's status was explained by David Kessler, Prime Minister Jospin's cultural adviser, in an interview with the author, April 5, 2001.

137 "Is the art genuine? . . ."   Ronald Lauder's comments were drawn from the official proceedings of the Washington Conference on Holocaust-Era Assets, November 30–December 3, 1998. See p. 468 of the proceedings published by the Department of State in April 1999. The emphasis is in the original.

137–38 a set of eleven principles   See pp. 971–72 of the official proceedings of the Washington conference.

138 In an early morning meeting   This account is based on interviews with State Department officials in Washington D.C., in March and June, 2001.

138 "You can't water down water."   Steinberg was quoted by Agence France Presse, December 2, 1998.

138 the Monet water lilies was returned   As reported by the *Boston Globe*, April 30, 1999.

138 One painting was sent back to Vienna   According to the *New York Times*, October 12, 1999, and March 17, 2001.

138 the fate of the MNR   This was brought to light by Hector Feliciano in his book *The Lost Museum* (New York: Basic Books, 1997). Kessler's comments are drawn from the author's interview in Paris on April 5, 2001.

139 "Those dark hours sully our history . . ."   See the speech by President Jacques Chirac on July 16, 1995, at public ceremonies commemorating *la grande rafle* of July 16 and 17, 1942. It is perhaps a sign of French denial of the Vichy years that these apparently obvious remarks had such an emotional impact in France.

140 Drancy became a transit point   See the interim Mattéoli report, published in January 1999.

140 individual government accounts   The accounts were kept at the Caisse de Dépôts et Consignations. Personal property was also held in vaults at the central bank, the Banque de France.

140 Chirac was horrified   The president made his feelings clear to Ady Steg, interviewed by the author in Paris, April 4, 2001.

140 Bousquet was killed   A year later, France continued its reexamination of Vichy with the trial and conviction of Paul Touvier, the head of a pro-Nazi militia in Lyon, who ordered the shooting of seven Jews.

140 "What Mitterand said . . ."   This is drawn from the author's interview with Claire Andrieu in Paris on April 4, 2001. All subsequent quotes by Andrieu are taken from the same source, unless otherwise stated.

141 Steg met with a group   This account is based on the author's interview with Ady Steg in Paris, April 4, 2001.

142 Steg told the new prime minister, Lionel Jospin   Based on the author's interview with David Kessler in Paris, April 5, 2001.

142 Jospin heard privately   See *Le Monde*, December 1, 1998.

143 The lawsuit accused the banks   See *Fernande Bodner v Banque Paribas et al*, December 17, 1997.

144 By his own admission McCallion explained his introduction to the Holocaust and the lawsuit in an interview with the author in New York, March 8, 2001.

144 In Weisberg's book See Richard H. Weisberg, *Vichy Law and the Holocaust in France* (New York: New York University Press, 1996), pp. 265–269.

145 He felt troubled by the Swiss bank litigation This account is drawn from the author's interview with Ken McCallion in New York, March 8, 2001.

145 infuriated by what she saw . . . This is drawn, along with the subsequent quotes, from the author's interview with Harriet Tamen in New York on March 28, 2001.

145 The French opted for a hardball defense See the banks' motion to dismiss, May 4, 1998.

146 the banks were also engaged This passage is based on the author's interview with Christian Schricke in Paris, April 3, 2001; as is the quotation preceding it.

147 "you can't lose this litigation . . ." This account is drawn from the author's interview with Fred Davis in New York, March 8, 2001.

148 "I'm based in Paris . . ." Samuels recalled the encounter in an interview with the author in Paris, April 2, 2001.

148 He took his message to the air This account is based on the author's interview with Shimon Samuels in Paris, April 2, 2001.

149 "There is something incestuous . . ." Samuels's comments were published by *Le Monde,* October 30, 1998.

149 "It's not just a problem for Jews . . ." This account of the exchange in the Matignon annex is based on the author's interviews with Israel Singer in New York, June 6, 2001; and David Kessler in Paris, April 5, 2001.

CHAPTER ELEVEN: AMERICANS AT THE GATE

150 They even distributed For example, see Kekst and Company press release of December 11, 1998, on behalf of French banks, detailing Jospin's speech to CRIF of November 28, 1998.

150 notably the Bader family This account is drawn from the author's interview with Owen Pell in Washington, D.C., January 27, 2001, which is also the source for his subsequent quotes.

151 Klein believed the bank's record Klein made his position clear in an interview with the author in Paris, April 3, 2001. His subsequent quotes are drawn from the same interview, unless otherwise stated.

151 In editorial columns See *New York Times,* December 15, 1998.

151 "a *goy* could tell me one day . . ." "Goy" is the sometimes derogatory Yiddish term for someone who is not Jewish.

151 Steinberg was convinced . . . This is based on the author's interview with Steinberg in New York on May 21, 2001. The subsequent quotes come from the same interview.

152 For just 335 Jewish clients The agreement was reported in the *Financial Times,* December 17, 1998.

152 Chase Manhattan declared See the Associated Press, December 17, 1998.

152 The French banks were incensed. See the press release by the French Bankers Association, December 17, 1998.

153 the victims' lawyers viewed This opinion is based on the author's interview with Ken McCallion in New York, March 8, 2001.

153 "The aim here is not to opt . . ." See p. 7 of the English version of the Mattéoli interim report, January 1999.

153 Now Steg and his fellow commission members See Mattéoli interim report, "Initial Recommendations," February 1999.

154 the WJC in New York was threatening to organize a boycott See Reuters, February 22, 1999.

155 the banks announced they would return See the press release by the French Bankers Association, March 24, 1999.

155 The banks were also monitoring . . . This is based on the author's interview with Christian Schricke in Paris on April 3, 2001. All subsequent quotes from Schricke are drawn from the same source, unless otherwise stated.

156 Jospin's office, grappling with the legal complexities This is based on the author's interview with David Kessler in Paris, April 5, 2001.

156 The apparently simple requests This account of the meeting in the Matignon annex is based on the author's interviews in Paris with Ady Steg, April 4, 2001, and David Kessler, April 5, 2001.

157 The prime minister had already indicated This is based on the author's interview with David Kessler in Paris, April 5, 2001.

157 Prime Minister Jospin signed a long-delayed decree See Agence France Presse, September 13, 1999.

158 Room 2128 of the Rayburn Office Building This passage is based on the author's observations and the House of Representatives Banking Committee transcript of the hearing. Steinberg's and Steg's quotes from the hearing are drawn from the same source.

159 Steg, listening in the corner Steg made his feelings clear in an interview with the author in Paris, April 4, 2001.

159 Steg was approached by someone This is based on the author's interview with Ady Steg in Paris, April 4, 2001.

159 They met for dinner at Le Marais This account of the dinner is based on the author's interviews with Ady Steg in Paris, April 4, 2001; Israel Singer in New York, June 6, 2001; and Elan Steinberg in New York, May 21, 2001.

160 But under French law This account of the Hevesi meeting is drawn from the author's interviews with Ady Steg and Claire Andrieu in Paris, April 4, 2001.

161 However, Singer confirmed his feelings This is drawn from the author's interview with Israel Singer in New York, June 6, 2001.

161 McCallion and Tamen accused the French This is based on the written presentation by Ken McCallion and Harriet Tamen to Alan Hevesi at the meeting.

161 Hevesi later took the chance According to the author's interview with Steve Newman in New York, March 17, 2001.

162 Hevesi appeared less aggressive According to the author's interview with Christian Schricke in Paris, April 3, 2001.

162 He and his aides marveled This account of Hevesi's trip to Paris is based on the author's interview with Steve Newman in New York, March 17, 2001.

162 Singer was in his element   Details of the meeting between Singer and the French prime minister are drawn from the author's interviews with Israel Singer in New York, June 6, 2001, and David Kessler in Paris, April 5, 2001.

CHAPTER TWELVE: ROUGH JUSTICE

164 To underline his strict control   See "Expectations and Requirements for Trial" by Judge Sterling Johnson, Brooklyn, N.Y., 2001, available at www.nyed.uscourts.gov/SJ-rules.pdf

164 When judges in his Brooklyn courthouse   See *New York Times*, October 15, 1998.

164 On March 15, 2000, the Holocaust lawyers   This account of the hearing is based on the court transcript of the day's proceedings.

166 believed they had lost their case   Samuels gave his account to the author in an interview in Paris, April 2, 2001.

166 the final Mattéoli report emerged   This passage is based on the introduction and foreword of the Mattéoli Commission report, published on April 17, 2000, as well as the summary of the report on financial spoliation and looting of apartments. It also draws on the report's general conclusion on the limits of restitution. The concept of spoliation is discussed in the sections entitled "Spoliation: Inspired by the Germans and Carried Out by the French" and "Looting: A German Affair."

168 "You know what you have done? . . ."   This is drawn from the author's interview with Ady Steg in Paris, April 4, 2001. The following comments from *Le Monde* were translated by the author.

169 to press for a special envoy   According to the author's interview with Christian Schricke in Paris, April 3, 2001.

169 Andréani was nevertheless infuriated   This is based on the author's interview with Jacques Andréani in Paris, April 2, 2001.

169 he found in favor of the victims   See Judge Sterling Johnson, memorandum and order in *Bodner et al v Banque Paribas et al*, August 31, 2000.

170 Harriet Tamen burst into tears   She gave her emotional account in an interview with the author in New York, March 28, 2001.

170 "It's now or never. . . ."   According to the author's interview with Fred Davis in New York, March 8, 2001.

171 J. P. Morgan paid   According to the author's interview with Harriet Tamen in New York, July 25, 2001.

171 Andréani meticulously laid out   This account of the meeting is based on the author's interviews with Jacques Andréani in Paris, April 2, 2001, and Stuart Eizenstat, March 15, 2001.

172 "For many Jews. . . ."   See the speech by Prime Minister Lionel Jospin on November 4, 2000.

173 They decided to treat the French   This is based on the author's interview with J. D. Bindenagel in Washington, D.C., March 6, 2001.

173 Eizenstat felt that his task   According to the author's interview with him in Washington, D.C., March 15, 2001.

173 The two sides met face-to-face   This account of the meeting is based on the author's interviews with Harriet Tamen in New York, March 28, 2001; Stuart

Eizenstat in Washington, D.C., March 15, 2001; Owen Pell in Washington, D.C., January 27, 2001; Ken McCallion in New York, March 8, 2001; and Claire Andrieu in Paris, April 4, 2001.

175 Meticulous records were made   According to Andrieu, a potentially far bigger figure was the number of dormant accounts in the northern occupied zone. There the banks may have held on to the savings of those murdered in the Holocaust. Using generous assumptions, she suggested the banks and government might have kept 360 million francs at the end of the war, worth around $87 million today. That was far less than the $105 million that the banks had already pledged to the foundation, in addition to paying any valid claims to individuals. There was just one exception—the unoccupied southern zone where few Jews lived and the records were poor. She estimated there might possibly be twelve hundred Jewish accounts belonging to people deported to concentration camps from the south.

175 Eizenstat met the prime minister   This account of the meeting is based on the author's interview with David Kessler in Paris, April 5, 2001.

176 There under the glass chandeliers   The account of this meeting is based on the author's interviews with Christian Schricke in Paris, April 3, 2001; Ken McCallion in New York, March 8, 2001; Owen Pell in Washington, D.C., January 27, 2001; Harriet Tamen in New York, March 28, 2001; Stuart Eizenstat in Washington, D.C., March 15, 2001; David Kessler in Paris, April 5, 2001; and other participants who wished to remain anonymous.

178 Eizenstat declared   See the Treasury press conference transcript on January 9, 2001.

178 Just down the hall from Eizenstat's talks   This encounter with Powell is based on the author's interviews with Owen Pell in New York, July 27, 2001; Stuart Eizenstat in Washington, D.C., March 15, 2001; and J. D. Bindenagel in Washington, D.C., July 26, 2001. In fact, Eizenstat had already lobbied the incoming administration to continue settling Holocaust disputes in an hour-long briefing with Powell. The briefing was supposed to concentrate on the international economy, but Eizenstat steered the talk to his highest policy priority.

179 Eizenstat made one last push   The account of these penultimate hours of talks is based on the author's interviews with Stuart Eizenstat in Washington, D.C., March 15, 2001; Owen Pell in New York, July 27, 2001, and Washington, D.C., January 27, 2001.

179 Over a bland hotel breakfast   This is based on the author's interview with Owen Pell in Washington, D.C., January 27, 2001.

180 They delivered their demands   This account of the final talks is based on the author's interviews with Stuart Eizenstat in Washington, D.C., March 15, 2001; Owen Pell in Washington, D.C., January 27, 2001; Michael Hausfeld in Washington, D.C., June 25, 2001; Harriet Tamen in New York, March 28, 2001; Fred Davis in New York, March 8, 2001.

182 "What we've now agreed to . . ."   See the official transcript of the press conference on January 18, 2001.

CHAPTER THIRTEEN: TO START A WAR

183 Stuart Eizenstat keeps a single vial   This passage on Eizenstat's family history and his interest in the Holocaust is drawn from his interview with the author in Washington, D.C., March 23, 2000.

185 Eizenstat could not resist the call   This is based on the author's interview with Stuart Eizenstat in Washington, D.C., March 23, 2000.

185 Meticulous about technical details   This portrait of Eizenstat was drawn with the help of several administration officials who asked to remain anonymous.

185 "deal *über alles"*   A quip by Martin Mendelsohn, interviewed by the author in Washington, D.C., March 2, 2001.

185 For some European officials   This is based on the author's interview with Stephan Keller in Berlin, April 18, 2001, and other European officials who wished to remain anonymous.

185 Eizenstat was so committed   See *New York Times,* May 13, 1999.

186 Eizenstat felt conflicted   This is based on the author's interviews in Washington, D.C., with Stuart Eizenstat on July 7, 2000, and Bennett Freeman on March 16, 2000.

187 his first reaction was to say no.   This is based on the author's interview with J. D. Bindenagel in Washington, D.C., on January 19, 2001.

188 The first class action lawsuit   This passage draws on *Iwanowa v Ford,* filed in March 1998.

188 Ford sent annual birthday gifts   See *Iwanowa v Ford,* March 1998.

189 Now Sturman seized   This passage, along with Sturman's family history and experiences in Germany, is based on the author's interview with Deborah Sturman in New York, May 8, 2001.

189 Fagan predicted his case   See *Newsday,* September 1, 1998.

189 To make matters even more embarrassing   See the Associated Press report on August 31, 1998.

190 "Once it became evident . . ."   This is drawn from the author's interview with Hausfeld in Washington on March 14, 2001.

190 "This is the same folly . . ."   Quoted from Mel Weiss's letter to President Clinton, January 28, 1999.

190 Eizenstat replied for the administration   Based on Stuart Eizenstat's letter to Mel Weiss, dated March 11, 1999.

192 he proposed that all companies   See *Süddeutsche Zeitung,* June 18, 1998. This passage also draws on the author's interview with Ludwig Stiegler in Berlin on April 24, 2001, which is the source for his subsequent quotes.

192 Two weeks before election day   The statement was made in a Green Party press release dated September 8, 1998.

192 Schröder responded a week later   See *Süddeutsche Zeitung* on September 15, 1998.

193 Kohl was not opposed   This is based on the author's interview with Wolfgang Gibowski, head of the former chancellor's press and information office, in Berlin, April 18, 2001.

193 His spokesman suggested   See Associated Press, August 26, 1998.

193 The first restitution law   This passage is based on a summary of German restitution on the U.S. State Department's website.

195 less than slaves   See Benjamin B. Ferencz, *Less Than Slaves* (Cambridge, Mass.: Harvard University Press, 1979).

195 It was there that Primo Levi.   Levi's classic account, *If This Is a Man,* is the most understated—and as a result the most powerful—account of life in Auschwitz. With a scientist's eye, Levi records the overwhelming suffering and observes the human condition with little regard for his own plight. This quotation is from p. 78 of the 1960 Orion Press edition.

196 After meeting with President Clinton   This account of Schröder's first contacts with German business leaders on the issue is based on the author's interview with Henning Schulte-Noelle in Munich, April 27, 2001.

196 The Jewish campaigners were overjoyed.   See the Claims Conference press release on October 20, 1998.

196 The new government and the industrial companies   See Associated Press, December 15, 1998.

197 Gentz feared the negotiations   This passage on Gentz's concerns—as well as the following account of his meeting with industrial executives in August 1998—is based on the author's interview with Manfred Gentz in Stuttgart, April 25, 2001.

198 Eizenstat took heart   This is drawn from the author's interview with Eizenstat in Washington on December 28, 2000. The subsequent quotes come from the same source.

198 Hombach was cautious   Hombach's first meetings were described to the author in interviews with Manfred Gentz in Stuttgart, April 25, 2001; Michael Geier in Berlin, April 19, 2001; and John Kornblum in Berlin, June 14, 2001.

198 The emotional wounds of the Holocaust   This account of the Walser/Bubis exchange was drawn from the *New York Times* report on November 10, 1998.

199 A friend of Bubis   Singer delivered an emotional eulogy for Bubis in Frankfurt on September 14, 1999, where he called Bubis's death a loss for Jews across the world. "Who will speak for us now?" he asked.

CHAPTER FOURTEEN: DOOMED TO SUCCEED

200 a damning report   See the OMGUS Finance Division report from November 1946.

201 "I'm not going to bother you . . ."   This is based on the author's interview with Israel Singer in New York, June 6, 2001.

201 Singer had earlier told the *Financial Times*   See *Financial Times,* January 2, 1999.

201 Singer then issued a new threat   See *Financial Times,* February 3, 1999.

201 Breuer swiftly tracked Singer down   According to Israel Singer in an interview with the author in New York, June 6, 2001.

201 The bank's historian   Deutsche employed several outside historians to examine its records, but its in-house specialist was Manfred Pohl. This account of the press conference is drawn from the *Financial Times,* February 5, 1999.

201 Breuer's lawyers were desperate   This is based on the author's interview with Klaus Kohler in Frankfurt, April 25, 2001.

201 their concerns appeared well founded   Hevesi's threats were reported in the *Financial Times,* December 8, 1998.

202 For Singer, the lawyers had crossed a moral line   Singer made his views clear in an interview with the author in New York, June 6, 2001.

202 a "loss leader"   This is drawn from the author's interview with Elan Steinberg in New York, June 29, 1999.

202 "This is a government-to-government affair . . ."   Michael Geier made his comments to the author in an interview in Berlin, April 19, 2001.

202 Eizenstat began by inviting the lawyers   This account of the meeting with Hombach is based on the participants' contemporaneous notes.

203 Hombach told Brown   This is based on the author's interview with Bobby Brown in Jerusalem, April 16, 2001.

203 Chancellor Schröder announced plans   This account of Schröder's press conference, and Weiss's response, is drawn from the *Financial Times* and *New York Times*, February 17, 1999.

204 Hombach confirmed that the Germans were focusing   This report is based on the participants' contemporaneous notes.

204 Germany did not want to damage its foreign policy   This is drawn from the author's interviews with Michael Geier in Berlin, April 19, 2001, and J.D. Bindenagel in Washington, D.C., January 19, 2001.

204 Polish officials had already issued   Janusz Stanczyk, the Polish under-secretary of state, issued the warnings, as reported by the Associated Press, January 15, 1999.

205 Eizenstat spoke of four "windows"   The account of the meeting is based on the participants' contemporaneous notes. Gentz's comments are drawn from an interview with the author in Stuttgart on April 25, 2001, as are his subsequent quotes, unless otherwise stated.

205 in talks with Polish diplomats   The relationship between Hausfeld and the Poles was explained in interviews with Michael Hausfeld in Washington, D.C., March 14, 2001, and Janusz Stanczyk in New York, July 5, 2001.

206 But to his fellow lawyers   According to the author's interview with Burt Neuborne in New York, March 24, 2000.

206 He drew up an agreement   See the Memorandum of Understanding between representatives of the World Jewish Restitution Organization and counsel for the plaintiffs, dated March 26, 1999.

206 "Reaching the stage of today's meeting . . ."   This is taken from the official State Department transcript of Eizenstat's press conference on May 12, 1999.

207 The Polish delegation was already furious   Based on the author's interview with Janusz Stanczyk in New York, July 5, 2001.

207 "Polish victims fear . . ."   This is based on a Republic of Poland position paper, May 11, 1999.

207 "I referred to it as the tale . . ."   Hausfeld's comments were made on the Cohen Milsten Hausfeld and Toll website, www.cmht.com, dated May 12, 1999.

209 The lawyers were also offended   According to a letter to Eizenstat and Westdickenberg from Hausfeld, Weiss, Mendelsohn, Cabraser and Levin, dated June 10, 1999.

209 In a joint statement they later attacked   See the plaintiffs' settlement statement, dated June 20, 1999.

209 While restitution laws had ordered   The Claims Conference made its arguments in a position paper on aryanization by banks, dated July 1999.

209 Gentz simply refused to accept their logic   The account of this exchange is based on the author's interviews with Manfred Gentz in Stuttgart, April 25, 2001, and Gideon Taylor in New York, May 8, 2001.

210 "What the banks did . . ."   In fact the bank itself had already accepted its moral obligation to pay some form of compensation. Three years earlier, Deutsche Bank had asked its historical institute to investigate the bank's role in handling looted gold in Switzerland. The historians reported that Deutsche had left 5.6 million deutsche marks of gold sitting in a bank vault in Switzerland until 1995, preferring to ignore it rather than decide how to dispose of it. As the Swiss banks scandal was emerging in 1997, Deutsche negotiated a settlement with Israel Singer. Half the cash went to the Claims Conference and the other half was donated to the March of the Living Foundation, educating Jewish teenagers about the Holocaust.

210 Hombach was spread too thin   Hombach's overload was described by Stuart Eizenstat in an interview with the author in Washington, D.C., December 28, 2000.

210 Hombach kept them out of the loop   According to the author's interview with Michael Geier in Berlin, April 19, 2001.

211 For the German companies   Their position was explained by their lawyer in Washington, D.C., Roger Witten, in an interview with the author on March 29, 2001.

211 Eizenstat would come to spend   Eizenstat's working habits were described to the author by Treasury officials who wished to remain anonymous.

211 they developed a mutual respect   According to the author's interview with Otto Graf Lambsdorff in New York, May 9, 2001.

212 effectively defusing the political debate   The political impact of Lambsdorff's appointment was explained to the author by Ludwig Stiegler in Berlin, April 24, 2001.

212 Eizenstat would stop by Lambsdorff's office   According to the author's interview with Otto Graf Lambsdorff in New York, May 9, 2001, and with Stuart Eizenstat in Washington on December 28, 2000.

212 felt the Jewish claims were "overdone"   Lambsdorff made his feelings clear in an interview with the author in New York, May 9, 2001.

212 Kent argued that anti-Semitism   Kent recalled the episode in an interview with the author in New York, January 26, 2001.

213 Gentz was aghast.   This description of the German reaction is based on the author's interviews with Michael Geier in Berlin, April 19, 2001, and Manfred Gentz in Stuttgart, April 25, 2001.

213 Eizenstat had struggled with the issue of money for weeks.   This passage on Eizenstat's assessment of the financial discussions is based on an interview with the author in Washington, D.C., December 28, 2000.

214 Only with such a large number   Stuart Eizenstat made this argument in a confidential briefing paper to President Clinton in October 1999.

214 "Impossible," said Gentz.   This exchange is based on the author's interviews with Manfred Gentz in Stuttgart on April 25, 2001, and Stuart Eizenstat in Washington on December 28, 2000.

214 "There is tremendous time pressure . . ."   Eizenstat's comments were quoted by Agence France Presse, August 27, 1999.

214 "We are doomed to succeed . . ."   Lambsdorff's comments were quoted in testimony by Burt Neuborne to the House of Representatives Banking Committee on September 13, 1999.

CHAPTER FIFTEEN: THE MAGIC NUMBER

215 Seated around him The participants included DaimlerChrysler's Jürgen Schrempp, Deutsche Bank's Rolf Breuer, Allianz's Henning Schulte-Noelle, and Volker Beck from the Greens.

215 First they talked about hard cash This account of the discussion is based on the author's interviews with Manfred Gentz in Stuttgart, April 25, 2001, and Wolfgang Gibowski in Berlin, April 18, 2001.

217 A new set of numbers These are drawn from Lutz Niethammer's report after the Florence meeting, dated September 4, 1999.

217 With such high numbers of survivors Otto Graf Lambsdorff conceded that Niethammer's numbers changed the German calculation, in his interview with the author in New York, May 9, 2001.

217 In large numbers This account of the Florence conference and its after-hours drinking is based on the author's interview with Michael Hausfeld in Washington, D.C., March 29, 2001.

218 Few in Germany . . . This is based on the author's interview with Michael Geier in Berlin on April 19, 2001.

218 In a 120-page opinion See Judge Joseph Greenaway's opinion in *Iwanowa v Ford Motor Company,* September 13, 1999.

218 In a separate ruling See Judge Dickinson Debevoise in *Burger-Fischer v Degussa* and *Lichtman v Siemens,* September 13, 1999.

219 "a small army of class action lawyers . . ." This comment is drawn from the author's interview with Burt Neuborne in New York on March 24, 2000. In fact, the dismissals did not discourage the class action bar from filing new lawsuits. Within two days, attorneys representing former U.S. prisoners of war filed class action lawsuits in California and New Mexico against Japanese companies for their use of slave labor.

219 A moral gesture would not be enough. See the testimony of Burt Neuborne to the House of Representatives Banking Committee on September 14, 1999.

219 Martin Mendelsohn claimed he saw According to his sworn deposition on November 3, 1999.

220 Weiss told journalists in Washington His comments were recorded in a B'nai B'rith press release at a news conference in Washington, D.C., October 5, 1999.

220 "We cannot guarantee . . ." These comments are taken from President Clinton's talking points for conversation with Chancellor Schröder in October 1999.

221 Weiss restrained himself His comments were reported in the *Financial Times,* October 8, 1999.

221 Summoning his best diplomatic powers See the statement by Stuart Eizenstat on October 7, 1999. Lambsdorff's comments are drawn from the same State Department transcript.

222 Gentz immediately confronted Lambsdorff Gentz made his anger clear in an interview with the author in Stuttgart, April 25, 2001. Gentz also voiced his anger in a speech at Humboldt University in Berlin, where he accused Lambsdorff of breaking his promise to stand firm.

222 Lambsdorff had lost the confidence This is taken from the author's interview with Wolfgang Gibowski in Berlin on April 18, 2001.

223 "We can't come to a defendable agreement . . ."   This exchange is based on the author's interview with Otto Graf Lambsdorff in New York, May 9, 2001.

223 a figure Gentz was convinced   This is based on the author's interview with Manfred Gentz in Stuttgart, April 25, 2001.

223 "This bill shows that Congress is serious . . ."   This is from the press release by Senator Charles Schumer on November 4, 1999.

224 Foxman turned his fire   See the speech by Abraham Foxman at the ADL dinner honoring Lufthansa, November 9, 1999.

224 "But we have to negotiate . . ."   This is drawn from the author's interview with Manfred Gentz in Stuttgart, April 25, 2001.

225 stretched the truth to breaking point   Eizenstat's tactics were detailed in the author's interviews with several U.S. officials who wished to remain anonymous.

225 "A negotiated settlement . . ."   Eizenstat's assertions and Gentz's insistence were reported in the *Washington Post* and *New York Times*, November 18, 1999.

225 continued to hold out for more   See Burt Neuborne's Memorandum to Counsel, dated November 22, 1999.

225 But Lambsdorff stood his ground   Lambsdorff made his position clear in a letter to Michael Hausfeld, dated December 1, 1999.

225 crunching through the numbers   This passage is based on the author's interviews with Michael Hausfeld in Washington, D.C., March 29, 2001; Martin Mendelsohn in Washington, D.C., March 2, 2001; Bob Swift in Philadelphia, July 30, 2001; and Deborah Sturman in New York, May 8, 2001.

227 a simple letter from President Clinton   The exchange between the two leaders is based on the letter from President Clinton to Chancellor Schröder on December 13, 1999, and Schröder's reply the next day.

227 "We close the 20th century . . ."   See President Clinton's statement outside the Oval Office on December 15, 1999. The president left Eizenstat to explain the details to the media in the White House briefing room.

228 "Nothing we could do now . . ."   See the statement by Madeleine Albright at the slave labor meeting in Berlin, December 17, 1999.

229 "This compensation comes too late . . ."   President Rau spoke in German—this is the official translation of his speech on December 17, 1999.

229 "I wonder why I am here . . ."   Kent's comments were taken from the official recording of the ceremony on December 17, 1999.

CHAPTER SIXTEEN: A PIECE OF RAW MEAT

230 At the outset.   This meeting has been reconstructed using the author's interviews with Israel Singer in New York, June 6, 2001; Michael Hausfeld in Washington, D.C., March 14, 2001, and June 25, 2001; Stuart Eizenstat in Washington, D.C., December 28, 2000; Deborah Sturman in New York, May 8, 2001; Roman Kent in New York, January 26, 2001; Gideon Taylor in New York, May 8, 2001; J. D. Bindenagel in Washington, D.C., April 19, 2001.

231 "since the first blood libels . . ."   The blood libels recurred from the late medieval times to the Renaissance, accusing Jews of killing Christian children to use their blood for making unleavened bread at the time of Passover. In many cases, they were the excuse for brutal pogroms.

232 Who did he think he was   Neuborne in fact compared Hausfeld to Metternich, the Habsburgs' foreign minister, who redrew the map of Europe after Napoleon's downfall. His letter to Hausfeld was dated December 13, 1999.

234 "We have the impression . . ."   Singer made his incendiary comments to the *Berliner Zeitung* in a report published on February 25, 2000.

234 Jewish survivors would receive   Under the Central and Eastern European proposals, property claims by Jews would receive just one-twentieth of that—4.64 percent of the funds, worth around $232 million.

235 A frazzled Eizenstat   This account is based on the author's interviews with Michael Hausfeld in Washington, D.C., March 29, 2001, and U.S. officials who wished to remain anonymous.

235 The Jewish negotiators had finally come   This description of the meetings on property—as well as Hansmeyer's position on insurance claims—is based on the author's interviews with Herbert Hansmeyer in Munich, April 23, 2001, and Gideon Taylor in New York, May 8, 2001.

237 All that was left   This argument was explained to the author in an interview with Elisheva Ansbacher in Jerusalem, April 18, 2001.

237 Eizenstat proposed a relatively low   This account is based on the author's interviews with Gideon Taylor in New York, May 8, 2001, and Manfred Gentz in Stuttgart, April 25, 2001.

238 even members of the German Bundestag.   This is from the statement by Otto Graf Lambsdorff to the German Bundestag committee on internal affairs on February 16, 2000.

238 The gap between Singer and Hansmeyer   This account of the meeting with Eagleburger is based on the author's interviews with J. D. Bindenagel in Washington, D.C., January 19, 2001; Herbert Hansmeyer in Munich, April 23, 2001; Manfred Gentz in Stuttgart, April 25, 2001; and Otto Graf Lambsdorff in New York, May 9, 2001.

239 Singer did most of the talking   This reconstruction of the Concorde lounge meeting is based on the author's interviews with Herbert Hansmeyer in Munich, April 23, 2001; Manfred Gentz in Stuttgart, April 25, 2001; and Israel Singer in New York, June 6, 2001.

CHAPTER SEVENTEEN: THE SPIDERWEB

241 "You can consider these doors . . ."   This account of the foreign ministry talks is based on the author's interviews with Stuart Eizenstat in Washington, D.C., on December 28, 2000; Michael Geier in Berlin, April 19, 2001; Stephan Keller in Berlin, April 18, 2001; and J. D. Bindenagel in Washington, D.C., February 6, 2001.

243 The one missing party   The labor and property talks were described to the author by Gideon Taylor in New York, May 8, 2001; Israel Singer in New York, June 6, 2001; J. D. Bindenagel in Washington, D.C., February 6, 2001; Otto Graf Lambsdorff in New York, May 9, 2001; and U.S. officials who wished to remain anonymous.

245 using cash appropriated by Congress   The Nazi Persecutee Relief Fund was established by the U.S. and U.K. governments at the London conference on

Nazi gold in December 1997, as they decided how to dispose of the remaining 5.5 tons of Nazi gold held by the Allies at the time. The gold was all that remained of a 330-ton stockpile seized by the Allies from Nazi Germany at the end of the war. The relief fund later attracted donations from more than a dozen countries, and the United States committed $25 million over three years, drawn from the State Department's budget. The cash remained under the control of the donor countries, which meant that Eizenstat effectively controlled how the U.S. contribution could be spent.

245 The Polish deal was sealed   Based on the author's interviews with Michael Hausfeld in Washington, D.C., March 29, 2001, and Linda Bixby in Washington, D.C., March 27, 2001.

245 For their part   According to Deutsche Bank's Klaus Kohler, in an interview in Berlin, April 25, 2001.

245 "This is a great day . . ."   See the statement by Stuart Eizenstat on March 23, 2000.

246 "neither humanitarian nor just compensation"   See *Jerusalem Post,* March 26, 2000.

246 bogged down in a legal quagmire   This account of the dispute over the U.S. government's statement of interest is based on the author's contemporaneous interviews with Wolfgang Gibowski, Michelle Smith, J. D. Bindenagel, and Michael Hausfeld.

247 Reparations claims might exist   See the statement by Stuart Eizenstat on May 22, 2000.

248 The executives leading the foundation   Manfred Gentz made clear his frustration in an interview with the author on April 25, 2001. Media companies proved even more frustrating for Gentz. While they were happy to denounce other media companies as meanspirited in the press, they proved less than willing to contribute on their own. It took several more personal interventions by Gentz to pressure companies such as Bertelsmann to join.

248 The foundation encountered   This is based on the author's interview with Wolfgang Gibowski in Berlin, April 18, 2001.

248 The substantial American contributions promised by Eizenstat . . .   Only Ford, on December 6, 2001, made a sizable contribution to a U.S. Chamber of Commerce fund for forced and slave laborers. After more than three years of archival study, the company claimed it had been "required" by the Nazi regime to use slave and forced laborers. Conceding that the practice was wrong, the company donated $2 million to the fund for survivors and another $2 million to a new center for the study of human rights issues.

249 The argument boiled down   This account of the argument over wording is based on the author's interviews with Wolfgang Gibowski in Berlin, April 18, 2001; Michael Geier in Berlin, April 19, 2001; and Otto Graf Lambsdorff in New York, May 9, 2001.

249 The solution was an agreement   See the letter to Michael Steiner, foreign policy adviser to Chancellor Schröder, from Sandy Berger, President Clinton's national security adviser, and Beth Nolan, White House counsel, dated June 16, 2000.

250 The class action lawyers arrived secure   The lawyers' fees were detailed in the German foundation arbitration plaintiff counsel awards, dated June 14, 2001.

250 he was traveling with a camera crew   Under a joint deal, the ABC exposé appeared at the same time on page one of the *New York Times*, September 8, 2000. Fagan later told the author, in a telephone interview on June 11, 2001, that he was taking legal advice on suing them.

250 Fagan staged a last-minute dispute   This account of the on-camera argument is based on the broadcast of ABC News's *20/20*, September 8, 2000, as well as the author's interviews with J. D. Bindenagel in Washington, D.C., February 6, 2001, and Stuart Eizenstat in Washington, D.C., December 28, 2000.

251 Eizenstat was so taken aback   Eizenstat made his feelings clear in an interview with the author in Washington, D.C., December 28, 2000. His speech is taken from the text of his remarks at the concluding plenary in Berlin, July 17, 2000.

251 The Claims Conference . . . agreed   See the text of Roman Kent's speech in Berlin, July 17, 2000.

251 Such noble words . . .   The subsequent comments are drawn from the author's interview with Klaus Kohler in Frankfurt on April 25, 2001; Herbert Hansmeyer in Munich on April 23, 2001; Michael Geier in Berlin on April 19, 2001, and Wolfgang Gibowski in Berlin on April 18, 2001.

CHAPTER EIGHTEEN: CLAIMS BY COMMITTEE

254 "We had a moral obligation . . ."   Eagleburger's quotes are drawn from a profile published in the *Financial Times*, "A Diplomat's Determination," November 30, 1998.

254 counting Edgar Bronfman   Bronfman refers to his friendship with Eagleburger in his book *The Making of a Jew* published more than a year before Eagleburger was appointed.

255 any consensus   Eagleburger described his emerging attitude to the commission in his speech to the Claims Conference in Washington, D.C., July 17, 2001. This account also draws on an interview with Neal Sher, his chief of staff, in Washington, D.C., in February 2001.

256 threatening to quit   Eagleburger quit his job for twenty-four hours in January 2002, reclaiming his position after winning fresh expressions of support from commission members.

256 a burgeoning bureaucracy   This comes from ICHEIC (International Commission on Holocaust Era Insurance Claims) internal documents.

257 Internal financial documents   See the *ICHEIC September Meeting Report*, 2000.

258 Israel's troubled politics.   New delegates arrived when Netanyahu's government fell in 1999, but Bobby Brown was allowed to keep his place by the incoming administration. Most of the delegation naturally looked to Sanbar.

258 Disgusted that the Swiss National Bank   Sanbar made his case against the SNB in Teitelbaum and Sanbar, *Holocaust Gold* (Tel Aviv: Moreshet, 2001). He was interviewed in Tel Aviv, April 17, 2001.

259 "I am more than slightly irritated . . ."   Eagleburger made these comments in an interview with the author on April 22, 1999.

260 "the conflict of constituencies . . ."   Hansmeyer was interviewed by the author in Munich, April 2001.

260 Two years earlier   See Chapter 9, "Falling like Dominoes."

261 Danny Kadden, an aide to Deborah Senn   Kadden provided notes on this incident.

263 if a claimant named Isaac   The 18 spellings are: Isaac, Izaac, Isaak, Isak, Izak, Izaak, Jsak, Jzak, Itzhak, Iszak, Izsak, Itschak, Isachar, Yitzhak, Jzchak, Itzik, Itzack, and Itzaakor.

263 The 1,398 variations   Yaacov Lozowick, Head of the Archives at Yad Vashem, provided this figure; he also lists 95 variations on the Jewish surname Berkowitz and 9 ways of spelling the Slovak city of Bratislava (Pressburg in German).

263 commission officials began to suspect   The examples are drawn from "Examples of Cases Denied on the Fast Track Process," a Memo by Geoffrey Fitchew, March 29, 2000.

263 a damning progress report   See *A Status Report on Holocaust-Era Insurance Claims, December 2000,* by Deborah Senn, Washington State Insurance Commissioner.

264 "I cannot become very emotional . . ."   See "The Last Victims," *Forbes,* May 2001.

264 This would reduce the available money   Eagleburger set out the proposal in a memo to all ICHEIC commissioners, alternates, and observers, June 11, 2001.

265 "A great big fat zero . . ."   All of these comments are drawn from Lawrence Eagleburger's speech to the Claims Conference, Washington, D.C., July 17, 2001.

Chapter Nineteen: In the Crossfire

266 "goodwill . . ."   Giovanni Perissinotto was interviewed by the author in New York, June 1, 2001.

267 Kenneth Bialkin, senior partner . . .   Bialkin was interviewed in his New York office on March 16, 2001. This is the source for all the quotes attributed to him.

269 The lawsuit recited   See Complaint, *Stern et al v Generali,* filed with the Superior Court for the State of California for the County of Los Angeles.

272 "I have had a heart attack . . ."   See *Jewish Bulletin of North California,* December 3, 1999.

272 Bronfman hosted Perissinotto   This account is based on interviews with Singer, Taylor, Perissinotto, Bialkin, and Bronfman.

273 "exclusive legal remedy"   See the ICHEIC press release of July 26, 2000.

274 it had made 271 "humanitarian" payments   These figures are taken from the letter of Martin Stern to the Israeli inspector of trusts, June 2001.

274 "Just to have Jews give refusals . . ."   Arie Zuckerman was interviewed in Jerusalem, April 26, 2001.

275 "This is a parliament . . ."   This conversation is drawn from Sanbar's recollection.

276 "You know and I know . . ."   This comment is as recalled by Arie Zuckerman.

277 Martin Stern may have settled   Stern based his objections on the following rough calculations. The trust had paid out $8.76 million on 816 policies by mid-2001, meaning that it paid an average of $10,735 per policy. The names of 22,000 Generali policyholders who might be Holocaust victims had been posted on the Internet. Assuming that the policies paid already were a representative sample, Stern reasoned that Generali's total liability could be more than $200 million. Others objected that the first claims were likely the strongest and so did not constitute a representative sample.

277 $75,000 for her father's policy   This number was quoted by Ed Fagan, her lawyer, and confirmed by Generali officials.

278 Shernoff's true target   See the Complaint, *Haberfeld v Generali*, filed by Shernoff, Bidart, Darras and Arkin, May 2001.

278 Shernoff had hired Michael Ovitz   Attempts to interview Mr. Shernoff for this book were originally denied by a lawyer acting for Mr. Ovitz's company, saying this would "interfere" with the project.

CHAPTER TWENTY: FREEDOM FIGHTING

280 "Austria, the home of my parents . . ."   Singer was speaking at Lincoln Square Synagogue on February 6, 2000. He also made his position clear at a working breakfast with Jewish community leaders in New York on February 11, 2000.

281 a stark monologue   See the opening address at the Stockholm International Forum on the Holocaust by Göran Persson on January 26, 2000.

281 But he had earned international notoriety   See *New York Times*, April 30, 2000.

282 He later apologized.   See *New York Times*, January 27, 2000.

282 Simon Wiesenthal uncovered the party's leader   See Hella Pick, *Simon Wiesenthal* (Boston: Northeastern University Press, 1996), pp. 259–262.

282 rebuilt his party with a new appeal   See *Foreign Affairs*, May/June 2000.

282 Hours before the opening ceremony   These comments are taken from the webcast of the press conference by Ehud Barak and Göran Persson on January 26, 2000. Viktor Klima's comments, which follow, are taken from the same source at www.holocaustforum.gov.se

283 the European Union took the unprecedented step   See *Financial Times*, February 1, 2000.

283 the United States was more cautious   U.S. policy, and Albright's remarks, were reported in the *New York Times*, February 5 and 6, 2000.

283 Schüssel professed to be baffled   As quoted by the Associated Press, January 31, 2000.

284 "France would never accept . . ."   Khol's comments were reported by the *New York Times*, July 23, 2000. Even the Green Party's leader, Alexander van der Bellen—no friend of the far right—warned that the sanctions would cause a backlash against "foreigners." Meanwhile, the Austrian media attacked foreign correspondents for dredging up Nazi images, citing a CBS News report about Haider that broadcast a picture of Hitler.

284 Most observers predicted   The predictions were published in the *Financial Times*, February 29, 2000.

284 "I am somewhat horrified . . ."   Haider's comments appeared on the Associated Press, on January 31, 2000.

284 Winkler offered Schüssel's government   This is based on the author's interview with Hans Winkler in Vienna, May 1, 2001.

284 he dashed off a letter   Wolfgang Schüssel wrote his letter to the Claims Conference on February 4, 2000.

284 "The federal government works for an Austria . . ."   See the Austrian government declaration: "Responsibility for Austria—A Future in the Heart of Europe," dated February 3, 2000.

284 Israel Singer was unimpressed.   Singer made his comments at a working breakfast of the World Jewish Congress on February 11, 2000.

285 warmly endorsed his presidential campaign   See *New York Times,* April 26, 1986.

286 Wiesenthal concluded that Waldheim had lied   See *New York Times,* May 17, 1986.

286 his opponent blamed the World Jewish Congress   See *New York Times,* June 9, 1986.

286 Waldheim blamed the campaign against him   See *New York Times,* June 12, 1996.

286 Martin Eichtinger had just joined . . .   This is taken from the author's interview with Eichtinger in Vienna on April 28, 2001. His subsequent quotes are drawn from the same interview, unless otherwise noted.

287 Thomas Klestil, visited the Israeli parliament   His comments were reported in the *Jerusalem Post,* November 16, 1994.

287 Hitler received a delirious welcome   See William L. Shirer, *The Rise and Fall of the Third Reich* (New York: Touchstone, 1981), p. 34.

287 Viennese Jews owned three-quarters   This account of Vienna in 1938 is based on Evan Burr Bukey, *Hitler's Austria* (Chapel Hill: University of North Carolina Press, 2000), pp. 131–136.

288 Moritz Fleischmann, a senior representative   See *Eichmann Trial,* April 24, 1961, Session 17; quoted in Martin Gilbert, *The Holocaust* (New York: Henry Holt, 1985), pp. 59–60.

288 The SS looted Jewish homes   See Shirer, *Rise and Fall,* p. 351.

288 It was, in the words of one historian   See Gerhard Botz, *"The Dynamics of Persecution in Austria, 1938–45"* in *Austrians and Jews in the Twentieth Century,* ed. Robert Wistrich (New York: St. Martin's Press, 1992), p. 202.

288 Within eighteen months, around two-thirds   See Robert S. Wistrich, *Austria and the Legacy of the Holocaust* (New York: American Jewish Committee, 1999).

288 Austrians represented only 8 percent   See Evan Burr Bukey, *Hitler's Austria* (Chapel Hill: University of North Carolina Press, 2000), p. 43.

289 After a long list of Austrian property   As detailed in the State Treaty for the Re-Establishment of an Independent and Democratic Austria, Article 26, May 1955.

289 Lawyers representing Jewish victims in the United States   This account is drawn from the author's interview with Seymour Rubin in Washington, D.C., March 27, 2001. It also draws on the letter from Seymour Rubin to Arthur Compton, State Department's Office of Western European Affairs, dated May 3, 1957.

290 The creation of the Austrian *Hilfsfond*   The Austrian foreign ministry estimates the fund—which was boosted in 1962 and 1976—paid out around

6 billion schillings ($370 million) by October 2000, according to a survey by Ernst Sucharipa.

290 Among his survivor friends This is based on the author's interview with Simon Wiesenthal in Vienna, April 30, 2001.

291 It would take another six months According to the author's interview with Martin Eichtinger in Vienna, April 28, 2001.

291 a ransom paid by Baron Louis de Rothschild See Shirer, *Rise and Fall,* p. 351.

291 National Socialism modernized Austria According to *Inventur 45/55. Österreich im ersten Jahrzehnt der Zweiten Republik,* ed. by Wolfgang Kos and George Rigele (Vienna: Sonderzahl Verlag, 1996), p. 310, quoted in Laurie Cohn, *Austrian Wartime Industrialization* (Vienna: Claims Conference, November 21, 2000).

291 Austrian officials believed that made suing them Martin Eichtinger made the government's position clear in an interview with the author in Vienna, April 28, 2001.

291 the archdukes were not seeking to regain This is based on the author's interview with Archduke Felix Habsburg-Lothringen in Washington, D.C., November 30, 1998.

292 told the companies that the problem This is drawn from the author's interview with Martin Eichtinger in Vienna, April 28, 2001.

292 With an election looming This is based on the author's interview with Hans Winkler in Vienna, May 1, 2001.

CHAPTER TWENTY-ONE: FIRST VICTIMS FIRST

294 Schüssel was seen as being too intellectual See *Neue Zürcher Zeitung,* February 28, 2000.

294 He turned to Schaumayer This account of the chancellor's relationship with Schaumayer—as well as Schaumayer's family background—is based on the author's interviews in Vienna with Hans Winkler on May 1, 2001, and Martin Eichtinger on April 28, 2001. The preceding characterization of Schaumayer is taken from the author's interview with Hans Peter Manz in Vienna on April 30, 2001.

294 Schaumayer laid down the ground rules This account of Schaumayer's first public event is based on the author's interview with her chief of staff, Martin Eichtinger, in Vienna, April 28, 2001.

296 Schaumayer was determined This is based on the author's interview with Martin Eichtinger in Vienna, April 28, 2001.

296 the Jewish side formalized its opposition As stated in a press release by the Claims Conference, dated March 16, 2000.

296 Singer was disgusted by the Austrian idea Singer made his comments in an interview with the author in New York, January 30, 2001.

296 He told Austrian officials Singer recounted the conversation in an interview with the author in New York, June 6, 2001.

297 a legal impossibility This is based on the author's interview with Hans Winkler in Vienna, May 1, 2001.

297 Singer hatched an awkward compromise This is drawn from the author's interview with Israel Singer in New York, June 6, 2001.

297 a thinly veiled warning   Eizenstat recounted the meeting in an interview with the author in Washington, D.C., March 15, 2001. He also explained how the Holocaust was a test for the Austrian government in his testimony before the Senate Foreign Relations Committee on April 5, 2000.

297 underlined by Secretary of State Madeleine Albright   The coordination between Albright and Eizenstat was detailed in a U.S. Treasury press release on March 20, 2000, and recounted by Hans Peter Manz in an interview with the author in Vienna, April 30, 2001.

297 Eizenstat knew he was being charmed   He admitted this in an interview with the author in Washington, D.C., March 15, 2001.

298 Eizenstat appeared jaded and misinformed   This section on his first meeting with Schaumayer is based on the author's interviews in Vienna with Martin Eichtinger on April 28, 2001, and Hans Winkler on May 1, 2001.

299 Fagan now claimed to have filed   According to his letter to Stuart Eizenstat, dated April 26, 2000.

299 Schaumayer said the figure   As quoted by ABCNews.com on April 17, 2000.

299 Eizenstat convened a Washington meeting   This account is based on a memorandum by Michael Hausfeld summarizing the Eizenstat meeting, dated April 28, 2000.

299 Schaumayer ended the debate in a stroke   Her performance—and thinking—was recalled in the author's interviews in Vienna with Hans Winkler on May 1, 2001, and Martin Eichtinger on April 28, 2001.

300 The chancellor had identified a huge surplus   Schüssel's financial creativity was explained to the author in interviews in Vienna by Hans Peter Manz on April 30, 2001, and Martin Eichtinger on April 28, 2001.

300 an unusual written statement   This is based on the U.S. Treasury press release, dated May 12, 2000, and the author's interview with Israel Singer in New York, June 6, 2001.

301 "I'm here to help do justice . . . "   This exchange and his talks with other Austrian ministers were recalled in the author's interview with Stuart Eizenstat in Washington, D.C., March 15, 2001. His comments are also drawn from his press conference with Maria Schaumayer in Vienna, May 17, 2000.

301 Everyone realized the labor issue   The events of the "reconciliation" session were detailed in the author's interviews in Vienna with Martin Eichtinger on April 28, 2001, and Hans Winkler on May 1, 2001.

301 Schaumayer claimed the talks   Her comments are drawn from her press conference with Stuart Eizenstat on May 17, 2000.

302 there was no invitation for anyone   This is based on the author's interview with U.S. officials who wished to remain anonymous.

302 accused his fellow attorneys   Hausfeld made his accusations in a memorandum to Central and Eastern European delegations, dated May 26, 2000.

302 the attorneys lashed out   This account is based on the lawyers' minutes of the meeting, dated June 7, 2000.

303 The Austrians themselves were modeling   According to the author's interview with Martin Eichtinger in Vienna, April 28, 2001.

303 Eager to prove Austrian complicity The debate over Mauthausen is based on the author's interviews with Gideon Taylor in New York, June 1, 2001, and Martin Eichtinger in Vienna, April 28, 2001.

303 In March 1944 See Martin Gilbert, *The Holocaust* (New York: Henry Holt, 1985), p. 679.

304 Austria received the absolution it was seeking Lambsdorff's role and comments were recalled in an interview with the author in Vienna by Martin Eichtinger on April 28, 2001.

304 His brief, as a special envoy Sucharipa's task—and prior experience—was explained to the author in interviews in Vienna with Hans Peter Manz on April 30, 2001, and Ernst Sucharipa on April 29, 2001. Sucharipa's subsequent quotes are drawn from these interviews, unless otherwise noted.

305 Some property issues were easy to identify According to the author's interview in Vienna with Ernst Sucharipa, April 29, 2001.

305 With such fuzzy talk This assessment was made by Hans Winkler in an interview with the author in Vienna, May 1, 2001.

306 Alan Hevesi warned See his letter to President Thomas Klestil, dated June 19, 2000.

306 Singer's reply was simple It came in the form of a letter from the Claims Conference to Stuart Eizenstat, dated July 24, 2000.

306 Eizenstat stepped in with his own framework These details are drawn from the State Department summary of his proposals, dated July 28, 2000.

306 Eizenstat came under intense pressure See the letter from the Foundation for Polish-German Reconciliation to Stuart Eizenstat, dated September 5, 2000.

306 Eizenstat presented a draft agreement This is based on the framework proposed by victims' representatives and agreed to by the U.S. government concerning negotiations regarding Austrian Nazi-era property, dated September 14–15, 2000.

307 A panel of experts The panel was led by the former Finnish president Martti Ahtisaari who earlier struck a peace deal with Slobodan Milosevic over the Kosovo conflict.

CHAPTER TWENTY-TWO: THE LAST WALTZ

308 close to his ancestral home Eizenstat traveled to Lithuania for a forum on looted cultural assets. On his trip to Vilnius, he visited the city's Jewish museum, where a plaque was dedicated to him for his work on Holocaust compensation. In his remarks on October 3, 2000, he underlined just how closely he identified with the European Jewish communities that were destroyed in the Holocaust: "I am proud to be a 'Litvak,' a descendant of the Jews who trace their origins in Lithuania back to the days of the Grand Duke Gediminas in the fourteenth century, and who eventually made Vilnius famous as the 'Jerusalem of the North.'"

308 It was not good news. This conversation is based on the author's interview with Hans Winkler in Vienna, May 1, 2001.

309 From Schüssel's office This account of the conference call negotiations—and the celebration afterward—is based on the author's interviews with

Hans Winkler in Vienna, May 1, 2001; Hans Peter Manz in Vienna, April 30, 2001; Israel Singer in New York, June 6, 2001; Gideon Taylor in New York, June 1, 2001; and government officials who wished to remain anonymous.

311 Eizenstat hailed the deal   His comments are drawn from the official text of his remarks at the signing of the Austrian labor agreement, on October 24, 2000.

311 Eizenstat struck a historic note   His comments are drawn from the official text of his remarks at the ceremony with Austrian President Klestil, October 24, 2000.

311 the two sides could agree   The exclusion of Jewish businesses was explained to the author in an interview with Ernst Sucharipa in Vienna, April 24, 2001. Details of the numbers of Jewish businesses—and the issue of the burden of proof—are based on a Claims Conference report on the inadequacies of the Austrian restitution process, dated 2000.

311 how to handle property taxes   This is drawn from the author's interview with Ernst Sucharipa in Vienna, April 24, 2001.

312 Martin Mendelsohn . . .   made his comments in an interview with the author in Washington, D.C., on March 7, 2001.

312 Eizenstat could barely contain his anger   This is drawn from the author's interview with Stuart Eizenstat in Washington, D.C., March 15, 2001, and his press statement at Vienna Schwechat Airport on October 25, 2000.

313 Schüssel held fast to the line   This is drawn from the author's interview with Hans Winkler in Vienna, May 1, 2001.

313 social security could be more valuable   Gideon Taylor explained the importance of the issue in an interview with the author in New York, June 1, 2001.

314 The American negotiators left Vienna   This is drawn from the press statement by Stuart Eizenstat on December 1, 2000.

314 the lawyers' demands more than halved   See the response of plaintiffs' counsel to the Austrian proposal of December 20, 2000.

314 Eizenstat carried a message of support   This is drawn from the author's interview with Stuart Eizenstat in Washington, D.C., January 5, 2001.

314 For the attorneys   This assessment of the lawyers' lack of confidence in the incoming administration was based on the author's interview with Deborah Sturman in New York on May 8, 2001.

314 Schüssel announced the final sum   This—and the following comment by the chancellor—is taken from the U.S.-Austrian press conference on Holocaust restitution negotiations on January 10, 2001.

315 Muzicant's demands appeared outlandish   This is based on the author's interviews in Vienna with Ernst Sucharipa, April 24, 2001, and Hans Winkler, May 1, 2001. Ariel Muzicant explained his demands in an interview with the author by telephone from Vienna, July 10, 2001.

316 Muzicant preferred to see his new lawyer   This is based on the author's interviews with Ariel Muzicant by telephone on July 10, 2001, and Charles Moerdler in New York, March 28, 2001. Eizenstat's one-liner was recounted by Deborah Sturman in an interview in New York, May 8, 2001, and by government officials who wished to remain anonymous.

316 he was prepared to work for Muzicant for free   This is based on the author's interview with Charles Moerdler in New York, March 28, 2001.

316 keep up the good work. According to Stuart Eizenstat in an interview with the author in Washington, D.C., March 15, 2001.

317 The Jewish negotiators were dismayed The debate over pensions was reconstructed through the author's interviews with Gideon Taylor in New York, June 1, 2001; Israel Singer in New York, January 30, 2001; and Ernst Sucharipa in Vienna, April 24, 2001.

317 Even as they prepared to sign the deal This account is drawn from the author's notes of the press conference by Stuart Eizenstat and Ernst Sucharipa in the State Department on January 17, 2001.

318 Muzicant scribbled a note According to the letter from Ariel Muzicant to Stuart Eizenstat, dated January 17, 2001.

318 He felt duped Muzicant explained his feelings and his thinking to the author in a telephone interview from Vienna on July 10, 2001. He also expressed his fears of the "liquidation" of the Jewish community in a letter to the State Department on February 13, 2001.

318 Schüssel wanted to force through This is based on the author's interview with Hans Winkler in Vienna, May 1, 2001.

319 "Jewish blood is dripping," Muzicant's comments were reported by Agence France Presse on February 2, 2001.

319 "pulled out of the air" Fenster was quoted by Reuters on February 26, 2001.

319 the first public intervention by Jörg Haider Haider's comments on the settlement were reported by the Associated Press on January 21, 2001. His comments on the Vienna elections were reported by Agence France Presse on March 2, 2001.

320 Haider blamed the party's defeat His explanation was reported by the *Financial Times*, March 29, 2001.

320 "Jews were afraid in Europe, . . ." Singer's comments were made at a working breakfast with Jewish leaders in New York, February 11, 2000.

321 Simon Wiesenthal spoke to the author in Vienna on April 30, 2001.

CHAPTER TWENTY-THREE: ASSIGNING GUILT

323 As 10:30 approached The account of events in Judge Kram's court is based on the author's contemporaneous notes.

323 Kram owed her elevation See "D'Amato Recommends 3 to Be U.S. District Judges," *New York Times*, August 19, 1982.

326 she turned to Jack Dweck Kram's prior relationship with Dweck is cited in the Memorandum of Law in Support of Motion to Recuse, In Re Austrian and German Bank Holocaust Litigation, filed by Jeffrey Barist, the lawyer for Deutsche Bank, on March 28, 2001.

327 shipments from Berlin This is taken from Moerdler's testimony at the Fairness Hearing on the Austrian Banks Settlement, November 1, 1999.

328 Swift's faction accused See the affidavit of Robert Swift, Southern District of Manhattan, November 13, 1998.

329 two thousand boxes of documents See the Testimony of John Rees at the November 1999 fairness hearing.

329 Moerdler happily agreed This version of events is confirmed by Moerdler and by Michael Hausfeld, interviewed June 25, 2001.

329 rival attorneys discovered the deal　See the letter from Stephen Whinston to Sara Bloomfield, October 12, 1999.

329 Hausfeld insisted　Letter from Michael Hausfeld to Judge Shirley Wohl Kram, December 16, 1999.

329 The Holocaust museum found the controversy　Letter from Sara Bloomfield to Stephen Whinston, December 10, 1999.

329 Singer arrived　The meeting at Claridge's was recounted by Moerdler, Singer, and Curtis Hoxter.

329 The typed paper　A copy of the Settlement Outline, January 26, 1999, is in the author's possession.

330 "They are out. . . ."　This is Moerdler's recollection. As a judge in control of a *sub judice* case, Kram was not available for interview.

331 struck dumb by the notion　Copies of the draft settlement papers are in the author's possession.

331 Couched in thick legalese　A further clause added: "Nor have the plaintiffs warranted that they will prosecute such claims or the manner in which they will do so." There was no guarantee that the plaintiffs would even follow up on the claims. The addendum is available on the *www.austrianbankclaims.com* website.

332 Moerdler followed with a passionate speech.　The account of the fairness hearing is drawn from the official transcript.

333 It explicitly waived　It is quoted in Jeffrey Barist's Motion to Recuse. This memorandum also gives a detailed account of how the plaintiffs' lawyers came to agree that the treaty voided the assigned claims, from which the following account is drawn.

335 But he was still game for a fight.　Neuborne made this comment in a contemporaneous interview with the author.

Chapter Twenty-four: Legal Peace?

336 Kram argued　See the Memorandum Opinion and Order, In Re: Austrian and German Bank Litigation, issued by Shirley Wohl Kram, March 7, 2001.

337 At Warsaw's State Jewish Theatre　As reported in the *Financial Times* on February 28, 2001.

337 German industrialists worried　Wolfgang Gibowski recounted this in an interview with the author in Berlin, April 20, 2001.

337 "A Judge with Courage."　See "Shirley Kram—Eine Richterin mit Mut," *Berliner Morgenpost*, March 9, 2001.

338 Hausfeld was uncomfortable　This account is based on interviews with Michael Hausfeld in Washington, D.C., June 25, 2001, and Burt Neuborne in New York, February 12, 2001.

338 the Berlin agreement　See Joint Statement on occasion of final plenary meeting, July 17, 2000.

338 a letter of explanation　Memo from Michael Hausfeld to Jerzy Kranz and Bartosz Jalowiecki, dated February 16, 2001.

338 without opening negotiations　The source is a telephone interview with Carol Makovich of IBM on February 13, 2001.

339 Neuborne filed his papers   See the Brief of Appellants and Petition for Writ of Mandamus, submitted by Burt Neuborne to Second Circuit Court of Appeals, March 20, 2001.

340 Famed for his near-photographic memory   See Boies's interview with the *Financial Times*, January 30, 1999. Boies's account of events is drawn from an author's interview in New York, June 12, 2001, which also involved his associate Ann Galvani. Hausfeld spoke about their negotiations to the author in Washington, D.C., on June 25, 2001.

342 They could do nothing more than promise   See the Memo from Michael Hausfeld to David Boies, April 30, 2001.

342 Hausfeld filed a declaration   See the Declaration in Support of Motion for Reconsideration by Michael Hausfeld, May 9, 2001.

343 "Urging is urging. . . ."   The account of the altercation is based on interviews with David Boies in New York, June 12, 2001; Michael Hausfeld in Washington, D.C., June 25, 2001; and Burt Neuborne in New York, June 8, 2001.

343 Kram greeted his presentation   The account of the hearing is drawn from the official transcript and from the author's contemporaneous notes.

344 Neuborne plucked up the courage   The account of Neuborne's confrontation with Kram comes from Burt Neuborne, interviewed in New York, June 8, 2001, and Michael Hausfeld, interviewed in Washington, D.C., June 25, 2001.

345 a one-paragraph press statement   It was issued by Andrew Frank on May 13, 2001.

345 "like stopping a tank . . ."   See the press release by Michael Hausfeld on May 13, 2001.

345 "Boies outsmarted him."   Sturman made the comment in a contemporaneous telephone interview with the author.

346 a totally different proposition   Neuborne expanded on this argument in his Supplemental Memorandum in Response to the Order of the District Court, May 14, 2001.

347 The Second Circuit heard the appeal   The account of the appeals court hearing and its aftermath is based on author's contemporaneous notes.

Chapter Twenty-five: The Judgment of Judah

350 Korman sat with lips pursed   The account of the courtroom scene is based on the author's contemporaneous notes of the hearing. Several details are drawn from the *Financial Times*, November 24, 2000.

351 "Jew.org embezzlement"   This is drawn from a press release issued by Gizella Weisshaus for the Union of Holocaust Survivors at the time.

352 the money would compensate four other groups of victims   These details can be checked in the Class Action Settlement Agreement, finally signed in January 26, 1999, but effectively ratifying the agreement that had been struck in Brooklyn in August the previous year. This and other essential legal documents are available on the website *www.swissbankclaims.com*.

353 the lawyers then agreed to add   The account of the struggle over which groups to define as victims is based on interviews with Burt Neuborne, July 9, 2001; Robert Swift, February 5, 2001; and Roger Witten, July 10, 2001.

353 the inclusion of political prisoners   The $200 million Swiss Humanitarian Fund, set up by the Swiss government in 1997, shows that adding political prisoners might have had a significant effect on the payout to Jews, while the other groups added would not. When the fund scoured Europe for "needy" victims of Nazi persecution, it found only 69 Jehovah's Witnesses, 32 disabled survivors, and 9 homosexuals. By comparison, it made handouts to 39,291 political prisoners. Details are in Annex V of the Gribetz Report.

354 a book on Holocaust history   See Judah Gribetz, Edward L. Greenstein, and Regina Stein, *The Timetables of Jewish History: A Chronology of the Most Important People and Events in Jewish History* (now out of print).

355 "The settlement changed the mentality . . ."   This is based on an interview with Michel Derobert, secretary of the Geneva Private Bankers Association, in Geneva, April 6, 2001. The association provided many of the other details that follow. Michael Bradfield, Paul Volcker's chief legal counsel, also discussed obstructive behavior by the banks in an interview with the author.

356 "We had no idea."   Hans Baer made these comments in an interview with the author in Zurich, April 2, 2001.

356 "in *Alice in Wonderland*"   Gasteyger was speaking in an interview with the author in Geneva, April 6, 2001.

356 "That issue was discussed vigorously . . ."   Bradfield made these comments in an interview in Washington, D.C., March 12, 2001.

356 During 1998 it employed more than a thousand people   This is based on an interview with Yaacov Lozowick, head of the archives at Yad Vashem, in Jerusalem, on April 22, 2001. The details on the number of Holocaust-related accounts and how they were calculated are drawn from Annex 4 of Volcker's final report, *Report on Dormant Accounts of Victims of Nazi Persecution in Swiss Banks* by the Independent Committee of Eminent Persons.

357 "Highly hypothetical figures . . ."   Rossier made these comments in a speech at Lausanne University, reprinted in *La Lettre,* newsletter of the Geneva Private Bankers Association, February 2000.

357 "no evidence of systematic destruction . . ."   This and the subsequent lengthy citation are from the introduction to the Volcker Report.

357 "not part of a master plan"   Volcker said this in an interview with the author in New York, March 19, 2001.

358 Banks levied fees on accounts   This material is drawn from Annex 5. Banks' names are not given in the report.

359 It refused to mandate   This is drawn from a letter from the Swiss Federal Banking Commission to Paul Volcker, in the possession of the author.

359 "the Volcker process could go on eternally."   Zulauf said this in an interview in Bern, April 4, 2001.

360 "a replay of the conduct . . ."   This is taken from the Memorandum and Order by Edward Korman, August 2, 2000. It is available on *www.swissbankclaims.com.*

360 memorials or museums   These submissions sometimes came at a price. Disability Rights Advocates, a San Francisco–based law firm, proposed that the fund should pay for a monument for the disabled Nazi victims, and simultaneously submitted a request for $311,649.02 in fees to cover the costs of the legal work they had done on the submission. This submission, along with many others like it and the other submissions quoted, are in the case docket in the Eastern District of New York in Brooklyn.

361 "The fear I have . . ."   See "Holocaust Claimants Grow Weary of Waiting," *Financial Times*, November 24, 2000.

362 payouts should be treated as charitable donations   See the Gribetz Report, p. 23.

362 Gribetz decided to allocate $90 million   Annex K of Gribetz's report details the experience of the Swiss Humanitarian Fund, which gives some basis for the 90 percent allocation to Jews. It found more needy Romani survivors than expected, and allocated 82 percent of their fund to Jewish survivors. Had they excluded political prisoners and righteous gentiles, and other groups excluded by the Brooklyn settlement, however, Jews would have received 94 percent, so Gribetz's recommendation allowed for the possibility of finding more Romani survivors. Gribetz's key findings on allocating between the different classes are on pp. 25–37 of the introduction to his report.

362 "I felt: why justify this?"   Ratner spoke in a telephone interview, January 29, 2001.

362 Volcker published a list   He did so at a press conference, February 5, 2001. The list of names appears on the *www.swissbankclaims.com* website.

363 Volcker established a Claims Resolution Tribunal   It took them four years to adjudicate on the 5,570 accounts in those lists, with 3,177 claimants eventually receiving 65 million Swiss francs. Fifty-five percent of accounts went unclaimed. Material on the tribunal is drawn from an interview in Zurich with Alexander Jolles, its secretary-general, and lawyers Heike Niebergall, Naomi Wolfensohn, and Kirsten Young in Zurich, April 2, 2001. At their request, names of claimants have been withheld.

363 "impossibly difficult."   Hans Baer was speaking to the author in Zurich, April 2, 2001.

364 It was not until November 2001   This information was provided by the Claims Conference. See also Stewart Ain, "At Last Heirs Get Swiss Money," *The Jewish Week*, February 1, 2001, for an article interviewing some of the first survivors to receive money in return for their Swiss bank accounts.

CHAPTER TWENTY-SIX: JEW VERSUS JEW

365 Jew versus Jew   The title for this chapter is borrowed from Samuel G. Freedman, *Jew versus Jew: The Struggle for the Soul of American Jewry* (New York: Simon and Schuster, 2000), a provocative analysis of the debate within the American Jewish community.

365 fake-leather-bound volume   See *Partners in History—A Tribute*, issued by WJC, September 11, 2000.

366 None was forthcoming.   The interview with Greta Beer was in Boston, February 21, 2001.

366 "a kick in the teeth."   Meili spoke in a telephone interview, Orange, California, May 21, 2001.

366 "hundreds of millions . . ."   See Joan Gralla, "Foundation to Manage Holocaust Restitution Funds," Reuters, August 24, 2000.

366 "HOW IS THAT AGAIN?"   Rechter's stream of consciousness appeared in the NACHOS newsletter, October 2000. His newsletter is also the source for Rositta Kenigsberg's quote.

367 Knesset speaker Avraham Burg.   He was speaking in an interview in Ramat Gan, Israel, April 18, 2001. Bronfman is quoted from his interview in New York in March 2001, and Kent from his interview in January of the same year, previously cited. Elan Steinberg was speaking in a telephone interview, June 2001.

369 "Their situation is so dire . . ."   See the Gribetz Report, Annex F.

369 a Yiddish theater company   Rechter made this comment in a speech to NACHOS, New York, June 24, 2001.

369 health care for American survivors   Gribetz had in fact closely considered this idea, advocated by many of his correspondents. For example Chaskel Besser, an Orthodox rabbi who sat on the board of the Swiss Humanitarian Fund, responsible for writing 61,000 equal checks for $502, complained that the gesture had been soon forgotten. He recommended that the money should be spent on health care for elderly survivors. Gribetz rejected the idea, following the precedent set in the settlement with victims of the U.S. armed forces' use of Agent Orange fifteen years earlier. The $1.25 billion could not possibly buy adequate health insurance for 800,000 elderly people.

369 "The American survivor community . . ."   Dubbin was speaking in a telephone interview with the author, August 2001.

370 "I can understand that sort of suspicion"   Schneider was speaking in a contemporaneous telephone interview.

370 ultimately unsuccessful campaign   After a strong start, Hevesi finished last among the four serious contenders in the Democratic primary, gaining only about 12 percent of the vote.

370 a religious occasion   The account of Hevesi's coffee-and-bagels meeting is drawn from the author's contemporaneous notes.

370 "last sound bite . . ."   Foxman first made this comment more than eighteen months earlier, when the dispute with the Swiss banks was at its height (see Chapter 7). He repeated the phrase many times.

372 Columbia University's law school   The account of Finkelstein and Singer's confrontation is drawn from the author's contemporaneous notes.

372 *The Holocaust Industry*,   Published by Verso in 2000.

372 whose tattooed number   Finkelstein volunteers the information on his website, *Normanfinkelstein.com*.

373 wanted the German government   Although the Claims Conference was responsible for processing claims, the German slave labor money was strictly controlled by the German foundation, "Remembrance, Responsibility and Future," and it is questionable whether the conference enjoyed any real discretion over how to spend it. If the Claims Conference found more laborers than it expected, the capped amount would be divided equally among them. If the conference found fewer, then any residue had to be returned to the German foundation, which would distribute it among Eastern Europeans.

375 "Mass murder. Horrible plunder. Slave labor. Let's eat."   Quoted on Finkelstein's website.

375 Avraham Hirschson   He was interviewed in Tel Aviv, April 17, 2001.

376 Holocaust Survivors' Foundation—U.S.A.   The statement of aims is drawn from a letter to academics sent by Leo Rechter.

377 "I would be ashamed of being Jewish"   Goldmann wrote this in his *The Jewish Paradox*, op.cit. p. 124.

EPILOGUE

378 Ben-Gurion, prime minister of the infant state of Israel   This account is based on the following sources: Tom Segev, *The Seventh Million*; Ehud Sprinzak, *Brother against Brother*, Nahum Goldmann, *The Jewish Paradox*; and Martin Gilbert, *Israel: A History*.

379 "Hast thou killed and also taken possession?"   This is the King James translation of the First Book of Kings, 21:19. The original Hebrew reads: *"Haratz-tachta vegam yarashta."* Ben-Gurion, in his speech, used a more florid translation which kept the sense of the original, as did Elie Wiesel in November 1998, at the opening of the Washington Conference on Holocaust-Era Assets. It was Wiesel's speech which gave this book its title.

380 the first recognition of their wartime suffering   It is not just the survivors in former Communist countries who were forgotten. In 1995, Israeli health officials admitted that hundreds of survivors had been needlessly incarcerated in mental institutions for fifty years.

380 "For the sole surviving daughter . . ."   This is taken from the presentation of Catherine Lillie at the National Archives conference in 1998.

380 the best settlement they obtained   This is drawn from the author's interview with Morris Ratner on January 29, 2001.

381 "a bastard a bastard."   Letter submitted to Judah Gribetz, in official case docket in Brooklyn.

381 "This subject had been on the wane . . ."   Singer made his comments in an interview with the author in Washington, D.C., on November 8, 2001.

382 Gentz vividly recalls   This is taken from the author's interview with Manfred Gentz in Stuttgart, April 25, 2001.

382 "Why did it work?"   Steinberg's comments were made in an interview with the author in New York on January 4, 2000.

383 looked back on their role   Lambsdorff dismissed the lawyers' efforts in his speech to the annual conference of the American Corporate Counsel Association in Berlin on June 25, 2001.

384 Theo Klein   was talking to the author in an interview in Paris on April 3, 2001.

384 Rabbi Marvin Hier   was talking in a telephone interview on March 27, 2001.

385 to make *Aliyah*   To emigrate to Israel.

385 Some, like Johnnie Cochran   Michael Hausfeld spoke of the contact with the slave reparations lawyers in an interview with the author in Washington, D.C., on March 3, 2001.

386 too old to be taken seriously   Some cases of slave labor in the South date back to the same period as the Armenian claims. According to a *Wall Street Journal* investigation published on July 16, 2001, African American prisoners in Alabama were forced to work in dangerous and inhuman conditions for companies such as U.S. Steel. Until the 1920s, African Americans convicted of minor offenses such as vagrancy were rounded up by Alabama's criminal justice system, which leased the prisoners to industry in exchange for cash. They were slaves in all but name.

387 shape foreign policy   See Anne-Marie Slaughter and David Bosco, "Plaintiff's Diplomacy," *Foreign Affairs*, September 2000.

388 As he agreed to the voluntary dismissal   This is taken from the opinion of Judge William Bassler dated December 5, 2000.

Note on Sources

This book is concerned with chronicling the compensation campaign of recent years rather than attempting to uproot the truth of what happened during and immediately after the war. The project grew out of our reporting for the *Financial Times* from New York and Washington. We were present at many of the public events described in these pages and interviewed many of the leading characters as the story was unfolding.

In writing this book, we have also conducted more than 150 interviews, mostly in person. This involved travel to Austria, France, Israel, Italy, Germany, and Switzerland. Many of the principal characters kindly consented to repeated interviews, showed us confidential documents detailing their work, and were exceptionally generous with their time.

Much of this book covers meetings that were either secret or closed to the press. In these cases, we have reconstructed dialogue with the use of participants' notes, where they were available. Otherwise we have restricted our reconstructions to details where there was agreement among those present as to what happened. All direct quotations in this book are drawn from our interviews unless otherwise stated in the Notes on Chapters.

Our interviewees, whom we cannot thank enough, are listed below:

IN AUSTRIA:
Martin Eichtinger
Hans Peter Manz
Ariel Muzicant
Ernst Sucharipa
Hans Winkler
Simon Wiesenthal

IN FRANCE:
Jacques Andréani
Claire Andrieu
Robert Gelli
Lucien Kalfon

David Kessler
Theo Klein
Shimon Samuels
Christian Schricke
Ady Steg

IN GERMANY:
Jörg Allgäuer
Emilio Galli-Zugaro
Michael Geier
Manfred Gentz
Wolfgang Gibowski
Herbert Hansmeyer

Stephan Keller
Kerstin Kiessler
Klaus Kohler
John Kornblum
Johanna Malz
Henning Schulte-Noelle
Ludwig Stiegler

IN ISRAEL:
Elisheva Ansbacher
Collette Avital
Zvi Barak
Bobby Brown
Avraham Burg
Avraham Hirschson
Michael Kleiner
Naphtali Lau LaVie
Yaacov Lozowick
Moshe Sanbar
Binyamin Shalev
Yair Sheleg
Edith Stern
Martin Stern
Dan Tichon
Arie Zuckerman

IN ITALY:
Guido Pastori
Giovanni Perissinotto
Alberto Tiberini

IN SWITZERLAND:
Hans Baer
Niklaus Blattner
Rolf Bloch
Michel Derobert
David Frick
Curt Gasteyger
Georg Krayer
Alexander Jolles
Heike Niebergall
Ulrich Pfister
Urs Roth
Flavio Romerio
Bernhard Stettler
Peter Widmer
Naomi Wolfensohn
Kirsten Young

Franz Zimmermann
Urs Zulauf

IN THE U.S.:
Philippe Autié
Jeffrey Barist
Greta Beer
Kenneth Bialkin
J. D. Bindenagel
Linda Bixby
David Boies
Michael Bradfield
Edgar Bronfman
Ramsay Clark
Hillary Rodham Clinton
Abraham Cooper
Frederick Davis
Sam Dubbin
Lawrence Eagleburger
Stuart Eizenstat
Ed Fagan
Abraham Foxman
Andrew Frank
Bennett Freeman
Ann Galvani
Jean Geoppinger
Judah Gribetz
Michael Hausfeld
Alan Hevesi
Karen Heilig
Marvin Hier
Andrew Hollinger
Curtis Hoxter
Greville Janner
Daniel Kadden
Saul Kagan
Alissa Kaplan
Roman Kent
Hillary Kessler-Godin
Helaine Klasky
Miriam Kleiman
Otto Graf Lambsdorff
Miles Lerman
Neil Levin
Francis Lott
Kenneth McCallion
Elizabeth McCaul
Jody Manning

Christoph Meili
Martin Mendelsohn
Charles Moerdler
Peter Moser
Irwin Nack
Burt Neuborne
Steve Newman
Owen Pell
Morris Ratner
Leo Rechter
Eric Rosand
Mendel Rosenfeld
Eli Rosenbaum
Jaime Rothman
Seymour Rubin
Audrey Samers
Andre Schaller
Greg Schneider
Deborah Senn
Neal Sher
William Shernoff

Israel Singer
Michelle Smith
Janusz Stanczyk
Elan Steinberg
Lisa Stern
Deborah Sturman
Robert Swift
Harriet Tamen
Jeffrey Taufield
Gideon Taylor
Mel Urbach
Scott Vayer
Paul Volcker
Harry Wall
Richard Weisberg
Martin Weiss
Melvyn Weiss
Gizella Weisshaus
Roger Witten
Eric Wollman

Acknowledgments

This book would not have been possible without Samuel G.
Freedman. I developed the first proposal for this book
along with a sample chapter as a participant in the rigorous book-writing seminar he runs at Columbia University's Grad-
uate School of Journalism. The class was deeply rewarding and
extremely hard (Professor Freedman accurately warns his students to forget about having a social life). He also introduced me
to a terrific agent, Kris Dahl of ICM, who had the faith and the
persistence to find a home for this manuscript. Alice Mayhew, the
legendary editor at Simon & Schuster, kindly gave me detailed
suggestions on an early proposal. I only hope that this book lives
up to Professor Freedman's standards of excellence.

If it does, this will be in large part due to the battalion of judi-
cious staff at HarperCollins who guided the publication, led by our
excellent editor, Tim Duggan. Tom Ward and Craig Shouldice of
the legal department helped rein in any excesses, as did David
Falk, who contributed a magisterially precise copyedit.

Special thanks must go to the Knight-Bagehot Fellowship in
Economics and Business Journalism, which offers reporters a year
at Columbia University. The fellowship enabled me to find a new
horizon in mid-career and its indomitable director, Terri Thomp-
son, became a beloved friend. My fellow Knight-Bagehot fellows
shared in the experience of planning for the book, especially Dan
Bases, Bruce Melzer, Mark Murphy, Anya Schiffrin, and Michael
J. Weiss, who passed on his wisdom as author of three books on

consumer trends. Special thanks must go to the George A. Wiegers Fellowship, which enabled me to complete an MBA at Columbia Business School while researching this book.

My colleagues at the *Financial Times* form a second group deserving of heartfelt thanks. Editors Robert Thomson and Richard Lambert granted me an extended sabbatical to attend Columbia and allowed me to work part time while writing the book, while news editor Julia Cuthbertson had the foresight to make coverage of the campaign for Holocaust retribution a priority for the newspaper. At her behest, I started reporting about dormant Swiss bank accounts in September 1996—more than five years before this manuscript was submitted.

I did much of the basic reporting for this book during my three years as the *FT*'s banking correspondent in New York during the launch of the paper's U.S. edition. My New York colleagues worked in an intense environment, helping to treble the paper's U.S. circulation in barely two years and having a lot of fun in the process. I am grateful to all of them, especially Daniel Bogler, Tracy Corrigan, John Labate, William Lewis, Rivka Nachoma, Richard Tomkins, and Richard Waters. Deborah Brewster and Elizabeth Wine uncomplainingly took up the slack during the book's final stages. Other *FT* journalists who collaborated on this story include Heather Bourbeau, Tobias Buck, Norma Cohen, Daniel Dombey, and Mark Huband. Graham Watts offered many helpful comments on the manuscript and even seemed to enjoy it.

The *FT*'s Zurich correspondent, Bill Hall, shared many bylines on this story and was a great host during my research in Switzerland. Avi Machlis of the Jerusalem bureau passed along many insights during his reporting of the story, helped orient me in Israel, and read through early drafts of several chapters. Danny Kopp, also of the *FT*'s Jerusalem bureau, arranged for me to talk to some of Israel's most powerful figures when they all had more troublesome matters on their minds.

A final *FT* journalist who must be thanked is, of course, my coauthor, Richard Wolffe. It was a pleasure working together and overcoming numerous travails, and our collaboration is testament also to the power of e-mail technology.

Many Swiss banks and European insurers were wholly cooperative with the writing of this book, despite their belief that the English-language press regularly treated them unfairly. Alberto Tiberini and Guido Pastori of Generali, in particular, were most gracious hosts in Trieste, as were Hans Baer in Zurich and Georg Krayer in Basel.

All the interviewees deserve thanks. Neil Levin, who was tragically killed in the World Trade Center on September 11, 2001, was open and always frank in his responses. He played a controversial role in the campaign, but he was without question a man of integrity who paused to question the moral complexities of both sides. With his death, New York lost a great public servant.

Among the other characters in the narrative, many gave more generously of their time than I could have asked. They include Bennett Freeman, Karen Heilig, Curtis Hoxter, Burt Neuborne, Steve Newman, Israel Singer, Elan Steinberg, Bob Swift, Gideon Taylor, and Eric Wollman. Martin Stern invited me to eat Passover matzoh with him on a Swiss mountain during a snowstorm, and weeks later he escorted me to a moving Holocaust remembrance ceremony at Yad Vashem. Leo Rechter kindly invited me to a meeting of child Holocaust survivors, which deepened my understanding of the strong feelings many have about the campaign run in their name.

Other people who do not appear as characters in the narrative were also crucially helpful: Alissa Kaplan and her successor, Hillary Kessler-Godin, of the Claims Conference; Andrew Frank, Jeffrey Taufield, and Harry Wall, who represented the accused European companies in New York; and James Nason of the Swiss Bankers Association. Danny Kadden, who became an activist in the Holocaust Survivors' Foundation, was a fount of information on insurance. The staff of the Brooklyn courthouse deserve several medals for their patience as I sifted through thousands of entries in their huge case docket on the Swiss litigation.

My parents, David and Janet Authers, were their customary pillars of strength. Their readings of early drafts also yielded many improvements.

I should also thank my fellow students in Professor Freedman's 2000 seminar for the many valuable comments they offered and salute those who also obtained book contracts. Sanghamitra Kalita is writing *Our Amrikan Dream* about the Indian immigrant experience in New Jersey, and Harry Bruinius is writing *Better for All the World* on the secret history of eugenics in America.

My final word of thanks must go to Sara Silver, to whom I became engaged while writing this book. She lived through the project with me for two years and proved to be a brilliant—albeit ruthless—editor. I now understand why authors so often end their acknowledgments with heartfelt thanks to their partner. Gracias, Sarita.

JA

Writing a book might sometimes seem like a solitary occupation, but the loneliness of the long-distance writer is little more than an illusion. There is nothing independent about this production. In many ways, this book is the collective work of all the individuals named below, whose goodwill and patience were both extraordinary and inexplicable.

First and foremost, it was a pleasure to work with John Authers, whose skills as a reporter are evident throughout his work. His unfailing enthusiasm for this book helped sustain it from its earliest days through some of its toughest deadlines.

This book was brought to life by our outstanding agent, Kris Dahl, who believed in us well before we believed in ourselves. Her judgment and understanding were flawless, and it was a real pleasure working with her and Liz Farrell at ICM.

But above all, this book was directed, shaped, and polished by the superb guiding hand of our editor, Tim Duggan. Tim's instincts were always on the mark, his suggestions perfectly placed, and his advice very gratefully received. He was both reassuring and deft in handling us and our copy. Thanks also to his assistant, John Williams, to the legal team led by Tom Ward, and to our meticulous copyeditor, David Falk. A special thanks to Cathy Hemming for her insightful comments on our initial manuscript, which hugely improved this book.

Inside the State Department, my reporting of this story was immeasurably improved by Bennett Freeman, whose political wisdom was matched only by his endless good humor. J. D. Bindenagel provided invaluable diplomatic knowledge and a rare voice of sanity in an overwrought debate. The book was also informed by the insights of Jody Manning and Eric Rosand, while my news reporting was aided by Susan Elbow and Jim Desler. At Treasury, Helaine Klasky and Michelle Smith were very supportive—not just of my reporting of this story, but for the full range of Treasury news.

In both departments, Stuart Eizenstat *was* the story. For the many hours of interviews he generously gave, I am eternally grateful. Those interviews did not stop even after he made it clear he was preparing his own book on the same events. That decision placed us both in an unusual situation, where the interviewee was also a rival author. But as always, he dealt with a sensitive situation as a consummate professional, with good grace and immense expertise.

Israel Singer's energy dances over almost every one of these pages. He granted us frequent, lengthy interviews, where it was always an education to hear the inside story of the long battle he waged. Without his support, this would be a far duller tale. Also thanks to Elan Steinberg, who was no less insightful, gifted with a turn of phrase, and generous with his time.

Among the lawyers, whose names were tarred so often, there were many thoughtful, engaging, and incredibly helpful sources. At the top of that list is Michael Hausfeld, who granted many hours of interviews in his frenetic schedule, to explain his particularly personal motivation for embarking on his litigation. Linda Bixby, his in-house historian, was exceptionally patient and informative and allowed full access to her impeccable records. Thanks also to Martin Mendelsohn for his insights and experience and especially for the introduction to Simon Wiesenthal.

At the Claims Conference, Gideon Taylor and Karen Heilig were incredibly cooperative in sharing their insights into the German and Austrian negotiations. Their energy and hard work is an impressive example of what a postwar generation can achieve for elderly survivors.

For my research in Europe, I am deeply indebted to the following people who were utterly invaluable in helping to organize interviews and acting as an introduction to sources: Wolfgang Gibowski in Germany; Philippe Autié in France; Martin Weiss in Austria. All provided exceptionally useful background information, which shaped not just my research but the writing of the book itself. Thanks also to Andrew Frank in New York for his constant guidance, and to Michael Geier in Berlin for his extensive help and for the introduction to Otto Graf Lambsdorff.

At the *Financial Times,* my second home for the last seven years, there are really too many people to thank. For allowing me to embark on this crazy project—and granting a long-delayed sabbatical to research this book—I am indebted to Robert Thomson, Richard Lambert, and John Ridding. For commissioning and editing the features that sparked the idea for the book, thanks to Julia Cuthbertson and Will Dawkins. For casting his truly expert eye over the manuscript, a special thanks to Graham Watts, who is simply the best copyeditor on the newspaper. And most important of all, for putting up with my endless moaning, rambling monologues, and my absence from the office, an enormous thanks to Gerry Baker, Steve Fidler, Deborah McGregor, Peter Spiegel, Ted Alden, Nancy Dunne, Perry Despeignes, Paulo Sotero, Nancy McCord, and Aida Atallah. It's a privilege to work with such a talented and hardworking team.

A very special thanks to Genna Lester, whose speedy, flawless, and tireless transcriptions were a godsend.

On my research tour across Europe, many friends were especially generous and supportive. In Paris, Anne-Laure-Hélène Lefort des Ylouses and Louis-Charles Viossat literally gave up their bed, while Nicolas and Elisabeth gave up something even more precious—their toys. Thanks also to Anne-Lorraine Bujon and Quentin Hirsinger for a fine dinner. In Munich, Silke and Thomas Glossner were wonderful hosts and provided a unique insight into the gastronomic delights of Bavaria.

In London, I could not have coped without the friendship of Will and Becca Lewis, James Harding, Julia Jenkinson and Andrew Palmer, Meike Hensmann, Tamara Russel, Gen and Tim West, Debbie and Jamie Heywood, Phil and Kelly Riggins, James Montgomery and Helen Branwood, Bob Sherwood and Kate Bowyer, Gwen Robinson, Kate McCarthy, and Justin Forsyth.

But it was at home in Washington where Paula and I relied most on the never-ending sympathy, patience, and support of our friends: José Bassat, Patrizia Tariciotti and Patrizio Nissirio, Danny Klaidman and Monica Selter, Stephanie Flanders, Mark Suzman, Heather Weston and Richard Delaney, Jill and Terry Neal, Anne Kornblut and Mark Orchard, John and Anne Dickerson, Frank Bruni, Campbell Brown, Nassrin Ghani and Kevin Flower. Frank's book-related advice was especially generous, inspirational, and labor-saving. A huge thanks to Andrea Dew—for her friendship and for opening the door to Hillary Clinton. Jake Tapper and Peter Bergen gave wise advice as fellow authors. Thanks also to Libby and Mark Gitenstein and John McInespie for their insights into the book world. In particular, an enormous thanks to Mary, David, Henry, and Gabriella Stevens for introducing us to Japan and being such warm and generous friends.

Most of all, I cannot thank enough José, Tichi, Carlota, and Inés Andrés—for all your friendship, food, and love.

An extra special thanks to all of Paula's mom friends who supported her while I was locked away with the book—Julie Diaz-Asper, Evy Mages, Becky Sachs, Rachel Allen, Kavita Singh, Mary Siddal, Cynthia Hacinli, and Katherine Landfield.

To Mum and Dad, you have been the most wonderful and inspirational parents. You gave me all the encouragement, confidence, and curiosity to discover the world. This is to say thank you for all those years of hard work and love which I never fully appreciated until Ilana came into our lives. To David and Dawn, Alain and Tracey, and Natasha and Ben, thank you for reminding me of my real place in the world—as a little brother. This is to say thank you for teaching me how to get dressed.

To Martha and Claudio, an enormous hug and *besos* for being the very best parents-in-law and friends. Your love and understanding have been amazing and unwavering. To Karina and Marcus, a huge thanks for giving up your bed in London and for your friendship across the Atlantic.

Acknowledgment seems such a poor word for the most important people in my life: my beautiful wife, Paula, and my adorable daughter, Ilana. Paula is my greatest inspiration, my best editor and my biggest champion. It was her spirit that turned my ideas into real writing, her unfaltering support that sustained me through exhaustion, and her selfless sacrifice that allowed me to spend so long in front of the computer. After a year of my absence on the campaign trail, she almost single-handedly loved and cared for our newborn baby as I disappeared once again into the book. I am in awe at her talent and her energy, her laughter, and her love. She truly deserves to be a coauthor of this book. Instead she has created and nurtured something infinitely more precious and miraculous: our vivacious daughter, Ilana. To Paula and Ilana, I dedicate this book with all my love.

RW

Index